BUYING

RETAIL

IS

STUPID!

Copyright © 1992 by Trisha King-Crumley, Deborah Newmark and Bonnie Cunningham. All rights reserved. No part of this work may be reproduced, stored in a retrieval system, or transmitted in any form or by any means, including electronic, mechanical, photocopying, or recording without express prior written permission from the authors and publisher.

Third Edition

Published by
Newmark Management Institute
18345 Ventura Boulevard, Suite 314
Tarzana, CA 91356

Printed by O'Neil Data Systems, Inc.
Los Angeles, CA

Cover designed by Steve Gussman

Library of Congress Catalog Number 92-060576

ISBN: 0932767-03-6

Printed in the United States of America

TENTH PRINTING

BUYING RETAIL IS STUPID!

By

TRISHA KING-CRUMLEY
DEBORAH NEWMARK
BONNIE CUNNINGHAM

ACKNOWLEDGEMENTS

My portion of this book is dedicated to all the very special people in my life who have loved, encouraged and supported me through a period of great change and upheaval.

A big thank you also goes to my friend, teacher and mentor, Jerry Newmark. I have learned and grown both personally and professionally due to his guidance and "blue pencil." LUCMOY!!!

– *Trisha King-Crumley*

I dedicate this book to my greatest fans:

My husband, partner and closest friend, Jerry, who encouraged me to become an author and supported me throughout the project.

My mom and dad, Anne and Harry, who taught me it was more important to get along with people than to get A's on my report card.

My older sister, Marcia, who taught me class and how to shop with style.

My younger sister, Gail, who taught me to feel from my heart.

And my younger brother Steve, who taught me that anyone can do anything if they really put their mind to it.

– *Deborah Newmark*

I dedicate this book to my co-authors, Trisha and Deborah, for their endless enthusiasm and commitment to putting together a quality product. I also dedicate this book to David Crumley and Jerry Newmark, for their vision and support. Last but not least, I dedicate this book to my partner in life, Jim, for his love and sense of humor which kept me going through the hard times.

– *Bonnie Cunningham*

TABLE OF CONTENTS OVERVIEW

FOREWORD

I. INTRODUCTION

USEFUL INFORMATION

GLOSSARY OF DISCOUNT TERMS

NOTES TO READER

II. SMART SHOPPING
WINNING STRATEGIES FOR SAVING MONEY AND TIME

MISCONCEPTIONS ABOUT DISCOUNT SHOPPING

ELEMENTS OF SMART SHOPPING

CONSUMER INFORMATION RESOURCES

III. DIRECTORY OF STORES & SERVICES

IV. DIRECTORY OF MAIL-ORDER COMPANIES

V. DIRECTORY OF CONSUMER INFORMATION RESOURCES

INDEX - STORES

INDEX - CATALOGUES

INDEX - STORES OFFERING DISCOUNT COUPONS

DISCOUNT COUPONS

ORDER BLANKS

TABLE OF CONTENTS

FOREWORD 1
I. INTRODUCTION 3
USEFUL INFORMATION 3
   ORGANIZATION & CONTENT 3
   DISCOUNT COUPONS 4
GLOSSARY OF DISCOUNT TERMS 5
NOTES TO READER 7
   FEEDBACK FROM YOU 7
   AUTHORS' NOTE 7
   LEGEND 8
   ADDITIONAL LOCATIONS 8
   CREDIT CARD ABBREVIATIONS* 8

II. SMART SHOPPING
WINNING STRATEGIES FOR SAVING MONEY AND TIME 9
MISCONCEPTIONS ABOUT DISCOUNT SHOPPING 9
ELEMENTS OF SMART SHOPPING 11
   BASIC STRATEGIES 11
      HIGHER-PRICED PRODUCTS & SERVICES 11
      ALL PRODUCTS & SERVICES 12
   MAIL-ORDER STRATEGIES 13
CONSUMER INFORMATION RESOURCES 14

III. DIRECTORY OF STORES & SERVICES
ANTIQUES & COLLECTIBLES 17
APPLIANCES 21
   ∞ SEWING MACHINES & VACUUM CLEANERS ∞ 25
   ∞ REPAIRS ∞ 27
   ∞ USED APPLIANCES ∞ 28
ART & ARTIFACTS 29
   ∞ ART DEALERS ∞ 29
   ∞ FRAMES & FRAMING SERVICES ∞ 30
ARTS, CRAFTS & HOBBIES 33
   ∞ ART SUPPLIES ∞ 33
   ∞ BEADS, RHINESTONES & CRYSTALS ∞ 34
   ∞ CRAFT & FLORAL SUPPLIES ∞ 35
   ∞ FABRICS & NOTIONS ∞ 39
   ∞ HOBBIES ∞ 44
      – Coins – 44
      – Model Trains – 45
      – Rubber Stamps – 46

ix

– Seashells –	47
AUTOMOBILES & VEHICLES	**49**
∞ ALARMS, STEREOS & TELEPHONES ∞	49
∞ BATTERIES ∞	53
∞ FLOOR MATS ∞	54
∞ PARTS ∞	54
– Used Parts –	56
∞ RV SUPPLIES & EQUIPMENT ∞	56
∞ REPAIR & MAINTENANCE ∞	57
– Body Work –	57
– Engine Work –	58
– Glass Replacement –	58
∞ SALES, LEASING & RENTALS ∞	58
∞ SERVICES ∞	60
– Driving School –	60
– Insurance –	61
– Road Service –	61
∞ TIRES ∞	62
BEAUTY SUPPLIES	**63**
∞ COSMETICS, FRAGRANCES & SUPPLIES ∞	63
∞ HAIRSTYLING ∞	67
∞ WIGS ∞	67
BOATING & MARINE PRODUCTS	**69**
BOOKS & MAGAZINES	**71**
∞ NEW & USED ∞	71
∞ USED BOOKS ∞	74
BUILDING & REMODELING	**77**
∞ AIR CONDITIONING & HEATING ∞	77
∞ BRICKS, BLOCKS & MASONRY ∞	78
∞ CABINETS, CLOSETS & COUNTERTOPS ∞	79
∞ CERAMIC & STONE TILE ∞	82
∞ DOORS, WINDOWS & MIRRORS ∞	86
∞ FLOOR COVERINGS ∞	87
∞ GATES & FENCING ∞	93
∞ HOME DESIGNS ∞	94
∞ ONE-STOP HARDWARE STORES ∞	94
∞ PAINT ∞	95
∞ PLUMBING & ELECTRICAL ∞	97
∞ REPAIR & WORK REFERRAL SERVICE ∞	100
∞ WALL & WINDOW TREATMENTS ∞	100
– Wallpaper –	100
– Window Treatments –	102
∞ TOOLS ∞	105
∞ WOOD STAINING & REFINISHING ∞	106
CLOTHING & ACCESSORIES	**107**

∞ ACTIVE WEAR ∞	107
∞ BRIDAL & FORMAL ∞	109
∞ FAMILY APPAREL ∞	112
∞ FASHION ACCESSORIES ∞	115
∞ INFANT'S & CHILDREN'S APPAREL ∞	118
∞ LARGE & HALF SIZES ∞	123
∞ LEATHER GARMENTS & FURS ∞	124
∞ LINGERIE ∞	126
∞ MATERNITY ∞	129
∞ MEN'S APPAREL & ACCESSORIES ∞	130
∞ MEN'S & WOMEN'S APPAREL∞	135
∞ RENTALS ∞	138
∞ RESALE STORES ∞	140
– Infants & Children –	140
– Family –	141
– Men's & Women's –	143
– Women's –	144
∞ SERVICES ∞	149
– Dry Cleaning –	149
– Tailoring –	150
∞ SHOES ∞	150
– Family –	150
– Men's –	154
– Men's & Women's –	154
– Women's –	156
– Work –	158
∞ SPECIAL SALES ∞	159
∞ SWIMWEAR ∞	160
∞ UNIFORMS ∞	162
∞ VINTAGE CLOTHING ∞	163
∞ WESTERN APPAREL ∞	165
∞ WOMEN'S APPAREL ∞	166
COMPUTERS	**175**
∞ HARDWARE & SOFTWARE ∞	175
∞ REPAIR & MAINTENANCE ∞	178
DEPARTMENT & WAREHOUSE STORES	**179**
DISCOUNT "SHOPPING CENTERS"	**185**
ELECTRONICS	**189**
∞ ENTERTAINMENT & COMMUNICATION ∞	189
∞ PARTS, SUPPLIES & EQUIPMENT ∞	193
FOOD & BEVERAGE	**197**
∞ BAKERY GOODS ∞	197
∞ DIETETIC & BULK FOODS ∞	198
∞ DINING DISCOUNTS ∞	199
∞ HEALTH FOODS & VITAMINS ∞	199

∞ MARKETS ∞	200
∞ MEAT & SEAFOOD ∞	202
∞ MEXICAN FOODS & PRODUCTS ∞	203
∞ NUTS & CANDY ∞	204
∞ SPIRITS ∞	206
∞ WAREHOUSES ∞	209
HOME FURNISHINGS	**211**
∞ CHINA, COOKWARE & SILVER ∞	211
∞ DECORATOR ITEMS ∞	215
∞ FURNITURE ∞	221
– Bedroom –	221
– Home –	228
– Infants & Children –	236
– Leather –	238
– Rattan & Wicker –	239
– Unfinished –	240
– Used –	241
∞ LAMPS & LIGHT FIXTURES ∞	241
∞ LINENS ∞	244
∞ RUGS ∞	247
∞ UPHOLSTERY SERVICE ∞	248
JEWELRY	**249**
∞ DIAMOND PURCHASING INFORMATION ∞	258
MEDICAL NEEDS	**259**
∞ DRUG STORES & PHARMACIES ∞	259
∞ SUPPLIES & EQUIPMENT ∞	260
∞ USED EQUIPMENT ∞	261
MUSIC & MOVIES	**263**
∞ CDS, RECORDS, TAPES & VIDEOS ∞	263
∞ CONCERTS & PLAYS ∞	267
∞ MOVIES ∞	268
MUSICAL INSTRUMENTS	**269**
∞ MUSIC STORES ∞	269
∞ PIANOS, ORGANS & KEYBOARDS ∞	273
∞ REPAIR ∞	276
OFFICE & BUSINESS NEEDS	**277**
∞ ONE-STOP SUPPLIERS ∞	277
∞ BUSINESS MACHINES ∞	280
∞ USED FURNITURE & EQUIPMENT ∞	281
∞ SERVICES ∞	283
– Printing –	283
– Secretarial –	284
OPTICAL SERVICES	**285**
PAPER & PARTY SUPPLIES	**287**
∞ BOXES ∞	287

- ∞ COSTUMES ∞ 287
- ∞ PARTY & PAPER SUPPLIES ∞ 288

PETS & ANIMAL SUPPLIES **291**
PHOTOGRAPHY **297**
PLANTS, LAWN & GARDEN **301**
- ∞ LAWNMOWERS ∞ 301
- ∞ NURSERIES ∞ 301
- ∞ POTS, PLANTERS & FOUNTAINS ∞ 304

POOL & PATIO **307**
- ∞ BARBECUES ∞ 307
- ∞ PATIO FURNITURE ∞ 309
- ∞ POOL SUPPLIES & SPAS ∞ 312

SAFES & VAULTS **313**
SERVICES **315**
- ∞ FLOWERS & BALLOONS ∞ 315
- ∞ HOME REPAIR & MAINTENANCE ∞ 317
- ∞ LEGAL SERVICES ∞ 317
- ∞ LIFE INSURANCE ∞ 318
- ∞ LOCKSMITH ∞ 318
- ∞ PARTY COORDINATING SERVICE ∞ 319
- ∞ PHOTOGRAPHERS ∞ 320
- ∞ USED MOBILE HOME SALES ∞ 321
- ∞ VIDEO TRANSFERS ∞ 321
- ∞ WEIGHT LOSS PROGRAM ∞ 322

SPORTS & RECREATION **323**
- ∞ BICYCLES ∞ 323
- ∞ EXERCISE EQUIPMENT ∞ 325
- ∞ GAME ROOM "TOYS" ∞ 326
- ∞ GOLF ∞ 328
- ∞ GUNS, AMMO & FISHING GEAR ∞ 331
- ∞ SPORTING GOODS & OUTERWEAR ∞ 332

SURPLUS **335**
TOYS, DOLLS & GAMES **337**
TRAVEL & VACATION NEEDS **339**
- ∞ LUGGAGE & TRAVEL ACCESSORIES ∞ 339
- ∞ TRAVEL ARRANGEMENTS & SERVICES ∞ 341

VARIETY & THRIFT STORES **343**
- ∞ GENERAL MERCHANDISE ∞ 343
- ∞ NEW & USED MERCHANDISE ∞ 346

IV. DIRECTORY OF MAIL-ORDER COMPANIES

CATALOGUES **351**
- ∞ ARTS, CRAFTS, & HOBBIES ∞ 351
  - – Art Supplies – 351
  - – Craft Supplies – 352

– Fabrics & Notions – 353
– Hobbies – 355
∞ APPLIANCES ∞ 355
∞ AUTOMOTIVE PARTS & ACCESSORIES ∞ 356
∞ BOOKS ∞ 357
∞ BUILDING & REMODELING ∞ 358
∞ CIGARS, PIPES & TOBACCO ∞ 359
∞ CLOTHING ∞ 359
∞ COSMETICS & WIGS ∞ 362
∞ ELECTRONICS ∞ 363
∞ FOOD & BEVERAGE ∞ 363
– Do-It-Yourself Kits – 365
– Health Foods & Vitamins – 366
∞ GENERAL MERCHANDISE ∞ 366
∞ HOME FURNISHINGS ∞ 367
– Decorator Items & Dishes – 367
– Floor Coverings – 370
– Furniture – 370
– Lamps & Light Fixtures – 371
– Linens – 372
– Wall & Window Treatments– 373
∞ JEWELRY ∞ 375
∞ LUGGAGE ∞ 375
∞ MEDICAL SUPPLIES ∞ 376
∞ MUSIC & MOVIES ∞ 377
∞ MUSICAL INSTRUMENTS ∞ 378
∞ OPTICAL PRODUCTS ∞ 379
– Contact Lens – 379
– Glasses & Sunglasses – 380
∞ OFFICE SUPPLIES & EQUIPMENT ∞ 381
∞ PARTY & PAPER PRODUCTS ∞ 381
∞ PET SUPPLIES ∞ 382
∞ PHOTOGRAPHY ∞ 382
∞ PLANTS, LAWN & GARDEN ∞ 383
∞ SPORTING GOODS ∞ 384
∞ TELESCOPES & BINOCULARS ∞ 386
∞ TRAVEL ∞ 386

V. DIRECTORY OF CONSUMER RESOURCES
CONSUMER INFORMATION 389
INDEX - STORES 393
INDEX - CATALOGUES 410
INDEX - STORES OFERING DISCOUNT COUPONS 413
DISCOUNT COUPONS 417
ORDER BLANKS 493

FOREWORD

With the publication of the third edition, BUYING RETAIL IS STUPID! has established itself as the basic "Shopper's Bible" for economy-minded consumers in Southern California. It has become a regional best-seller and a staple item in Southland bookstores.

As the most comprehensive discount shopping guide of its kind in this area, BUYING RETAIL IS STUPID! has achieved the status of "essential shopping companion" for consumers who seek to stretch their dollars. It enables shoppers to buy more, spend less, and get more for their money. BUYING RETAIL IS STUPID! contains hundreds of stores and services where you can buy almost EVERYTHING from A to Z–appliances, art work, cars, cellular phones, clothes, furniture, groceries, jewelry, luggage, musical instruments, pets, stereos, travel services, wallpaper, zippers—and at savings from 20–80% off retail prices. By buying brand-name, quality goods at 20–80% off retail prices, the buyer has more disposable dollars for additional purchases or for savings.

BUYING RETAIL IS STUPID! has appealed to almost every segment of the buying public—all age, socio-economic, occupational and ethnic groups. The recession has given considerable impetus to consumer and media interest in BUYING RETAIL IS STUPID!. It has been featured on Fox KTTV Channel 11 News, AM Los Angeles KABC-TV, KABC Talk Radio Michael Jackson show, KFI Tom Leykis show, KNX-CBS radio and most other major talk shows; BUYING RETAIL IS STUPID! has been written up in Entrepreneur magazine, Orange Coast magazine, Valley magazine, L.A. West magazine, The Savvy Shopper—Insiders Guide to Shopping Around the World and in newspapers throughout the Southland.

BUYING RETAIL IS STUPID! co-authors Trisha King-Crumley and Deborah Newmark are the regular bargain columnists for the Daily News. Their weekly column (Thursdays, L.A. Life section) has developed a wide following which continues to grow. Their research for the column enables them to locate exciting new discount stores and services which are included in this new edition of BUYING RETAIL IS STUPID!; also, in this way the authors are able to keep their hands on the bargain shopping pulse.

This updated, expanded and revised third edition includes over 200 new discount stores, new manufacturer's outlet malls, over 100 new discount mail-order catalogue houses and extra money-saving bonus coupons from 151 stores. It also has a new chapter on "Smart Shopping" which offers winning strategies for saving money and time.

In addition to covering the major areas of Los Angeles, Orange, Riverside and San Bernardino counties, more stores have been added to Palm Springs, Ventura, and San Diego. Other areas which have been added to the third edition include Palmdale and Lancaster, plus the Santa Clarita, Conejo and Simi valleys.

Whether or not prices continue to rise and people continue to feel pressed economically, thrifty buying appears to be here to stay. Time Magazine (July 23, 1990) calls it a mini revolution. The 1990s has been heralded as the decade of the discount shopper. We trust BUYING RETAIL IS STUPID! will continue to serve as an essential tool for every shopper, irrespective of budget, who wants to find the right product, at the right price, with the greatest ease.

Have a great time as you explore the joy and benefits of discount shopping!

Gerald Newmark
Publisher
Newmark Management Institute

I. INTRODUCTION

Here we are again with a new edition of BUYING RETAIL IS STUPID!—our third. Since the last edition, we have been busy writing a weekly bargain column for the Daily News and doing a considerable number of TV and radio shows and speaking engagements. Our research for these activities, and our own normal shopping excursions, have enabled us to discover some exciting new stores, services and references related to discount shopping; we are happy to share them with you here. Many of you have sent us leads which also have added to the richness of this edition, and our chapter on "smart shopping" should help you save more money than ever and have more fun in the process. Here's what you'll find on the following pages and how to make best use of the material.

USEFUL INFORMATION

Organization & Content

The glossary of discount terms provided in this chapter will help you understand terminology in this book and also in other publications dealing with shopping.

In Chapter II on "smart shopping," we describe winning strategies which we have discovered for becoming an aware, knowledgeable and economical shopper. These recommendations are designed to assist you in engaging in value shopping with ease and confidence.

Chapter III, Directory of Discount Stores & Services, is the heart of the book. Here we describe stores and services with enough information to give you a good feel for what each one offers, how it operates and where it is located. Many stores sell items that you will not find in a shopping mall and at prices that will make you smile.

Chapter IV is devoted to discount catalogue firms from throughout the United States. This enables you to engage in discount shopping beyond the borders of Southern California without leaving home. Mail-order shopping has become very popular because it is convenient, fun and cost effective.

Chapter V provides you with a directory of consumer information resources. This will guide you in starting your own consumer library—

one that you'll enjoy referring to often and will find most valuable as you experience the joys of discount shopping.

The Table of Contents, listed by products, and the alphabetical store, catalogue and coupon indexes make it easy to locate whatever you are looking for.

Discount Coupons

For extra savings, don't forget your BUYING RETAIL IS STUPID! coupons in back of the book. Every store designated with a double asterisk will give you an additional percentage off their regular discount prices upon presentation of the coupon. The percentage of discount is indicated on the coupon.

The Ideal Gift

Think about BUYING RETAIL IS STUPID! as an ideal gift because it fits everyone and everyone can use it—friend, relative, business associate, student—anyone you want to remember you as they save money and have fun with discount shopping throughout the year.

So, here's wishing you "Happy Shopping and Terrific Savings."

Trisha King-Crumley
Deborah Newmark
Bonnie Cunningham

GLOSSARY

The following are some of the terms most commonly used in connection with discount shopping:

- *Bankrupt Stock*: When a business goes bankrupt, the stock on hand is sold in lots at lower than wholesale or manufacturer's prices in order to pay off creditors.
- *Close-outs:* Usually odds and ends or last season's merchandise sold at discounted prices in order to make room for new inventory.
- *Cost*: Either the price incurred manufacturing an item or the wholesale price a business pays for items to be resold.
- *Cost Plus*: The cost of an item to the dealer plus his or her percentage of profit. When calculating cost, a dealer is likely to also include operating expenses—shipping, rent, advertising, etc.—and then add an override of about 10%
- *Coupons*: Specified discounts or rebates on forms redeemable in person or by mail.
- *Department Store Outlet*: Remaining merchandise from all of a company's stores brought together in one location (either in a separate facility or a designated area of one of their larger stores). Includes items that aren't selling, seconds, slightly damaged goods, returns, floor models, demonstration models and mismatched goods.
- *Discontinued or Manufacturer's Close-out*: A product no longer being manufactured that is sold at a discount to make room for current goods. Quality of the merchandise is not affected.
- *Discount*: A percentage or dollar amount reduced from the manufacturer's suggested retail price
- *Flea Market and Swapmeet*: Groups of vendors in individually rented areas. Low overhead usually means lower mark-ups on new and used merchandise. Sellers will often negotiate price.
- *Floor Sample*: A model used for display in the store.
- *Freight Damage*: Items that are broken, burned, chipped, marred, or otherwise affected during shipment. The merchandise may be noticeably damaged, but often it is in top condition.
- *Garage Sale*: Accumulated unwanted "stuff" people sell at very low prices in front of their homes or apartments. Sometimes excellent "buys" can be found.
- *In-season Buying*: Most retailers buy merchandise months in advance (summer items are purchased in winter). Discounters often purchase goods during the season (winter items are bought in winter) relieving the manufacturer of goods from cancelled orders or overruns.

- *Inventory Reduction:* A business will have a big sale to improve cash flow rapidly and make room for new merchandise. Also, reduced stock means fewer man hours will be needed to take inventory.
- *Irregular*: Merchandise with minor imperfections, often barely discernable.
- *Job Lot*: Miscellaneous goods gathered for sale as one quantity.
- *Jobber*: A person who buys or imports quantity goods from manufacturers and then sells the merchandise to dealers.
- *Liquidated Stock*: When a business is in financial trouble, their goods are sold by the lot at less than wholesale prices to convert assets into quick cash.
- *Loss Leader*: An item purposely priced low to attract customers into the store.
- *Manufacturer's Outlet*: A store containing a single manufacturer's products at discounted prices. The merchandise may include discontinued lines, unsold merchandise, overruns, irregulars, seconds and sometimes lines made specifically for the outlet.
- *Manufacturer's Outlet Mall:* A number of outlet stores located together.
- *Odd Lot*: A small quantity of unsold merchandise that remains after orders have been filled at the wholesale level.
- *Overrun*: An excess of quantity over the actual amount the manufacturer wanted to produce.
- *Past-season or Last-season Goods*: Items left over from a previous season.
- *Rebate*: A refund, usually a certain dollar amount, offered from the manufacturer when your purchase one of their products.
- *Resale Stores:* Generally a store selling used clothing, but some also sell used furniture and miscellaneous items. Quality varies from store to store. Some stores will only carry certain brands, others carry anything and everything   Goods in most stores are sold on consignment.
- *Retail*: The selling of goods directly to the customer or end user.
- *Sample*: An item shown by a salesperson to prospective buyers.
- *Second*: An item with either cosmetic or functional flaws.
- *Suggested Retail*: The price of an item the manufacturer recommends the retailer charge the consumer..
- *Surplus or Overstock*: A quantity in excess of what is needed by a dealer or manufacturer.
- *Thrift Stores*: Second-hand items which are resold at very low prices.
- *Wholesale Price*: The actual cost of an item to the retailer.

NOTES TO READER

Feedback From You

We want to hear from YOU! If you know of any other great discount businesses not already included in this book, please send us their name, address and telephone number. We'd like to include them in future editions of BUYING RETAIL IS STUPID! And if you have any comments about any of the shops listed in this book, we'd like to hear those, too. This book is for YOU. Please write to us at BUYING RETAIL IS STUPID!, 18345 Ventura Boulevard, Suite 314, Tarzana, CA 91356. Also, you can order additional copies of the book for yourself, friend, family, and for business associates by simply completing the order form in the back of the book. We look forward to hearing from you.

Authors' Note

The information in this book has been compiled to the best of our ability. Although we have visited and/or contacted almost all the stores, we have relied principally on data supplied by the businesses themselves. We are not responsible for any misinformation, or if a store has closed, moved or changed policies since publication. This book is intended solely as a guide and does not imply endorsement of any business.

Legend

Additional Locations

Wherever any of the listed stores has from one to five other locations in Southern California, the cities, addresses and the telephone numbers have been included following the description of the store. Where any store has six or more additional locations, only the number of locations is indicated. In this case, please consult your local telephone directory for a store located near you. Note: Store hours may vary from location to location. Check with store for hours.

Credit Card Abbreviations*

AE	= American Express	MC	= MasterCard
DC	= Diners Club	OPT	= Optima
DISC	= Discover	V	= Visa

* Other forms of payment are also listed if a vendor doesn't accept credit cards.

Stores Accepting Coupons

Stores that accept BUYING RETAIL IS STUPID discount coupons are designated by double asterisks (**) placed at the end of the store name.

II. SMART SHOPPING
WINNING STRATEGIES FOR SAVING MONEY AND TIME

MISCONCEPTIONS ABOUT DISCOUNT SHOPPING

The question is sometimes asked, "How can discounters compete with the buying power of large retail operations (department stores, supermarket chains, etc.)?" Basically, it is a combination of some of the following factors: low profit margins (profit comes from sales volume); low overhead (absence of large corporate staffs & executive salaries); limited or no advertising; fewer personnel; less expensive locations; flexible buying approach (not restricted by specific procedures, formula, tradition; can buy anything at any time of year and take advantage of opportunities); attention to detail (management often closer to the operation and can keep expenses down).

The following are some of the misconceptions associated with discount shopping:

Quantity & Location
(Discount stores are few in number and are usually located in out-of-the-way, hard-to find locations.)

In larger cities such as Los Angeles, the opposite is true. There is an incredibly large number of discount entities, and they are everywhere—downtown areas, suburbs, main streets, back streets, exclusive areas, industrial parks, malls, small shopping centers, and manufacturer outlet parks.

Size & Type
(Discount stores are generally small, "mom and pop" type operations.)

On the contrary, a tremendous variety exists in the discount field including small, single owner, one item specialty stores; large specialty stores (of almost every kind: books, plants, clothes, food, etc.); small and large department type stores selling everything; local and national chain stores; resale stores; manufacturer's outlets; and membership warehouse companies; plus hundreds of mail-order, discount catalogue businesses throughout the U.S.A.

Quality
(Discount stores carry products of inferior quality—seconds or "knock offs" of name-brand goods.)

Almost every top-quality and name-brand product can be purchased at discounts from 20-80%. Some stores do carry seconds or slightly damaged goods, but these are usually marked. (The buyer does have to be careful of unscrupulous discounters who would pass these off as new.)

Service & Atmosphere
(When buying discount, you have to give up service and atmosphere.)

In many of the larger operations (e.g., membership warehouse clubs) staffs are smaller and you'll do more waiting on yourself. (However, how much attention are you getting in the typical retail department store these days?) The decor will often be simple or barren. On the other hand, there are numerous discount stores where you will be waited on by the owners themselves or some dedicated employees. And, many of them will be in beautiful settings where coffee, soft drinks and snacks are served.

Selection
(Limited selection is available when buying discount.)

Almost everything produced, from A to Z (including hay for horses), can be bought at a discount—also, a considerable number of services. In large specialty stores, which carry a wide selection of a single product category, you are more likely to find the size, color and style you want than at the typical department store.

Convenience
(You have to give up convenience to buy discount—travel far distances to seek out places since they don't advertise).

With books such as BUYING RETAIL IS STUPID! and weekly bargain columns such as the one Trisha and Deborah write for the Daily News in Los Angeles, the work has been done for you. They make it easy for you to find what you want at the right price. And frequently you can find places in the vicinity of your home or work. In addition, given the large number of mail-order discount companies, sometimes you do not even have to leave home to get a bargain.

ELEMENTS OF SMART SHOPPING

Do you consider yourself a smart shopper? Would you like to become a smart shopper or at least smarter than you are now? What is meant by smart shopping? Smart shopping generally includes the following:

- Saving money (getting good "buys"—obtaining merchandise or services at the most favorable prices)
- Conserving time and energy (spending several hours driving around in a car to save a few dollars is not smart shopping)
- Getting value for your money (quality of product must be consistent with price or better than what one could expect realistically for a given price; cheaper is not always a bargain; a lower-priced product (a so-called bargain) that lasts half the time or doesn't work well, is not value; also includes avoiding rip-offs by knowing what you are getting)

Smart shopping, then, should enable the consumer to make wise decisions—to be able to spend less and buy more with greater ease, convenience and confidence in having received value for one's dollar. Smart shopping involves formulating an approach to shopping and following it. The strategies and information discussed below take into account all the basic elements discussed above.

Basic Strategies

Higher-Priced Products & Services

- Check the rating of the model you want in "Consumer Reports" (available at your local library)
- Check for things to look for and pitfalls to avoid in books such as: "Better Business Bureau's A to Z Buying Guide" and "The Frugal Shopper" (see section on Consumer Information Resources)
- Call retail stores for their prices (also see newspaper ads)
- Locate discount stores which potentially carry item. Use discount resource guide such as BUYING RETAIL IS STUPID! (also check yellow pages, newspaper ads, etc.) Look for nearest locations.
- Telephone discount stores to check on availability of item and price. (Some discount stores will not give a price on the phone; however, if you specify a price, they will usually tell you if they can beat it.)
- Ask if they guarantee lowest price and what you need to bring to store to verify the lowest offer you've received.
- Check on return policy.

- Check on whether item is in stock and quantity available before going to store.
- If item is in short supply, ask to have item held for you.

All Products & Services

To the above, add the following for all products and services, as appropriate:

- Select favorite store(s) and frequent them regularly.
- Establish a relationship with a particular salesperson and/or manager. They will level with you—give you good information and advice and personal attention.
- Have store notify you when they have a special sale and when items or brands of interest to you arrive.
- Identify discount stores that are near each other (e.g., clusters, outlet malls) so that you can visit several on one trip.
- Find out the best time to buy certain items (e.g., January white sales). Unless there is an urgent need, wait for that time.
- Buy what you need. Avoid buying something because it is a bargain if you don't need it.
- An exception to the above is "creating your own gift shop." Throughout the year there are always gifts to be given—births, birthdays, anniversaries, graduations, weddings, showers, and of course Christmas. Whenever you find a "super bargain," buy it and store it. When a gift is needed for someone, get it from your own gift shop. This will reduce the number of last minute, costly gift purchases you will have to make.

Mail Order Strategies

Buying from catalogues is a huge part of the consumer scene and growing all the time. Mail-order purchasing has become significant to individuals who want to buy conveniently (from their home), locate articles that may not be readily available in stores, and save money through discounts and low prices due to reduced overhead (no sales people or fancy facilities needed).

Initially, people may be hesitant to send money to an unknown entity for something they haven't seen, touched or tried on—especially with the publicity sometimes given to rip-offs. However, with increased numbers of people reporting positive experiences and with guaranteed satisfaction and return policies, reservations are diminishing. Once someone overcomes hesitancy and becomes a first-time buyer, that person frequently becomes a regular mail-order purchaser.

The following strategies are aimed at maximizing benefits and minimizing risks. As you use these suggestions you will probably find, like millions of others, that mail-order buying can be convenient, fun and cost-effective.

- Start your own discount mail-order library by writing for catalogues (free in most cases) of businesses and merchandise that interest you, using the BUYING RETAIL IS STUPID! catalogue section (and other sources) as a resource.
- As the catalogues arrive, have fun looking through them. Mark those items that you may be interested in purchasing. Make a separate list indicating the business name, page number, item and cost.
- Compare retail price for desired items with mail-order price.
- From those that appear to be "good buys," experiment by first ordering a few low or medium-priced items.
- Before ordering, call (many have 800 numbers) to verify delivery, return, and satisfaction guaranteed policies.
- For higher-priced items—especially involving companies with which your experience is limited—you may want to ask for the names of one or two purchaser references. Prepare specific questions and contact these references.
- Develop confidence with particular companies; establish your favorites from among these and deal with them regularly.
- Establish relationship with a specific person to deal with.

CONSUMER INFORMATION RESOURCES

Becoming a "smart shopper" involves rational (rather than emotional) decision making. Whether purchasing a product or seeking services, there are a number of questions to be asked. How do I get the best value for my money? What do I need to know about the purchase in question to make an informed decision? What pitfalls do I need to avoid? What recourse do I have when I am dissatisfied?

Fortunately, an increased number of excellent publications are available to assist you in answering these questions. The smart shopper will create a home consumer library of pertinent books, periodicals, catalogues, pamphlets and articles. For a nominal cost (in some cases free), these publications can help you become a knowledgeable shopper, one who is more likely to make sound decisions, avoid mistakes and save thousands of dollars.

Chapter V, Directory of Consumer Information Resources, contains numerous recommendations and descriptions. Included in this chapter are such publications as: "Consumer Reports" (monthly magazine reporting results of comparative field tests of a wide variety of products); "The Better Business Bureau A to Z Buying Guide," and "The Frugal Shopper" by Ralph Nader & Wesley J. Smith (both provide consumers with essential information to make sound, economical purchasing decisions on hundreds of products and services); U.S. Government catalogues containing hundreds of materials assisting with living more wisely, effectively, economically and healthily (most of these are free or inexpensive); "Consumer Action" (a consumers services guide that details resources available for dissatisfied consumers); "The AAA Car Buyer's Handbook!" (contains everything you need to know about getting the most for your money in buying a new or used car).

Upon obtaining these materials, become familiar with them by glancing through the table of contents and reading the texts superficially. You are certain to find some interesting and intriguing information; even this casual reading will make you a more knowledgeable consumer and will enable you to know where to look for specific information before buying. Over the course of a year, you will probably refer to these resources often and will find them invaluable.

III

DIRECTORY

OF

DISCOUNT STORES

&

SERVICES

ANTIQUES & COLLECTIBLES

THE ANTIQUE CLOCK SHOP
1060 Hamner Ave.
Norco, CA 91760
714/736-9598
HOURS: MON-FRI: 8:30-5
CREDIT CARDS: CASH OR CHECKS ONLY

At The Antique Clock Shop you will find over 100 elegant antique clocks for sale. The owner, John Cox, has turned his hobby into a business. As antique clocks in working condition are very expensive, Mr. Cox buys old clocks in need of repair. After working his magic, the clock is placed for sale in the store. Because of the low prices paid originally for the clocks, you'll find the prices far below what you would pay in an antique or jewelry store. If you have an antique clock in need of repair, John Cox's repair work is first-rate. So if you are looking for an antique clock, this is the place to start!

ANTIQUE HOUSE
2865 Foothill Blvd.
La Crescenta, CA 91214
818/957-3166
HOURS: TUES-THUR, SAT: 10-6   FRI: 10-7   SUN: 12-5
CREDIT CARDS: DC, DISC, MC, V

You'll save money and be amazed at the buys in antiques here. There are 3,000 square feet filled with lovely, turn-of-the-century American Oak pieces, country pine imports from Denmark, elegant mahogany and walnut from 1860 to 1930, European and American period pieces. You'll find prices between 20 to 40% less than you can expect at most antique stores. You can spend hours looking over quality antique furniture, art, sterling, cut glass, primitives, glassware, trunks, quilts, books, jewelry, china, lighting, clocks, mirrors, and more. Delivery and shipping services are available. They offer full service antique restoration and repair, and quality consignments are accepted. Antique House will buy one piece or your entire estate. For your convenience, they have a lay away plan (four month maximum) and instant financing on approved credit.

ANTIQUES & COLLECTIBLES

COLLECTOR'S EYE
21435 Sherman Way
Canoga Park, CA 91303
818/347-9343
HOURS: MON-SAT: 10-6
CREDIT CARDS: AE, MC, V

This is definitely one of our favorites. Walking into the Collector's Eye is like walking through a rainbow and finding the pot of gold. All of their elegantly displayed vintage jewelry is arranged by colors and/or style. You might find an antique vanity draped in pearl necklaces, brooches, earrings, bracelets, chokers and rings. Another display might consist of 75 various styles in shades of blue or perhaps, sterling silver. The antique jewelry, real and costume, is from the early 1800s up through the early 1960s and all at 50–70% below retail. You can literally spend hours browsing through this oasis of jewelry acquired from estate sales, swapmeets and retirement homes. The Collector's Eye offers jewelry repair and will also buy your vintage jewelry. A definite stop when in the San Fernando Valley!

ESTATE HOME FURNISHINGS
11901 Holser Walk, Suite 300
Oxnard, CA 93030
805/983-2211
HOURS: MON, WED-SUN: 10-6 (CLOSED TUES)
CREDIT CARDS: MC, V

Why pay retail when you can take advantage of outstanding values and quality merchandise at Estate Home Furnishings? Browsers and buyers alike will be delighted roaming through 17,000 square feet of momentos and memories. Whether you're looking for furniture, antiques, collectibles, glassware, jewelry, paintings, sterling, clothing, china, lamps or pianos, Estate Home Furnishings has it all. They are also noted for their large collection of antique dolls. With three estates arriving weekly, the selection of merchandise is always changing. So, if you're in the mood for a drive, it would be well worth your while to head up to Estate Home Furnishings. They offer great terms, too.

ANTIQUES & COLLECTIBLES

RAY FERRA'S IRON & ANTIQUE ACCENTS
342 N. La Brea Ave.
Los Angeles, CA 90036
213/934-3953

HOURS: TUES-FRI: 10-5   SAT: 10-3
CREDIT CARDS: MC, V

If you've been looking for replacement glass for an old antique lamp, then Ray Ferra can come to your rescue. If the problem isn't replacement glass, he also does rewiring for most lamps, ceiling fixtures, and crystal chandeliers. Commercial and residential lighting are two of his specialties. He carries both reproduction and original Tiffany lamps, handles, and many hard to find lighting items. He's been providing excellent service since 1967, and savings run 20% or more off retail prices, even if you could find it elsewhere. You'll find parking in back of the store.

GRUBB & GRUBB'S GENERAL STORE
18523 Sherman Way
Reseda, CA 91335
818/996-7030

HOURS: MON-SAT: 9:30-5:30
CREDIT CARDS: AE, MC, V

This is a one-stop shop for vintage clothing and antiques. Grubb & Grubb's General Store has an extensive line of clothing for men and women, costume jewelry, vintage shoes, purses and hats. After you have put together the perfect outfit, you can explore their antique furniture, kitchenware, and art.

KING RICHARD'S ANTIQUE MALL
12301 E. Whittier Blvd.
Whittier, CA 90602
310/698-5974

HOURS: MON-WED: 12-6   THUR-FRI: 12-8   SAT: 10-6   SUN: 12-5
CREDIT CARDS: DISC, MC, V

King Richard's is located in a 1902 orange packing house. With over 70,000 square feet and 230 antique dealers on site, they boast being the largest antique mall in Southern California. Almost anything can be found here, and the competition of the dealers insures you can get a good price on most items. Usually the larger the purchase, the larger the discount. You can find a lamp repair shop, also glass and wicker furniture repairs and restorations. Soon they will be opening a deli so you can rest and get something to eat before you continue your search for that special item.

ANTIQUES & COLLECTIBLES

PENNY PINCHERS
4265 Valley Fair St.
Simi Valley, CA 93063
805/527-0056
HOURS: MON-SAT: 10-5 SUN: 11-5
CREDIT CARDS: DISC, MC, V

There are 60 individual antique dealers in this 10,000 square foot antique mall. The prices are so good here that you may see antique dealers from the more expensive parts of Southern California shopping here. Penny Pinchers has been in business since 1966 featuring furniture, porcelain, pottery, linens, paintings, lamps, figurines, rugs, jewelry and just about anything else normally found in an antique store. There is a central sales register and you can take advantage of their 30 day layaway plan. Plenty of parking is available, and there is a small refreshment area.

SOMETHING OLD SOMETHING NOUVEAU
1303 Lincoln Blvd.
Santa Monica, CA 90401
310/395-8088
HOURS: TUES-SAT: 11-5
CREDIT CARDS: MC, V

All merchandise is on consignment here. Items are dated upon arrival and discounted 20% after the first two months. Each month thereafter another 10% is taken off. This store is a cozy 1918 bungalow that sells collectibles, antiques, furniture, silver, china, glass and linens. The second Saturday of every month there is a collector's jamboree sale where 35 dealers set up stalls along the house and in the parking area. Shopping at Something Old Something Nouveau can lead to some truly marvelous finds.

APPLIANCES

ALBEE'S DISCOUNT APPLIANCES
6305 Wilshire Blvd.
Los Angeles, CA 90048
213/651-0620
HOURS: MON-SAT: 9:30-7 SUN: 11-6
CREDIT CARDS: AE, DISC, MC, V

It would be easier to list what Albee's doesn't carry. They sell everything and at about 10% above cost. The savings are terrific on television and video sets, stereos, washers, stoves, refrigerators, sewing machines, hair dryers, cameras, vacuum cleaners, fans, computers, fax machines, and hundreds of other items. They have a vast selection from all the top name brands.

BARRETT'S APPLIANCES
2723 Lincoln Blvd.
Santa Monica, CA 90405
310/392-4108
HOURS: MON-FRI: 8-6 SAT: 8-5
CREDIT CARDS: MC, V

Since 1946, Barrett's Appliances has been offering low price guarantees on every major appliance for your kitchen and laundry room. Buying their inventory as part of a national buying group, they are able to pass on the huge volume discounts they receive. Brand names include Maytag, Amana, Whirlpool, Speed Queen, Westinghouse, Wolf, Creda, and many more. Their award winning service department and friendly sales people have one thing in mind—making sure their customers are satisfied! While credit cards are accepted, you'll receive an additional 3% discount paying by cash or check. Another reason to shop here is their low price policy. If within 30 days of purchase you see the same item advertised for less by any appliance dealer, Barrett's will gladly refund you the difference upon presentation of the ad. They pride themselves in being involved with their local community activities.

APPLIANCES

BAY CITY APPLIANCES
8151 Beverly Blvd.
Los Angeles, CA 90048
213/651-2800
HOURS: MON-FRI: 9-6 SAT: 9-5:30
CREDIT CARDS: MC, V

This is not your usual whitegoods store. Bay City carries major appliances, televisions, and housewares at discounts of 20 to 50%. They also have plumbing fixtures. They have six experienced salespeople to help you and there is parking in front and back of the store. This store is a favorite for those who want to find everything under one roof.

HERB BEAN SALES CO.
8920 Melrose Ave.
Los Angeles, CA 90069
213/655-5878
HOURS: MON: 9-7 TUES-FRI: 9-6 SAT: 9-5
CREDIT CARDS: MC, V

At Herb Bean Sales Co. you can buy a refrigerator and appliances for your kitchen, stereo for your den, washer and dryer for your laundry room and a bed to sleep on. There are 7,000 square feet filled with a wide variety of merchandise to choose from, namely Calpholon cookware, Sub-Zero refrigerators, Thermador major cooking appliances, Sealy mattresses, Whirlpool, Amana and Maytag washers and dryers. Herb Bean has been offering great deals since 1964. You'll save 15 to 20% off retail on appliances and 50 to 80% on beds. Financing is also available.

CARLSON'S T.V. & APPLIANCES**
1342 Fifth St.
Santa Monica, CA 90401
310/393-0131
HOURS: MON-SAT: 9-6 SUN: 11-4
CREDIT CARDS: AE, MC, V

Carlson's carries a large stock of brand name televisions and appliances, at just 10% above cost. They say their prices are lower, on an overall basis, than their best known competitors. On display are over 100 refrigerators, 20 freezers, 40 washers, 20 air conditioners, 30 ranges and 20 dishwashers. You'll find Westinghouse, Frigidaire, Hot Point, RCA, Gibson, Maytag and others. In the same location since the late 1930s, they're proud of their reputation "built on service." Fast delivery is also available. If you use your BUYING RETAIL IS STUPID coupon, you'll save an additional $10! Deals don't get any better than this.

APPLIANCES

NAT DIAMOND EMPIRE FURNITURE**
4431 W. Adams
Los Angeles, CA 90011
213/732-8128
HOURS: MON, FRI: 10-7 TUES-THUR: 9:45-6:30 SAT: 9:30-6
CREDIT CARDS: AE, DISC, MC, V

This store has been in business over 50 years selling furniture and appliances at 20 to 50% below retail prices. They carry a huge inventory of General Electric appliances which include refrigerators, freezers, stoves, washers, dryers, and more. Nat Diamond Empire Furniture also carry the latest furniture trends and styles. You'll save an additional 10% off their already terrific prices by using your BUYING RETAIL IS STUPID coupon.

FATOR'S APPLIANCES & PLUMBING
436 S. Robertson Blvd.
Los Angeles, CA 90048
213/386-1743
HOURS: MON-FRI: 8:30-5:30
CREDIT CARDS: MC, V

Family owned and operated, Fator's offers major appliances for the home at 5–10% above cost. Knowledgeable salespeople are always happy to give useful information and to point customers in the right direction. They also have microwaves and gas barbecues. If you're going to install your new dishwasher yourself, you'll be relieved to know they carry a complete line of plumbing materials.

FRIEDMAN'S–THE MICROWAVE SPECIALISTS
5515 Stearns
Long Beach, CA 90815
310/598-7756
HOURS: MON-SAT: 10-6 SUN: 12-5
CREDIT CARDS: AE, DISC, MC, V

"I have more time for lovin' since I got my microwave oven," is the motto at Friedman's. And we kid you not, Judy Hatzger is in love! She gives free cooking classes in the store every Tuesday for anyone who purchases a microwave. And you can come back to the classes as many times as you want. They'll give you a lifetime price guarantee which means if in your life-time you find your microwave at a lower price, they'll refund the difference. With over 100 microwaves on display, if you can't find what you want, it hasn't been invented yet. If by any chance, even after knowing about all of the wonderful services Friedman

APPLIANCES

extends, you're still not satisfied, they'll give you your money back after 30 days. Now that's what we call real old fashion service!
Additional Locations: 8 other stores throughout S. CA

PASQUINI
1501 W. Olympic Blvd.
Los Angeles, CA 90015
213/739-8826

HOURS: MON-FRI: 8-5 SAT: 9:30-2
CREDIT CARDS: MC, V

If you like coffee, espresso and cappuccino, visit Pasquini for the finest in home machines. You'll save at least 15% off retail prices on their wonderful selection of machines. They've been in business since 1956 and their secret is personalized service. They'll show you how to use your new machine, and you can purchase grinding machines and coffee beans here too. Repairs and service are also available for their machines.

SEARS CONTRACT SALES
866 N. Hilldale Ave., Suite 5
Los Angeles, CA 90069
800/767-1311, ext. 7210

HOURS: MON-FRI: 9-5
CREDIT CARDS: SEARS OR CHECKS

For Kenmore appliances—refrigerators, ranges, dishwashers, washers, dryers—it's hard to beat the savings (25 to 40% off retail) at Sears Contract Sales. This is the commercial division of Sears, and when you buy appliances from them, you receive the same warranties offered by Sears' department stores. Because they don't have a luxury showroom, you place your order by telephone. You can order anything carried by Sears department stores. All you need to do is give them the item, model number and color. If you don't have access to the necessary information, call them for one of their catalogues.

VINOTEMP INTERNATIONAL
134 W. 131st
Los Angeles, CA 90061
310/719-9500

HOURS: MON-FRI: 8:30-6 SAT: 9-6
CREDIT CARDS: ALL MAJOR

If you have a wine collection or are thinking about creating one, then you want to see the folks at Vinotemp International. They manufacture the Vinotemp wine cellar. Owner Alvin Patrick says, "Compare first then come see us. We will not be undersold." Whether you want your wine

APPLIANCES

cellar built-in or free standing, Vinotemp can help you. They will visit your home and give you an estimate on which wine storage device is best for you. You'll save at least 20% or more off the retail price.

WAREHOUSE DISCOUNT CENTER
30621 Canwood St.
Agoura, CA 91301
800/334-4WDC (800/334-4932)
HOURS: MON-FRI: 9-9 SAT: 9-5 SUN: 10-5
CREDIT CARDS: DISC, MC,V

Warehouse Discount Center has one of the largest display showrooms (33,000 square feet) in Southern California. They carry almost every major appliance, in-home electronics and kitchen and bath plumbing needs. You'll find brand names such as G.E., RCA, Yamaha, Maytag, Hitachi, Kohler, Whirlpool, Magic Chef, Viking, Kenwood and much more on items like microwave ovens, ranges, ovens, washers, dryers, dishwashers, freezers, bathtubs, toilets, jacuzzis, big screens and stereo equipment. Their policy is to meet or beat competitor's prices. They also have a small section in the store that has freight-damaged goods at even greater savings.

∞ SEWING MACHINES & VACUUM CLEANERS ∞

ORANGE APPLIANCE & VACUUM**
12845 Chapman Ave.
Garden Grove, CA 92640
714/750-3151
HOURS: MON-FRI: 10-6 SAT: 10-3
CREDIT CARDS: ALL MAJOR

As an authorized factory service center for more than 30 manufacturers, Orange Appliance & Vacuum is able to extend discounts of 20 to 50% off retail on vacuum cleaners and small household appliances. Brand names include Bissell, Black & Decker, Eureka, General Electric, Proctor Silex, Royal, Toastmaster, Hamilton Beach, Ultra Flex (Krups), Sharp, Whirlpool and many others. They're so sure their prices are the lowest on vacuum cleaners they guarantee to beat any advertised price. For added savings on your purchase, you'll receive an additional 5% discount by using your BUYING RETAIL IS STUPID coupon. And, if your purchase happens to be a vacuum cleaner, you'll also receive a free year's supply of bags and belts.

APPLIANCES

RAINBOW VACUUM CENTER
634 E. Colorado Blvd.
Glendale, CA 91205
818/247-1943

HOURS: TUES-SAT: 10-6
CREDIT CARDS: AE, MC, V

The last time you were on a nuclear submarine, did you happen to notice how clean and dust free it was? The Rainbow Vacuum is purchased by the U.S. Navy for the super clean environment that must be maintained on their subs. Doctors recommend the same product for their allergy patients needing their homes to be dust free. They'll beat anybody's price on brand names such as Hoover, Eureka, Electrolux, Panasonic, Royal, and rebuilt Kirbys. Warranty and repair work is done on the premises. Their 1,600 square foot showroom always has over 400 vacuums in stock. Senior citizens always receive an extra 10% discount.

SINGER BURBANK SEWING CENTER
150 N. San Fernando Blvd.
Burbank, CA 91502
818/845-8311

HOURS: MON-SAT: 9-5
CREDIT CARDS: AE, DISC, MC, V

Not only are sewing machines priced 20 to 50% below retail, when you buy a new Singer, free lessons are included. If you've seen what sewing machines can do today, you know how important it is to have lessons. Their machines are guarantied for 25 years against fattory defects (2 years on electrical and 3 months on anything else). They also sell Singer vacuum cleaners and cabinets, and take trade-ins. All repair work is done on the premises. If you inherited your grandmother's old Singer and you'd like to restore it, you can find the parts you need here.

U.S. SEW-N-VAC
21430 Sherman Way
Canoga Park, CA 91303
818/348-6014

HOURS: MON-SAT: 9-6
CREDIT CARDS: MC, V

Why not check out U.S. Sew-N-Vac the next time you need a sewing machine, vacuum cleaner or typewriter? You can save 10 to 40% off retail. They specialize in Royal, Eureka, Panasonic and Hoover vacuum cleaners and are an authorized Riccar dealer. In addition to sales, they offer same-day repair service on sewing machines and vacuums with free pick-up and delivery. Trade-ins are accepted and financing is available.

VACUUM & SEWING CENTER
21360 Devonshire Blvd.
Chatsworth, CA 91311
818/998-6988

HOURS: MON-FRI: 9:30-5:30 SAT: 9:30-5
CREDIT CARDS: MC, V

New, rebuilt and used vacuum cleaners made by Hoover, Eureka, and Royal, and sewing machines by Riccar and Singer are some of the brands found at the Vacuum & Sewing Center. You can select from over 100 different vacuum cleaners and 10 different models of sewing machines in stock. They guarantee their service and merchandise for one full year. With friendly salespeople and a skilled technician on the premises you can't go wrong. Free pick-up and delivery is also available. Savings run 20–50% below retail.

∞ REPAIRS ∞

ALTO APPLIANCE SERVICE
44809 Genoa Ave.
Lancaster, CA 93534
805/948-8779

HOURS: MON-SUN: 8-6 (CLOSED SAT)
CREDIT CARDS: CASH OR CHECKS ONLY

If you live in Antelope Valley and need repairs or service on your appliances or heating and air conditioning units, you should give Alto Appliance Service a call. They are a family-owned business that has little overhead so they can pass on the savings to their customers. There are never any service charges; they charge for parts and labor only. This will save you at least $30 per service call. Seniors get a 10% discount; their work is guaranteed in writing, and they will make calls on Sundays or evenings at no extra charge! They also sell used appliances which are guaranteed in writing.

APPLIANCES

∞ USED APPLIANCES ∞

A APPLIANCE FACTORY
3851 Pyrite St.
Riverside, CA 92509
714/681-5300
HOURS: 9- 6 SEVEN DAYS A WEEK
CREDIT CARDS: ALL MAJOR

Washers, dryers, refrigerators, stoves, freezers or dishwashers, this is truly an appliance recycling factory with 10,000 square feet of showroom and 5,000 square feet of factory. Save at least 50% off what the same item would cost brand new! There are always at least 300 reconditioned units for sale and at least 3,000 units on hand. (Reconditioned means they replace all worn parts.) You won't find any plastic appliances, only metal, because appliances made out of metal last much longer than the ones made of plastic. If you see a unit not yet reconditioned, you can "stake your claim," and it will be moved up to the front of the line for reconditioning. Included in the sale price is a 30 day warranty, and you can purchase their service warranty for six months or one year ($35 every six months) which includes parts and labor service in home. If the unit can't be fixed, you'll receive a replacement. Also, if your service agreement is renewed every year, the price stays the same as the original contract price. There is usually something on special; if they are overstocked on some items, those units can be on special for 30% below what they charge normally. They will also paint the appliances for you should you desire a different color.

ART & ARTIFACTS

∞ ART DEALERS ∞

H. LEWIS REX FINE ART**
6701 Variel Ave., #C48-49 (Valley Swap Meet)
Canoga Park, CA 91303
818/715-9980
HOURS: SAT & SUN: 10-6
CREDIT CARDS: MC, V

Choose from over 200 pieces of fine original oil paintings with savings of 25 to 40%. They carry artists such as Domina, Parnel, Millet, Perry and Mario, and have a large selection of Southwestern art. Get on their mailing list to be notified about special sales. They sell to the public only at the Valley Swap Meet in Canoga Park. You can paint yourself an extra 10% discount using your BUYING RETAIL IS STUPID coupon!

PANG!**
18530 Oxnard St.
Tarzana, CA 91356
818/344-7611
HOURS: MON-SAT: 10-6
CREDIT CARDS: AE, MC, V

Are you an art lover but can't afford the price of original oils or signed lithographs? Pang! (Poster Art N Graphics!) frames graphic arts to look like lithographs at prices 30–50% off retail. A 24 x 36-inch Mark King landscape, in a 2-inch oak frame with triple matting was $95 here. A local store had the same item, unmatted, for $165. On the floor, you'll find 700 to 1,000 prints already framed and matted. Most are double matted in a laminate frame. If you spot a picture you like, but the frame color or matting doesn't go with your decor, the staff will help you select somthing more to your liking. As long as it's just a change in frame color, not style, there's no extra charge. Otherwise, the price is adjusted up or down, depending on the frame. PANG!, family owned and operated, believes in great service and low prices. They've been in business since 1978 and have never raised their prices. All materials used are first quality. You'll receive a 10% discount on stock items and custom framing with your BUYING RETAIL IS STUPID coupon.
Additional Locations:
Costa Mesa–1835-D Newport Blvd., Suite 159, 714/646-8603

ART & ARTIFACTS

EDWARD WESTON FINE ARTS
19355 Business Center Dr.
Northridge, CA 91324
818/885-1044
HOURS: MON-FRI: 8-6
CREDIT CARDS: AE, MC, V

This is a showroom of wholesale art that generally deals with gallery owners. If you are an art connoisseur this is your kind of place. They have posters, limited edition graphics, original oils and sculptures, pottery, photography, Southwestern art and artifacts all at 20% to 50% off retail prices. You can find Picasso, Miro, Chagall, Bragg, Bert Stern, George Barris and hundreds of other artists here. If your schedule doesn't fit into their posted hours, call to arrange an evening or Saturday appointment.

∞ FRAMES & FRAMING SERVICES ∞

ACTA FAST FRAME
16052 Sherman Way
Van Nuys, CA 91406
818/786-9336
HOURS: MON-FRI: 10-6 SAT: 10-5
CREDIT CARDS: AE, MC, V

Look no further for a store that specializes in museum quality custom framing at competitive prices. They also sell art, limited editions, posters and ready-made frames. Acta Fast Frame carries a large variety of over 1,000 different frames from which to choose. Discounts range from 10 to 45% off retail prices. They have year-round specials on framed art posters, some as low as $29.95.
Additional Locations:
Redondo Beach–1622 S. Pacific Coast Hwy., 310/316-2881

DISCOUNT FRAMES
12811 Victory Blvd.
North Hollywood, CA 91606
818/763-6868
HOURS: MON-SAT: 9:30-5:30
CREDIT CARDS: MC, V

This is the solution you've been searching for if you need your paintings reframed to match your new decor. Discount Frames has one of the biggest selections of frames in Los Angeles, and you can take advantage of the tremendous savings they offer on every size, color, style and shape. They also provide excellent custom framing.
Additional Locations:
Tarzana–18561 Ventura Blvd., 818/343-5566
Woodland Hills–22713 Ventura Blvd., 818/884-0500

DISCOUNT PICTURE FRAMES
102 S. Manchester
Anaheim, CA 92802
714/956-0121
HOURS: MON-FRI: 10-6 SAT: 10-5
CREDIT CARDS: AE, MC, V

Do you have an unframed painting that has been sitting in the back of your closet for a while? All ready-made frames are discounted 10–20% off retail, and Discount Picture Frames stocks over 15,000 frames! Now that's what we call a selection! Their customers drive a long distance for their custom framing service, too. Owner Mike Neben has been in business since 1970, and his courteous staff will take care of everything for you. No seconds or close-outs here, just first quality merchandise and service.

FRAMEX
4054 Laurel Canyon Blvd.
Studio City, CA 91604
818/509 0700
HOURS: MON-SAT: 10-6
CREDIT CARDS: DISC, MC, V

Why take photographs if they're only going to end up in a box under your bed? Get some enlargements made and take them over to Framex, where you can save 20 to 60% off retail on custom framing. Lots of framing shops subcontract work, but not here. All work is done on the premises using the latest equipment. With lower prices than so called discount chains, you can be sure your pictures are getting framed, not you.

ART & ARTIFACTS

FRAMING OUTLET**
8301 W. 3rd St.
Los Angeles, CA 90048
213/655-1296
HOURS: MON-SAT: 10-6
CREDIT CARDS: MC, V

In business for more than five years, Framing Outlet provides professional custom framing and has ready-made frames as well. You can also purchase posters at bargain savings of 50% off retail. This is great place to shop for special frames to adorn your desk or credenza. With their wide variety in brass, silver, porcelain and marble, they have the largest selection of picture frames in Los Angeles. Their trained staff will help you design a framing layout that will fit perfectly in any room of your home. You will regularly save 10 to 20% on your custom framing at Framing Outlet, and you will save an additional 10% when you present your BUYING RETAIL IS STUPID discount coupon.

GREY GOOSE
111 N. La Brea Ave.
Los Angeles, CA 90036
213/931-8087
HOURS: MON-FRI: 9-5 SAT: 10-6
CREDIT CARDS: MC, V

Everything you want in custom framing at competitive prices can be found at the Grey Goose. A metal frame measuring 24" x 36", including dry mounting and glass of your choice, is runs just $39.50 and is available in 25 different colors. Shoppers will generally save 50% on what others charge for metal frames. Check out all their other varieties of frames, too.
Additional Locations:
Los Angeles–615 N. La Cienega, 310/652-0273

ARTS, CRAFTS & HOBBIES

∞ ART SUPPLIES ∞

AMSTERDAM ART
160 S. La Brea Ave.
Los Angeles, CA 90036
213/936-8166
HOURS: MON-THUR: 9-8 FRI-SAT: 9-6 SUN: 12-5
CREDIT CARDS: AE, MC, V

You will encounter two floors with 10,000 square feet filled with a variety of supplies and equipment necessary for fine art, illustration art and production art. Experienced salespeople at Amsterdam Art will assist you in solving any problem you might have with graphic layout and design work. Make sure you check out their special retail prices. They have been serving the art community in the Los Angeles area since the late 1960s.

THE ART STORE
11450 S. Ventura Blvd.
Studio City, CA 91604
818/505-1383
HOURS: MON-FRI: 9-7 SAT: 9:30-5:30 SUN: 11-4
CREDIT CARDS: DISC, MC, V

Here's the place to go for a complete selection of artist materials, graphic supplies, fine art, furniture, custom framing and much more. You will be gratified to find their salespeople very knowledgeable about their products. Whether you are into art as a hobby, or you are a seasoned professional, The Art Store offers terrific discounts of 20 to 40% off suggested retail prices. Make sure you get on their mailing list for notification of special sales and general information.
Additional Locations: 6 other stores throughout S. CA

ARTS, CRAFTS & HOBBIES

∞ BEADS, RHINESTONES & CRYSTALS ∞

BOHEMIAN CRYSTAL
812 S. Maple
Los Angeles, CA 90014
213/627-9554
HOURS: MON-SAT: 9-5:30
CREDIT CARDS: MC, V

Bohemian Crystal has one of the largest selection of beads, rhinestones, pearls, metal parts, trimmings, apparel embroidery products, appliques, and all the accessories needed to make custom jewelry. Crystal accessories and chandeliers are also available. At Bohemian Crystal you can save 10 to 40% off retail prices. They have been in business since 1944 and occupy 5,000 square feet of property. You can purchase quality items made of Bohemian crystal from Czechoslovakia or Austria. Whether you're buying a set of crystal stemware for yourself, or a crystal ball for your favorite fortune teller, you can't go wrong shopping here for price and selection.

KLEIN'S BEAD BOX**
309 N. Kings Rd.
Los Angeles, CA 90048
213/651-3595
HOURS: MON-FRI: 10-5 SAT: 10-4
CREDIT CARDS: AE, MC, V

Put together your own designs with wholesale merchandise from Klein's Bead Box. You can be as creative as you want with beads, Swarovski crystals, rhinestones, glass jewels, pearls, sequins and appliques. A professional skater we know from Orange County tells us that Klein's is the only place that carries what she needs for her costumes. Make earrings and necklaces or spice up that basic black dress hanging in the back of your closet! You'll also find a large selection of buttons. Get free advice from the designers that shop at Klein's and don't forget to check out the close-out table for even better buys. Call them for a catalogue and for information on classes they offer. Take your BUYING RETAIL IS STUPID coupon with you for an additional 5% discount.

ARTS, CRAFTS & HOBBIES

∞ CRAFT & FLORAL SUPPLIES ∞

BEV'S CRAFTS & LACE
7620 Tampa Ave.
Reseda, CA 91335
818/881-2257
HOURS: MON & WED: 10-8 TUES, THUR-SAT: 10-6
CREDIT CARDS: CASH OR CHECKS ONLY

Are you envious of creative friends who decorate their homes with handmade seasonal items? If you want to try your hand at crafts, you can get started with supplies at discount prices. Create your own items or borrow some ideas from the samples all over the store. You'll find lots of beads, rhinestones, studs, Christmas boutique supplies, and just about any item you need for creating holiday and special occasion centerpieces. For both sewing and crafts, an entire wall of the store is devoted to lace. Depending on the time of year, 725 to 950 colors and varieties of flat and ruffled lace are available at rock bottom prices. On display throughout the store are items of wearable art so beautifully decorated you might think they were made by a professional artist, but don't let that intimidate you. The staff is very helpful; they can assist you in getting started on your own work of art. Also at discounted prices is a full line of miniatures for doll houses.

CRAFTS PLUS**
19401-7 Parthenia St.
Northridge,CA 91324
818/709-7581
HOURS: MON-SAT: 10-8 SUN: 11-6
CREDIT CARDS: DC, MC, V

Crafts Plus is more than just a discount craft supply store. They offer classes on how to do t-shirt decorating, lace appliques and work with dried flowers. They also offer another service—the Stamp Hut produces decorative stamps at low prices, 20% above wholesale. Wholesalers are welcome; they have a great selection of lace, pearls, ribbons, flowers, paints, baskets and transfers. The classes are free, except for the material costs. The customer can get extra help whenever needed and service is friendly. Be sure to take your BUYING RETAIL IS STUPID discount coupon with you to get an additional 10% off on your purchase.

ARTS, CRAFTS & HOBBIES

CRYSTAL'S LACES & GIFTS**
18215 Parthenia St.
Northridge, CA 91325
818/701-0168
HOURS: MON-SAT: 10-5 TUES: 10-8
CREDIT CARDS: MC, V

Wall decorations can add a lot of warmth to your home, especially with your own personal touch. You can get ready-made items here at about 25% below retail, but you'll save even more if you provide the labor. Crystal's is a large boutique filled with everything needed for crafts and floral arrangements (no needlework). Every Thursday they have a free class called Thursday Treats and it runs from 10:30 a.m. to 3 p.m. There is a huge 99¢ sale every Thanksgiving weekend where most items are sold at cost or below. In October, they hold a "bring your own bag" sale where you'll save an additional 15% off on anything and everything you can fit into your bag. You can bring any size bag you want. October 1st is the beginning of the winter season and Crystal's turns into a Christmas store. Remember to take in your BUYING RETAIL IS STUPID coupon and you'll save an extra 15% off your purchase.

GRASON'S ART CRAFTS AND FLORAL SUPPLIES
31143 Via Colinas, No. 508
Westlake Village, CA 91362
818/707-6008
HOURS: MON-SAT: 10-5:30
CREDIT CARDS: MC, V

Do you get a sense of satisfaction when you complete an arts and crafts project? Whether you are a novice or an old hand at do-it-yourself creativity, you'll find just what you need for almost any project at Grason's priced 10 to 50% off retail. Brides-to-be on a budget will find supplies for party favors, decorations, bridal veils, headdresses, centerpieces and even umbrellas for bridesmaids. If you'd like to start an arts or crafts hobby, but have no idea where to begin, call Grason's for a schedule of classes. Students can buy their supplies (if not already included in the price of the class) at an additional 10% discount off their regularly low prices. The store in Lancaster is called Rainbows and Ribbons.
Additional Locations:
Chatsworth-20816 Plummer St., 818/773-0910
Lancaster-1036 W. Ave. K, 805/945-5644

H & H CRAFT & FLORAL SUPPLY CO.
1885 N. Tustin
Orange, CA 92665
714/998-4460
HOURS: MON-FRI: 9-9 SAT: 9-7 SUN: 10-6
CREDIT CARDS: MC, V

H & H Craft & Floral Supply carries a tremendous line of craft and floral supplies. If you are in need of styrofoam, art supplies, candles, party supplies, macrame, rattan, silk trees, plants and flowers, beads and sequins, floral arrangements, wedding decoration rentals, plasterware, dried flowers, arts and craft books, needlecraft supplies, cake and candy making supplies, wrapping paper or ribbon, this is the place to go. They even have craft and art classes. Last but not least, H & H extends a 10% discount to senior citizens.

Additional Locations:
Garden Grove–12091 Harbor Blvd., 714/750-9222
Mission Viejo–25310 Marguerite Pkwy., 714/770-5001
Palm Desert–72885 Hwy, 111, 619/779-1535
Riverside–6230 Van Buren, 714/359-1091
Temecula–26447 Ynez Rd., 714/695-3308

KIDS' ART SPACE
12532 Riverside Dr.
North Hollywood, CA 91607
818/752-9767
HOURS: TUES-FRI: 10:30-5:30 SAT-SUN: 10:30-5
CREDIT CARDS: MC, V

If you'd like to get your children involved in a wholesome activity and at the same time have someone else clean up the mess, then this is your kind of place. You'll find approximately 1,000 white plaster sculptures at 20% off retail, plus all necessary paints and brushes. Owners Al and Vicky Abrams go one step further. Included in the price of any plaster piece is studio space, paints, brushes and a smock. They'll even store the project for free until it's finished. You will find plaster pieces such as statues, cookie jars, plaques, animals and fantasy characters. Parents can join in the fun or relax watching cable TV or reading periodicals and newspapers. Free popcorn, coffee and tea are also provided.

ARTS, CRAFTS & HOBBIES

MIJANOU'S SILK DESIGNS**
718 E. Imperial Hwy.
Brea, CA 92621
714/990-3601

HOURS: MON-SAT: 9-6
CREDIT CARDS: MC, V

Mijanou's is a place that specializes in silk designs. They buy in quantity and pass the savings on to their very satisfied customers. Everything you need in silk greenery, trees, and flowers can be found here for only 15% above cost. They also carry vases, baskets, floral supplies, and brass. If you are a lover of silk arrangements, you'll find them here. Should you want to design your own arrangement, free consultation is available. In addition, Mijanou's makes certain they not only have a great selection of variety and color, but also take pride in stocking the unusual. Take your BUYING RETAIL IS STUPID coupon with you for an extra 5% discount.

POTTERY AND FLORAL WORLD**
3352 San Fernando Rd.
Los Angeles, CA 90065
213/254-5281

HOURS: 8:30-7 SEVEN DAYS A WEEK
CREDIT CARDS: MC, V

Pottery and Floral World has one of the West Coast's largest selections of pots, pottery, dried and silk flowers, and all the accessories that go along with them. They have great macrame supplies, gourmet ware, baskets and wrought iron. They are both a factory outlet and a direct importer, so you can expect discounts of 20 to 50% off retail prices found elsewhere. They have close-outs weekly, so you always find a changing inventory. If you're looking for Christmas decorations, they carry a complete line. You will get an additional 10% off your purchase price when you use your BUYING RETAIL IS STUPID discount coupon.
Additional Locations: Out of the area (San Francisco & Las Vegas)

ROBERTSON'S INC.
18217 Parthenia Ave.
Northridge, CA 91325
800/CRAFTYU (Orders Only)

HOURS: MON, WED-FRI: 8-5 TUES: 8-8 SAT: 10-5
CREDIT CARDS: MC, V (PURCHASE OVER $100 ONLY)

Robertson's is a wholesaler to craft stores all over the country. If you belong to Price Club, Costco, Pace or have a resale number, you can shop in their ware-house. Prices are at least 50% off retail. There is a minimum $50 first order and $10 on future purchases. There is so much to

ARTS, CRAFTS & HOBBIES

see that you may lose track of time. This 10,000 square foot warehouse is full of wedding supplies (headpieces, center pieces, favors, trimmings), ceramics, paper mache figures ready to be decorated, t-shirts, styrofoam, ribbon (wired, painted, lace and satin) and items in any seasonal theme you can imagine. The Christmas items alone fill two long aisles. The bins all have prices clearly marked and some offer multiple discounts. If you don't belong to one of the membership stores mentioned above or have a resale number, once a year they open the warehouse to the public. It happens on Thanksgiving weekend during their annual "99¢ Sale."

SILK WAREHOUSE**
7651 Sepulveda Blvd.
Van Nuys, CA 91405
818/988-5970

HOURS: MON-SAT: 10-6   SUN: 10-5
CREDIT CARDS: MC, V

Savings run 20 to 40% off retail at Silk Warehouse on single stems or ready-made trees and arrangements. With 20,000 square feet of silk flowers and foliage, you can design away to your heart's content. For a minimal fee they offer classes on flower arranging. After completion of a class, you'll receive a card for a 15% discount on silk flowers and supplies. There is always a sales corner filled with super discounted items too. Take in your BUYING RETAIL IS STUPID coupon and you'll receive an extra 20% discount.

∞ FABRICS & NOTIONS ∞

BIG Y YARDAGE OUTLET
440 S. Main St.
Orange, CA 92668
714/978-3970

HOURS: MON: 9:30-9 TUES-FRI: 9:30-6 SAT: 9:30-5:30
CREDIT CARDS: MC, V

After you have decorated your house with new furniture, stop by Big Y Yardage Outlet for do-it-yourself assistance in making new draperies, bedspreads, valances, tablecloths, cushions, pillows and more. You'll find a large assortment of decorator drapery and upholstery fabrics, along with a sales force knowledgeable about the right fabric to use for your needs. For those of us less creative than others, Big Y Yardage Outlet also offers made-to-order services on the items mentioned above. Miniblinds and shades can be ordered here, too. You'll save at least 25 to 50% off the retail price, and remnants are offered at just 25¢ a yard.

ARTS, CRAFTS & HOBBIES

CALICO CORNERS
3830 Foothill Blvd.
Pasadena, CA 91107
818/792-4328
HOURS: MON: 10-7 TUES-SAT: 10-6 SUN: 12-5
CREDIT CARDS: MC, V

Wouldn't you love to own a quilted bedspread? Well, you can at 30 to 60% above cost when you shop at Calico Corners. They carry designer fabrics, slip covers, tablecloths, feather and down pillows. Upholstery fabrics and books on upholstering are for sale, plus books on slip covers and windows. They have tape for making Roman and Austrian shades, and pleating tape for making curtains. Get on their mailing list so you'll know about their really big sales.

D/M YARDAGE OUTLET
16510 Hawthorne Blvd.
Lawndale, CA 90260
213/772-1800
HOURS: MON-SAT: 9:30-6
CREDIT CARDS: DISC, MC, V

Any day of the week you can save up to 70% off retail prices at D/M Yardage Outlet on thousands of in-stock fabrics, plus discounts on their special order fabrics, too. D/M Yardage Outlet will custom make your draperies and your bedspreads, if you like. They have a beautiful selection of upholstery and drapery fabrics, ready-made draperies, wallpaper, and even discounted mini-blinds.

DESIGNER FABRIC SHOWCASE
10199 Hole Ave.
Riverside, CA 92503
714/354-6684
HOURS: MON-THUR: 10-6 FRI: 10-4 SUN: 12-4
CREDIT CARDS: MC, V

Designer Fabric Showcase is the place to go for spectacular savings on decorative fabrics for the home. They always have at least 1,000 bolts of first quality fabric to choose from. Their fabrics are all kept on rollers enabling you to actually pull out the fabric for a total visual concept rather than only having a little square to look at. If you don't want to do the job yourself, you can order custom draperies, bedspreads and upholstery work. With savings at 50% below manufacturers list and 25% less for labor, you can't go wrong.

ARTS, CRAFTS & HOBBIES

FABRIC WAREHOUSE
11612 W. Olympic
West Los Angeles, CA 90024
310/477-7023
HOURS: MON-FRI: 10-8 SAT: 10-6 SUN: 11-5
CREDIT CARDS: DISC, MC, V

For those of us still interested in taking the time to sew our own clothes, decorate our own homes or just feel like being creative, Fabric Warehouse is definitely the place. You'll be in fashion with the newest fabrics purchased from many of the top clothing manufacturers in New York. Their inventory is constantly changing year round, so you will always find the latest in fabrics and prints, along with their exclusives such as silk prints from St. Gillian. You will find they carry cotton, linen, wool, silk, drapery and upholstery fabrics, as well as notions and patterns. Some of their fabrics are imported. Whatever you do, don't miss out on any of their special sales by making certain you get on their mailing list.

Additional Locations:
Costa Mesa–1805 Placentia, 714/646-4040
Northridge–19536 Business Center Dr., 818/349-3988
Torrance–21303 Hawthorne Blvd., 310/543-5588
Valencia–23152 Valencia Blvd., 805/254-8300

FOAM MART**
628 N. Victory Blvd.
Burbank, CA 91502
818/848-FOAM (3626)
HOURS: MON-SAT: 9-6
CREDIT CARDS: AE, MC, OPT, V

If you're in the market for foam, look no further. Foam Mart has the largest selection around for replacing foam in your sofa and chair cushions. Prices are about 10-20% off retail, but what makes this a super deal is that they'll install the foam for free if you bring in the cushions. In addition to foam, there are several other departments in this 8,000 square foot store. Italian tapestries are about 50% off retail, and most of the other fabrics found here are 40% off retail. You'll also find down and polyester pillow forms in all sizes, furniture and marine vinyls, canvas in all widths and colors, burlap, felt and simulated furs. Foam Mart, in business since 1964, will give you an additional 10% discount when you take in your BUYING RETAIL IS STUPID coupon. The coupon is good only on nonsale items.

ARTS, CRAFTS & HOBBIES

GOLDEN FLEECE DESIGNS INC.**
441 S. Victory Blvd.
Burbank, CA 91502
818/848-7724
HOURS: MON-FRI: 8-5
CREDIT CARDS: AE, MC, V

Canvas, canvas and more canvas. Anything made from canvas can be found here. Canopies, flags, duffle bags, boat covers, sailboat accessories, nautical gift items, marine hardware and hats. They will also custom make any canvas item to suit your needs. You can purchase industrial canvas by the yard and you can also silkscreen and embroider on any item. If you remember to use your BUYING RETAIL IS STUPID coupon you can sail off with an additional 15% discount.

KAGAN TRIM CENTER
750 Towne Ave.
Los Angeles, CA 90021
213/627-9655
HOURS: MON-THUR: 8-5 FRI: 8-4:30
CREDIT CARDS: CASH OR CHECKS ONLY

Anyone that does their own sewing or tailoring will find this store to be truly amazing. If you can imagine it, Kagan Trim Center has it. Apparel construction and fashion products is the proper description of the merchandise they carry. Translated, that means you'll find things like beads, laces, pearls, ribbon, appliques, tassels, webbing, netting, fringe, ruffling and anything else you need. You have the convenience of finding everything you need under one roof, and because they are wholesalers, you can count on exceptional savings. Please note, they only sell their merchandise in full rolls or boxes, no cut yardage and no samples.

MICHAEL LEVINE, INC.
920 S. Maple
Los Angeles, CA 90015
213/622-6259
HOURS: MON-FRI: 9-5:30 SAT: 9-4:30
CREDIT CARDS: MC, V

Michael Levine, Inc. has been in business since the late 1960s; their store occupies one entire block near 9th and Maple in the heart of LA's garment district. Everything you need in fabrics can be found under one roof. They offer a complete bridal department, upholstery products, and drapery goods. Fun furs, piece goods, and other apparel necessities are also available. Everything is priced at 20–50% below retail. Parking is validated for 30 minutes or with a $15.00 minimum purchase.

ARTS, CRAFTS & HOBBIES

LINCOLN FABRICS
1600 Lincoln Blvd.
Venice, CA 90291
310/396-5724

HOURS: TUES-FRI: 10-6 SAT: 10-5:30
CREDIT CARDS: AE, DISC, MC, V

This family business has been in this location since 1955. Their warehouse, so big it covers an entire block, contains over a million yards of fabric. Lincoln Fabrics has drapery fabrics and hardware, hall runners, and upholstery fabrics. You'll be happy to know that you'll be paying at or below wholesale prices! They also carry art and marine canvas, cottons, linens, silks, foam rubber, vinyl, leather, natural burlap and more. You get good service along with a massive selection of merchandise. It's no wonder they've been around for so many years!

OFF THE BOLT
6812 De Soto Blvd.
Canoga Park, CA 91303
818/999-0441

HOURS: MON-FRI: 9-6 SAT: 10-5
CREDIT CARDS: MC, V

All major mills are represented here. Off The Bolt has about 75,000 yards of fabric for your selection. This is a wonderful place to browse through and you can save about 50% off the retail prices. Their selection of decorative fabrics are perfect for drapery and upholstery projects. The salespeople here are most perceptive about your needs, and you really should check out their clearance and remnant tables where you can unearth great fabrics for as low as 50¢ a yard.

ORIENTAL SILK CO.
8377 Beverly Blvd.
Los Angeles, CA 90048
213/651-2323

HOURS: MON-SAT: 9-6
CREDIT CARDS: MC, V

The Oriental Silk Company has exceptional buys on elegant silks and wools. You will discover a large selection of different colors and patterns in this 2,600 square foot store. They import their own products in large quantities and pass the savings on to their customers. You will not only save about 25% off what you'd pay in a fabric store at the mall, but you'll have a lot more to choose from. Call George every now and then to make sure you don't miss out on anything. He'll tell you about his current stock or when his next shipment will be arriving.

ARTS, CRAFTS & HOBBIES

STERN'S DISCOUNT DRAPERY CENTER
226 E. 9th St.
Los Angeles, CA 90015
213/622-3564, 213/622-4894
HOURS: MON-SAT: 9-4
CREDIT CARDS: MC, V

Stern's Discount Drapery Center is a leading wholesaler and retailer (since 1952) of drapery and upholstery fabrics. You will save 40 to 50% off retail and even more on unclaimed items. Custom-made draperies are available, but the savings aren't quite as much as they are on fabrics. Look for their special close out selection of fabrics for more savings.

THE VELVET TOUCH
5666 W. 3rd St.
Los Angeles, CA 90036
213/933-8363
HOURS: TUES-FRI: 10-5   SAT: 10-3
CREDIT CARDS: MC, V

In business since 1959, Yehuda Handel knows what the public wants when it comes to beautiful drapery and upholstery fabrics. He'll also create window coverings for you. Drapery and upholstery fabrics, drapery hardware, mini-blinds, pleated shades, window shades and roman shades are all available here at savings of at least 20 to 50%.

∞ HOBBIES ∞

– COINS –

ASSOCIATED FOREIGN EXCHANGE, INC.
433 N. Beverly Dr.
Beverly Hills, CA 90210
310/274-7610
HOURS: MON-FRI: 9-4:30   SAT: 10-4
CREDIT CARDS: CASH OR CASHIERS/TRAVELERS CHECKS ONLY

Even if you are buying money, why should you pay retail? Yes, Associated Foreign Exchange sells Krugerrands, Mexican Pesos, Credit Swiss bars, silver coins and bullion, and U.S. gold coins and foreign currency. AFEX offers these foreign currencies and precious metals at the lowest market price available. They buy and sell all gold, silver and platinum investment products, with no commission charges and handle over 120 foreign currencies.

ARTS, CRAFTS & HOBBIES

– MODEL TRAINS –

ALLIED MODEL TRAINS
4411 S. Sepulveda Blvd.
Culver City, CA 90230
310/313-9353, 310/475-0463
HOURS: MON-THUR, SAT: 10-6   FRI: 10-9
CREDIT CARDS: AE, MC, V

We have discovered the world's largest model train store! They carry all brands and all sizes of kits, tools, scenery supplies, and automobile and aircraft models. Most everything you see is priced at 20 to 50% off retail. You'll see name brands such as Lionel, LGB, American Flyer, Aster, Athearn and more. Allied Model Trains has 11,600 square feet for hobbyists to explore! For your enjoyment, they have several very interesting, extremely detailed operating displays. Expert repairs are available, and they also buy old trains and toys.

DISCOUNT TRAIN WAREHOUSE**
777 W. Imperial Hwy.
Brea, CA 92621
714/255-0185
HOURS: MON-FRI: 11:30-7:30   SAT: 11-5   SUN: 12-4
CREDIT CARDS: AE, DISC, MC, V

Located 2 miles west of the 57 Freeway on Imperial Highway in the city of Brea, is Southern California's most complete discount model train store. The Discount Train Warehouse carries thousands of items for the model train hobbyist in their 3,500 square foot store—everything for the beginner to expert. Some brand names you'll find are LGB, Lionel plus many more. They are also an authorized Lionel dealer. If you make tracks to this store, they will give you an additional 5% discount when you use your BUYING RETAIL IS STUPID coupon.

THE ROUNDHOUSE TRAIN STORE**,
12804 Victory Blvd.
North Hollywood, CA 91606
818/769-0403
HOURS: MON-THUR, SAT: 8:30-6   FRI: 8:30-9   SUN: 12-5
CREDIT CARDS: AE, DISC, MC, V

No longer are electric train sets a pastime strictly for children. Adults who enjoy collecting trains can be found browsing at one of the largest train stores in Southern California. The Roadhouse Train Store carries such brand names as LGB, Playmobil, Lionel, American Flyer, HO, N &

ARTS, CRAFTS & HOBBIES

Z Gauge and more. Thousands of HO scale-detail parts are in stock. As a matter of fact, the movie industry is constantly buying parts to be used for special effects. Different specials are run every week in addition to their regular discounted prices. Whatever you do, don't forget to bring your BUYING RETAIL IS STUPID coupon for added savings of 10%. Make certain to get on their mailing list for updates on their sales and new merchandise arrivals.

SAN-VAL DISCOUNT INC.
7444 Valjean Ave.
Van Nuys, CA 91406
818/786-8274
HOURS: MON-FRI: 7:30-6 SAT: 8-5
CREDIT CARDS: AE, DISC, MC, V

Youngsters and oldsters alike can get toy trains, buildings and all the necessary accessories at San-Val Discount. Savings run 10-40% off list prices on brand names such as LGB, USA Trains, Rea, Pola, Delton, Lionel, Dan, Regner and many more. They guarantee the lowest prices around and if you show them an advertised price that's lower than their's, they'll beat it! Mail order, shipped the same day, is available. They've been in business since 1980. You can also get aircraft parts and supplies at Sun-Val Discount.

– RUBBER STAMPS –

CRAFTS PLUS**
19401-7 Parthenia St.
Northridge,CA 91324
818/709-7581
HOURS: MON-SAT: 10-8 SUN: 11-6
CREDIT CARDS: DC, MC, V

Crafts Plus is more than just a discount craft supply store. They offer classes on how to do t-shirt decorating, lace appliques and work with dried flowers. They also offer another service—the Stamp Hut produces decorative stamps at low prices, 20% above wholesale. Wholesalers are welcome; they have a great selection of lace, pearls, ribbons, flowers, paints, baskets and transfers. The classes are free, except for the material costs. The customer can get extra help whenever needed and service is friendly. Be sure to take your BUYING RETAIL IS STUPID discount coupon with you to get an additional 10% off on your purchase.

ARTS, CRAFTS & HOBBIES

PARTY KING
6038 Reseda Blvd.
Tarzana, CA 91356
818/343-3343
HOURS: MON-FRI: 8:30-8 SAT: 8:30-6 SUN: 9-5
CREDIT CARDS: MC, V

This 4,000 square foot store has a huge selection of party supplies for every occasion and theme imaginable. Party King consistently has over 150 patterns and fashion colors, including an incredible selection of juvenile ensembles, decorations and party favors. You can expect to save 25% off retail prices on wedding invitations, Bar Mitzvah invitations, and 20% off all greeting cards. Rubber stamp collectors will find "Stamp Castle," a-store-within-a-store, filled with novelty rubber stamps, ink pads, paper and other accessories.

STAMP 'N' DOODLE**
18709 Sherman Way
Reseda, CA 91335
818/881-1366
HOURS: TUES-FRI: 11-7 SAT: 11-6 SUN: 12-5
CREDIT CARDS: MC, V

You'll find at least 2,000 different designs of rubber stamps at Stamp 'N' Doodle. Prices run about 20% off retail on rubber stamps, ink pads in all colors (they will even customize rainbow pads while you wait), markers and paper goods. Merchandise comes from companies such as All Night Media, Hero Arts, Marvy Markers, Printworks, Stamp Francisco, Rubber Stampede, Stampendous and many others. They have free stamping demonstrations and classes are available for $5 (materials included). Use your BUYING RETAIL IS STUPID coupon to receive a free stamp pad with the purchase of three stamps.

– SEASHELLS –

FERGUSON'S MARINE SPECIALTIES**
617 N. Fries Ave.
Wilmington, CA 90744
213/775-1696
HOURS: MON-FRI: 8-4:30 SAT: 8-3
CREDIT CARDS: CASH OR CHECKS ONLY

Shells, shells and more shells—several million in over 500 varieties—is what you'll find at Ferguson's Marine Specialties. Whether you're a collector or use seashells in arts and crafts projects, you'll find them in every

ARTS, CRAFTS & HOBBIES

shape, size and color at discounted prices. They also have nets, ropes and net floats guaranteed to add a touch or realism to a room or party with a nautical theme. The next time you're in the area take in your BUYING RETAIL IS STUPID coupon for a 10% discount and a free carved cowrie shell.

AUTOMOBILES & VEHICLES

∞ ALARMS, STEREOS & TELEPHONES ∞

AHEAD STEREO
7422 Beverly Blvd.
Los Angeles, CA 90036
213/931-8873
HOURS: MON-FRI: 11-7 SAT: 10-6
CREDIT CARDS: MC, V

Here are discount prices for car stereos and cellular phones, with personalized service, in a store that stocks everything. Their inventory includes names such as Technics, Kenwood, ADCOM, Denon, A.D.S., and lots more. "We dare you to beat our prices," they say. You'll appreciate the full service provided by the nice sales staff. All of this, and they guarantee the best price, too.

AUTO STEREO WAREHOUSE
8376 W. Beverly Blvd.
Los Angeles, CA 90048
213/655-5521
HOURS: MON-FRI: 9-5:30 SAT: 10-4
CREDIT CARDS: AE, DISC, MC, V

They have been doing business since 1977. The wide variety of discounts at Auto Stereo Warehouse (5 to 50%) is attributed to manufacturer close-outs and volume purchasing. Specializing in custom installation, they offer auto stereo systems in such names as Alpine, Blaupunkt, ADS, Fosgate, Denon and Becker. Auto alarm systems are available in passive and manual arming, keypad style, remote control, and pagers. Their auto alarm systems are made by Vehicle Security, Derringer 2, Stealth, Quantum, Alpine, Clifford and more. All brands of cellular phones are heavily discounted due to volume buying. Working models of stereos are on display in their carpeted, soundproof showroom for a more accurate and personal selection. In addition to installing stereos, Auto Stereo Warehouse offers custom woodwork and upholstery. Also available are free estimates for insurance replacement work.

AUTOMOBILES & VEHICLES

CELLULAR WHOLESALERS**
4200 Lincoln Blvd.
Marina del Rey, CA 90292
310/827-8885
HOURS: MON-FRI: 7:30-5:30   (CALL FOR SATURDAY HOURS)
CREDIT CARDS: AE, MC, V

Cellular Wholesalers specialize in cellular phones for cars, boats and also handle portable units, fax machines, beepers and car alarms. They offer savings of 20% off retail on all major brands such as Mitsubishi, Oki, NEC and Motorola. They have one of the largest customer service departments in Los Angeles, and installers will come to your premises. They can furnish a mobile number from Pacific Bell or LA Cellular, and have it hooked up anywhere in the U.S. Ask about their "buy 1 get 1 free" plan, and about their special plan designed for large corporations. Your BUYING RETAIL IS STUPID coupon will save you an extra 5%!

INTERSPACE ELECTRONICS, INC.
10854 Washington Blvd.
Culver City, CA 90232
310/836-6018
HOURS: MON-FRI: 10-5   SAT: 10-3
CREDIT CARDS: MC, V

Save from 20 to 50% off retail prices on communications equipment, citizen band radios, scanners, alarm systems for automobiles, and even radar detectors. While we haven't begun to name everything Interspace Electronics has in their inventory, we're sure you get the general idea.

ITC ELECTRONICS**
2772 W. Olympic Blvd.
Los Angeles, CA 90006
213/388-0621
HOURS: MON-SAT: 9-6
CREDIT CARDS: MC, V

ITC Electronics is a full-line authorized distributor of electronic supplies, auto sound products and electronic test equipment. They also carry close-outs and special purchases You can save anywhere from 10 to 60% off retail on such brand names as Sansui, Pyle and Pioneer. Special pricing is available for quantity purchases and don't forget your BUYING RETAIL IS STUPID coupon for an extra 5% discount.
Additional Locations:
Chatsworth–9229 De Soto, 818/700-0900
Oxnard–2320 Vineyard Ave., 805/983-4115)
Torrance–20368 Hawthorne Blvd., 310/370-6211)

AUTOMOBILES & VEHICLES

OLYMPIC ELECTRONICS
6310 Hollywood Blvd.
Hollywood, CA 90028
213/467-4752
HOURS: 10-9 SEVEN DAYS A WEEK
CREDIT CARDS: MC, V

Olympic Electronics is right on the corner of Hollywood and Vine. They promise the lowest prices in the area on AM-FM portable radios, cameras, and stereos for the home or car. They have a store full of electronic wonders from all the major manufacturers, and most are priced at just 5 to 10% over cost. They are wholesale to the public so shop here and save.

RADIOLAND/INGLEWOOD ELECTRONICS
4701 W. Century Blvd.
Inglewood, CA 90304
310/671-7761
HOURS: MON-FRI: 9:30-6 SAT: 9-5 SUN: 12-4
CREDIT CARDS: AE, V

Radioland/Inglewood Electronics offers discount prices on name brands seven days a week. Their customers save from 25 to 50% off retail on radio and television tubes, transistors, TV antennas, cable TV accessories, as well as stereos and CB radios for vehicles. A few of the other items available here are portable radios, phonograph needles, and most electronic parts.

ROGERSOUND LABS
8381 Canoga Ave.
Canoga Park, CA 91304
818/882-4600
HOURS: 10-10 SEVEN DAYS A WEEK
CREDIT CARDS: AE, MC, V

Rogersound Labs carries speaker systems, audio-video components, car stereos, and much more. They have discounted prices on such brand names as Sony, Kenwood, Yamaha, Mitsubishi, and JVC. You can count on finding a helpful, professional staff at any of their stores. By the way, the salespeople don't work on commission. Also at the Canoga Park location is their outlet store where you'll find discontinued items at greater discounts.

Additional Locations: 10 other stores throughout S. CA

AUTOMOBILES & VEHICLES

SOUNDS GOOD STEREO
7218 Topanga Canyon Blvd.
Canoga Park, CA 91303
818/999-4523
HOURS: MON-SAT: 9-6
CREDIT CARDS: AE, MC, V

This discount store offers you a selection of stereo systems for your car or truck, cellular telephones and automobile alarms. You'll find their merchandise priced at about 30 to 40% off retail. Since 1978, Sounds Good Stereo has been featuring low prices and high quality with such names as Alpine, Rockford, JBL, Fosgate, Concord, and more. They're equipped for repairs and are very proud of their professional, award winning installation department. Sounds good to us.

SPEAKER CITY
10615 Vanowen St.
Burbank, CA 91505
818/508-1908
HOURS: MON-SAT: 10-6
CREDIT CARDS: MC, V OR CASH ONLY (NO CHECKS)

We've discovered a virtual candy store for speaker enthusiasts and audiophiles, filled with speakers for the home and complete sound systems for vehicles, at savings of at least 50%! All components needed to build speakers from scratch, and also complete kits for speaker systems can be found here. They do "X-overs" too. One of the great things about Speaker City is you know exactly what you are buying. The price of a speaker already built is no longer a mystery because lining the walls are the individual components that went into the speaker, along with the cost of each item. Though they only carry speakers for the home (no stereos), they do stock complete sound systems for your car (no installations). Customized speaker systems are available for both home and vehicles. Names you'll recognize include Focal, Dynaudio, Vifa, Peerless and Pyle. If you need any technical advice, talk to Wally Noss. He's not only an expert on sound systems, he's also a professional musician.

AUTOMOBILES & VEHICLES

∞ BATTERIES ∞

BATTERY DEPOT
9118 Glenoaks Blvd.
Sun Valley, CA 91352
818/768-7802

HOURS: MON-FRI: 8-6 SAT: 8-3
CREDIT CARDS: CASH OR CHECKS ONLY

New and rebuilt batteries are sold here for autos, trucks, and RVs. On new batteries you'll save 50% off retail. In addition to batteries, they sell starters and alternators. The friendly people you'll meet at Battery Depot will do an electrical check for you at no charge. Major brands include Delco, GNB, and many more.

BATTERY SPECIALIST CO.
21303 Sherman Way
Canoga Park, CA 91303
818/884-2288

HOURS: MON-FRI: 9-6 SAT: 9-1
CREDIT CARDS: ALL MAJOR

The Battery Specialist Co. carries over 1,000 batteries for all applications at extremely competitive prices. Most all major brands are included. Considering themselves problem solvers of any kind of battery needs, they will analyze your problem or concern, recommend a product and check the equipment for you. The Canoga Park store is closed on Sundays, but their Van Nuys store is open every day. Call them for their hours on Sundays.
Additional Locations:
  Van Nuys–7444 Van Nuys Blvd, 818/988-2288

LYNWOOD BATTERY MFG. CO., INC.
4054 E. Washington Blvd.
Los Angeles, CA 90040
213/263-8866

HOURS: TUES-FRI: 7-3:30
CREDIT CARDS: CASH OR CHECKS ONLY

Just as the name implies, the Lynwood Co. manufactures their own batteries. They've been selling their merchandise to the trucking industry and marine dealers in California, Arizona and Colorado since the 1930s. Even though they use only the highest quality materials, you can buy your battery at 20 to 50% over cost! That should give you a charge.

AUTOMOBILES & VEHICLES

∞ FLOOR MATS ∞

ULTIMAT CAR MATS
16673 Roscoe Blvd.
North Hills, CA 91343
818/895-6287
HOURS: MON-FRI: 9-5:30   SAT: 10-3
CREDIT CARDS: MC, V

Ultimat Car Mats specializes in mats for any make or any model automobile. If you're sprucing up your car or have just bought a brand new one, you can purchase mats to match from their assortment of 20 colors. They offer same day service for both standard and custom monograms. Look for discounts at 20 to 25% below retail at this factory outlet.

∞ PARTS ∞

ABC AUTO PARTS DISTRIBUTING
21360 Deering Court
Canoga Park, CA 91304
818/883-3021
HOURS: MON-FRI: 8-6   SAT: 8-5   SUN: 9-4
CREDIT CARDS: MC, V

ABC Auto Parts sells all brake parts, shock absorbers, clutches, brake drums, disc rotors, power steering components, machine drums, and fly wheels. Name brands include, among others, Bendix, TRW, KYB, and Wagner. Started in 1968, this family operation is reputed to be the most knowledgeable in the business. They have the largest inventory in the San Fernando Valley and offer their customers savings between 20 to 30% off retail prices found elsewhere.

BOB'S AUTO SUPPLY
1539 W. Manchester Ave.
Los Angeles, CA 90047
213/759-1155
HOURS: MON-FRI: 8-6   SAT: 8-5
CREDIT CARDS: CASH OR CHECKS ONLY

Instead of running all over town, do-it-yourself mechanics can find everything they need at Bob's Auto Supply. Savings run 30 to 50% on all auto parts and machine shop services. They carry quality AC-Delco parts, brake drums, and can provide engine repair and parts—foreign and domestic. Complete engines are also available for sale.

AUTOMOBILES & VEHICLES

RAP DISCOUNT AUTO PARTS & MARINE SUPPLY
21407 Vanowen St.
Canoga Park, CA 91303
818/884-3370
HOURS: MON-FRI: 8-9 SAT: 8-5 SUN: 9-5
CREDIT CARDS: AE, DISC, MC, V

Rap is the specialist in reconditioning of cylinder heads for automotive or marine engines. They carry a complete line of spare parts for engines of all types and sell them at 30 to 70% below retail. You'll find welding goods, and products made by Cannon, Adesco and Ditzler. In addition to foreign and domestic parts, they have a complete machine shop for engine work, and they make hydraulic, air conditioning and power steering hoses.

SONNY'S RADIATOR EXCHANGE**
34996 Yucaipa Blvd.
Yucaipa, CA 92399
714/790-1991 800/551-3388
HOURS: MON-FRI: 8:30-5 SAT: 8:30-1
CREDIT CARDS: MC, V

This warehouse distributor stocks more than 3,000 radiators. They also discount items such as headers, air condition condensers, shock absorbers, transmission oil coolers, mufflers and fan clutches. Some of the brand names they carry are K.Y.B., Modine, Blackstone, Mando, Stuart and Daniels. Prices quoted are cash prices. You'll receive a 10% discount when you purchase a radiator and a free container of Permatex Sealant by using your BUYING RETAIL IS STUPID coupon.

SURPLUS CITY JEEP PARTS
11796 Sheldon St.
Sun Valley, CA 91352
818/767-3666
HOURS: MON-SAT: 9-6
CREDIT CARDS: MC, V

Whether your Jeep is new or used, this is the place to go for all your jeep needs. Expect to find their prices 20–30% below dealer prices. Your vehicle may be all terrain, but you won't need to go over hill and dale to find good prices—just stop here.

AUTOMOBILES & VEHICLES

– USED PARTS –

MARV'S U.S.A. AUTO DISMANTLING
11021 Tuxford St.
Sun Valley, CA 91352
818/767-6615, 213/875-2781
HOURS: MON-FRI: 8-5
CREDIT CARDS: MC, V

Marv's U.S.A. Auto Dismanting carries over 45,000 item numbers in their computerized used parts inventory. All their parts (domestic only) are cleaned and tested and carry a six month guarantee. They have 20 experienced countermen to help you find the part you need. You can save 50 to 65% off the cost of new parts when you buy from Marv's. Why spend more on new parts when Marv's are less and are guaranteed?

∞ RV SUPPLIES & EQUIPMENT ∞

SHELL CENTER OF THOUSAND OAKS, THE
3242 E. Thousand Oaks Blvd.
Thousand Oaks, CA 91362
805/373-0259
HOURS: MON-FRI: 8:30-5 SAT: 9-4
CREDIT CARDS: AE, MC, V

When we first heard of this place we pictured it to be a store, with a tropical sort of decor, filled with exotic seashells from all over the world. Boy, were we wrong! The Shell Center of Thousand Oaks carries shells for any kind of pick-up truck. Some of the names carried are Snug Top Brahma, Stockland, Vista and others. First you start out with a barebones shell and then add factory options You can expect to find about 110–150 shells in stock.

SIX-PAC FACTORY OUTLET
1450 Pomona Rd.
Corona, CA 91720
714/735-2402
HOURS: MON-FRI: 9-5 SAT: 9-4
CREDIT CARDS: MC, V

Since 1938 Six-Pac Factory Outlet has been serving the RV industry with great buys on RV parts, accessories and shells. Depending on what you are buying, savings run from 5 to 25%. They have unadvertised specials, so call to check out their best deals.

VAN DE CAMPER**
7801 Noble Ave.
Van Nuys, CA 91405
818/780-6361
HOURS: MON-FRI: 9-5 SAT: 10-3
CREDIT CARDS: MC, V

Okay you van enthusiasts, Van De Camper is the place to get a complete van conversion—everything from running boards, seats, windows, carpeting, drink trays, paneling, televisions, refrigerators, and all the other products needed for the self-contained vehicle. You can do the work yourself, or you can let Van de Camper build and install to your specifications. While there, look at their catalogues for automobiles, trucks, vans, and performance and racing cars. Their catalogues feature aftermarket items, accessories and replacement parts. You can save between 30 to 50% off dealer prices. With your BUYING RETAIL IS STUPID coupon, you can save an extra 5% on van supplies, or an extra 10% off catalogue orders!

∞ REPAIR & MAINTENANCE ∞

– BODY WORK –

ASSOCIATED AUTO BODY**
11803 Sherman Way
North Hollywood, CA 91605
818/764-5884
HOURS: MON-FRI: 8-5 SAT: 9-12
CREDIT CARDS: DISC, MC, V

Associated Auto Body mainly does contract work for insurance companies, combining high quality with thoroughness and consistency. Luckily, they also welcome the individual customer and give them a discount on the labor charges. Serving the public in this area since the late 1960s, they do complete frame, auto body repair, and repainting. Price and time estimates are given in advance. The job usually gets done in the promised time, but if it doesn't, they will let you know. Not only will you find the people accommodating and friendly, their work is guaranteed. You'll save an extra 5% discount on labor charges with your BUYING RETAIL IS STUPID coupon.

AUTOMOBILES & VEHICLES

– ENGINE WORK –

FRANCO'S ENGINE REBUILDERS
4989 N. Huntington Dr.
Los Angeles, CA 90032
213/225-4129
HOURS: MON-SAT: 8-6 SUN: 8-4
CREDIT CARDS: CASH ONLY

A professional engineer supervises the remanufacturing of the engines, and you also get factory-direct, wholesale prices. Franco's services domestic and foreign engines; plus they have a large inventory of engines and a complete line of auto parts. They offer a good warranty and have been in business since 1975.

– GLASS REPLACEMENT –

ALL STAR GLASS
7535 Woodley Ave.
Van Nuys, CA 91406
818/902-1511
HOURS: MON-FRI: 8-5 SAT: 8-12
CREDIT CARDS: DISC, MC, V

All Star Glass specializes in windshield replacement for automobiles. Free mobile service is provided, which means, they'll do the work at your home at no extra charge. If you need an estimate, All Star Glass will give you one on the phone. They provide written guarantees and have qualified technicians/installers, maintaining factory standards.
Additional Locations: 14 other shops throughout S. CA

∞ SALES, LEASING & RENTALS ∞

GAYNOR'S CYCLE SALES
11916 S. Prairie Ave.
Hawthorne, CA 90250
310/644-2900
HOURS: MON-FRI: 8-6 SAT: 8-5
CREDIT CARDS: DISC, MC, V

If you're looking for a low cost means of transportation or just fun on the week-ends, visit California's largest selection of used motorcycles at Gaynor's Cycle Sales. You can choose from 500 cycles with such brand names as Suzuki, Yamaha, Kawasaki and Honda.

MICKEY'S AUTO SALES & LEASING
5554 Reseda Blvd.
Tarzana, CA 91356
818/996-9601, 800/882-AUTO
HOURS: BY APPOINTMENT ONLY MON-FRI: 9-5:30
CREDIT CARDS: CASH OR CASHIER'S CHECKS ONLY

Since 1957, Mickey's Auto Sales & Leasing, the oldest discount auto broker in Los Angeles, has helped thousands of people save time and money on the purchase and lease of new vehicles. This licensed and bonded dealer, through it's computerized dealer network, researches hundreds of dealers to find your new vehicle, in your choice of color and equipment, at the lowest price possible. They handle all makes and models, foreign and domestic, including vans and trucks. Trade-ins are welcomed. Low cost financing is available or they'll work with your credit union or bank. Substantial discounts are available on aftermarket items such as alarms and telephones. Mickey's charges no service fee! Decide on the make, model, color and options you want and call for an appointment. At your meeting, you'll find out how nice it is to get your next car without the hassling and haggling usually associated with purchasing or leasing a new vehicle.

NATIONAL AUTO BROKERS, INC.
23011 Moulton Pkwy., Suite I-11
Laguna Hills, CA 92653
714/770-7441
HOURS: MON-FRI: 9-6:30
CREDIT CARDS: MC, V, CASHIERS CHECKS

National Auto Brokers (NAB) has serviced Southern Californians for more than a decade . They have sold and leased thousands of cars and trucks to customers at enormous savings. They sell all makes and models, domestic or foreign. Their volume allows them to purchase new vehicles at the lowest prices, and because they operate on a low fixed fee, the savings are really remarkable. You can save $500 to $5,000 depending on the make or model. They take trade-ins and provide financing and leasing OAC. Leases can be tailored to the buyer's specifications, and they offer the lowest cost "bumper-to-bumper" extended warranty available anywhere. Cashiers checks are preferred, but bank drafts are accepted.

AUTOMOBILES & VEHICLES

RENT-A-WRECK
12333 W. Pico Blvd.
Los Angeles, CA 90064
310/478-0676, 800/423-0676
HOURS: MON-SAT: 7-7 SUN: 8-4
CREDIT CARDS: MC, V

Why not go to Rent-A-Wreck where you can save on car rentals by renting a vintage beauty at 20 to 40% less than standard. You can also rent a van, pick-up truck or classic convertible. Their used cars rent for as little as $19.95 a day, some have free mileage. If you're curious, they'll send additional information.
Additional Locations: 25 other offices in S. CA–Call 800/535-1391

UGLY DUCKLING RENT-A-CAR
10620 Venice Blvd.
Culver City, CA 90230
310/837-7752
HOURS: MON-FRI: 8-6 SAT: 9-5
CREDIT CARDS: AE, MC, V

Save a buck, rent a duck. That's their slogan, not ours. But the fact remains that Ugly Duckling will meet or beat other prices in town. You won't know until you call. All cars are used.

∞ SERVICES ∞

– DRIVING SCHOOL –

FORD DRIVING SCHOOL
4624 Hollywood Blvd.
Los Angeles, CA 90027
213/660-1212
HOURS: MON-FRI: 8AM-9:30PM SAT: 9-5 SUN: 9-3
CREDIT CARDS: CASH OR CHECKS ONLY

This is a full driving school service promising the lowest possible rates in town. Ford says they'll save adults taking their courses 50% and savings run 40% for courses designed for teenagers. Need a traffic school because of a speeding ticket? You'll save 20% at Ford's traffic school. In addition to their 18 years of experience, they have dual control cars, male and female instructors and can handle all languages. They also have fast, economy courses where teens can take driver's education and training in one week at their special, low price.

AUTOMOBILES & VEHICLES

– INSURANCE –

SURVIVAL INSURANCE
6301 Sunset Blvd., #104
Hollywood, CA 90028
800/441-5533 or 213/957-8010

HOURS: MON-FRI: 9-9 SAT: 9-6
CREDIT CARDS: MC, V

Survival Insurance says they'll save you 15 to 20% on auto insurance if you give them a call. Even if you drive an exotic car or have a few tickets, they say they can still save you money on your insurance needs. Remember, you have to have insurance on your car in California, it's the law! So in order to survive, you may want to call Survival Insurance.
Additional Locations:
Santa Ana–2112 N. Tustin Ave., 714/285-2900
Sherman Oaks–14396 Ventura Blvd., 818/382-7100
Torrance–17228 Hawthorne Blvd., 310/793-1000
Upland–345 Mountain Ave., 714/931-3000

– ROAD SERVICE –

AUTOMOBILE CLUB OF SOUTHERN CALIFORNIA
2601 S. Figeroa
Los Angeles, CA 90007
213/741-3330

HOURS: MON-FRI: 9-5
CREDIT CARDS: MC, V

How many times have you locked your keys in the car or had a flat tire on the road? Being a member of the Automobile Club of Southern California would have solved your problems easily. Today the Automobile Club's 3.7 million members benefit by the organization's emergency road services; travel planning with maps, tourbooks and reservations; automotive testing and analysis; automobile buying services; auto pricing information and competitively priced auto insurance. Most services (not insurance) are free with your annual membership. All this for a first-time membership fee of $58. Members rejoining pay only $38 each year. With just one road service tow, you'll probably recoup your investment. Membership entitles you to four free tows a year. When you're planning a trip, stop by and pick up some of their excellently written tour books. They have a wealth of information, and can suggest many places to use your membership card for additional discounts while traveling.
Additional Locations: 78 other sites in S. CA

AUTOMOBILES & VEHICLES

∞ TIRES ∞

BOB'S TIRE TOWN
2478-2484 W. Washington Blvd.
Los Angeles, CA 90018
213/731-6389
HOURS: MON-FRI: 7:30-5:30 SAT: 7:30-3:30
CREDIT CARDS: AE, MC, V

Bob's Tire Town offers B.F. Goodrich, Pirelli, Uniroyal, Michelin, Solar Shocks at 10 to 20% above cost. They also offer brake repair, alignment and front-end work at significant savings. There are great buys on custom wheels for those of you with real hot "rides."

BOB MIRMAN'S WESTCOAST TIRE AND BRAKE
2239 Pontius Ave.
West Los Angeles, CA 90064
310/477-7057
HOURS: MON-FRI: 8-5:30 SAT: 8-3
CREDIT CARDS: MC, V

If your tires are looking a little bald then head on over to Bob Mirman's. He'll meet or beat any price in town. To remove any doubt, current ads from their discount competitors are posted for do-it-yourself price comparisons. There are 14 lines of brand-name tires in stock and special orders are no problem. In addition to tires, you can have your vehicle aligned in the four-wheel computer alignment center; completion within one hour is guaranteed. Other services include brakes, struts, shocks, air conditioning and heating, radiators, and batteries. Mirman's also provides a waiting room complete with cable TV, refreshments and a courtesy telephone for local calls. You'll save more paying by cash or check.

TELETIRE
17622 Armstrong Ave.
Irvine, CA 92714
714/250-9141
HOURS: MON-FRI: 7-6 SAT: 8-1
CREDIT CARDS: MC, V

Teletire is a mail and phone order operation that will save you 40–60% off retail on tires from Bridgestone, Dunlop, Continental, Pirelli, Michelin and Yokohama. You can also order wheels from Euki and American Racing. They're a division of 4-Day Tire, based in Irvine, CA. With their phones staffed by tire experts, not just order clerks, you can feel comfortable placing an order.

BEAUTY SUPPLIES

∞ COSMETICS, FRAGRANCES & SUPPLIES ∞

BALL BEAUTY SUPPLIES
416 N. Fairfax Ave.
Los Angeles, CA 90036
213/655-2330

HOURS: MON-SAT: 8:30-5:30
CREDIT CARDS: MC, V

Ball Beauty Supplies carries everything for your hair and manicuring needs, and you'll save 30 to 50% off retail by shopping there. They have been serving the public for over 35 years and know what their customers like. You will find everything from hair coloring to curling irons. Excuse the pun, but you'll have a ball shopping at Ball Beauty Supplies.

CROWN DISCOUNT BEAUTY SUPPLY**
19228 Ventura Blvd.
Tarzana, CA 91356
818/344-8307

HOURS: MON-FRI: 9:30-6 SAT: 9:30-5:30
CREDIT CARDS: AE, DISC, MC, V

Crown Discount Beauty Supply has been serving their customers for the past seven years with hair care, nail care and hair accessories at 10 to 15% off retail. You'll find products such as Sebastian, Paul Mitchell and Mastey. Most of Crown's experienced staff have their hair and nail care licenses. You can "trim" an additional 10% off the purchase price when you shop with a BUYING RETAIL IS STUPID coupon here!

FRAGRANCE BOUTIQUE
44413 Valley Central Way
Lancaster, CA 93536
805/723-7001

HOURS: MON-SAT: 10-7 SUN: BY APPOINTMENT ONLY
CREDIT CARDS: MC, V

For the ladies in Antelope Valley, Fragrance Boutique features fabulous custom-blended versions of over 100 of the world's most sought after perfumes, for the low-low price of $29.95. You can also get your man his favorite cologne at the same price. Also featured at Fragrance Boutique is a unique service—a fragrance compatibility test. This test deter-

BEAUTY SUPPLIES & COSMETICS

mines which fragrances are best suited to a woman's body chemistry—no more guess-work or frustration and expense in "trial and error." An appointment is recommended for the compatibility test. There is plenty of free parking, and a mail order service is available.

LACE & SCENTS
9140 Owensmouth Ave.
Chatsworth, CA 91311
818/718-3900

HOURS: MON–FRI: 9–5
CREDIT CARDS: AE, MC, V

This is a great place to buy fragrances for men and women at 10 to 50% off department store prices. Brand names include Passion, Opium, Obsession, Lagerfeld, Chanel, Aramis, Chloe, Eternity, Poison, and many more. Don't forget to check out the large selection of designer lingerie priced 50 to 75% below retail. We can't name names, but you'll recognize the same items found in department and lingerie stores.

LORA BEAUTY CENTER
18737 Ventura Blvd.
Tarzana, CA 91356
818/705-4030

HOURS: MON-SAT: 9:30-6:30
CREDIT CARDS: MC, V

Looking for the best prices in town on Lancome products? Sean Miles, the owner of Lora Beauty Center, guarantees to beat anyone's price on Lancome products and fragrances. In addition to Lancome, they carry a complete line of beauty supplies and professional hair care products. You'll also find name brand fragrances such as Halston, Fendi, Chanel, Polo, and many others. You'll save 10 to 50% off retail shopping here. The store in Los Angeles is called Bel Air Discount Beauty Supply.
Additional Locations:
Los Angeles–11677 San Vicente Blvd., 310/826-6159

MAX FACTOR OUTLET**
1666 N. Highland Ave.
Hollywood, CA 90028
213/463-6164

HOURS: MON-SAT: 9-5
CREDIT CARDS: AE, MC, OPT, V

Here's a wonderful opportunity to buy cosmetics bearing one of the world's most famous names. When shopping at Max Factor Outlet you can save 25% off retail on cosmetics worn by so many stars and many of

BEAUTY SUPPLIES & COSMETICS

the world's most beautiful women. This wonderful outlet carries the entire line of Max Factor, including products such as nail polish and fragrances. They also have beauty advisors if you need assistance. It's located next door to the Max Factor of Beauty Museum. You'll save an extra 5% when you use your BUYING RETAIL IS STUPID coupon.

PARIS PERFUME
21727 Sherman Way
Canoga Park, CA 91303
818/348-4780
HOURS: MON-SAT: 9-7
CREDIT CARDS: ALL MAJOR

Do you feel as though you're not completely dressed without a dab of perfume or eau de toilette here and there? You can buy all your favorite scents at Paris Perfume at 20 to 50% off retail. In addition to the newer fragrances that abound in today's market, they stock classics that have been around for many years like Shalimar, Joy, White Shoulders and even Jungle Gardenia. You will also find a large selection of men's scents such as Aramis, Bijan, Brut, Boss and many others, too.

PERFUME CITY
12215 Ventura Blvd., No. 204 (Times Square Center)
Studio City, CA 91604
818/763-1875
HOURS: MON-SAT: 10-7   SUN: 12-5
CREDIT CARDS: MC, V

Whether you're looking for men's or women's fragrances, Perfume City has hundreds of scents at 10 to 60% off retail. Brand names include Ysatis, Bijan, Beverly Hills, Tiffany, Montana, Kenzo, Opium, Joy, Safari, Red, Calyx, Clinique Aromatics and lots more. If you happen to be glancing through a fashion magazine and spot a new perfume, chances are that Perfume City will have it in stock before the department stores receive their shipments. They also carry many scents no longer carried by many retailers. Miniature collectors will have to control themselves when they see the selection here. This neatly organized boutique is always on the look-out for super buys to pass on to their satisfied customers. Gift wrapping is free and if you're buying for several people, they will put removable stickers on each package so you'll know what's what when you get home. All purchases come with a 30-day money-back guarantee.

BEAUTY SUPPLIES & COSMETICS

PRESTIGE FRAGRANCE & COSMETICS
100 Citadel Dr. (Citadel Outlet Connection)
Los Angeles, CA 90040
213/887-1135
HOURS: MON-SAT: 9-9 SUN: 11-6
CREDIT CARDS: MC, V

Revlon, Max Factor, Ultima II, Germaine Monteil, Borghese, Jean Nate, Ciara, Norrell, Maroe, Bill Blass cosmetics and fragrances can be found at 10 to 60% off retail at PFC Fragrance & Cosmetics. They are a factory-direct outlet, so make it a point to check out their prices, service and quality. Additional health and beauty aids and gift items can also be found here. Prestige Fragrance & Cosmetics are all located in factory outlet malls. The Ontario store is in Plaza Continental Factory Stores and the San Ysidro store is located at San Diego Factory Outlet Center.
Additional Locations:
Ontario–3700 E. Inland Empire Blvd., 714/944-5881
San Ysidro–4498 Camino de la Plaza, 619/428-4480

STERLING BEAUTY SUPPLY CO.
1244 N. Vine St.
Hollywood, CA 90028
213/463-6801
HOURS: MON-SAT: 9-6 SUN: 11-5
CREDIT CARDS: MC, V

Save 20 to 40% off retail prices on one of the largest selections of brand-name beauty products, shampoos, hair coloring, permanents, and any other products to make you more beautiful. They also carry products like TCB and Lustra-Silk. You will find that Sterling Beauty Supply Company has a friendly, knowledgeable staff to give you expert advice.
Additional Locations: 7 other stores throughout S. CA

WILSHIRE BEAUTY SUPPLY CO.
5401 Wilshire Blvd.
Los Angeles, CA 90036
213/937-2000
HOURS: MON-FRI: 9-8 SAT: 9-6 SUN: 11-5
CREDIT CARDS: MC, V

Your hair really is your crowning glory. You can have on an unbelievable outfit, but if your hair isn't together, forget it. At Wilshire Beauty Supply Company you can purchase all the hair products you need for 20% above cost. If you'd like to try a new product someone there will be happy to recommend something suitable for your type of hair. You will also find a selection of cosmetics and nail products. They have a

BEAUTY SUPPLIES & COSMETICS

monthly catalogue for professional cosmetologists, as well as seminars and educational classes.
Additional Locations:
Arleta–8915 Woodman Ave., 818/891-5745)
Beverly Hills–153 S. Beverly Dr., 310//276-0627
Simi Valley–2311-G Tapo St., 805/526-2281
W. Los Angeles–10863 W. Pico Blvd., 310/475-3531

∞ HAIRSTYLING ∞

C.E.N.T.R.E. SALON
6109 De Soto Ave.
Woodland Hills, CA 91367
818/347-1900
HOURS: CALL FOR HOURS
CREDIT CARDS: NONE

If you want your hair snipped into the latest fashion, you can get it done here for free. Twice a month they have training programs in up-to-date hair fashions for Sebastian's new stylists. They'll let you know what the styles are and if they don't happen to to your liking or if your hair isn't the right length for your cut, they'll put you on their mailing list for future cuts. Although they only do this twice a month, you sure can't beat the price. It's free!

∞ WIGS ∞

SHAKY WIGS OF HOLLYWOOD
6364 Hollywood Blvd.
Hollywood, CA 90028
213/461-8481
HOURS: MON-SAT: 10-7 SUN: 1-5
CREDIT CARDS: AE, MC, V

If you are looking for that perfect wig, hair accessory or even hairspray, go straight to Shaky Wigs of Hollywood. We flipped our wigs when we saw over 100 wigs to choose from! Don't be shy! Go ahead and try on any number of their wigs which are discounted 10 to 20% off retail. By the way, this store isn't just for women. Men will find wigs and toupees made from 100% human hair. Other services offered are braiding and weaving.

BEAUTY SUPPLIES & COSMETICS

WILSHIRE WIGS, INC.
13213 Saticoy St.
North Hollywood, CA 91605
818/983-0874
HOURS: MON-FRI: 9-5:30 SAT: 9-4
CREDIT CARDS: ALL MAJOR

Men and women alike will find whatever they need in wigs and hairpieces (synthetic and human hair) at Wilshire Wigs priced 40 to 70% off retail. They have 6,000 square feet filled with 800 models with brand names such as Eva Gabor, On-Rite, Alan Thomas, Tony of Beverly Hills, Adolfo, Rene Paris and many others. You can buy ready-made items or you can have something customized just for you. If you're new at this, the staff can help you find the right style and color.

BOATING & MARINE PRODUCTS

B & B MARINE EQUIPMENT & SERVICE, INC.
2701 W. Coast Hwy.
Newport Beach, CA 92663
714/646-8901
HOURS: MON-SAT: 9-5
CREDIT CARDS: MC, V

B & B has been doing business at this Newport Beach location since 1977. They carry a full line of communication and navigation equipment, paint and finishes, safety equipment, and all boating accessories. In fact, they say, "Call us for anything marine." Next day delivery is available and also installation service. They carry all major brands including Raytheon, 3M, Furuno, Micrologic, Data-marine, Apelco, Marinetech, Sterling, and many others. Call around. All of their products are discounted and the best price is guaranteed. Orders are taken over the phone so, if you already know what you need, give them a call.

GOLDEN FLEECE DESIGNS INC.**
441 S. Victory Blvd.
Burbank, CA 91502
818/848-7724
HOURS: MON-FRI: 8-5
CREDIT CARDS: AE, MC, V

Canvas, canvas and more canvas. Anything made from canvas can be found here. Canopies, flags, duffle bags, boat covers, sailboat accessories, nautical gift items, marine hardware and hats. They will also custom make any canvas item to suit your needs. You can purchase industrial canvas by the yard and you can also silkscreen and embroider on any item. If you remember to use your BUYING RETAIL IS STUPID coupon and you can sail off with an additional 15% discount.

LYNWOOD BATTERY MFG. CO., INC.
4054 E. Washington Blvd.
Los Angeles, CA 90040
213/263-8866
HOURS: TUES-FRI: 7-3:30
CREDIT CARDS: CASH OR CHECKS ONLY

Just as the name implies, the Lynwood Co. manufactures their own batteries. They've been selling their goods to the trucking industry and marine dealers in California, Arizona and Colorado since the 1930s.

BOATING & MARINE PRODUCTS

Even though they use only the highest quality materials, you can buy your battery at 20 to 50% over cost! That should give you a charge.

RAP DISCOUNT AUTO PARTS & MARINE SUPPLY
21407 Vanowen St.
Canoga Park, CA 91303
818/884-3370
HOURS: MON-FRI: 8-9 SAT: 8-5 SUN: 9-5
CREDIT CARDS: AE, DISC, MC, V

Rap is the specialist in reconditioning of cylinder heads for automotive or marine engines. They carry a complete line of spare parts for engines of all types and sell them at 30 to 70% below retail prices. You'll find Cannon, Adesco parts, Ditzler paints and supplies, welding supplies, and marine accessories. In addition to foreign and domestic auto parts, they also have a complete machine shop for any kind of engine work, and they make hydraulic, air conditioning and power steering hoses.

BOOKS & MAGAZINES

∞ NEW & USED ∞

BODHI TREE ANNEX
8585 Melrose Ave.
Los Angeles, CA 90069
310/659-3227
HOURS: 11-7 SEVEN DAYS A WEEK
CREDIT CARDS: MC, V

The Bodhi Tree Annex specializse in homeopathic remedy, herbs, and all metaphysical books. Discounts of 50% off retail are not unusual. They buy and sell, and they have a substantial inventory of used books. It's a fun place to browse, especially if you are philosophically undernourished.

BOOK MART U.S.A.
12152 Victory Blvd.
North Hollywood, CA 91606
818/980-2241
HOURS: TUES-SAT: 10-5:30
CREDIT CARDS: CASH OR CHECKS ONLY

You've been playing the game all your life. Now learn "How to Win at Bingo." This is probably the only store that carries this manual of current Bingo games. Along with this book, you can get complete Bingo game supplies. Book Mart stocks over ten thousand separate titles of paperback books at 20 to 70% off the publisher's printed price.

BOOKSTAR
3005 El Camino Real (Tustin Marketplace)
Tustin, CA 92630
714/731-3166
HOURS: 9AM-11PM SEVEN DAYS A WEEK
CREDIT CARDS: ALL MAJOR

Books, books and more books! Newly located in California, Bookstar is one of the largest suppliers of discounted books. Their regular savings are 5% on paperbacks and 33-1/2% on bestsellers. When you purchase a $10 yearly membership, savings are increased to 15% on paperbacks and 40% on bestsellers. Make sure you check out their bargain table for additional savings.

Additional Locations: 12 other stores throughout S. CA

BOOKS & MAGAZINES

CROWN BOOKS
3790 Tyler St.
Riverside, CA 92503
714/688-6231
HOURS: MON-SAT: 10-9   SUN: 10-6
CREDIT CARDS: MC, V

You save 10 to 50% off retail on current books, magazines and books on tape at Crown Books and they have convenient locations all over Southern California. If you're a book browser, every store has a section filled with books—usually hardbacks—with even deeper discounts. All Crown Books have a great selection, but for mega selection, be sure to pay a visit to one of the much larger Super Crowns. Along with more books, the Super Crowns have places to sit.
Additional Locations: 96 other stores throughout S. CA

DISCOUNT READER BOOKSTORE
8651 Lincoln Blvd.
Los Angeles, CA 90045
310/410-1069
HOURS: MON-FRI: 9:30-8   SAT: 9:30-7:30   SUN: 10-5
CREDIT CARDS: MC V

Discount Reader Bookstore offers a 10% discount on paperbacks and a 20% discount on hardcovers. If a book is on the NY Times Best Seller list, you'll get 25% off paperbacks and 35% off hardcovers! They are distributors for North Point Press, one of the best small publishers in California. You can save up to 70% in a special close-out section of books.

DUTTON'S BOOKS
5146 Laurel Canyon Blvd.
North Hollywood, CA 91605
818/769-3866
HOURS: MON-FRI: 9:30-9   SAT: 9:30-6   SUN: 11-5
CREDIT CARDS: AE, MC, V

Dutton's Books carries a huge stock of new, used and rare books. This is a book lovers paradise! With a half a million books in stock, you can also trade in your used books and get a 40% discount toward your purchase. They also carry publishers overstock at tremendous discount prices, research and scholarly books on nearly every subject and category, and children's books. To top it all, they have free gift wrapping.
Additional Locations:
Brentwood–11975 San Vicente at Bundy, 310/476-6263
Burbank–3806 W. Magnolia, 818/840-8003
Los Angeles–5th & Flower (Arco Plaza), 213/683-1199

BOOKS & MAGAZINES

ENCYCLOPEDIAS BOUGHT & SOLD
14071 Windsor Pl.
Santa Ana, CA 92705
714/838-3643
HOURS: DAILY BY APPOINTMENT ONLY: 10-10
CREDIT CARDS: CASH OR CHECKS ONLY

E N C Y C L O P E D I A—remember when you knew you could spell when you sang Encyclopedia? Well Kathleen Italiane has been singing this song for the last 27 years. She has one of the largest and most varied collection of encyclopedias in the Western United States dating from the late 1800s to current editions. Her collection consists of Britannia, Americana, Colliers, World Book, New Book of Knowledge, Compton, Academic American, and she'll sell them at a savings of 10-60% on used sets and at least 40% on new sets. Harvard Classics and Time-Life books are also available.

VALLEY BOOK CITY
5249 Lankershim Blvd.
North Hollywood, CA 91601
818/985-6911
HOURS: MON-THUR: 11-7 FRI-SAT: 10-8 SUN: 11-6
CREDIT CARDS: MC, V

There are over 100,000 new and used books here, and you can save 30-90%! That's right—because all new hardback books are sold for 30% off cover price. It pays to become a regular because Valley Book City issues their hardcore patrons a 20% courtesy discount card, and that means savings of 50%! Bargain shelves inside the store and on the sidewalk have hardcover books for as low as 29¢. They buy, sell and trade new, used, rare and collectable books. Here's where you can find scarce and out-of-print titles. They have thousands of new, used, and rare paperbacks, too, at 50% off cover price (some exceptions). Their books are arranged in over 400 categories. They not only accept cash, checks and credit cards, they've been known to haggle on occasion as well. You will find all of this in a quiet, relaxed atmosphere that encourages browsing.

BOOKS & MAGAZINES

∞ USED BOOKS ∞

ACRES OF BOOKS
240 Long Beach Blvd.
Long Beach, CA 90802
310/437-6980
HOURS: TUES-SAT: 9:15-5
CREDIT CARDS: CASH OR CHECKS ONLY

Acres of Books, in business since 1934, has an overwhelming selection of books. With 13,000 square feet of floor space and 750,000 books, it's about the largest store of its kind. In fact, it's so big there are maps strategically placed around the store to help their customers find their way around. Acres of Books attracts bookworms from all over Southern California. Head on down to Long Beach if you are searching for a particular book no longer in print. If you love books, you'll find a visit a real treat, and they get new shipments every day.

BOOK CASTLE INC.
200 N. San Fernando Rd.
Burbank, CA 91502
818/845-1563
HOURS: 10-6 SEVEN DAYS A WEEK
CREDIT CARDS: DISC, MC, V

There are over 200,000 used hardbacks, 100,000 paperbacks, and 500,000 magazines stocked in this massive, concrete building that does resemble a castle, and you'll save 20 to 60%. There's a large inventory of comic books and a large, full-service newsstand that has over 1,000 periodicals on sale monthly. Right next to the main store is Book Castle's Movie World store, devoted to selling items of all description related to the history and lore of the cinema. Included in their inventory are photographs, movies posters, lobby cards, movie and TV scripts, books and other memorabilia.

BOOK CITY
6627 Hollywood Blvd.
Hollywood, CA 90028
213/466-2525
HOURS: MON-SAT: 10-10 SUN: 10-8
CREDIT CARDS: MC, V

This truly is a city of books—literally thousands and thousands of them. You can save 20 to 50% on your purchases, and in addition, Book City has one of Southern California's largest selection of used books. If you

BOOKS & MAGAZINES

have a little time to spare, just browse through the book stacks and find reading treasures for as little as 49¢. And, if you are a movie or music buff, then you must visit their separate collectibles store next door where you can find photos, autographs and the like, dating back to 1900!
Additional Locations:
Burbank–308 N. San Fernando Blvd., 818/848-4417

THE BOOKANEER
6755 Tampa Ave.
Reseda, CA 91335
818/881-6808
HOURS: TUES-SAT: 10-6
CREDIT CARDS: CASH OR CHECKS ONLY

Opened in 1974 by Jim and Shirley, genuine bookworms will have a hard time leaving this used bookstore. The Bookaneer has over 150,000 titles in their collection of paperbacks, hardbacks, comic books, biographies, science fiction, romance, western, nonfiction, and of course children's books. They buy, sell and trade 500 books a day, so their stock is always changing. Upon purchase of a few paperbacks no longer in print, we received book credits good towards future purchases. Though not the largest used bookstore in the area, it's definitely the friendliest. Jim's sense of humor seems to rub off on his customers.

BOOKSVILLE
2626 Honolulu Ave.
Montrose, CA 91020
818/248-9149
HOURS: 9:30-7:00 SEVEN DAYS A WEEK
CREDIT CARDS: CASH OR CHECKS ONLY

The proprietress of this charming bookstore is Shirley McCormick. You'll be able to find special buys in used books for every member of the family. Start your search here for treasures at bargain prices.

COSMOPOLITAN BOOK SHOP
7007 Melrose Ave.
Los Angeles, CA 90038
213/938-7119
HOURS: MON-SAT: 11:30-6
CREDIT CARDS: CASH OR CHECKS ONLY

After 33 years in business, and 20 years at their present location, nothing is new at Eli Goodman's Cosmopolitan Book Shop. There is, however, for those who enjoy rummaging through one of the West Coast's largest collections of used, out-of-print and antiquarian books, the possibility of

BOOKS & MAGAZINES

finding the rare, the unusual and the different. Included in the 3,000 square feet of space are paperbacks, select copies of magazines, and LPs of every description. Top prices are offered for whole collections, or they'll make acceptable trades. A customer can expect to save as much as 50% on books in print, and it's even possible to buy a book for as little as 50¢.

PAPERBACK TRADER
511 Wilshire Blvd.
Santa Monica, CA 90401
310/394-8147
HOURS: MON-THUR: 10-8 FRI-SAT: 10-10 SUN: 12-8
CREDIT CARDS: CASH OR CHECKS ONLY

The Paperback Trader likes to say they sell recycled books, not used ones. Regardless of the view you happen to take, savings run 50% off retail on recycled reading material. They have an excellent selection of hardbacks and lots of books on science fiction, mystery, romance and horror. You can also save about 10% off retail on new books.

BUILDING & REMODELING

∞ AIR CONDITIONING & HEATING ∞

AIR CONDITIONING EXCHANGE**
6900 San Fernando Rd.
Glendale, CA 91201
213/849-2495, 818/845-8544, 800/540-EASY
HOURS: TUES-SAT: 8:30-5
CREDIT CARDS: DISC, MC, V

You can find everything you need for central heating and air conditioning equipment at the Air Conditioning Exchange. Whether you are installing a complete system or fixing an old one, you will find prices at 20 to 50% above their cost. Not only do they carry major brand names such as Carrier, Lennox, Day & Night, Tempstar, Heil, and Payne, they stock supplies and parts in their 10,000 square foot warehouse. They also fabricate custom sheet metal. For super bargains, don't overlook the factory closeouts or items that are scratched or dented. This family-owned and operated business has been serving the community since 1959. You'll receive an additional 10% discount plus a free tape measure when you use your BUYING RETAIL IS STUPID coupon.

HOME COMFORT CENTER**
18419 Vanowen St.
Reseda, CA 91335
818/345-9557
HOURS: MON-FRI: 10-6 SAT: 10-4
CREDIT CARDS: MC, V

If you are the handywoman or handyman in your household, you will definitely want to head over to Home Comfort Center, a place geared toward home owners. They carry everything you'll need for do-it yourself heating and air conditioning at savings of 50 to 60% off retail prices. Whether you're doing repair work or installing an entire system, you'll find everything at Home Comfort Center. Experts on their staff will help you every step of the way, and it's all free. Their showroom has extensive displays designed especially to be unintimidating to do-it-yourselfers, and they will go out of their way to make you feel comfortable doing this kind of work. You'll find extra comfort saving an additional 10% when you use your BUYING RETAIL IS STUPID coupon.

BUILDING & REMODELING

NUTONE PRODUCTS DISTRIBUTOR
14670 Firestone Blvd., #410
La Mirada, CA 90638
310/921-8933
HOURS: MON-FRI: 8-10   SAT: BY APPOINTMENT ONLY
CREDIT CARDS: CASH OR CHECKS ONLY

These people are the factory distributors for all Nutone products. You'll save 25 to 30% off the retail price on heaters, exhaust fans, paddle fans, track lighting, intercoms, security systems, door bells, bath cabinets, mirrors, food centers, central vacuum systems, and more. They have been in business over 17 years, and they offer shipping on all items.

∞ BRICKS, BLOCKS & MASONRY ∞

BRICK CORRAL
24100 Orange Ave.
Perris, CA 92370
714/657-1807
HOURS: TUES-FRI: 7-4   SAT: 7-2 (OCT-APR) 7-4 (MAY-SEPT)
CREDIT CARDS: MC, V

Brick Corral is a division of New Davidson Brick Company. This is their outlet for seconds and overruns so you pay prices that are far below wholesale! Some of the brick products are 5–15¢ less than what a contractor would pay. These bricks, blocks and pavers, all structurally sound, and are perfect for patio and garden projects.

ELLIOTT PRECISION BLOCK CO.
157 N. Rancho Ave.
San Bernardino, CA 92410
714/885-6581
HOURS: MON-FRI: 7-4   SAT: 7-NOON
CREDIT CARDS: MC, V

Elliott Precision Block Co. has been around since 1946 offering first quality materials for the do-it-yourselfer at factory direct prices. Their customers are generally professional contractors needing materials for projects such as building walls, fences and courtyards. They carry blocks, brick, cement, pavers, sand, steel and everything needed to build a fireplace from scratch. If you know exactly what you need, they will be happy to quote you prices over the phone.

BUILDING & REMODELING

SHIPS CONCRETE COMPANY
6925 Cherry Ave.
Long Beach, CA 90805
310/630-1775
HOURS: MON-FRI: 7-5:30 SAT: 7:30-NOON
CREDIT CARDS: DISC, MC, V

Okay, how many times have you been looking for just the right place to buy sand, cement and masonry supplies? Well, search no more because Ships Concrete Company carries all the sand, cement and masonry supplies you need. They have firsts and seconds here at low low prices. Parking is available and free.

∞ CABINETS, CLOSETS & COUNTERTOPS ∞

FAIRFAX KITCHEN CABINETS
935 N. Fairfax Ave.
Los Angeles, CA 90046
213/656-1133
HOURS: MON-FRI: 7-4 SAT: 8-4:30
CREDIT CARDS: CASH OR CHECKS ONLY

Fairfax will plan your cabinets for kitchen and bath. Custom woods include oak and birch, or Fairfax will refinish your existing cabinets with formica or wood. They also do countertops and wardrobes. With their free consultations and expert planning, you will save 30 to 40% on the work—an incredible bargain!

FROCH'S WOODCRAFT SHOP, INC.
6659 Topanga Canyon Blvd.
Canoga Park, CA 91303
818/883-4730
HOURS: AE, MC, V
CREDIT CARDS: MON-THUR: 9-6 FRI: 9-5 SAT: 9-6

Froch's Woodcrafts Shop, a large store with standard and unusual pieces, is by far the best unfinished furniture store we've ever seen. They manufacture their unfinished furniture in the San Fernando Valley with their own craftsmen. This allows for fantastic savings of 50% off retail. You can remodel or build your kitchen with cabinetry available in different styles and sizes. If you're ready to revamp your closets, Froch's has various units you can mix and match to suit your own particular needs. Everything is all wood, and you won't find any particle board.
Additional Locations:
Panorama City–7945 Van Nuys Blvd., 818/787-3682

BUILDING & REMODELING

INTERIOR RESOURCES
8523 Canoga Ave., Units E & F
Canoga Park, CA 91304
818/700-1891
HOURS: MON-FRI: 8-6   SAT: 10-4
CREDIT CARDS: CASH OR CHECKS ONLY

Allow Interior Resources, a factory-direct outlet, to bring your old kitchen into the 21st century. They have European kitchen specialists, complete professional design service and a full line of traditional and custom cabinets available. Their prices usually run 20 to 40% below retail.

THE KITCHEN & BATH WAREHOUSE**
2149 W. Washington Blvd.
Los Angeles, CA 90018
213/734-1696
HOURS: MON-SAT: 9-5
CREDIT CARDS: MC, V

Kitchen and bathroom cabinets of all qualities and price ranges, from ultra contemporary to old-world traditional, and from cherry to oak are all available at The Kitchen & Bath Warehouse. They also have marble and formica counter tops. All of this at savings from 10 to 60% off retail! Come in and bring your room measurements with you. An expert kitchen designer will help you create a beautiful kitchen or bathroom, one that maximizes storage space and work flow, while creating a room that you will be proud of. And, believe it or not, the designing is absolutely free! Save another 5% by using your BUYING RETAIL IS STUPID coupon.

MARBLE PRODUCTS OF FULLERTON**
112 W. Commonwealth, Bldg. A
Fullerton, CA 92632
714/738-4384
HOURS: MON-FRI: 10-5
CREDIT CARDS: CASH OR CHECKS ONLY

Vanity tops for bathrooms, shower pans, walls, window sills and table tops can be found here, and John Mezei promises to be 10% lower than anyone in Orange County. They manufacture their own products so they are able to make anything of any size or color. Don't forget your BUYING RETAIL IS STUPID coupon at home or you'll miss out on an additional 5% discount.

BUILDING & REMODELING

NISSAN WOODWORKS INC.
2150 W. Washington Blvd.
Los Angeles, CA 90018
213/731-4883
HOURS: MON-SAT: 10-5
CREDIT CARDS: CASH OR CHECKS ONLY

Alfred Nissan specializes in standard and custom cabinetry for your kitchens, bathrooms, bars, and garages. Whether it's wood or laminate cabinets you are looking for, you will find them here at 20 to 40% below retail prices.

PANEL-IT DISCOUNT STORES
6322 W. Slauson
Culver City, CA 90230
310/839-5213
HOURS: MON-FRI: 8:30-8 SAT: 8:30-5:30 SUN: 9:30-3
CREDIT CARDS: MC, V

Panel-It Discount Stores specialize in prefinished kitchen cabinets at 50% off retail prices. In addition, you will also find bathroom vanities, glass enclosures, counter tops, doors and windows. Panel-It offers you Diamond and Merillat Cabinets, Formica Counter Tops, and Z Brick. You will be pleased dealing with their well-trained, professional sales staff.

THRIFTY KITCHENS, INC.
16147 Runnymede St.
Van Nuys, CA 91406
818/286-0984
HOURS: MON-FRI: 8-5
CREDIT CARDS: MC, V

For the complete kitchen remodeling job, Thrifty Kitchens offers up to 25-50% off! Along with great quality, they guarantee the best prices. They offer kitchen remodeling, refacing new counter tops, and they supply design ideas as well as all materials and labor. Look for familiar names such as Formica, DuPont and Corian, to name a few. So, whether you want your kitchen cabinets refaced with a new look, or want to tear out everything and start over again, Thrifty Kitchens could be the solution.

BUILDING & REMODELING

∞ CERAMIC & STONE TILE ∞

CALIFORNIA WHOLESALE TILE
1656 S. State College Blvd.
Anaheim, CA 92806
714/937-0591
HOURS: MON-FRI: 7:30-5 SAT: 8-4:30 SUN: 9-4
CREDIT CARDS: MC, V

Whether you're looking for bathroom, kitchen, entryway or patio tiles, California Wholesale Tile is the place to shop. You will find quarry tile, terra cotta tile, pool tile, hand painted tile, small mosaic tile and Italian decorative floor and wall tile at one of the largest ceramic tile showrooms in Orange County. They have over 6,000 square feet of showroom filled with great buys. Although the store names are different, they have another locations in the same area of Anaheim called Tile Importers. So, if one of their stores doesn't have exactly what you have in mind, it's a short distance to another showroom.

Additional Locations:
Anaheim–Tile Importers, 1320 S. State College Blvd., 714/533-9800

D'MUNDO TILE
36660 Bankside Dr., Suite G
Cathedral City, CA 92234
619/328-4646
HOURS: MON-FRI: 7-5 SAT: 7-3
CREDIT CARDS: MC, V

D'Mundo Tile imports most of their tile from Italy, Spain, Brazil and Mexico, and they also have a few American-made lines. They specialize in rustics perfect for southwest decor. In business since 1984, D'Mundo Tile has a 6,000 square foot showroom along with a 36,000 square foot warehouse filled with tile, furniture and pottery priced 40 to 60% off retail. In stock are over 40 styles of pavers and nearly 100 patterns in handpainted Talavera tiles. Custom work is available (you may bump into landscapers and interior designers when shopping here), and they'll send you a free brochure filled with tile and furniture to get your creative juices flowing.

Additional Locations:
Palm Desert-77725 Enfield Ln., #170, 619/360-0097

BUILDING & REMODELING

DISCOUNT TILE CENTER
8627 Venice Blvd.
Los Angeles, CA 90034
310/202-1915, 310/202-1939
HOURS: MON-FRI: 8-5:30 SAT: 9-5
CREDIT CARDS: MC, V

This is a great wholesale, factory-direct center for ceramic tiles of all kinds. Discount Tile Center has tiles imported from all over the world. Hand painted tiles come with such names as Huntington Pacific, Marazzi USA, Royal Tiles of Italy, Monarch and Soto Mexican Pavers. Everything is in stock or can be obtained in just a few days. You'll save at least 30-50% off retail prices all the time, and they also feature special sales during the year where you could be paying less than wholesale!

NEW METRO TILE COMPANY
5477 S. Alhambra Ave.
Los Angeles, CA 90032
213/221-1144
HOURS: MON-FRI: 7-5 SAT: 8-2:30
CREDIT CARDS: MC, V

This store handles imported and domestic tiles of all major brands like H & R Johnson, Huntington/Pacific, and many more. This is a real do-it-yourselfers headquarters. You can save 20 to 50% on your purchases and they have extra special prices on their discontinued items and seconds. When you buy their tile, you can leave a deposit, and they will loan you tools to complete the job.

OBALEK TILE & WALLPAPER
2301 S. Hill St.
Los Angeles, CA 90007
213/748-4664
HOURS: MON-FRI: 8-6 SAT: 9-5
CREDIT CARDS: MC, V

If you want to find great discount prices on a huge stock of tiles from around the world, visit Obalek Tile & Wallpaper. They have approximately 500,000 square feet of ceramic and vinyl tiles in stock. The savings found here are fantastic. For example, tiles that retail for $1.79 to $1.89 at other stores cost as little as 59¢ to $1.29 per tile. In addition to tile, they stock 250,000 rolls of wallpaper. They carry all the tools necessary for do-it-yourselfers, and their professional staff will be glad to instruct you on the how-to. General manager Bill Cochran and his staff are extremely helpful.

BUILDING & REMODELING

TILE FOR LESS**
8369 Topanga Canyon Blvd.
Canoga Park, CA 91304
818/704-7961
HOURS: MON-FRI: 10-6 SAT: 10-5 SUN: 11-5
CREDIT CARDS: MC, V

If you're ready to redo the tile in your home you should take a look at the inventory at Tile for Less. Most of the inventory (over 200 styles of ceramic tile) consists of manufacturer overruns or close-outs. Prices for wall tile start at 69¢ and floor tile begins at 89¢. If you're long on energy, but low on experience, the staff will give you any advice you may need. If your purchase is over $100, you'll get a free bag of grout with your BUYING RETAIL IS STUPID coupon.

TILE OUTLET
1551 S. State College Blvd.
Anaheim, CA 92806
714/937-1818
HOURS: MON-FRI: 7:30-5 SAT: 8-4:30
CREDIT CARDS: MC, V

This 1,500 square foot showroom is filled with ceramic tiles and marble at savings of 25 to 50% off retail. Tile Outlet is an importer with a 23,000 square foot warehouse. You will find prices that should make you very happy at this outlet.

TILE, MARBLE & GRANITE WAREHOUSE**
7118 Reseda Blvd.
Reseda, CA 91335
818/881-1056
HOURS: MON-FRI: 8-6 SAT: 9-5
CREDIT CARDS: MC, V

You'll find miles of tiles at this business based entirely on great service! And, their prices are still 30% below most discount tile stores. Owner Jeff Joss imports most of the tile and passes the savings on to you. You will be pleased with the selection of tile, marble and granite for your floors, walls, counters, kitchen, bathrooms, pool or spa. They have in-house designers and all the supplies needed for installation. Not only do they offer free professional advice, they also offer free use of tools. Take in your BUYING RETAIL IS STUPID coupon and they'll give you an extra 10% discount. Now that's a deal carved in stone!
Additional Locations:
Glendale–1264 S. Central Ave. (N. of Los Feliz), 818/240-7555

TILECLUB**
6945 Reseda Blvd.
Reseda, CA 91335
818/345-2276
HOURS: MON-FRI: 9-7 SAT: 9-5 SUN: 10-4
CREDIT CARDS: MC, V

Tileclub caters to the homeowner. They have a large inventory, and there is no more than a five to seven day wait on non-stock items. You will find ceramic tile, some marble and granite, and related products for counters, walls and floors. Their staff will teach you how to install ceramic tile, and they have rental equipment and offer tile cutting service too. Savings run 20 to 50% off retail, and you can save more at their January clearance sale. Whatever you do, don't forget to bring along your BUYING RETAIL IS STUPID coupon for an additional 10% discount!

Additional Locations:
Anaheim–1833 S. State College Blvd., 714/385-1717
Encinitas–260-B N. El Camino Real, 619/632-1178
Escondido–2122 W. Mission, 619/745-9123
La Mesa–8177 Alvarado Rd., 619/697-6400
San Diego–1022 W. Morena Blvd., 619/276-0271

VALLEY TILE DISTRIBUTORS
1618 S. San Gabriel Blvd.
San Gabriel, CA 91776
213/283-5085
HOURS: MON-SAT: 9-5
CREDIT CARDS: MC, V

One of the largest ceramic tile showrooms in Southern California, Valley Tile is never undersold. Their savings range from 20 to 80% (the 80% is on their close-outs), and they are really "wholesalers to the public". They carry the biggest names, give instructions to the do-it-yourselfers, cut tile, and have tools and setting materials. Valley Tile has been selling tiles from around the world for everything from your kitchen to your swimming pool since 1965.

BUILDING & REMODELING

∞ Doors, Windows & Mirrors ∞

ACTION SCREEN & DOOR**
24619 Arch St.
Newhall, CA 91321
805/254-6794

HOURS: TUES-FRI: 8:30-5 SAT: 10-4
CREDIT CARDS: CASH OR CHECKS ONLY

Whether you're remodeling or just adding new screens, Action Screen & Door is a great way to save money. Homeowners can buy all kinds of doors and windows at 20-25% above cost. Brand names include Superior Aluminum, Andersen, Velux Skylites, California Classic, Phifer Sun Screen and more. Everything is special ordered and Action Screen & Door handles all the follow-up. If you remember to use your BUYING RETAIL IS STUPID discount coupon, you'll receive a 15% discount and one free window screen when you order four or more screens.

ALL STAR GLASS
7535 Woodley Ave.
Van Nuys, CA 91406
818/902-1511

HOURS: MON-FRI: 8-5 SAT: 8-12
CREDIT CARDS: AE, DISC, MC, V

All Star Glass specializes in windshield replacement for autos. Free mobile service is provided, which means, they will do the work at your home at no extra charge. Also available are residential or commercial table tops, shower enclosures, wardrobe sliders, doors, quarters, and vents. If you need an estimate, All Star Glass will give you one on the phone. They provide written guarantees and have qualified technicians/installers, maintaining factory standards.

Additional Locations: 14 other shops throughout S. CA

ALL VALLEY SHOWER DOOR CO.
14665 Arminta St.
Van Nuys, CA 91402
818/782-7477

HOURS: MON-FRI: 8-5 SAT: 8-12
CREDIT CARDS: CASH OR CHECKS ONLY

Marilyn Singer is the manager of this establishment that offers standard and custom shower enclosures, mirrors, wardrobe doors, and anything in glass. Contractors are welcome. You'll find brochures and samples on display.

BUILDING & REMODELING

PREFERRED GLASS
18319 Napa St.
Northridge, CA 91325
818/886-4610, 213/628-6902
HOURS: MON-FRI: 8-6 SAT: 10-3
CREDIT CARDS: CASH OR CHECKS ONLY

Preferred Glass is your one stop glass shop. Whether you happen to be looking for window panes, mirrors, store fronts, sliding glass doors, or tub and shower enclosures, you'll find them here at about 30% below retail prices. They give free estimates and also one-day mobile service on automobile glass repair.
Additional Locations: 7 other shops throughout S. CA

∞ FLOOR COVERINGS ∞

AAA CARPET EXCHANGE
4120 Crenshaw Blvd.
Los Angeles, CA 90008
213/290-3414
HOURS: MON-SAT: 8:30-5:30
CREDIT CARDS: MC, V

Levelor blinds are oh-so-chic. Apartment owners even advertise them as rental features. You can get Levelor and mini-blinds at AAA Carpet Exchange as well as vinyl, wood and tile flooring, draperies and a full line of carpeting. Save 20-70% on most everything! This huge showroom/warehouse stocks miles and miles of carpets, plus thousands of remnants in all sizes and colors. Special sales occur all the time, so check often for extra savings on their vast and varied merchandise. All employees are professionally trained and are most helpful.

ABLE CARPETS
8854 Pico Blvd.
Los Angeles, CA 90035
310/859-1522
HOURS: MON-FRI: 8:30-6 SAT: 9-5
CREDIT CARDS: DISC, MC, V

All major brands of carpets are discounted for you and they have been in business here since 1959; quotes are cheerfully given. You can carry out your carpet purchases, or they will deliver. They have expert installation service, plus a good selection of vinyl flooring and mini-blinds to complement your decor. In addition to the huge stock of full rolls, there are always good remnants to check out.

BUILDING & REMODELING

CARPET BAZAAR
7833 Canoga Ave.
Canoga Park, CA 91304
818/713-9220
HOURS: MON-FRI: 9-6   SAT: 10-5
CREDIT CARDS: MC, V
With over 15,000 square yards of carpet in stock and hundreds of styles and colors to choose from, in a showroom/warehouse of 6,600 square feet, the Carpet Bazaar is a place you should shop before making a decision. Special prices on mill close-outs and slightly irregulars are below their everyday low prices. Their truckload buying power saves you money. They offer volume discounts, and prompt installations are available. Name brands include Royale Weave, Royalty and Classique.
Additional Locations:
Agoura–30615 Canwood St., 818/706-2353

CARPET COLLECTION**
12124 Sherman Way
North Hollywood, CA 91605
818/982-4554
HOURS: MON-FRI: 8-6   SAT: 9-5   SUN: 11-5
CREDIT CARDS: MC, V
Carpet Collection carries a large inventory of floor coverings—carpeting, vinyl, tile and linoleum—and also window coverings. According to the owners, any carpet a customer might want is available and for any budget. They say they will beat any legitimate price. Service is emphasized and immediate installation is available. They carry a large selection of name brands such as Philadelphia, Salem, Royalty, El Dorado, Catalina, Armstrong, Horizon and more. Their 3,500 square foot showroom is housed in a 10,000 square foot warehouse. The public is welcome and special low discounts are offered to contractors and interior decorators. You can save an additional 5% off your purchase price when you use your BUYING RETAIL IS STUPID coupon.

CARPET LAND MILLS
6951 Reseda Blvd.
Reseda, CA 91335
818/609-0339
HOURS: MON-FRI: 10-8   SAT: 10-6
CREDIT CARDS: CASH OR CHECKS ONLY
In their 1,500 square feet of showroom, there are more than 100 mills represented and over 2,000 samples from which to choose. They also carry hardwood, vinyl and tile flooring, and vertical or mini-blinds.

BUILDING & REMODELING

Prices are at about 5% above cost and phone quotes are welcomed. Among the brands carried are Stainmaster and Weardated carpets. They offer immediate delivery. Don't forget to ask about their 18 month replacement guarantee.

CARPET MANOR**
5900 Kester Ave.
Reseda, CA 91335
818/344-2277

HOURS: MON-FRI: 9-6   SAT: 10-5   SUN: 12-4
CREDIT CARDS: MC, V

In business since 1953, Carpet Manor offers a wide selection of carpets, remnants, wood and vinyl flooring and window coverings. Prices are up to 70% off retail, and they guarantee best price. They carry all major brands in their 5,000 square foot store and offer prompt delivery and service as well as free advice to ambitious customers who want to do it themselves. They'll roll out the carpet for an extra 5% discount if you use your BUYING RETAIL IS STUPID coupon!

CARPET MARKET OUTLET
5916 Kester Ave.
Van Nuys, CA 91411
818/989-0940

HOURS: MON-SAT: 9-5:30
CREDIT CARDS: AE, MC, V

The Carpet Market Outlet is just what their name describes—they are an outlet for most major brands of carpeting, linoleum, and ceramic tile. They carry only major brands such as Anso V, Stainmaster, and DuPont Certified. Joe Zeldin says he has the guaranteed best price anywhere.

CULVER CARPET CENTER
4026 S. Sepulveda Blvd.
Culver City, CA 90230
310/398-2458

HOURS: MON-FRI: 8:30-6   SAT: 8:30-5
CREDIT CARDS: MC, V

Culver Carpet Center is a large discount carpet and vinyl warehouse, one of LA's largest volume dealers. You can save 25 to 40% off retail on first-quality, name-brand rolls and remnants of carpets. You'll also find a complete line of custom wood flooring, linoleum and a fine vinyl selection. They have a department for window coverings, too, and these experts can install everything they sell. In business since 1952, they offer selection, service, and big savings.

BUILDING & REMODELING

FLOOR COVERING UNLIMITED
8480 W. 3rd St.
Los Angeles, CA 90048
213/651-5290
HOURS: MON-FRI: 7-5:30
CREDIT CARDS: MC, V

Whatever you want to put on the floor, including the floor, Floor Covering Unlimited has it and at wholesale prices. Custom hardwood floors, vinyl and tile, Levelor blinds, wallpaper and draperies are available in an almost limitless array of choices. They have been in business since 1971 and give free estimates. There's always a pile of carpet doormats and remnants for $1 to $2.

FLOORMART
437 Fernando Crt.
Glendale, CA 91204
818/243-6242, 213/245-3374
HOURS: MON-FRI: 7:30-4:30 SAT: 8:30-3:30
CREDIT CARDS: CASH OR CHECKS ONLY

Because Floormart is a specialist in buyer close-outs, most of their inventory is priced below cost. They handle carpeting and vinyl coverings and you'll pay less than department store sale prices on items they have in inventory. If you want to special order floor coverings, you can expect to pay 12% above cost. Installation is also available.

LESTER CARPET CO., INC.
7811-7815 Beverly Blvd.
Los Angeles, CA 90036
213/934-7282
HOURS: MON-SAT: 8-5
CREDIT CARDS: MC, V

Whether you want to cover your floors, windows, or doors, Lester Carpet Co. guarantees the lowest price! They've been in business since 1954; with that kind of experience and over 13,000 square feet of warehouse, they definitely know how to buy in volume and pass the savings on to you. You can carpet your home with name brands such as Tuftex, Armstrong, Hollytex, Tarkett, and Queen. Other items carried are draperies, blinds, shutters, mini-blinds, vertical blinds, quilts, upholstery, linoleum sheets, tiles and wood flooring. Custom work is available as well.

LINOLEUM CITY
5657 Santa Monica Blvd.
Hollywood, CA 90038
213/469-0063, 463-1729
HOURS: MON-THUR: 8:30-5:30   FRI: 8:30-7   SAT: 9-5
CREDIT CARDS: DISC, MC, V

Since 1948, Linoleum City has been serving the needs of L.A.'s shoppers for floor coverings. They have a combination warehouse and showroom in Hollywood of over 10,000 square feet. Claiming to have the largest selection of vinyls and carpeting in the city, you can find brand names such as Armstrong, Mannington, Tarkett, Kentile, Hartco, Caronet, Wellington, as well as many others. In addition to the thousands of rolls of vinyl floor covering in stock, they have a huge inventory of commercial and residential tiles, rolls of carpets, and hundreds of carpet samples. Their sales staff is very knowledgeable and installation is available through independent contractors.

M & H CARPETS
16842 Stallion Pl.
Riverside, CA 92504
714/780-7624
HOURS: MON-FRI: 9-5   SAT: 10-4
CREDIT CARDS: MC, V

Don't worry if the kids spill chocolate sauce on your white carpets, M & H Carpets carries Anso V Worry Free Carpets and Genesis, as well as several other brand names, at 40% below retail. Bring in any written estimate and they will beat the price.

MELROSE DISCOUNT CARPET
7951 Melrose Ave.
Los Angeles, CA 90046
213/653-4653
HOURS: MON: 9-7   TUES-FRI: 9-5
CREDIT CARDS: MC, V

If you're going to replace your old vinyl floor in the kitchen, here's the place for you. Melrose Discount Carpet carries carpet, hardwood flooring, linens, tile, and area rugs. You can save 50% over most places, and they have remnants for sale. They are located one block west of Fairfax and parking is on the street only.

BUILDING & REMODELING

PICO CARPET CO.
1647 S. La Cienega Blvd.
Los Angeles, CA 90035
310/274-7846
HOURS: MON-FRI: 8-5   SAT: 8:30-4
CREDIT CARDS: CASH OR CHECKS ONLY

Pico Carpet Company is a discount warehouse selling carpets primarily from major mills at 20 to 50% off retail. In addition to the many rolls of carpet in stock, they also have remnants, linoleum, wood flooring, custom blinds, and expert installation. Make the time to look here before you make your next carpet purchase.

ROYAL DISCOUNT CARPETS
529 N. Fairfax St.
Los Angeles, CA 90036
213/655-4343
HOURS: MON-SAT: 9-4
CREDIT CARDS: CASH OR CHECKS ONLY

This shop is stuffed with wonderful buys on carpeting, loose rugs and oriental carpets. Most of the merchandise is priced at 10% over cost. If you're looking for carpeting, then this shop is a must because the prices are really hard to beat. Go on over and check out what Royal Discount Carpets has to offer.

WESTPORT CARPET INDUSTRIES
18314–6 Oxnard St.
Tarzana, CA 91356
818/344-3291
HOURS: MON-FRI: 8-05   SAT: 9-4
CREDIT CARDS: MC, V

If you're in the market for new carpeting or flooring of any sort, you can save big bucks at Westport Carpet. This is where interior designers, architects and contractors shop. Westport's warehouse has a library of more samples than one would ever imagine existed. They literally have thousands of samples of domestic and imported carpets—from the usual to the very unusual—such as a carpet with several different textures sewn in a wave pattern. Hobbyists will find large hooped carpet in lots of textures, perfect for large wall hangings. Have you ever seen a beautiful rug in a model home or a hotel lobby and thought that you'd love to have something similar, but done a little differently? Westport has one section with sample books of area rugs that you design yourself. There are a multitude of patterns from which to choose—e.g., a very simple bordered sculpted rug to one with an intricate floral design. The best part is, you get to pick the color and texture combinations. With the exception of remnants, everything is special ordered. If for some reason you can't find the exact color needed, you can have the carpet you choose dyed to your specifications for an extra 5%.

∞ GATES & FENCING ∞

FENCE FACTORY
29414 Roadside Dr.
Agoura, CA 91301
818/889-2240
HOURS: MON-FRI: 8-5 SAT: 9-3
CREDIT CARDS: MC, V

Save 10–50% below retail on wood fences, ornamental iron fences, chain link fences, fittings, gates, poultry wire and more at the Fence Factory. They have a superb staff to install everything for you, or provide the do-it-yourselfer with all necessary materials. Custom work is available, too.
Additional Locations:
Goleta–60 S. Kellogg, 805/965-2817
Santa Maria–2709 Santa Maria Way, 805/928-5848
Ventura–1441 Callens Rd., 805/485-8831

J & Y WELDING & IRONWORKS
11151 S. Avalon Blvd.
Los Angeles, CA 90061
213/756-9215
HOURS: MON-FRI: 8-5 SAT: 8-12
CREDIT CARDS: CASH OR CHECKS ONLY

J & Y Welding has been in business since 1980 installing motorized gates for guarded estates or apartments. Specializing in ornamental ironworks such as gates, window bars, pool fences, and handrails, they will also custom design and build to specifications. You can expect savings of at least 15% over what others would charge.

∞ HOME DESIGNS ∞

HIAWATHA HOMES**
16706 Bollinger Dr.
Pacific Palisades, CA 90272-1148
310/454-4809
HOURS: MON-FRI: 10-5
CREDIT CARDS: CASH OR CHECKS ONLY

Looking to save money on building your own home? The first thing you should do is place an order with Hiawatha Homes. Six books filled with 1,000 designs for single family homes will cost you a total of $19.00. After you decide on the home of your dreams, order a set of four working drawings and two outline specifications at a cost ranging from $95 to $600. Some of these plans could easily cost $3,000 to $5,000 prepared by a designer or architect as a custom plan, and yet the quality would be no better than the plans you can buy from Hiawatha Homes. Their plans are designed primarily for the West and meet California building codes. Save time and money on building your next home, and build in an additional 15% discount using your BUYING RETAIL IS STUPID coupon. Remember, the coupon works with the plans, not the house.

∞ ONE-STOP HARDWARE STORES ∞

A-WAHL'S BUILDING MATERIALS
11501 Tuxford St.
Sun Valley, CA 91352
818/767-9400
HOURS: MON-FRI: 7-5 SAT: 8-4 SUN: 9-3
CREDIT CARDS: DISC, MC, V

This family owned and operated business is on five and a half acres and has been serving the public for the past 30 years. They carry such brand names as Skil, Makita, Milwaukee, and Armstrong. Everything related to building projects of every kind can be found at A-Wahl's. You'll find great prices on power tools, lumber, roofing material, hardware, sand and gravel, fencing, plumbing materials, electrical, and paint. You name it, and if it has to do with building, they probably have it. Savings run at least 50% off retail.

BUILDING & REMODELING

BUILDER'S DISCOUNT
20914 Nordhoff St.
Chatsworth, CA 91311
818/341-3646
HOURS: MON-FRI: 7-9 SAT: 7-8 SUN: 8-6
CREDIT CARDS: MC, V

This place has everything at low discount prices year round on name brands for the person who knows exactly what he needs. Builder's Discount carries a complete supply of lumber, paneling, cabinets, vanities, toilets, faucets, hand and power tools, doors and windows, water heaters, light fixtures, drill bits, pipes and fittings, all at savings of 20 to 70%. You'll recognize top name brands such as Dasco, Skil, Makita, Georgia Pacific, GE, Kwikset, and many others.

Additional Locations:
Los Angeles–4550 W. Pico Blvd., 213/938-5656
N. Hollywood–12580 Saticoy St., 818/982-5900
Simi Valley–1855 Cochran St., 805/522-2725)

L.A. WRECKING COMPANY
810 E. 9th St.
Los Angeles, CA 90021
213/622-5135, 213/623-3646
HOURS: MON-SAT: 8-4:30
CREDIT CARDS: MC, V

It's not what you think. You don't hire these people to wreck your house. L.A. Wrecking Company has all you need in the way of plumbing fixtures and supplies, and screens. Save 20 to 50% on these items plus an additional 5% discount on purchases of $100 or more paid in cash. Checks are taken with purchases of $25 or more and credit cards are accepted on purchases over $15.

∞ PAINT ∞

A. A. BAKER'S PAINT & HARDWARE
3925 San Fernando Rd.
Glendale, CA 91204
818/242-7467
HOURS: MON-FRI: 7:30-6 SAT: 7:30-5 SUN: 9-4
CREDIT CARDS: MC, V

Baker's is an institution in Glendale, having been there since 1915. They offer the best discount prices on paint and hardware needs.

BUILDING & REMODELING

PAR PAINT COMPANY INC.**
1801 W. Sunset Blvd.
Los Angeles, CA 90026
213/413-4950
HOURS: MON-FRI: 7:30-5 SAT: 7:30-2:30
CREDIT CARDS: MC, V

Talk about guys that know paint? Par Paint Company has been in business since 1949 selling paints, lacquers, varnishes, compliances coatings, automotive paints, industrial paints and supplies at wholesale prices. They represent 3M, Lilly Industrial, Gemstar, Guardsmen, Purdy, Pittsburgh, Spectrum, Krylon, Zynolite, Nason, and Ellis. They also have rollers, spray cans, covers, brushes, and all acoustical supplies. Whatever you need in this department, they've got, and their prices are 20% below retail. You will save an additional 5% when you use your BUYING RETAIL IS STUPID coupon.

SCOTCH PAINTS FACTORY STORE
555 W. 189th St.
Gardena, CA 90248
310/329-1259
HOURS: MON-FRI: 7-5 SAT: 8-12
CREDIT CARDS: MC

Scotch Paints Factory Store is the place to go when you know what you want and are eager to get up to 75% off retail. The paints you purchase here are manufactured at their own plant and are the same ones they sell to million dollar construction companies. They have a selection of 32 exterior and 16 interior colors from which to choose. You'll also find everything in equipment and supplies needed for house painting such as ladders, brushes, rollers, drop clothes, and lots of other things. Because Scotch Paints caters mainly to professionals, the best buys come in five gallon containers. If you don't need quite that much, one gallon containers are available for just a few cents more.

Additional Locations:
Hesperia–11873 Hesperia, 619/244-3477
Lancaster–42620 10th St. West, 805/945-8080
Temecula–41860 Enterprise Circle South, #C, 714/694-9498

BUILDING & REMODELING

∞ PLUMBING & ELECTRICAL ∞

A J SPECIALTY BATH PRODUCTS
702 Thousand Oaks Blvd.
Thousand Oaks, CA 91360
805/497-1678
HOURS: TUES-THUR: 1-5 FRI: 10-5 SAT: 10-2
CREDIT CARDS: MC, V

Is there anything more relaxing than soaking in a whirlpool tub? Tubs at A J Specialty Products—by Hydrosystems and Custom Home Spa—are 35 to 50% off retail. Everything here is first-quality merchandise. If they happen to get an outstanding buy from the manufacturer, they pass the savings on to their customers, which can sometimes produce discounts higher than 50% off retail. Whirlpool tubs aren't as difficult to install as one might think. They are installed just like a regular tub, except for a simple electrical wiring connection to the motor. Something else that might interest you is a portable steam bath for one person. The steam bath is on rollers and can be easily moved from one room to another. It runs on a regular 110 outlet and comes in several colors. Make sure you call them for store hours. The above hours change during the summer and, for your convenience, appointments are available for times other than posted hours. Delivery is free to the Ventura and San Fernando Valley areas. There is a nominal charge per trip for deliveries outside of these areas.

FATOR'S APPLIANCES & PLUMBING
436 S. Robertson Blvd.
Los Angeles, CA 90048
213/386-1743
HOURS: MON-FRI: 8:30-5:30
CREDIT CARDS: MC, V

Family owned and operated, Fator's offers all major appliances at 5 to 10% above cost. They carry a large display of refrigerators, washers, dryers and dishwashers. Knowledgeable salespeople are always happy to give useful information and to point customers in the right direction. If you're going to install your new dishwasher yourself, you'll be relieved to know that Fator's carries a complete supply of plumbing materials.

BUILDING & REMODELING

LARRY & JOE'S PLUMBING SUPPLIES
10955 Sepulveda Blvd.
Mission Hills, CA 91345
818/365-9394
HOURS: MON-FRI: 8-6 SAT: 8-5 SUN: 9-5
CREDIT CARDS: DISC, MC, V

In business since 1967, these people know what they are doing. Whatever you happen to need in plumbing, electrical and hardware supplies, they have at 20 to 30% off normal retail prices. They offer free professional advice to all of you do-it-yourselfers and will provide installation, if that's what you need. Service is their priority and service is what you get at Larry & Joe's Plumbing Supplies.
Additional Locations:
Northridge–8916 Corbin, 818/349-2540
Reseda–18446 Vanowen, 818/345-6103
Simi Valley–1560 Los Angeles Ave., 805/584-6800

LE ELEGANT BATH
470 Princeland Court
Corona, CA 91719
714/734-8084, 800/454-BATH
HOURS: MON-FRI: 8:30-5 SAT-SUN: BY APPOINTMENT ONLY
CREDIT CARDS: MC, V

Pamper yourself and relax in one of Le Elegant's beautiful bathtubs. Prices start at $395 and go to just under $2,000. The $2,000 tub is a two person whirlpool with 10 jets and 2 separate air controls. This price includes all hardware and the on/off switch (located on the tub itself) for the air pump. Another two person whirlpool that measures 6' x 42", has 8 jets, and sells complete for $1,398. All of their tubs are nonporous and easy to clean. They use the same suppliers and the exact materials (100% acrylic) that American Standard, Jacuzzi and Kohler use for their products. If you have priced whirlpool tubs lately, you know these prices are amazing. Any color is available on their seven models, and if they don't have it in stock, they will make one up for you. If the color isn't a standard color, bring in a sample so they can custom blend the color for you on the premises. At savings of at least 50% off retail, depending on the model you select, you can save hundreds or thousands of dollars at Le Elegant.

BUILDING & REMODELING

MC NALLY ELECTRIC
10792 Los Alamitos Blvd.
Los Alamitos, CA 90720
310/598-9438, 714/761-0692
HOURS: MON-FRI: 9-5
CREDIT CARDS: DISC, MC, V

Whatever your lighting needs, McNally Electric can satisfy them. Table and floor lamps, fluorescents, incandescents, HID, track or recessed lighting, low voltage, indoor or outdoor, you'll find them here at 20–50% savings. Whether your needs are commercial, residential, or office, their trained sales personnel will help you with your purchase. They also carry all the "stuff" that goes behind the light fixture such as switches, breakers, fuses, and PVC. If you have a favorite lamp that needs repair, bring it in. We can't begin to list all of the brand names they carry, but some of the brand names they carry are Tivoli, Fredrick Ranond, Hilite, Nutone, Plantation, Melissa, Angelo, Dinico, and Halo Lighting.

SAVE–MOR PLUMBING SUPPLIES
3361 Hamner Ave.
Norco, CA 91760
714/735-8310
HOURS: MON-SAT: 8-5:30
CREDIT CARDS: DISC, MC, V

At Save-Mor Plumbing Supplies, every employee can take the do-it-your-selfers by the hand and help them with their projects. These projects can range from installing a garbage disposal to plumbing an entire house. While their showroom is only 900 square feet, their inventory of supplies and equipment takes up 2-1/2 acres! Prices run about 20 to 40% below prices at hardware chain stores. They have three plumbers that make calls at far less than most since they are the material suppliers. Another plus for shopping here is that their personnel appears to be genuinely pleased to serve you.

WAREHOUSE DISCOUNT CENTER
30621 Canwood St.
Agoura, CA 91301
800/334-4WDC (800/334-4932)
HOURS: MON-FRI: 9-9 SAT: 9-5 SUN: 10-5
CREDIT CARDS: DISC, MC,V

Warehouse Discount Center has one of the largest display showrooms (33,000 square feet) in Southern California. They carry almost every major appliance, in-home electronics and kitchen and bath plumbing needs. You'll find brand names such as G.E., RCA, Yamaha, Maytag,

BUILDING & REMODELING

Hitachi, Kohler, Whirlpool, Magic Chef, Viking, Kenwood and much more. There policy is to meet or beat competitor's prices. There's also a small section with freight-damaged goods at even greater discounts.

∞ REPAIR & WORK REFERRAL SERVICE ∞

END RESULT
818/784-1572
HOURS: 9-9 SEVEN DAYS A WEEK
Do you need some work done on or in your home? End Result has been referring people to trustworthy tradesmen—with down to earth prices—since 1979. Whether you need a roofing contractor or a handy man, End Result will refer you to someone thoroughly screened and reliable. They have nearly 10,000 satisfied clients including some of the biggest names in Hollywood. There is no charge to the customer for this service.
Additional Locations:
Orange County Referral Service: 714/546-6008

∞ WALL & WINDOW TREATMENTS ∞

– WALLPAPER –

DISCOUNT WALLPAPER & INTERIORS
67802 E. Palm Canyon Dr.
Cathedral City, CA 92234
619/321-9652
HOURS: MON-FRI: 10-6 SAT: 10-2
CREDIT CARDS: DISC, MC, V

You can save up to 50% off suggested retail prices on designer wallpaper. They have hundreds of rolls in stock from companies such as Schumacher and Waverly. The patterns are up-to-date and there are always bargain close-outs featuring single rolls of wallpaper for $1.

OBALEK TILE & WALLPAPER
2301 S. Hill St.
Los Angeles, CA 90007
213/748-4664
HOURS: MON-FRI: 8-6 SAT: 9-5
CREDIT CARDS: MC, V

Obalek Tile & Wallpaper has approximately 250,000 rolls of wallpaper in stock. They carry all the tools necessary for do-it-yourselfers, and their professional staff will be glad to instruct you on the how-to. General manager Bill Cochran and his staff are extremely helpful.

WALLPAPER BIN
8969 Tampa Ave.
Northridge, CA 91324
818/886-1291
HOURS: MON-SAT: 10-6
CREDIT CARDS: MC, V

If you're looking for "high-quality" decorator and famous maker wallcovering, how would you like to save 50 to 80% off original book prices! That's exactly what you can save on items in stock at Wallpaper Bin. They carry brands like Mitchell Designs, James Seamans, Astor, Sinclair, Waverly, Schumacher, King Fisher, Cherry Hill, Bolta, Sanitas and many more. You'll be able to make your selection from a variety of vinyls, mylars, textures, handprints, strings, grass cloths and more. Most all of these absolutely marvelous buys are from factory, mill and distributor inventories (out of production goods). Wallpaper Bin is the very best resource for quality in-stock wallpaper. Both stores now have a clearance section with wallpaper priced at $3.99 a roll. The rolls in this special area originally sold for $18.95 to $50 retail per roll. There are also bagged lots of two double rolls (4 rolls of paper) for $10, or three double rolls for $20.
Additional Locations:
Ventura—4255 E. Main St., 805/642-6422

WALLPAPER CITY
1320 Lincoln Blvd.
Santa Monica, CA 90401
310/393-9422
HOURS: MON-FRI: 8:30-5:30 SAT: 9-5
CREDIT CARDS: MC, V

There are more than 1,000 rolls of different wallpaper in stock at any one time, 800 wallpaper books to order from, and you can save 20–60% on your selection. Manager Lotte Hanock has this large stock of wallpaper which she can match to shades and drapery treatments. Fabric can also be ordered to match your designer paper from companies such as Schumacher, Waverly and Charles Barone. At Wallpaper City you can purchase vinyls, grass cloths, custom bedding, pillows and window coverings, all at big savings.

– WINDOW TREATMENTS –

AERO SHADE
8404 W. 3rd St.
Los Angeles, CA 90048
213/655-2411
HOURS: MON-FRI: 8:30-5
CREDIT CARDS: MC, V

Aero Shade has everything for windows, except drapes. If you're looking for pleated or laminated shades, shutters, Levolor or vertical blinds, they have a complete stock and quick service. You're buying factory direct at Aero Shade, and can save 10 to 25%. Some of the styles available are custom, decorative and simple. They'll provide new rollers or put the new cloth on your old rollers. You can also have your fabrics laminated. They've been in business for over 50 years.

BEVERLY WESTERN INTERIORS
336 N. Western Ave.
Los Angeles, CA 90004
213/463-3192
HOURS: MON-FRI: 8-6
CREDIT CARDS: CASH OR CHECKS ONLY

Save 20 to 40% and get the best of interior design selection, too. Beverly Western has draperies, carpeting, bedspreads and furniture for your consideration. Your draperies will be custom-made and of the finest quality at factory-to-you prices. Established in 1965, you receive expert advice and years of experience.

BLUE CHIP DRAPERY, INC.
2139 Stoner Ave.
Los Angeles, CA 90025
800/BLUE-CHP, 310/477-2421
HOURS: MON-SAT: 8-5
CREDIT CARDS: DISC, MC, V

You will usually save 50% or more on draperies and blinds at Blue Chip Drapery. This company is California's largest discount drapery manufacturer, with eight window covering showrooms throughout greater Los Angeles and Orange counties. There are 120 sizes of ready-to-hang draperies in a great variety of textures and colors, always available at factory-direct prices in each showroom. All ready-mades (standard, elegant, luxury and close-out lines) are sold on a satisfaction guaranteed

BUILDING & REMODELING

basis, allowing a 10 day exchange or refund. When you order custom draperies from their huge stock of discounted decorator fabrics, there is no labor charge added to most selections. Major brands of mini blinds, verticals, and other window treatments are also discounted.

Additional Locations: 7 other stores in S. CA–Call 800/BLUE-CHP

BRITE AND SHINE, INC.
7625 Hayvenhurst Ave.
Van Nuys, CA 91406
818/782-5326
HOURS: MON-FRI: 8:30-4:30
CREDIT CARDS: MC, V

Brite and Shine offers name-brand window coverings with bottom line, lowest prices. They carry such brand names as Levolor, Graber, Louverdrape, Hunter Douglas, Del Mar, Kirsch and Verosol. A 6 foot sliding glass door can be covered with vertical blinds for as little as $101.75, including a valance. Brite and Shine offers fast delivery and lifetime warranties on all their merchandise. They specialize in mini-blind cleaning using ultra sound. With prices up to 70% below retail, you'd be "brite" to shop here!

DIAMOND V INTERIORS
4145 Indus Way
Riverside, CA 92503
714/736-6055
HOURS: MON-FRI: 8-5
CREDIT CARDS: CASH OR CHECKS ONLY

Diamond V Interiors carries custom draperies and bedspreads direct from the manufacturer. They have thousands of samples to choose from, and you can save 20% off retail on your purchases. They've been in business for over 10 years, so you can expect to find knowledgeable help.

INTERIOR MOTIVES
8362 W. 3rd St.
Los Angeles, CA 90048
213/658-6017
HOURS: MON-FRI: 9-5
CREDIT CARDS: MC, V

Interior Motives is really a window covering specialist, but they also offer 20 to 50% discounts on office furniture, carpets and window tinting. You'll find an extensive selection of mini-blinds, vertical blinds, woven blinds, shutters, Levolors, Roman shades, pleated shades and custom

BUILDING & REMODELING

draperies. In business since 1979, they offer free estimates, and also a home shopping service.

MELROSE DRAPERIES
7748 Santa Monica Blvd.
Los Angeles, CA 90046
213/653-1601
HOURS: MON-FRI: 8:30-5
CREDIT CARDS: AE, DISC, MC, V

These folks have been in business over 30 years selling, manufacturing, and installing window coverings. Want your bedspread to match your bedroom drapes? Look no further! Want to see how the fabrics will look in your home? They'll bring out samples to your home. Draperies, bedpreads, window shades, and true discount prices. What a combination!

MORAN WAREHOUSE STORE
4631 S. Huntington Dr.
Los Angeles, CA 90032
213/221-4141
HOURS: MON-SAT: 10-6 SUN: 10-5
CREDIT CARDS: DISC, MC, V

You can get ready-made draperies, quality custom-made draperies, bedspreads, sheets, curtains, panels, mini-blinds, vertical blinds, drapery yardage, and remnants at 40 to 75% below retail prices. They buy direct from their vendors and pass these savings on to you.

STAR DRAPERIES MFG.**
319 N. Western Ave.
Los Angeles, CA 90004
213/463-1574, 800/541-7827
HOURS: MON-SAT: 9-5:30
CREDIT CARDS: AE, DISC, MC, V

Star will come to your home, measure your windows and give you a free estimate. When your order has been completed, their pro will handle the installation. Vertical blinds are their specialty and they make mini-blinds, pleated shades and wood blinds. Draperies are also custom-made. Look forward to factory direct prices with savings as much as 60 to 70% off retail prices. They have been in business since 1974. Don't forget to use your BUYING RETAIL IS STUPID coupon for a 10% discount.
Additional Locations:
Van Nuys–14551 Erwin St., 818/787-7841

BUILDING & REMODELING

SUPERIOR WINDOW COVERINGS, INC.**
10731 Chandler Blvd.
North Hollywood, CA 91601
818/762-9033
HOURS: MON-SAT: 9-5
CREDIT CARDS: MC, V

Wholesale prices on draperies, vertical blinds, mini-blinds, pleated shades, wood blinds, shutters, draperies, roman shades, balloon shades, cloud shades and cornice boxes are found in Superior Window Coverings' factory showroom. They carry such brand names as Bali, Duette, and Superior. You'll find special liquidation sales during January and February, and again in October and November. Bring in your BUYING RETAIL IS STUPID coupon for an extra 10% discount!

VASONA INTERIORS
8323 De Celis Pl.
North Hills, CA 91343
818/993-9248
HOURS: MON-SAT: 8-5:30
CREDIT CARDS: MC, V

Vasona Interiors has window coverings to fit any room in your house. They can fix you up with mini-blinds, shades, vertical blinds, and verosol blinds with brand names such as Levolor, LouverDrape and Kirsch. You can also get draperies, bedspreads, wallpaper and personalized service. All orders are custom-made. Service is most important to them. Customer satisfaction is guaranteed. You can expect a 50% discount off retail items.

∞ TOOLS ∞

POST TOOLS
3838 Santa Fe Ave.
Vernon, CA 90058
213/588-1255
HOURS: MON-SAT: 8-5 SUN: 10-3
CREDIT CARDS: AE, DISC, MC, V

Previously known as Santa Fe Tool & Supply, this is the undisputed leader in discount prices for tools. They say they have no competition because they will beat all prices. What's more, Post Tools guaranties everything they sell. What do they sell? TOOLS—power tools, hand tools, air tools, auto tools and shop tools—including such names as Skil,

BUILDING & REMODELING

Hitachi, Makita and the rest. They also sell work gloves and work brushes too. Ask to be put on their mailing list so you can hear about special sales. Any day you visit Post Tools you'll save 30 to 50% off retail prices. Free parking is available alongside the store.

Additional Locations: 18 other stores throughout S. CA

∞ WOOD STAINING & REFINISHING ∞

RAY'S WOOD FINISHING
10465 San Fernando Rd., Unit 3
Pacoima, CA 91331
818/899-1488
HOURS: MON-FRI: 8-4:30 SAT: 9-3
CREDIT CARDS: CASH OR CHECKS ONLY

Want to add more cabinets to your kitchen? If you do but have had second thoughts because of the cost, or you couldn't match the stain, Ray's Wood Finishing may be just the ticket. Ray Camacho, a man that loves his work, can help you with the finish of any kind of wood, new or antique. He also does minor repair work, but if the job is too big, he will find someone to do it for you. Ray's guarantees the best price around. He's been in business for nine years, and the money you save will surprise you.

CLOTHING & ACCESSORIES

∞ Active Wear ∞

CHEAP FRILLS**
8325 W. Third St.
Los Angeles, CA 90048
213/653-9997
HOURS: MON-SAT: 11-6
CREDIT CARDS: AE, DISC, MC, V

If you want to be a hit at your local gym, stop by Cheap Frills. Their expert sales staff will help coordinate your entire workout outfit. They carry dance, swim, athletic and sportswear for women and children, a small men's collection, aerobic shoes, ballet and jazz shoes, body hugging cotton/lycra clothing (mini-skirts), leggings, sport bras and bags. All this at 10 to 20% off retail prices and up to 50% off on sales items. Brand names include Dance France, Danskin, Flexatard, Nike, Kicks, Marika, Baryshnikov, Olga, EG Smith and Avia. And if you can't stop by the store, they have a catalogue for mail orders. You'll be in the pink, tights that is, when you use your BUYING RETAIL IS STUPID coupon here to save an extra 5%!

DESERT EMPIRE GOLF CENTER
74-121 Hwy. 111
Palm Desert, CA 92260
619/568-4644
HOURS: MON-SAT: 9-5 (10-4 DURING JUNE, JULY, AUGUST)
CREDIT CARDS: MC, V

If you like to golf you will want to look good walking or riding the course. Here's the place to get top name-brand golf wear for both men and women at savings of 20% to 50% off retail. Desert Empire has been in business for 14 years and has a 2,800 square foot store. You can expect personal service even though the prices are sliced, and it won't be rough to find additional savings during the summer or other seasons. You'll find yourself on the right course for golf shoes, shirts, slacks, warm-ups, tops, shorts, skirts and sweaters, but don't get teed off because they carry clothing only. Desert Empire has grown through word of mouth which is the best kind of advertising.

CLOTHING & ACCESSORIES

LOVE MATCH TENNIS SHOP
21781 Ventura Blvd.
Woodland Hills, CA 91364
818/348-8866
HOURS: MON–SAT: 10-6
CREDIT CARDS: AE, MC, V

As the name suggests, this store offers a huge selection of tennis clothing, shoes, and accessories. From arm bands to warm-up suits, you'll find whatever you need for the family. Almost everything is 15% off retail, and don't overlook their special price racks for even greater savings!

MOVE IT
308 Rosecrans Ave.
Manhattan Beach, CA 90266
310/545-6455
HOURS: MON, FRI: 11-6 WED, THUR: 11-7 SAT: 10-6 SUN: 11-5
CREDIT CARDS: MC, V

Move It is an outlet for a local active wear manufacturer that sells primarily to the midwest and east coast. Most of the merchandise is a cotton/lycra blend. You'll find leggings, leotards, catsuits, stir-up pants and bicycle pants all at about 20% above cost. You'll save even more money when you buy in quantity. For example, items that sell for $9.99 individually are sold three for $25. You won't find anything priced over $30 at Move It. They also have a line of active wear for girls sizes 4 to 14.

OLGA WARNER'S MANUFACTURER'S OUTLET
15750 Strathern
Van Nuys, CA 91406
818/994-7963
HOURS: MON–SAT: 9–5 SUN: 12–4
CREDIT CARDS: AE, MC, V

For bargains on ski wear for men and women, it's hard to beat the prices at the Van Nuys Olga Warner's Outlet. This store has a large selection of Edelweiss bibs, shells, ski pantsuits and powder jackets. Discounts start at about 30% below retail prices. If you happen to go in before the beginning of ski season, you will find some real bargains on last year's ski clothes. On our last visit we spotted a White Stag parka that originally retailed for $200 tagged at $66.

CLOTHING & ACCESSORIES

SANDLER OF THE VALLEY**
19009 Ventura Blvd.
Tarzana, CA 91356
818/881-6999

HOURS: MON-SAT: 10-5:30
CREDIT CARDS: DISC, MC, V

Women and children can find shoes discounted 10–20% at Sandler of the Valley. Dancewear is also available and has been since 1969. You'll find Jumping Jacks, Keds, L.A. Gear, Capezio and many other brands. Take in your BUYING RETAIL IS STUPID coupon for a 10% discount.

SHELLY'S DISCOUNT AEROBIC & DANCE WEAR
2089 Westwood Blvd.
Westwood, CA 90025
310/475-1400

HOURS: MON: 10-8 TUES-SAT: 10-6 SUN: 11-4
CREDIT CARDS: AE, DISC, MC, V

You'll save from 50 to 70% on leotards, tights and active wear that are perfect for dancing and those strenuous aerobic workouts. Shelly Seeman has them in all sizes and styles and colors—even for mothers-to-be and for children. She has extra specials going on all the time Brand names include Rachelle, Softouch, Marika and Cathy George, to name a few. You'll find a complete selection of costumes and accessories, dance shoes and dancewear in this 3,000 square foot store. Dressing rooms and parking are available.
Additional Locations:
Tarzana–Apparel Warehouse, 6010 Yolanda St., 818/344-3224

∞ BRIDAL & FORMAL ∞

AFFAIR OF THE HEART**
Newbury Park, CA 91320
818/715-0570   805/498-9338

HOURS: BY APPOINTMENT ONLY
CREDIT CARDS: CASH OR CHECKS ONLY

Affair of the Heart can save you 20 to 40% off retail on the gown of your choice! All you need is the manufacturer's name, style number and color. If you can't decipher the sales tag at a bridal boutique, you can send them a picture of a dress from a bridal magazine (don't forget to specify the issue and name of the magazine). The service also extends the same savings on accessories, bridsmaids and flowergirl dresses, mother-of-the-bride dresses and special occasion gowns. The dress must

CLOTHING & ACCESSORIES

be paid for in full before they will place the order, and you also pay for shipping and insurance. If payment in full makes you a little nervous, Affair of the Heart will provide references. If you order invitations—discounted 25% off retail—you'll receive 100 personalized napkins for free with your BUYING RETAIL IS STUPID coupon.

BRIDAL FACTORY OUTLET**
3334 Eagle Rock Blvd.
Los Angeles, CA 90065
213/259-1740

HOURS: SAT: 10-3
CREDIT CARDS: MC, V

Open only on Saturdays, this is a factory outlet full of wedding gowns and accessories like headpieces, veils, petty coats and shoes. You'll also find a variety of dresses for bridesmaids, mothers-of-the-bride, proms and special occasions. The labels found here are their own, and they specialize in ruffled wedding gowns. Savings run 50 to 70% off retail on sizes 4 to 20. Because it's a warehouse, it's not a fancy place to shop, but the savings are well worth it. You'll save an extra $25 if you use your BUYING RETAIL IS STUPID coupon.

THE BRIDE'S ALTERNATIVE
19449 Ventura Blvd.
Tarzana, CA 91356
818/345-8702

HOURS: MON-WED, FRI: 12-6 THUR: 12-8 SAT: 10-6
CREDIT CARDS: MC, V

Finally, a bridal store that offers an alternative—bridal attire and bridesmaid gowns that you can afford! The Bride's Alternative features low prices (10 to 30% off retail) on designer gowns and headpieces, with superior attention to detail and alterations to make your wedding attire the best you've ever seen. Mom and Dad, this is one store that won't put you on the path to the poorhouse!

ROBERT ELLIS**
12524 Ventura Blvd.
Studio City, CA 91604
818/769-9666

HOURS: MON-WED, FRI-SAT: 9:30-6 THUR: 9:30-8
CREDIT CARDS: AE, MC, V

If you want to look like a million dollars, then Robert Ellis (formerly called Poor Snob) is for you. They carry the "look," not necessarily the label. Designer styles without designer prices is what you'll encounter here. Get your famous designer look-alike for $800 instead of $7,000 to $10,000. While this boutique isn't inexpensive, it may just be one of the best values in BUYING RETAIL IS STUPID. The collection of clothing reflects their philosophy of, "The best dressed women know that style means everything, and labels don't matter." For sophisticated clothing you really must come here! You'll save an additional 10% if you remember to use your BUYING RETAIL IS STUPID discount coupon.

GALAXY OF GOWNS**
2292 Tapo St.
Simi Valley, CA 93063
805/526-4696

HOURS: MON-THUR: 10-5 FRI-SAT: 10-6 SUN: 12-5
CREDIT CARDS: AE, MC, OPT, V

Galaxy of Gowns has literally thousands of gowns and dresses (in 3,700 square feet) you can buy right off the rack. The tags are cut out of the dresses, but if you've been shopping around, you'll recognize the brands. Gowns that retailed for $1,800 can be found here for $675. How do they do it? They buy samples from bridal boutiques and close-outs from manufacturers. Many times gowns are discontinued at the beginning of a season, so often you'll find dresses still advertised in a current issue of a bridal magazine. Sizes usually run 8, 9, 10 and 12 (sample sizes). By the way, as long as a dress fits you in the shoulders, the dress can be altered to fit. If you're handy with a needle and are making your dress, check out the bargain room. This is a great way to buy expensive appliques and lace. They also carry bridesmaid, pageant, mother-of-bride and cocktail dresses. Galaxy of Gowns has quarterly sales to make room for new inventory. During the sale, prices are cut another 50%. Call for an appointment if their regular hours don't fit into your schedule. You'll get an extra 20% discount with your BUYING RETAIL IS STUPID coupon.

HALF-PRICE HOUSE
12152 Brookhurst
Garden Grove, CA 92640
714/537-1231

HOURS: MON-FRI: 10-9 SAT: 10-6 SUN: 10-5
CREDIT CARDS: MC, V

This missy store is the oldest discount house in Orange County, and it's no wonder it's so popular. New merchandise arrives almost daily from cities like New York, Miami and Chicago. Many are designer originals and samples—plus dresses, sportswear coordinates, and swimwear. Their specialty is special occasion dresses, both long and short. All items are available in regular, large and half-sizes at 50 to 70% below retail.

CLOTHING & ACCESSORIES

LEON MAX FACTORY OUTLET
3535 S. Broadway
Los Angeles, CA 90013
213/234-0510

HOURS: MON-FRI: 10-6 SAT: 10-4
CREDIT CARDS: MC, V

Ladies, here's the store for you. Leon Max used to sell his designs through Bullocks and Nordstrom; he now has two retail stores in Brentwood and Santa Monica. Fortunately for BUYING RETAIL IS STUPID readers, he has a factory outlet where you will find terrific buys. You can buy an entire silk outfit for around $100. From casual to formal wear, for the missy to the matronly, you can find all styles at less than wholesale. They also have markdowns once a month on already discounted clothing.

PRICE-LESS BRIDALS**
6633 Fallbrook Ave., Suite 204
West Hills, CA 91307
818/340-6514

HOURS: MON-FRI: 1-9 SAT: 10-6 SUN: 12-5
CREDIT CARDS: AE, DISC, MC, V

Price-Less Bridals is a factory-direct discounter with prices 15–75% below retail! They carry clearance gowns off the rack in sizes 4–20, and also offer a full line of bridals to order at 15–20% below retail. There is a style for every bride at an affordable price. Dresses range run $99 to $1,999. You'll find a huge selection of bridesmaid dresses in many colors and sizes. Prom dresses and mother-of-the-bride dresses are also available at great savings. Take in your BUYING RETAIL IS STUPID coupon for an extra 5% discount.

∞ FAMILY APPAREL ∞

CALIFORNIA JEANS
1228 Obispo Ave.
Long Beach, CA 90804
310/494-1300

HOURS: 11-7 SEVEN DAYS A WEEK
CREDIT CARDS: MC, V

California Jeans always has low prices on Levis, Lee and Wrangler jeans, jackets, shirts, coveralls, and overalls. Prices for jeans range from $16.00 to $32.00. You'll also find great buys on additional men's, children's and women's wear. Free parking and dressing rooms are available.

CLOTHING & ACCESSORIES

CALIFORNIA SOCKS
401 Ocean Front Walk
Venice, CA 90291
310/399-7818

HOURS: MON-SUN: 9-6
CREDIT CARDS: MC, V

California Socks has one of the largest selections of discounted socks in Los Angeles. Yes, we said socks. Not only will you find some of the most unusual socks in town, but they also have socks featuring every state in the United States. Instead of collecting spoons for every state, you can now collect socks.

COOPER BUILDING
860 S. Los Angeles St.
Los Angeles, CA 90014
213/622-1139

HOURS: MON-SAT: 9:30-5:30 SUN: 11-5
CREDIT CARDS: CASH OR CHECKS ONLY*

This place is incredible! The Cooper Building is a "Tall Mall" 11 stories high with 8 selling floors all bulging with exciting merchandise in the heart of the wholesale garment district. You'll find quite a collection of outlet stores representing various manufacturers, famous retail stores and discount stores. Whether you shop at the Cooper Building once a month or once a year, you always save 25 to 75% off retail prices every single day of the week. Quality and value prevail in over 70 stores featuring current designer and brand-name fashions for men, women and children of leather fashions, shoes, handbags, fashion accessories, lingerie and home fashions all under one roof. Why spend twice the amount on prestigious labels carried in expensive department stores when you can save a bundle buying the identical item at the Cooper Building?
*Some vendors accept credit cards.
Additional Locations: 70 stores at one location

NORDSTROM RACK
3900 S. Bristol St.
Santa Ana, CA 92704
714/751-5901

HOURS: MON-FRI: 9:30-9:30 SAT: 9:30-7 SUN: 10-6
CREDIT CARDS: MC, NORDSTROM, V

The Nordstrom Rack stores are filled with last season's sensational garb from their mall stores. You'll find shoes, clothing and accessories for the entire family. This is also the perfect place to pick up designer labels at generic prices. One of the authors had the opportunity to attend the

CLOTHING & ACCESSORIES

Academy Awards and wore a chic ensemble she purchased at Nordstrom Rack. She paid just $89 for an outfit that originally retailed for over $300. Prices run 30–70% off retail.
Additional Locations:
Chino–5537 Philadelphia St., 714/591-0551
San Diego–824 Camino del Rio, 619/296-0143
Woodland Hills–21490 Victory Blvd., 818/884-6770

REAL CHEAP SPORTS
36 W. Santa Clara
Ventura, CA 93001
805/648-3803

HOURS: MON-SAT: 10-6   SUN: 11-5
CREDIT CARDS: AE, MC, V

This is where you'll find Patagonia outdoor clothing. Prices start at about 30% below retail. The merchandise consists of discontinued merchandise from the previous season and overruns and seconds from the current season. The seconds are clearly marked, and the flaws are always cosmetic, never functional ones. There are always at least half-dozen items on special at low low prices, and the sale items change every two weeks. In addition to ski pants, parkas, sweats, polo shirts, long underwear and other wearables, you'll also find various types of outdoor equipment such as down sleeping bags and a large variety of backpacks.

ROSS DRESS FOR LESS
4315 Pacific Coast Hwy.
Torrance, CA 95050
310/373-0784

HOURS: MON-SAT: 9:30-9   SUN: 11-7
CREDIT CARDS: ALL MAJOR

Ross Dress for Less is the perfect place to go if you want to outfit the entire family with quality merchandise at savings of 10–60% off retail. They attempt to accommodate everyone—infants, children, men and women will find clothing for petite to larger sized women. You can satisfy many needs at Ross stores including shoes, hosiery, handbags and popular name-brand fragrances. Since their price tags note the Ross price compared to the suggested retail price, you will enjoy knowing just how much you are saving. You won't lose out on any of the amenities that you find at major department stores because Ross offers exchanges, cash refunds and private dressing rooms.
Additional Locations: Over 50 stores throughout S. CA

CLOTHING & ACCESSORIES

WAREHOUSE OUTLET
100 N. Maclay
San Fernando, CA 91340
818/361-0292

HOURS: 8:30-5:30 SEVEN DAYS A WEEK
CREDIT CARDS: CASH OR CHECKS ONLY

Barry Seeman and family own and operate this quaint store, keeping expenses to a minimum. This 3,500 square foot store is tightly packed with excellent values. Men's and children's casual wear, jeans, underwear, jackets, coats, shirts, screen printed t-shirts and thermals are all 30 to 50% off retail. They carry Levi's, Wrangler, Fruit of the Loom, Zeppelin, and Pipeline. Levi's basic 501 denims are stocked in sizes 0–50. In addition, they carry a full range of Levi's pants, jackets, cords, 501's in all colors, and Levi's Nuvos, to mention a few.

∞ FASHION ACCESSORIES ∞

ANTELOPE
12212 Ventura Blvd.
Studio City, CA 91604
818/980-4299

HOURS: MON-SAT: 9:30-6:30
CREDIT CARDS: AE, DISC, MC, V

Antelope carries all kinds of leather goods and purses, especially 24K gold plated evening bags. With about 2,000 bags on display, even the most finicky of shoppers are bound to be satisfied. If they have only one remaining of a certain style bag, it's usually sold at cost. They also carry briefcases, attache cases, organizers, wallets, and overnighters. On most items you'll pay 20 to 50% off retail. In business since the early 1970s, they know how to make their customers happy by standing behind their merchandise for one year. Whether the stitching starts to unravel or the hardware falls off, Antelope will fix it or replace it within one year of purchase. They also repair leather clothing and accessories. Some of the brand names they carry are Viva, Pinky, Il Bisonti, and Marco Ricci.

CLOTHING & ACCESSORIES

BAG LADY
31954 San Luis Rey
Cathedral City, CA 92234
619/323-7272

HOURS: MON-SAT: 9:30-5   SUN: 11-4
CREDIT CARDS: AE, MC, V

Claiming to have the largest selection in the entire Cochella Valley, Bag Lady has women's handbags, leather jackets, leather accessories and fashion jewelry at great savings 20 to 50% off retail. Carrying at least 4,000 handbags, it would be nearly impossible to walk out without finding that perfect handbag. You will always find a great selection filled with buys on the bargain table.

FASHION WEST
71-846 Highway 111
Rancho Mirage, CA 92270
619/773-3361

HOURS: MON-SAT: 9:30-5   SUN: 11-4
CREDIT CARDS: AE, MC, V

Famous designer labels highlight this great fashion accessory shop. Fashion West is geared toward personal service for your personal style! You can look forward to savings of 20 to 40% off retail prices on ladies accessories, handbags, jewelry, belts, scarves and small leather goods. This is where you need to go to spruce up or complete your wardrobe.

MARLENE GAINES HANDBAGS**
6000 Reseda Blvd.
Tarzana, CA 91356

818/344-0442

HOURS: MON-SAT: 10-5:30
CREDIT CARDS: MC, V

As the name implies, Marlene Gaines Handbags specializes in handbags and jewelry. You'll find buys at 30 to 50% off the retail prices department stores charge. They carry brand names such as Susan Gails, Aspects, Lissette, and Pantera. The quality handbags are all leather, and they have sales in June and December with prices discounted even more. You'll find Marlene has an unbelievable selection, including white handbags year round. There are hundreds of bags, including great knock-offs, and each style comes in several colors. They also carry one-of-a-kind jewelry, making this store a worthwhile shopping venture. Take in your BUYING RETAIL IS STUPID coupon for an extra 10% discount on any nonsale item.

CLOTHING & ACCESSORIES

HANDBAG HANGUP
8580 Washington Blvd.
Culver City, CA 90232
310/559-4705

HOURS: MON-SAT: 10-5:30
CREDIT CARDS: DISC, MC, V

Someone definitely gave this store the right name. It's hard to visualize, but on the average, Handbag Hangup carries 20,000 to 30,000 handbags! Prices range from $1 to $300. In addition to all of those handbags, they also carry a small selection of small leather goods, and travel accessories. All merchandise is 25% off retail prices set by manufacturers.

HOSIERY OUTLET, INC.**
19410 Business Center Dr.
Northridge, CA 91324
818/885-6331

HOURS: MON-FRI: 10-6 SAT: 10-5
CREDIT CARDS: MC, V

If it seems as though you are opening a new package of pantyhose every time you turn around, then Hosiery Outlet can save you loads of money. This 2,600 square foot store carries pantyhose in every texture and color you can imagine for regular, petite and queen-sized women. Discounts run 20–50% off retail on brand names such as Round the Clock, Christian Dior, Isotoner, Givenchy, Hanes and more. You can also get pantyhose or stockings customized with rhinestones or pearls. Whenever you buy a dozen pair of stockings, you receive an extra pair free. They accept C.O.D. orders, and you can order by telephone with a credit card. There are always unadvertised specials and whatever you do, don't forget to use your BUYING RETAIL IS STUPID coupon for an extra 10% discount.

LE CLUB HANDBAG CO.
860 S. Los Angeles St.
Los Angeles, CA 90014
213/623-8709

HOURS: MON-FRI: 9:30-5 SAT: 9-6 SUN: 11-5
CREDIT CARDS: MC, V

You can find every major brand of handbag at Le Club Handbag that you would find in your major department stores. They also carry accessories, gloves, hats, costume jewelry, watches, and small leather goods. Their prices average 25 to 90% off department store prices. You can save even more during their semi-annual sales. If you don't see what you're looking for ask Bill Reich, the owner, and he'll help you out!

CLOTHING & ACCESSORIES

MILLIE'S HANDBAGS AND SHOES
101 W. 9th St.
Los Angeles, CA 90015
213/623-6175
HOURS: MON-SAT: 10-6
CREDIT CARDS: AE, DISC, MC, V

Across the street from the California Mart, and one block from the Cooper Building, lies Millie's Handbags and Shoes. Millie carefully follows the world of fashion, and makes certain her 2,000 square foot store has the accessories to complement the latest styles. She's just waiting to put the finishing touches on the new outfits you've found while shopping in the garment district. You'll find discounts of 20 to 50% off the retail price on famous brand names such as Liz Claiborne, Anne Klein, Jazz, 9 West, What's What and many more. This is the place to go to make your new threads shine!

∞ INFANT'S & CHILDREN'S APPAREL ∞

C.W. DESIGNS
18720 Oxnard St., #106
Tarzana, CA 91356
818/343-0823
HOURS: MON, TUES & FRI: 9-3:30 WED-THUR: 9-5 SAT: 9:30-3
CREDIT CARDS: CASH OR CHECKS ONLY

For the most part, you'll find special occasion dresses for little girls and preteens here. C.W. Designs are found in specialty stores all over the country. The dresses that retail for $130 to $200 are 20 to 50% off retail here. What you'll find mostly are overruns. There is also a custom boutique where young women can create a dress that reflects their own personalities and measurements. If you have an extremely picky teen who's impossible to please, C.W. Designs might just be the solution.

CHARADES OF CALIFORNIA
1035 S. Maple Ave.
Los Angeles, CA 90015
213/748-9409
HOURS: MON-SAT: 9-5 SUN: 10-4
CREDIT CARDS: MC, V

This 3,500 square foot warehouse is stacked floor to ceiling with children's wear, sizes newborn to 14 in boys and girls. Charades has a large selection of short sets, dresses, pants, dress suits, shirts, slacks, jeans, jogging suits, coats, diaper bags, blankets, caps, belts and accessories,

CLOTHING & ACCESSORIES

pajamas, socks, underwear, robes, t-shirts, tops and bathing suits. You'll find savings of 20 to 50% off regular department store prices on such brands as Polly Flinders, Baby Togs and Healthtex. You won't need to wave your arms around to get attention here.

DAVID'S CHILDREN'S WEAR
712 S. Los Angeles St.
Los Angeles, CA 90014
213/683-1622
HOURS: MON-SAT: 9:30-6 SUN: 11-5
CREDIT CARDS: AE, MC, V

David's Children's Warehouse has been offering great savings on children's clothing since 1940. Sizes start with infants and go to 14, preteens, slim, regular and husky. The basement is dedicated to a fantastic selection of boy's wear. With 5,000 square feet of clothing at savings of 20 to 50% off retail, this place is a must for mothers with young children.

FLAP HAPPY KIDS
3516 Centinela Ave.
Los Angeles, CA 90066
310/398-FLAP (3527)
HOURS: MON-FRI: 10-5 SAT: 10-4
CREDIT CARDS: AE, DISC, MC, OPT, V

This small factory outlet is a good place to buy Flap Happy clothing—and hats—for babies and toddlers. Savings run about 20 to 40% off retail on the same items found in department stores. Much of the merchandise consists of Flap Happy seconds, but you'll also see overruns and closeouts from other manufacturers.

FOR KIDS ONLY
19367 Victory Blvd. (Loehmann's Plaza)
Reseda, CA 91335
818/708-9543
HOURS: MON-WED, FRI-SAT: 10-6 THUR: 10-7 SUN: 12-5
CREDIT CARDS: MC, V

How often do you say, "I can't believe how quickly the baby is growing?" Well, For Kids Only is the place to keep taking your babies until they reach size 16. You'll find fine European and American clothing priced 40 to 60% lower than your better clothing stores. With the most up-to-date fashions in stock, your young ones will be the best dressed children on your block.
Additional Locations:
Los Angeles–746 N. Fairfax, 213/650-4885

CLOTHING & ACCESSORIES

KIDS CLUB OUTLET**
215 N. Moorpark Rd., "E"
Thousand Oaks, CA 91360
805/496-6989

HOURS: MON-WED & SAT: 10-6   THUR-FRI: 10-8   SUN: 10-5
CREDIT CARDS: MC, V

We can't mention names, but you'll find name-brand children's clothing here at 30 to 70% off prices found in boutiques and department stores. Boys sizes run newborn to size 7 and girls sizes run newborn to preteen. If you use your BUYING RETAIL IS STUPID discount coupon, you'll receive an additional $5 off on a purchase of $25 or more.
Additional Locations:
West Hills–6633 Fallbrook Ave., #408 (Fallbrook Mall), 818/888-4665
Oxnard–1843 Ventura Blvd., 805/983-1173

MARCIA'S RAINBOW FACTORY OUTLET
1111 Rancho Conejo Blvd., Suite 201
Newbury Park, CA 91320
805/375-1415

HOURS: MON-FRI: 10-4
CREDIT CARDS: CASH OR CHECKS ONLY

Normally only found in very pricey boutiques around the country, now you can get Marcia's Rainbow clothing at their factory outlet in Newbury Park. Discounts are about 50% off retail for girl's sizes infant through preteen. Occasionally they have clothing for little boys, but for the most part the clothing is geared towards little girls. During their bi-annual sales, the outlet marks everything down an additional 20 to 50%.

SACKS SFO KIDS
7018 Melrose St.
Hollywood, CA 90036
213/935-2590

HOURS: MON-TUES: 10-6   WED-FRI: 10-7   SUN: 11-6
CREDIT CARDS: MC, V

Sacks SFO Kids is right next door to the main Sacks SFO. Here you will find high fashion and low prices for tots to teens. They cater to children as young as 3 months and as old as 14 years. Dare we hope that one day they will tell us what SFO means?
Additional Locations:
Burbank–1439 W. Olive, 818/840-0571
Tarzana–18600 Ventura Blvd., 818/609-9282

CLOTHING & ACCESSORIES

SEE ME COLOR**
625 E. Cochran St.
Simi Valley, CA 93065
805/527-9573

HOURS: MON-FRI: 9-5 SAT: 9-12
CREDIT CARDS: CASH OR CHECKS ONLY

This is a factory outlet filled with overruns priced at or under $11. You'll find the hottest styles in either 100% cotton or stretch clothing made of a cotton/lycra blend. Children's sizes run 2 to 14 with the largest selection devoted to little girls. Women's and junior styles are available in small, medium and large. They have leggings, tops, shorts, dresses and stretch pants at 20 to 50% below retail prices. Don't forget your BUYING RETAIL IS STUPID coupon for savings of an extra 10%.

SEYMOUR FASHIONS**
7040 Darby Ave.
Reseda, CA 91335
818/705-1911

HOURS: MON-FRI: 9:30-5 SAT: 10-4
CREDIT CARDS: MC, V

Save money and customize your little girl's wardrobe (sizes 2 to 14) at the same time at Seymour Fashions. Just about everything is made to be mixed and matched. Most of the tops are appliqued, and there is a large assortment of bottoms (shorts, pants, leggings, and skirts) made from the same fabric used in the appliques. Not only can you mix and match, you can actually have anything you see in the store made in one of many available fabrics. If you find a top and can't find a bottom to match the fabric in the applique, they'll make one for you at no extra charge. As the manufacturer, Seymour Fashions is able to do all alterations on the premises, sometimes while you wait. The clothing here is not only versatile but also very well made. By the way, women's clothing, with the same mix-and-match theme, comprises more than half the store. Take in your BUYING RETAIL IS STUPID coupon for an extra 10% discount.

SID'S DISCOUNT BABY FURNITURE
8338 Lincoln Blvd.
Los Angeles, CA 90045
310/670-5550

HOURS: MON-THUR: 10-6 FRI: 10-7:30 SAT: 10-6
CREDIT CARDS: MC, V

Sid's is an institution where you can find everything in baby furniture and clothing for infants. There are all the necessities, of course, like strollers and car seats. Sid's carries major brands like Simmons, Lul-

CLOTHING & ACCESSORIES

labye, Childcraft, Bassett, Pride and Babyline. They offer free layaway, free shower registry, a most knowledgeable staff and big savings! Families have been shopping for their baby needs at Sid's since 1951.

STAR BABY**
5675 E. Telegraph Rd., #100A (Citadel Outlet Connection)
City of Commerce, CA 90040
213/888-2781
HOURS: MON-SAT: 9-8 SUN: 10-6
CREDIT CARDS: AE, MC, V

When it comes to well-made clothing for infants and toddlers, it's hard to beat Star Baby. Popping up all over the country, their durable clothing is all made of 100% cotton and is designed and manufactured right here in the U.S.A., including the fabric. Everything in the store is current, first-quality merchandise. On occasion they do have seconds but they are clearly marked. Sizes run newborn to 6X for girls and to size 7 for boys. You'll see a lot of the same items found in department and specialty stores at 20 to 50% off retail. The only difference being the brand name in the clothing because Star Baby sells their line to better department stores. There's always a huge selection of infant rompers, and thankfully all have snap-crotches. If you're new at this, Star Baby has ready-to-give gift packages already wrapped for newborns, baby showers and birthdays. They also provide free pamphlets with lots of helpful information. Grandparents, take note: You get an additional 10% discount every Wednesday. The stores maintain a birthday list and will send the birthday boy or girl a 15% discount coupon. Take in your BUYING RETAIL IS STUPID coupon for an extra 10% discount (nonsale items only).
Additional Locations:
Los Angeles–10250 Santa Monica Blvd., Bldg. 2 , 310/286-7984
San Ysidro–4498 Camino de la Plaza 619/690-5270

THE STORK SHOP
1868 S. La Cienega Blvd.
Los Angeles, CA 90035
310/839-2403
HOURS: MON-SAT: 10-5:30
CREDIT CARDS: MC, V

The Stork Shop promises a fun visit. They have everything you could possibly want in furniture and clothes for your baby. In fact, they also carry over 50,000 garments for boys and girls up to age 14. Their layettes are beautiful and you'll love the many designer styles of furniture items and accessories. You'll save 20 to 50% off retail prices on most of your purchases too!

CLOTHING & ACCESSORIES

∞ LARGE & HALF SIZES ∞

THE BIG, THE BAD & THE BEAUTIFUL**
2976 Los Angeles Ave.
Simi Valley, CA 93065
805/582-1921
HOURS: MON, TUES, THUR-SUN: 10-7 WED: 10-8
CREDIT CARDS: MC, V

Wouldn't it be great to have clothing that looks fantastic no matter how much your weight fluctuates up or down? This store has contemporary clothing at low prices for women wearing up to size 60 (to 500 pounds). Owner Marsha Alexander's motto is "Dare to be beautiful." A size 32 herself, Marsha opened The Big, the Bad & the Beautiful because she was tired of going into department stores and ending up with three of four outfits she hated because she was stuck buying what fit, not what she liked. Sound familiar? The clothes are really one-size-fits-all. For example, on one visit to the store, four women, ranging from size 4 to 32, tried on the same French-lace jacket. It looked terrific on all of them with a minor adjustment to the shoulder pads. To maximize shoppers' wardrobes, most of the merchandise is made to be mixed and matched or reversed. There are dresses and tops that have a normal scoop neck on one side and a much deeper neckline on the other side. All you have to do is reverse the article of clothing for an entirely different look. One of the most popular items is comfortable pants that fit. You'll find clothing for every occasion from casual to dressy, and they have lots of sexy lingerie for big, bad, beautiful women. Don't forget to take in your BUYING RETAIL IS STUPID coupon for an additional 10% discount.
Additional Locations:
Lancaster–44337 Challenger Way, 805/723-1554
Reseda–7634 Tampa Ave., 818/345-3593

ESTHER'S FULL FASHIONS
18147 Ventura Blvd.
Tarzana, CA 91356
818/996-8323
HOURS: MON-SAT: 10-6
CREDIT CARDS: AE, MC, V

Esther's Full Fashions caters to the large size woman with a fine selection of blouses, dresses, sweats, skirts, jackets, office wear, undergarments and accessories. Sizes range from 14 to 52, and prices are 20% off the retail prices department stores charge, if you can find the right size.

CLOTHING & ACCESSORIES

HALF-PRICE HOUSE
12152 Brookhurst
Garden Grove, CA 92640
714/537-1231
HOURS: MON-FRI: 10-9 SAT: 10-6 SUN: 10-5
CREDIT CARDS: MC, V

This missy store is the oldest discount house in Orange County, and it's no won-der it's so popular. New merchandise arrives almost daily from cities like New York, Miami and Chicago. Many are designer originals and samples—plus sportswear coordinates, swimwear and casual dresses. Their specialty is special occasion dresses, both long and short. All items, in regular, large and half-sizes, are priced 50 to 70% below retail.

∞ LEATHER GARMENTS & FURS ∞

LEATHER CAPITOL
223 E. 9th St.
Los Angeles, CA 90015
213/629-5079
HOURS: MON-SAT: 9-5
CREDIT CARDS: AE, MC, V

Looking for that special leather jacket for your husband or wife? The Leather Capitol has fine quality leather clothing at discounts of 20 to 30%! Save on purchases of leather skirts, pants, or handbags. They've been in business since 1973, so you know you can count on quality and service. Their other store, located in the Cooper Building, is called Leather Express
Additional Locations:
Los Angeles–860 S. Los Angeles St., 213/627-3883

LEONORE'S FUR OUTLET**
228 S. Beverly Dr., Suite 200
Beverly Hills, CA 90212
310/278-4001
HOURS: MON-SAT: 10-5 SUN: BY APPOINTMENT ONLY
CREDIT CARDS: CASH OR CHECKS ONLY

This is the place for fine furs, new and preowned. The family has been in the fur business since 1927 and have fine fur salons throughout the country. They carry the same merchandise found in most of your high end department stores. Some name brands include Christian Dior, Bill Blass, and Oscar de la Renta. You'll find sable, lynx, mink and other varieties of fur in every design imaginable. The store is small but carries at least

300 fur garments at all times. When you purchase a fur at Leonore's, you'll receive a furrier cover as well as your name or initials monogrammed in the lining. If you can't decide between sable or chinchilla, you can experiment by renting a fur from Leonore's. In addition to selling and renting, Leonore's also buys new and nearly new furs. There is metered parking on the street and free two hour parking two doors north of the store in the Beverly Hills multilevel parking structure. Don't forget your BUYING RETAIL IS STUPID coupon for an extra 10% discount.

WHOLESALE LEATHER APPAREL**
1406 E. Katella Ave.
Anaheim, CA 92805
714/937-8924
HOURS: MON-SAT: 10-6
CREDIT CARDS: AE, MC, V

This store carries leather jackets for men and women at 20 to 50% less than the prices found in most department stores. Wholesale Leather Apparel buys directly from the manufacturer; like other companies, they have their own labels put into the merchandise. They also have a store—actually a warehouse—in Long Beach with different business hours, so give them a call before you make the trip. And, you'll receive an extra 5% discount if you present your BUYING RETAIL IS STUPID coupon.
Additional locations:
Long Beach-838 W. 12th St., 310/432-8203

WILSONS LEATHER OUTLET STORE
1033 N. Hollywood Way
Burbank, CA 91505
818/841-7789
HOURS: WED-FRI: 12-7 SAT: 10-7 SUN: 11-7
CREDIT CARDS: AE, DISC, MC, V

Have you wanted a leather coat for quite a while but haven't found anything reasonably priced? This outlet has all kinds of leather garments at up to 75% off original retail prices. There are lots of jackets, skirts, tops and accessories consolidated from Wilson stores all over the country. Some of the buys we've seen were $25 gloves for $10, first-quality leather suede skirts in several colors for $5, and full length men's coats for $150 instead of $450. The front of the store has racks and tables of first-quality clearance items. The rest of the store consists of seconds, returns and damaged merchandise. All sales are final (no refunds or exchanges), so go over your purchases with a fine-tooth comb before leaving the store. Customers with valid military identification receive an additional 10% discount.

CLOTHING & ACCESSORIES

∞ LINGERIE ∞

AMORE CREATIONS
645 S. Los Angeles St.
Los Angeles, CA 90014
213/624-8048
HOURS: MON-SAT: 10-5:30
CREDIT CARDS: AE, MC, V

Everyone loves lingerie! Especially when you can buy all those gorgeous creations (Bras, girdles, panties, garter belts, G-strings, teddies and peignoir sets) at 40–75% off retail prices. They have 5,000 square feet of lingerie and are always getting new items. Amore Creations stocks the standard lines from most of the major manufacturers like Playtex, Bali, and many others. Sometimes they're able to buy an entire discontinued line, which means more savings for their customers. As an extra touch, they'll always let you know if what you are buying is a regular item or one that has been discontinued. They're open Sundays during the holiday season. Call in November or December for holiday hours.

CHIC LINGERIE OUTLET
693 High Lane
Redondo Beach, CA 90236
310/372-9352
HOURS: MON-FRI: 7:30-4
CREDIT CARDS: CASH OR CHECKS ONLY

This is a factory outlet where you will find savings from 40–50% on sleepwear, lingerie and loungewear. Their merchandise is the same found in most of your budget department stores. Any flaws are clearly marked. Don't hesitate to try on anything from a selection of 15,000 garments. They've been in business for 50 years, saving people lots of money on their "unmentionable" products!
Additional Locations:
Los Angeles–3435 S. Broadway, 213/233-7121

CREATIVE WOMAN
1530 S. Myrtle Ave.
Monrovia, CA 91016
818/358-6216
HOURS: MON-FRI: 10-7 SAT: 10-6:30 SUN: 11-5:30
CREDIT CARDS: AE, DISC, MC, V

Located off the Myrtle Avenue exit from the 210 Freeway, this wholesale and discount store is run by the very personable Ed and Bonnie Kaufman. They carry lingerie in all sizes, garter belts, stockings, corsets, and feathers. Feathers? They even have a department with sexy costumes. Corsets range in sizes 32A–46DD and backless strapless bras come in sizes 32A–48DD. They also have custom fitted bras in sizes 26BB–52HH. Now that's a selection!! Alterations are done on the premises.

LACE & SCENTS
9140 Owensmouth Ave.
Chatsworth, CA 91311
818/718-3900

HOURS: MON–FRI: 9–5
CREDIT CARDS: AE, MC, V

Although we can't name names, Lace & Scents has designer and brand name lin--priced 50 to 75% below department store and boutique prices. Most of the merchandise is sized small, medium and large with some petite sizes. They have weekly shipments so check in often for changes in the inventory. While there, check out their discounted fragrance

LINGERIE FOR LESS
2245 S. Sepulveda Blvd.
West Los Angeles, CA 90064
310/477-1898

HOURS: MON–SAT: 10–7 SUN: 11–6
CREDIT CARDS: MC, V

Lingerie for Less offers luxurious lingerie at discount prices of 20–70% off retail. Although we have been asked to omit brand names, they carry the same merchandise found in most major middle-of-the-road to high-end department stores. Each store caters to the area they are in, so if you don't find something you like at one store, chances are you'll find something to your liking at another location. You can choose styles from simple and conservative or slinky and exotic. They have everything from bras and panties to sexy peignoir sets and feathered satin slides. If you're into silk, you'll like their prices on silk lingerie for men and women.
Additional Locations: 15 other stores throughout S. CA

LORE
15515 Califa St.
Van Nuys, CA 91411
818/901-8549

HOURS: MON-FRI: 10-6 SAT: 11-6
CREDIT CARDS: CASH OR CHECKS ONLY

It's difficult to find a fabric more luxurious or expensive than silk, but we've found a place tucked away in an alley that offers a variety of silk items at unbelievably low prices. Bikini panties that normally retail for

CLOTHING & ACCESSORIES

$30 to $40 are $12 at Lore, a well known name in pricey boutiques and high-end department stores. You may have also seen their tastefully provocative ads in magazines such as Vogue. This is a genuine factory outlet. Everything hangs in protective plastic on garment racks in the factory itself. You pay less than retailers for the lingerie because the merchandise for sale consists of close-outs, odds and ends, samples, and overruns. For example, retailers that buy from Lore pay $68 for an exquisite chemise in peach silk with black Chantilly lace. You can get it here when available, for $42. In addition to silk lingerie, they sometimes have beautiful items made from 100% Swiss cotton. Selection varies from visit to visit. Sometimes you'll have hundreds of items to choose from and other times there will be much less.

OLGA WARNER'S MANUFACTURER'S OUTLET
743 Baker St.
Costa Mesa, CA 92626
714/957-1214

HOURS: MON–FRI: 10–6 SAT: 10–5 SUN: 12–5
CREDIT CARDS: AE, MC, V

There is no longer any reason to buy your Olga and Warner lingerie at department stores when you can go to their outlet and save a minimum of 30% off retail. Other brand names include Scassi, Ungaro and Valentino. Most of the merchandise is first quality. Seconds are clearly marked and in a separate section of the store. Many items in this area have nothing wrong with them except perhaps something like a rose applique instead of a daisy sewn on to a bra.

Additional Locations:
Van Nuys–15750 Strathern; 818/994-7963

THE ROBE OUTLET
2233-1/2 S. Sepulveda Blvd.
West Los Angeles, CA 90064
310/478-0197

HOURS: MON-SAT: 10-6 SUN: 12-5
CREDIT CARDS: MC, V

The Robe Outlet has some of the most gorgeous robes for men and women. You can save 30–70% below retail prices on not only robes, but also on loungewear, career dresses, sundresses, warm-up suits, swimsuits, and sleepwear in sizes petite to extra large. They have special sales several times a year, so ask to be put on their mailing list. Their merchandise is current; you can find them in department stores or speciality shops, so come here and save.

Additional Locations: 6 other stores throughout S. CA

CLOTHING & ACCESSORIES

∞ MATERNITY ∞

DAN HOWARD'S MATERNITY FACTORY
22817 Hawthorne Blvd.
Torrance, CA 90505
310/375-2640
HOURS: MON, THUR: 10-9 TUES-WED, FRI-SAT: 10-6 SUN: 12-5
CREDIT CARDS: AE, DISC, MC, V

Everything an expectant mother needs in the way of apparel is available through this factory outlet which designs and manufactures their own maternity clothing. There's always a wide selection from sportswear to evening wear, in sizes 4 to 24, at 25% off retail Professional women will be pleased with the attire they carry suitable for the office. Lingerie and pantyhose are also available. Dan Howard's Maternity Factory has been producing stylish and quality maternity clothes for over 50 years.
Additional Locations:
Cerritos–11326-1/2 South St., 310/402-1953
Montclair–5027 S. Plaza Ln., 714/626-6516
San Diego–252 Fashion Valley, 619/296-9221
Santa Ana–3930 Bristol St., 714/557-4342
Woodland Hills–20929 Ventura Blvd., 818/887-6317

MOM'S THE WORD**
1008-1/2 Fair Oaks Ave.
South Pasadena, CA 91030
818/441-9692
HOURS: MON-FRI: 10:30-7 SAT: 10-6
CREDIT CARDS: MC, V

Mom's the Word has a fabulous selection of discounted clothing (25–60% off retail) from top designers for every occasion. They carry current styles and are able to offer low prices by purchasing their goods during the season. (Most retailers place their orders with manufacturers two seasons ahead.) We've been asked not to name names, but everything is extremely tasteful and well-made with lots of attention to detail. Shipments arrive weekly, so the inventory is always changing. The store carries cruise wear and swimsuits, plus dressy outfits year-round. If you aren't very far along, they'll loan you a pillow so you get an idea of how the outfit will look in the future. If you're already in an advanced stage of pregnancy, you'll appreciate the roomy private dressing rooms. They have outfits made specifically for nursing, and nursing bras run sizes 34B to 40G. Children are welcome, and there are plenty of toys to keep them occupied. Alterations are complimentary and you'll receive an additional 10% discount if you take in your BUYING RETAIL IS STUPID coupon.

CLOTHING & ACCESSORIES

SHELLY'S DISCOUNT AEROBIC & DANCE WEAR
2089 Westwood Blvd.
Westwood, CA 90025
310/475-1400
HOURS: MON: 10-8 TUES-SAT: 10-6 SUN: 11-4
CREDIT CARDS: AE, DISC, MC, V

You'll save from 50 to 70% on leotards, tights and activewear that are perfect for dancing and those strenuous aerobic workouts. Shelly Seeman has them in all sizes and styles and colors—even for mothers-to-be and for children. Brand names include Softouch, Marika and Cathy George, to name a few. Dressing rooms and parking are available.
Additional Locations:
Tarzana–Apparel Warehouse, 6010 Yolanda St., 818/344-3224

∞ MEN'S APPAREL & ACCESSORIES ∞

ACADEMY AWARD CLOTHES, INC.
811 S. Los Angeles St.
Los Angeles, CA 90014
213/622-9125
HOURS: MON-SAT: 9-5:30
CREDIT CARDS: MC, V

Known as the Gucci of Los Angeles Street, Academy Award Clothes has been in business since 1949. They stock thousands of men's suits, sport coats, slacks, formal wear, and haberdashery, with most designer names available. As you enter the front door you will be assigned a salesman to assist you in your selection. Parking is validated with a $100 purchase.

C & R CLOTHIERS
6301 Wilshire Blvd.
Los Angeles, CA 90048
213/655-6466
HOURS: MON-FRI: 9:30-9 SAT-SUN: 10-6
CREDIT CARDS: AE, MC, V

If you want a complete selection of handsome men's wear from all the major labels at savings of 10 to 50% every day, then you can't beat C & R Clothiers. They carry an incredible selection of men's suits, jackets, slacks, and accessories—fashions you'd normally find in designer salons and specialty stores often priced at twice the price. Ask to be put on their mailing list so you will be notified of special sales throughout the year.
Additional Locations: 62 other stores throughout S. CA

CLOTHING & ACCESSORIES

COMPAGNIA DELLA MODA INC.
31192 La Baya Dr., #F
Westlake Village, CA 91362
818/706-8177
HOURS: MON-FRI: 9-5 SAT:10-4
CREDIT CARDS: MC, V

Now you can look as though you've just stepped out of GQ dressed in classically styled, Italian men's clothing of the highest quality without paying Beverly Hills' men's store prices. A local television host said, "This is LA's best kept secret!" He is absolutely right. You'll find 4,000 square feet consisting of suits, sport coats, slacks, shirts, and sometimes formal wear priced 50 to 60% below intrinsic value. Most of the garments are made of wool, silk or cotton and you can forget about finding any polyester. Believe me, if you want to wear the very best, and we do mean the very best, it's well worth a trip to Westlake Village. Please note: Even at savings of 50–60%, this clothing is NOT inexpensive.

COOPER & KRAMER, INC.
1401 Santee St.
Los Angeles, CA 90015
213/747-5816
HOURS: MON-FRI: 9-4:30 SAT: 9-4
CREDIT CARDS: MC, V

Whether you're looking for career apparel or something a little more on the casual side, Cooper & Kramer will fit the bill. With over 7,000 American-made suits in their 8,000 square foot warehouse, you're bound to find plenty of new additions to your wardrobe. Clothing for men runs 30 to 50% off retail and women's clothing is discounted 30 to 60%. We can't name names, but if you're curious give them a call and they'll fill you in. They've been in business since 1932.

GHQ OUTLET
19413 Victory Blvd. (Loehmann's Plaza)
Reseda, CA 91335
818/708-8999
HOURS: MON-FRI: 10-9 SAT: 10-6 SUN: 11-6
CREDIT CARDS: ALL MAJOR

Would you mind saving 30 to 70% on GHQ clothing? We've discovered a gold mine in modern men's clothing. Everything is first quality, no seconds. The clothing is shipped from the mall stores as room is needed for new merchandise. We know of several young men in their twenties who won't shop anywhere else.

CLOTHING & ACCESSORIES

LEONARDO'S ITALIAN FASHION**
336 N. Beverly Dr.
Beverly Hills, CA 90210

310/275-6677

HOURS: MON-SAT: 10-6
CREDIT CARDS: AE, DISC, MC, V

Leonardo's is a direct importer, so they can pass on some real savings on men's suits, slacks, jackets, dress shirts, sport shirts, and accessories such as shoes, ties, belts, and socks. Even though their store is in Beverly Hills, they have some very good buys. Paying $99 for two pair of Italian loafers is what we call a buy! They carry St. Moritz, Cavalini, Bucatchi, and other brand names. Madeleine, the owner, tells us she has quite a following of stars, so you may run into one of your favorites if you shop there! Don't forget your BUYING RETAIL IS STUPID coupon for your additional 10% savings.

MAX LEVINE & SON, INC.
845 S. Los Angeles St.
Los Angeles, CA 90014

213/622-2446

HOURS: MON-FRI: 9-5:30 SAT: 9-5
CREDIT CARDS: MC, V

Max Levine & Sons has been around since 1936 evolving into a discount operation selling men's clothes. You can always find a selection of 6,000 to 8,000 suits and slacks here. They also carry sport coats, formal wear, belts, shoes, ties, and other fashion accessories. Designer names such as Ralph Lauren, Calvin Klein, Yves St. Laurent are available in shorts, regulars, longs, and extra longs, in sizes 35 to 50. The savings are generally 40% below retail department stores.

MEN'S CLOTHIERS–MANUFACTURERS' OUTLET
1427 S. Village Way
Santa Ana, CA 92705

714/667-5110

HOURS: FRI: 10-7 SAT: 10-6 SUN: 11-5
CREDIT CARDS: DISC, MC, V

If there's one person who knows about men's clothing it's Bob Correnti, founder and former chairman of the board at C & R Clothiers. Bob now owns Men's Clothiers–Manufacturers' Outlet store that has over 7,500 suits and sportcoats, thousands of shirts and ties, dress socks and formal wear at less than half the normal retail price. Plan your shopping accordingly since they're only open Fridays, Saturdays and Sundays.

CLOTHING & ACCESSORIES

MEN'S FASHION DEPOT
3730 Sports Arena Blvd.
San Diego, CA 92110
619/222-9570

HOURS: MON-FRI: 10-9 SAT: 10-6 SUN: 12-5
CREDIT CARDS: DISC, MC, V

You won't find any brand names here because they rip out the labels. What you will find are discounts of up to 50% off retail on men's suits, sport coats, slacks, shirts, ties, warm-up suits and even tuxedos. With 6,500 square feet of clothing, you're bound to find something to your liking. Sizes range from 34 x-short to 60 long, and suits are $69 to $229.

ROSEMAN & ASSOCIATES
2211 E. Olympic Blvd.
Los Angeles, CA 90006
213/622-6266

HOURS: MON-SAT: 10-6 SUN: 11-5
CREDIT CARDS: MC, V

Roseman & Associates is another men's clothing wholesaler that offers quality name brand men's wear at prices from 50 to 72% below retail. They carry names such as Nino Cerruti, Pierre Cardin, Jamar, Louis Roth, Adolfo, Givenchy, and many more. Their 15,000 square foot location offers suits, sport coats, dress slacks, sports slacks, shirts, and accessories. There are 10 dressing rooms and plenty of free parking. Tailoring is also available. You'll want to get on their mailing list for advance notice of their warehouse sales.

THE SHIRT MARKET
2207 Honolulu Ave.
Montrose, CA 91020
818/248-0788

HOURS: TUES-FRI: 10-4 SAT: 12-4
CREDIT CARDS: MC, V

The Shirt Market is a manufacturer's outlet for shirts and ties sold to better specialty stores all over the United States. Savings run at least 50% off retail on dress shirts (sizes 14-1/2 32/33 to 17-1/2 34/35), sport shirts (small, medium, large, x-large and xx-large), and ties. Prices range from $9.99 to $29.99. There are shirts to try on for size, and the salespeople will make sure you get a good fit. By the way, The Shirt Market had originally planned to sell shirts by the pound, hence the butcher shop decor, but that would have involved the Department of Weights and Measures. Oh well, another good idea bites the dust.

CLOTHING & ACCESSORIES

STEVEN CRAIG WHOLESALE CLOTHIERS
19365 Business Center Dr.
Northridge, CA 91324
818/701-7473

HOURS: WED-SAT: 10–5
CREDIT CARDS: MC, V (PURCHASES OVER $100 ONLY)

Gentlemen, are you ready for some new clothes? Steven Craig is the place to buy the same high-quality suits found in major department stores at about 40% off retail. The clothing is first-quality, current merchandise, not carry-overs from last season. Most of the suits are made in Italy of fine wools—no polyester or blends. Some of the brands include Pierre Cardin, Jones of New York and Modena. Sizes run 38–42 regular, 38–44 short and 40–48 long. They also carry gabardine slacks, and tuxedos.

ROGER STUART CLOTHES, INC.
729 S. Los Angeles St.
Los Angeles, CA 90014

213/627-9661

HOURS: MON-SAT: 9-5:30
CREDIT CARDS: MC, V

When it comes to price and selection, it's hard to beat Roger Stuart Clothes. They carry brands such as Cavelli, Ferrine, San Remo, and many others. Their prices are usually 25 to 62% below retail, so you could pay from $266 to $525 for a $700 Italian wool suit. They have over 6,000 square feet of men's clothing and 12 dressing rooms, so you can be sure of the fit. Alterations is not a service they provide, but they'll recommend a nearby tailor so you can get your purchases altered the same day. Their customer files are kept on computer, so gifts or accessories can be matched up with previous purchases. They have a huge sale every year; it's worth getting on their mailing list. Gentlemen, unless unusually large or small, will be able to find a good fit here. They carry almost every size (35–54 Regular, 38–54 Long, 42–54 X-Long, 35–46 Short, 35–42 X-Short) in suits, sport jackets, shirts, ties, and slacks.

ZACHARY ALL
5467 Wilshire Blvd.
Los Angeles, CA 90036

213/931-1484

HOURS: MON-FRI: 10-6:30 SAT: 9-6 SUN: 10-5
CREDIT CARDS: MC, V

This fabulous men's store is half a block long and is filled with everything the well-dressed man could want. Save 20 to 40% off the retail price on men's suits, jackets, coats, sweaters, shirts, tuxedos, slacks, and all the accessories. They have every size you can imagine and do their own alterations. Plenty of free parking is available in the rear of the store along with good service and courteous attention, too.

∞ MEN'S & WOMEN'S APPAREL∞

3RD FAZE CLOTHING COMPANY
411 Rose Ave.
Venice, CA 90291
310/392-9599
HOURS: MON-SAT: 10-8 SUN: 11-7
CREDIT CARDS: AE, MC, V

What a place! This clothing store for men and women is always filled with clothing reflecting current fashion trends. You can buy everything from an award winning Italian suit to a casual pair of shorts. To give you a idea of what their merchandise is like, Point Zero is one brand name they carry, and Shang-Hai is another. For those of you allergic to synthetics, most of the clothing in the store is made from natural fabrics. We saved the best part for last. The average price you'll pay at 3rd Faze Clothing Company is a whopping 80% off retail!

Additional Locations:
West Hollywood–1157 N. La Brea Ave., 213/851-5447

CARMEN'S VERANDA
100 State St.
Santa Barbara, CA 93101
805/962-0836
HOURS: 10-6 SEVEN DAYS A WEEK
CREDIT CARDS: MC, V

Carmen's Veranda distributes products they have made in Indonesia to stores all over the United States and Caribbean; this is their factory outlet. Brand names include Fit-To-Be-Tied (scarves, ties, 100% rayon separates such as dresses, jackets, shorts, skirts, shirts, and more), Sarong's (shoes) and Flamingo (brightly painted wood jewelry). Everything is priced at least 50% off retail. During the summer they're open later, and by the way, Carmen Miranda was the inspiration for Carmen's Viranda!

CLOTHING & ACCESSORIES

FUNKY & DAMNEAR NEW
123 S. 1st St.
La Puente, CA 91744
818/330-0303

HOURS: WED-SAT: 10-6 SUN: 12-5
CREDIT CARDS: MC, V

Their specialty is "remanufactured", repaired and new Levi's. What's great about this place is that you don't have to worry about how the pants you buy will fit after you wash them. All new Levi's at Funky & Damnear New are laundered and high heat dried to remove shrinkage. And, if you have a backlog of old Levi's, trade them in for Funky Bucks which can be spent on anything in the store. You'll also find Levi jackets and shirts. Custom length alterations are available on the spot for $3.00.

H R D DISTRIBUTORS**
18318 Oxnard St., Unit 4
Tarzana, CA 91356
818/708-1941

HOURS: MON-SAT: 9–5:30
CREDIT CARDS: MC, V

This is a clothing outlet that is hard to find, but is well worth the hunt. Hidden away in an alley in Tarzana, H.R.D. Distributors specializes in sportswear for men and women, and unisex clothing at discounts that run 40–80% off retail! You'll find a large variety of 100% cotton sweaters, sweat pants, sweat shirts, jeans, t-shirts, and more. New stock arrives at least twice a week providing constant change in the inventory. You never know what brand names you may find. In the last year, we've seen labels from Le Roy Knits, Loubella, Gap, Pierre Cardin, and Bugle Boy. One brand name you'll find consistently is Long Johns, a 100% cotton line made right here in Southern California. For extra savings make sure to redeem your 10% BUYING RETAIL IS STUPID discount coupon.

HARRIS & FRANK CLEARANCE CENTER
13451 Sherman Way
North Hollywood, CA 91605
818/764-4872

HOURS: MON-SAT: 9-5
CREDIT CARDS: ALL MAJOR

This 6,000 square foot outlet store gives you the best buys on Harris & Frank clothing. Merchandise is brought in from their 19 stores, so you'll find top quality men's and women's clothing with names such as Halston, Lanvin, Cricketeer, Jaymar and Dior. Discounts of 35% off retail are guaranteed at this outlet.

CLOTHING & ACCESSORIES

PIC-A-SHIRT
10918 W. Pico Blvd.
Los Angeles, CA 90064
310/475-0088

HOURS: MON-SAT: 10-5:30
CREDIT CARDS: AE, MC, V

Without even trying, you can save at least 20 to 30% on shirts, athletic sweats, t-shirts, and short sleeved dress shirts. But, if you look a little harder you'll find savings up to 75% on men's and women's shirts. Nate Lasner has been in business for over 20 years. His people are helpful, and they'll even do custom lettering and transfers on your t-shirts.

PILLER'S OF EAGLE ROCK
1800 Colorado Blvd.
Los Angeles, CA 90041
213/257-8166

HOURS: FRI-SAT: 10-5:30   SUN: 12-5
CREDIT CARDS: MC, V

Would you like to find a good deal on men's or women's clothing? How about 50% off the retail price of nationally advertised brands? No hole-in-the-wall, Piller's of Eagle Rock has 25,000 square feet of merchandise. During the year they have sales with prices up to 90% off retail. In the shoe department, you'll find about 25,000 pairs with brand names like Bruno Magli, Bally, and more. Dressing rooms are provided, so you can be sure of the fit. Piller's has been in business since 1949, so you know they're reliable.

SACKS SFO INC.
652 N. La Brea
Hollywood, CA 90036
213/939-3993

HOURS: MON-FRI: 10-8   SAT: 10-7   SUN: 10-6
CREDIT CARDS: MC, V

You can save a bundle of money all the time on men's and women's fashionable and trendy clothing. Save 40 to 70% on great ready-to-wear items with a special emphasis on natural fibers. Much of their merchandise is designer clothing. Sacks SFO also has leather jackets, pants, and fashion accessories such as jewelry, belts and ties. For your convenience they have private dressing rooms. Get on their mailing list for bi-monthly fashion newsletters and sales notices. If you'd like, they'll even coordinate your wardrobe for you. David Sacks goes out of his way to make certain he has the nicest salespeople in all Sacks SFO stores.
Additional Locations: 6 other stores in S. CA

CLOTHING & ACCESSORIES

∞ RENTALS ∞

DRESSED TO KILL
8762 Holloway Dr.
West Hollywood, CA 90069
310/652-4334

HOURS: BY APPOINTMENT ONLY MON-SAT: 11-7 SUN: 10-6
CREDIT CARDS: AE, MC, V

How many times have you wished you could wear a knock-out designer gown for just one evening? Well, your wish can come true because Dressed To Kill offers you just that, an opportunity to rent a gorgeous haute couture gown for just pennies on the dollar. Rental fees run between $75–350 per day for gowns that retail in the four and sometimes five figure range. In addition to the gowns, you can also rent matching accessories. So, when the next invitation to an important gala arrives in the mail, make an appointment at Dressed To Kill. You'll knock 'em dead when you make your appearance in your Bob Mackie or Chanel evening gown. Dressed to Kill has added a full line of bridal wear which includes designer wedding gowns (up to $25,000 retail), accessories, and mother-of-the-bride dresses.

LEONORE'S FUR OUTLET**
228 S. Beverly Dr., Suite 200
Beverly Hills, CA 90212
310/278-4001

HOURS: MON-SAT: 10-5 SUN: BY APPOINTMENT ONLY
CREDIT CARDS: CASH OR CHECKS ONLY

This is the place for fine furs, new and preowned. The family has been in the fur business since 1927 and have fine fur salons throughout the country. They carry the same merchandise found in most of your high end department stores. Some name brands include Christian Dior, Bill Blass, and Oscar De la Renta. You'll find sable, lynx, mink and other varieties of fur in every design imaginable. When you purchase a fur at Leonore's, you will receive a furrier cover as well as your name or initials monogrammed in the lining of the garment. If you can't decide between sable or chinchilla, you can experiment by renting a fur from Leonore's. In addition to selling and renting, Leonore's also buys new and nearly new furs. There is metered parking on the street and free two hour parking two doors north of the store in the Beverly Hills multilevel parking structure. Don't forget your BUYING RETAIL IS STUPID coupon good for an additional 10% savings.

CLOTHING & ACCESSORIES

ONE NIGHT AFFAIR GOWN RENTALS
2370 Westwood Blvd., Suite H
Los Angeles, CA 90064
310/474-7808

HOURS: BY APPOINTMENT ONLY TUES-FRI: 11-7 SAT: 10-7
CREDIT CARDS: MC, V

Why pay hundreds or thousands of dollars for a dress—including bridal gowns—you can be seen in only once? One Night Affair has over 250 wedding gowns for rent ranging in sizes 2 to 26. And while we're on the subject, if you've ever been a bridesmaid, have you ever had the opportunity to wear the dress afterwards or would you even want to be seen in it again? We never have either. One Night Affair has rental bridesmaids gowns available in 24 styles and 16 colors. In addition to bridal wear, they also have formal gowns (500 in sizes 2-30) and cock-tail dresses (350 in sizes 2-26). To really complete the outfit you can rent shoes, gloves, jewelry, and evening bags. Some of the labels you'll see include Bob Mackie, Oleg Cassini, Scaasi, Oscar de la Renta and Victor Costa. Make sure to call for an appointment because they don't take walk-ins.

STARLIT SOIREE
8950 W. Olympic Blvd., Suite 213 (Beverly Hills Plaza)
Beverly Hills, CA 90211
310/275-5570

HOURS: MON-SAT: 10-6
CREDIT CARDS: AE, MC, V

Most of us don't have the patience to spend days looking for a special occasion dress and then additional hours trying to put it all together with shoes and accessories. So why not let a professional dress you from head to toe at a fraction of what a new dress would cost? Starlit Soiree rents complete ensembles guaranteed to make you look and feel like a million dollars. They have a seamstress for alterations to make certain the dress is a perfect fit. And, they keep records of what outfits they've rented so you won't have to worry about seeing your dress on someone else. You'll find dresses (first-quality purchased directly from the designers) that are simple and elegant to real show stoppers. Sizes range from 3 to 22 and rental rates are $45 to $250. If you were to purchase the dresses carried here, you'd pay $300 to $2,000 retail. In addition to dresses, you can rent shoes (in black satin or velvet and gold or silver in two heel heights), jewelry (lots designed to match certain dresses), evening bags, wraps and capes. Twice a year they have a special inventory sale, and there are always retired rental dresses for sale. You can also save lots of money when prom season rolls around. At this time they bring in lots of dresses geared to teenagers.

CLOTHING & ACCESSORIES

∞ RESALE STORES ∞

– INFANTS & CHILDREN –

EVERYTHING FOR KIDS
24407 Hawthorne Blvd.
Torrance, CA 90505
310/373-4863

HOURS: TUES-SAT: 10-5
CREDIT CARDS: CASH OR CHECKS ONLY

Located near the Palos Verdes area, this store gets a lot of look-like-new clothing and furniture for babies to teenagers. All of the items in the store are sold on consignment. This results in customers paying a fraction of the original price. There are dressing rooms and a play area for the kids. You'll find many top name brands here, and friendly service is always available. Mark the 1st and the 15th of every month on your calendars for their markdown sales. If you have some items you'd like to put on consignment, call Pat Benson to set up an appointment.

KID'S CLOSET
5316 Lankershim Blvd.
North Hollywood, CA 91601
818/505-8555

HOURS: MON-SAT: 10-5
CREDIT CARDS: CASH ONLY

You'll find some new items, but most are used quality names in children's clothing from sizes 0 to 14. You'll pay at least half of what you would pay if purchasing the items new. There is also a selection of baby furniture such as high chairs, playpens, cribs, car seats, and walkers. Call Kid's Closet, too, if you are selling your goods. They pay cash.

MOTHER GOOSE GARMENT EXCHANGE
22478 Barton Rd.
Grand Terrace, CA 92324
714/783-4666

HOURS: TUES-SAT: 10-5 :30
CREDIT CARDS: CASH OR CHECKS ONLY

Mother Goose Garment Exchange, located outside of Riverside, is very selective about the clothing it carries. The selection of resale merchandise will clothe a mother to be and her newborn. Sizes for children run from infant to size 14. In addition to clothing, you will find an assortment of baby necessities such as car seats, receiving blankets, walkers,

CLOTHING & ACCESSORIES

carriers. The selection varies from visit to visit. Sometimes they even have baby furniture. If you have items you no longer need, you may be able to exchange them for store credits to be used in the store at your convenience (by appointment only).

SOMETHING FOR BABY**
1359 N Hill Ave.
Pasadena, CA 91104
818/791-3314
HOURS: TUES-SAT: 11:30-6
CREDIT CARDS: CASH OR CHECKS ONLY

Something For Baby is a resale/consignment children's store. They buy good quality used clothing such as Osh Kosh, Carters, Healthtex, Buster Brown, Little Me and many other names; their sizes are newborn to 7, and their prices range from $2 to $15. They also carry baby equipment such as cribs, bassinets and strollers. Inventory on consignment, usually means good quality. Their prices are 50% to 75% below retail, so you can shop for baby and still have a little left over to spend on yourself. If you use your BUYING RETAIL IS STUPID coupon you'll save an additional 10%.

– FAMILY RESALE –

BACK ON THE RACK**
21506 Sherman Way
Canoga Park, CA 91367
818/704-8303
HOURS: MON-FRI: 10:30-6:30   SAT: 10:30-5   SUN: 1-5
CREDIT CARDS: MC, V

Here's a resale store for the entire family that has been growing by leaps and bounds. They have had to move into larger quarters three times over the past eight years. Their specialty is children's used clothing that are like new, as well as infants, ladies, maternity and men's clothing. They also carry shoes, baby furniture and toys. So, when you want Guess, Levi's, Osh Kosh, Espirit, Liz Claiborne, or Evan Picone brand clothing, your best bet is Back On The Rack for 50 to 80% discounts compared to buying the same clothing new. They also buy clothing that is up-to-date and in excellent condition, by appointment only. You can also bring your BUYING RETAIL IS STUPID coupon for a 10% discount.

CLOTHING & ACCESSORIES

RAVE REVIEWS-KIDS COTTAGE**
3415 W. Magnolia Blvd.
Burbank, CA 91505
818/562-1331

HOURS: MON-WED: 10-6   THUR-FRI: 10-6:30   SAT: 10-5:30
CREDIT CARDS: MC, V

Rave Review deserves just that for offering men, women and children's contemporary resale clothing at 1/3 the original retail price. All the clothing has been cleaned and inspected and look just like new. If their merchandise has not sold after 30 days, it is marked down an additional 15% to 50%. Much of their clothing comes from production companies and costume designers. You'll be delighted to find many of your favorite brand names; for kids: Guess, Osh Kosh, Esprit, Baby Dior and Polo; for the ladies: Liz Claiborne, Carole Little, Donna Karan, and Victor Costa; for men: Polo, Nordstrom's brand, Bullocks' brand and Armani. Don't hesitate to bring the kids along because they have a great play area, and they provide a changing table too. They even display the kids art work! Bring the BUYING RETAIL IS STUPID coupon for a 10% discount on items not already marked down.

TWICE TREASURED
530 New Los Angeles Ave., Suite 117
Moorpark, CA 93021
805/529-0010

HOURS: MON-FRI: 10-6   SAT: 10-4
CREDIT CARDS: CASH OR CHECKS ONLY

Twice Treasured has 1,300 square feet of carefully hand-picked clothing. Ninety percent of their merchandise is on consignment. They stock women's and junior, missy and plus sizes, children's sizes 0-14, and all accessories such as shoes and purses to complete your outfit. To go along with the baby clothing, Twice Treasured also carries baby furniture and new or craft items at reasonable prices. Their inventory changes every month so you will constantly see new items when you shop here. Some of the brand-names they sell are Liz Claiborne, Ellen Tracy, Jones New York, Healthtex, Levis and Baby Guess.

CLOTHING & ACCESSORIES

– MEN'S & WOMEN'S RESALE –

BAILEY'S**
109 E. Union St.
Pasadena, CA 91103
818/449-0201

HOURS: TUES-SAT: 11-5
CREDIT CARDS: AE, MC, OPT, V

If you'd like designer names, but without the pricey price tags, Bailey's is going to become your favorite place to shop. This resale store is full of men's suits, sport coats, dress and casual shirts, sweaters, shoes, and accessories at 1/3 of the original retail price. Some of the labels at Bailey's include Valentino, Armani, Hugo Boss, Lavin, Ralph Lauren, Calvin Klein and many more. Take in your BUYING RETAIL IS STUPID coupon and you'll receive an additional 10% discount.

GENTLEMEN'S EXCHANGE
24066 Neece Ave.
Torrance, CA 90505
310/375-4148

HOURS: TUES-SAT: 11-5
CREDIT CARDS: CASH OR CHECKS ONLY

Let Patricia Benson, owner of Gentlemen's Exchange, dress you in her gently worn suits, sportswear, shoes and accessories. The labels you'll find will include Nino Cerruti, Nordstrom, Daniel Hechter, Christian Dior, and Hart. Half-off sales are held four times a year. She also takes men's clothing on consignment by appointment.

RECYCLED RAGS
2731 E. Coast Hwy.
Corona del Mar, CA 92625
714/675-5553

HOURS: MON-TUES, FRI-SAT: 10-6   WED-THUR: 10-8:30   SUN: 12-5
CREDIT CARDS: MC, V

When Audrey Patterson set up her shop in Corona del Mar before 1969, she was one of the first to specialize in recycled designer clothing. With such a major price difference between new and worn only once or twice, why not wear designer clothes previously owned by the rich and famous? She carries both men's and women's clothing, all at a fraction of the original cost. This shop has clothing, furs, and jewelry from many of the world's top designers. On the last Sunday of every month, she has a parking lot sale where you save even more. She serves hot dogs and lemonade, and holds a drawing for $100 of free merchandise.

CLOTHING & ACCESSORIES

– WOMEN'S RESALE –

THE ADDRESS
1116 Wilshire Blvd.
Santa Monica, CA 90403
310/394-1406

HOURS: MON-SAT: 10-6 SUN: 12-5
CREDIT CARDS: AE, MC, V

The AdDress, considered to be one of the most elegant women's resale shops in Southern California, features after-five clothing for those special occasions. Some of the accoutrements found here may have been previously owned by one of your favorite Hollywood stars. In addition to resale, they also have new designer samples discounted 25-30%. You won't be disappointed by the selection, savings, service or hospitality.

CHERIE'S SECRETS
12526 Ventura Blvd.
Studio City, CA 91604
818/508-1628

HOURS: MON-SAT: 10-6
CREDIT CARDS: AE, OPT, MC, V

Cherie's Secrets shop should not be kept a secret. It is an upscale women's resale store that carries current, in-season designer clothing and accessories at tremendous savings. Some of the labels you'll find here are Chanel, Escada, Ungaro, Armani, Donna Karan, Liz Claiborne as well as Opera-Soprano. Her sales people are very friendly and enjoy helping their customers put together complete outfits along with that "just right" piece of jewelry or hat. You won't have to wait around for a dressing room since they have five.

CLOTHES HEAVEN
110 E. Union St.–Pasadena Old Town
Pasadena, CA 91107
818/440-0929

HOURS: TUES-SAT: 11-5
CREDIT CARDS: AE, DISC, MC, V

Owner Larayne Brannon says, "Clothes Heaven is where good clothes go when they're passed on." They have been serving their long term clientele for the past seven years with a store filled primarily with gently worn designer clothing. Some of the garments, with store tags still intact, have never been worn. Their women's designer clothing and accessories have been passed on from some great closets in New York, Scottsdale, San

CLOTHING & ACCESSORIES

Francisco, La Jolla, Santa Barbara and Los Angeles. Their labels include Anne Klein, Yves St. Laurent, Valentino, Ungaro, Armani, Calvin Klein, Diane Freis, Fendi, Chanel, Maud Frizen, Nancy Heller, Liz Claiborne, Carole Little, Ellen Tracy, and many other well-known designer names. You can save about 67% off the original purchase price shopping here. They are experts in making customers feel special, as well as helping to coordinate their wardrobe. It's been said that Clothes Heaven is a dangerous place, because shopping there can become an addiction (price wise, designer wise and service wise).

DRESS UP
2043 Westcliff Dr., #102
Newport Beach, CA 92660
714/631-8290

HOURS: MON-WED, FRI: 10-6   THUR: 10-8   SAT: 10-5   SUN: 12-4
CREDIT CARDS: MC, V

Dress Up is well established (since 1981) and well known in Newport Beach. They take in only better merchandise and do many buy-outs from other shops (brand new goods at greatly discounted prices). The store is neatly organized by size, including a selection of petite and full-figured clothing. Dress Up caters to professional women with name brands such as Anne Klein, Carole Little and Paul Stanley. You can accessorize you new outfits with Dress Up's fine and costume jewelry. They also have a small area of the store devoted to costumes and vintage clothing. The last Saturday and Sunday of every month they have an 80% off sale on already low priced goods (this is on selected merchandise)..

THE GREAT NAME
311 Wilshire Blvd.
Santa Monica, CA 90401
310/395-2217

HOURS: MON-SAT: 11-6
CREDIT CARDS: MC, V

About 18 years ago, the five Frost sisters had a great idea; they opened The Great Name and have been stocking it ever since with new and barely-used designer clothing and accessories for women. You can save 50 to 80% off retail prices on such labels as Yves St. Laurent, Missoni, Calvin Klein, Perry Ellis, Chloe, Kamali, Dior, Chanel, Halston, Givenchy, and many more. You'll love the natural fabrics (silks, woolens and cottons) that are featured, and you'll find clothes ranging from casual to formal in sizes 4 to 14. This is a bright, cheerful shop with private dressing rooms and a helpful staff.

CLOTHING & ACCESSORIES

JEAN'S STARS' APPAREL**
15136 Ventura Blvd.
Sherman Oaks, CA 91403
818/789-3710
HOURS: TUES-SAT: 10-6
CREDIT CARDS: AE, MC, V

This is one of the nicest resale boutiques we've seen. The store is extremely neat with everything organized by size and style. Nothing is crammed on to unruly racks. Shopping here is like shopping in a very expensive boutique. And, unlike expensive boutiques, the very professional staff offers lots of sincere, personal service. According to owner Janet, the store was started in 1958 and stocks only the finest designer fashions previously owned by wealthy women. Prices are 60-90% below original cost. You'll find women's wear from dressy to casual (with a selection of shoes, handbags and fashion jewelry), from Ungaro, Yves Saint Laurent, Anne Klein, Chloe, Adolfo, Ralph Lauren, Bill Blass, and more. Some of these items are less than a couple of months old. Women have actually flown across the country just to buy clothes from Jean's. Why? The savings are astronomical. A Chanel evening gown that retailed for $9,000 and worn only once for a photo session sold for $400!!! You might find a $5,000 Valentino gown tagged at $350, a $1,600 Adolfo suit priced at $140 and a pair of $300 shoes priced as low as $20. Is the picture a little clearer now? Jean's Stars' Apparel caters to a woman's every whim and fantasy by offering exclusive attire for every occasion, sizes range from 3 to 14, and all at affordable prices. A 45 day layaway plan is available and while shopping you can munch on cheese, crackers and beverages. Jean's Stars' Apparel invites you to come in and indulge yourself. And whatever you do, don't forget your BUYING RETAIL IS STUPID coupon for an extra 10% discount.

LABEL'S HI-FASHION RESALE
6268 W. 3rd St.
Los Angeles, CA 90036
213/938-8868
HOURS: MON-FRI: 11-6   SAT: 10-6   SUN: 12-5
CREDIT CARDS: AE, DISC, MC, V

This store is so popular that it just keeps expanding, so hurry to see the fabulous selection of current fashions. Most of the fashions here are for ladies priced at least 1/3 off the original prices. Would you like an example? How about Mary McFadden dresses that retail for $3,000? At Label's you'd pay $600. There are unique items from movie sets, fashion houses and actresses. You'll find a large variety of famous designers including Anne Klein, Joanie Char, YSL and Krizia.

CLOTHING & ACCESSORIES

PATSY'S CLOTHES CLOSET
1525 N. Main St.
Santa Ana, CA 92706

714/542-0189

HOURS: TUES-FRI: 10-5:30 SAT: 10-4
CREDIT CARDS: MC, V

Like designer clothing but can't stand the prices? Patsy's Clothes Closet is the place for you. How about an Albert Nipon dress for as little as $40, or a two-piece Carole Little silk for $45. Half of Patsy's stock consists of designer samples; the remainder is slightly used, gently worn resales. In the center of the store is a large case of sample and vintage jewelry, and all at good discounts. In the same location since 1972, you'll find Patsy's Clothes Closet in what used to be a large, rambling home, built after the turn of the century. There are seven rooms to explore, and six dressing rooms. Should you need a bit of a rest, hot coffee is always available.

P.J. LONDON**
11661 San Vicente Blvd.
Los Angeles, CA 90049

310/826-4649

HOURS: MON-THUR, SAT: 10:30-6 FRI: 10:30-6:30 SUN: 12-5
CREDIT CARDS: AE, MC, V

This is the place to go to purchase top designer clothing on a bargain basement budget. All their merchandise has barely been worn and is in perfect condition. They carry resale clothes by the top names in the world—Chanel, Donna Karan, Vittadini, and more. Sizes range from 4 to 14, and they feature four sales a year in order to clear out all items that have been around for more than 90 days. These sales cut the prices by more than 50% and on the final day, all items are $5 and $10. So it's possible to buy a $1,500 dress for $10! In addition, you can find furs, jewelry and accessories. Don't forget to bring your BUYING RETAIL IS STUPID coupon for a 10% discount.

THE PLACE & COMPANY
8820 S. Sepulveda Blvd.
Los Angeles, CA 90045

310/645-1539

HOURS: MON-SAT: 10-5:30
CREDIT CARDS: MC, V

Newsweek says, "This is the finest resale store in the country." The Place is regularly featured on local television shows with names such as Ungaro, Adolfo, Chanel, and Valentino. Owner Joyce Brock has over

CLOTHING & ACCESSORIES

3,000 square feet of everything from formals to sportswear. She carries furs, jewelry, shoes, and handbags. Get on her mailing list to be informed of the super sales. There's free parking, so come on down.

SECOND TIME AROUND #2
432 32nd St.
Newport Beach, CA 92663
714/675-2864

HOURS: MON-SAT: 10-6
CREDIT CARDS: MC, V

Second Time Around is a resale store that deals in consignments. They accept like-new garments, shoes, purses and jewelry. Sizes in clothing range from 5-20. There are savings of 25 to 50% on names like Picone, Anne Klein, Dior, Blackwell and more. All items are carefully inspected before being accepted for sale. Give them a call to find out about their sales held at the end of each month.

SILENT PARTNER
99 E. Union.
Pasadena, CA 91103
818/793-6877

HOURS: TUES-FRI: 11-5 SAT: 11-4
CREDIT CARDS: AE

Alice Doney's Silent Partner is just what the name implies. If you want to dress professionally, but really can't afford the usual price tags for St John, Diane Freis or Chanel, then here's where your Silent Partner can help you. They have clothes for every occasion, from casual to ball gowns; they also carry shoes, purses and accessories. Here's even better news—Alice's daughter has a store in Claremont, Silent Partner East. The prices are usually about 33% of original retail. They also carry new clothes from eight different boutiques that are discounted.
Additional Locations:
Claremont–372 S.Indian Blvd., 714/624-0696

STARS & DEBS**
12424 Ventura Blvd.
Studio City, CA 91604
818/980-7433

HOURS: TUES-FRI: 1-5;30 SAT: 10-5:30
CREDIT CARDS: AE, OPT

Stars & Debs is just the place you can go to be fitted from head to toe in excellent resale women's clothing. They handle a wide selection of sweaters, blouses, hats, scarves, pant suits, skirt suits, and dresses. You can't go wrong with designers like Georgio Armani, Sonia Rykiel, Calvin Klein, Perry Ellis, Diane Freis and Carole Little. They also carry shoes by Kenneth Cole, Bruno Magli and Ferragamo just to name a few. If you enjoy fantastic bargains, but love impressive labels, Stars & Debs holds three half-price sales a year. For example, an Escada jacket that retails for $1,000 can be had for $100 to $150 here. So bring along your BUYING RETAIL IS STUPID coupon for an additional 10% discount.

THAT SPECIAL SHOP
8749 La Tijera Blvd.
Westchester, CA 90045
310/670-3441
HOURS: TUES-SAT: 10-5:30
CREDIT CARDS: AE, DISC

Want to meet some great guys? You will here. Ralph Lauren, John Henry, Calvin Klein, Willy Smith, Perry Ellis, Oscar De la Renta are all hanging around this store, and it won't cost you a fortune to get them to come home with you either. You will also find a few creative women hanging around these guys, too. Liz Claiborne has been known to drop in, as well as Carol Little, Anne Klein and Diane Freis. This store's sportswear, shoes, hats, handbags, formals, jewelry, and lingerie are up to 70% off retail prices. The staff at That Special Shop emphasizes courtesy, friendliness, and very special care of their customers. That's probably how they got their name. Their clothes sizes range from 0 to 22-1/2.

∞ SERVICES ∞

– DRY CLEANING –

JASMINE CLEANERS
9130 Reseda Blvd.
Northridge, CA 91325
818/349-3293
HOURS: MON-FRI: 7-7 SAT: 8-6
CREDIT CARDS: CASH OR CHECKS ONLY

Now that you've bought your clothing at a discount from stores in BUYING RETAIL IS STUPID, where do you go to get them dry cleaned at a bargain? Try one of the Jasmine cleaners. They will dry clean your clothes for $1.50 per item (does not include suede or leather). Orders must be prepaid and they accept only cash or checks.
Additional Locations:
Tarzana–18151 Ventura Blvd., 818/342-5806
Woodland Hills–19749 Ventura Blvd., 818/340-7061

CLOTHING & ACCESSORIES

RITZ DRY CLEANERS
6022 Woodman Ave.
Van Nuys, CA 91401
818/902-1108
HOURS: MON-FRI: 7:30-6:30 SAT: 8:30-5
CREDIT CARDS: CASH OR CHECKS ONLY

Tired of paying more than $5 for your suits or dresses to be cleaned? If your answer is yes, then Ritz Cleaners is where you'll want to take your dry cleaning from now on. With the exception of suede, leather, or formal wear, most garments are cleaned for $1.50. Ritz has another topper—no extra charge for one day service.

– TAILORING –

INTERNATIONAL CUSTOM TAILORS**
12075 Ventura Pl.
Studio City, CA 91604
818/509-9032
HOURS: MON-FRI: 10:30-6 SAT: 10-5
CREDIT CARDS: CASH OR CHECKS ONLY

Instead of buying new clothes, why not have your old ones let out or taken in? This family-owned business hasn't raised their prices since the 1970s. In addition to low-priced, high-quality tailoring, they also do custom work. You can have your fittings done at the store or they will come to your home or office. With your BUYING RETAIL IS STUPID coupon you'll get a 10% discount and a pair of pants hemmed for free with $25 of incoming alterations.

∞ SHOES ∞

– FAMILY –

CONVERSE FACTORY OUTLET
423 S. Lincoln Blvd.
Venice, CA 90291
310/396-0719
HOURS: MON-FRI: 10-6 SAT: 10-6 SUN: 11-6
CREDIT CARDS: MC, V

This is the only Converse Factory Outlet in Southern California. You'll find 25 to 70% savings off retail on most types of sport shoes from infant size to 17. And if you have a group, school or business that wants to buy in quantity, you'll receive an even greater discount. They have a knowledgeable staff to help you

CLOTHING & ACCESSORIES

FOOT FIESTA**
19168 Soledad Canyon Rd.
Santa Clarita, CA 91351
805/298-4291

HOURS: MON-FRI: 10-8   SAT: 10-6   SUN: 11-5
CREDIT CARDS: MC, V

You can find athletic shoes for the entire family at Foot Fiesta at up to 40% off retail. Brand names include Nike, Avia, Vans, Reebok, New Balance and Keds. There are shoes for aerobics, basketball, tennis, cross training, and running; they can order specialty shoes or certain models not in stock. A layaway plan is also available. You can save an extra 5% if you use your BUYING RETAIL IS STUPID coupon.
Additional Locations:
Chatsworth-10206 Mason Ave., 818/886-4966

FOOT MART SPORTS**
8575 Knott Ave.
Buena Park, CA 90620
714/827-8540

HOURS: MON-FRI: 9-9   SAT: 9-8   SUN: 9-7
CREDIT CARDS: AE, DISC, MC, V

If you find yourself spending lots of money for all those many feet in your household, this is surely the place you'll want to go. They carry all the major brands: Reebok, Nike, Adidas, Puma, New Balance, Avia, and British Knight—all at savings of 30% or more below retail. Their 12,000 square foot warehouse has all sorts of sports shoes for infants, children, women and men. In addition, they handle specialty shoes for soccer, basketball, and running. Free shuttle service is offered from many Orange County hotels to the store. Don't forget to bring along your BUYING RETAIL IS STUPID coupon for an extra 5% discount.
Additional Locations:
Huntington Park–7020 Pacific Blvd., 213/583-9926
Corona–406 N. Main St., 714/278-3901

PRICE BUSTERS SHOE WAREHOUSE**
5100 E. Whittier Blvd.
Los Angeles, CA 90022
213/265-4141

HOURS: 10-7 SEVEN DAYS A WEEK
CREDIT CARDS: AE, DISC, MC, V AND NO CHECKS ACCEPTED

This large store is known for their "two-fers." What in the world is a two-fer? Well, most of the athletic shoes are sold two pairs for $50, $60 or $70. Depending on what shoes you select, discounts range from 20 to

CLOTHING & ACCESSORIES

70% off retail. You'll find shoes—Nike, L.A. Gear, British Knights, Fila, Avia, Converse, K-Swiss, Vans and others—for the entire family. Take in your BUYING RETAIL IS STUPID coupon and you'll receive a free six-pack of socks with your purchase.

SAV-MOR SHOES
16919 Devonshire St.
Granada Hills, CA 91344
818/360-4488
HOURS: MON-THUR: 9:30-7 FRI: 9:30-8 SAT: 9:30-6 SUN:11-5
CREDIT CARDS: MC, V

You'll find brand shoes for the entire family at Sav-Mor Shoes. Don't be surprised when you see name brands such as Rockport, SAS, Bass, Sperry Topsider, Naturalizer, French Shriner, Candies, Cherokee, Penalgo, Fila, Nike, Reebok, L.A. Gear, Avia, Keds and New Balance. They also carry wide and extra wide shoes. Sav-Mor offers sale racks of odds and ends, too. If you join their Lucky 13 Club, you'll get the 13th pair of shoes you buy for FREE! At the same location since 1964, Sav-Mor Shoes is family owned and operated by the father and two sons.

SHOE OUTLET**
7835 Canoga Ave.
Canoga Park, CA 91304
818/702-6833
HOURS: MON-SAT: 9:30-5
CREDIT CARDS: MC, V

Does it seem that whenever you turn around it's time to lay out some money for a new pair of tennies? You'll find name-brand athletic shoes for everyone in the family for 15 to 30% off retail at Shoe Outlet. Name brands include Converse, Reebok, Nike, Tiger, Avia, Adidas, Kaepa, Puma and L.A. Gear. They even carry cheerleader shoes for women. Brand names and styles change constantly, so stop in every now and then to see what's new as shipments arrive twice a week. They also carry casual and dress shoes for the entire family, but the largest selection is devoted to women's shoes. Returns are accepted for store credit only. You'll receive a 10% discount with your BUYING RETAIL IS STUPID coupon.

CLOTHING & ACCESSORIES

SHOES INC.
19015 Parthenia St.
Northridge, CA 91324

818/772-4697

HOURS: MON-SAT: 9:30-6:30 SUN: 10-6
CREDIT CARDS: MC, V

You'll find prices at 20 to 50% below retail at Shoes Inc. on men's, women's and children's shoes, boots and athletics. All the great name brands can be purchased at Shoes Inc. You can also look forward to $1.00 sales, Red Dot sales and 1/2 price sales. Be sure to get your name on their mailing list, so you will be notified in advance about all of their special sales.

SPORTS SPECTACULAR
8859 W. Pico Blvd.
Los Angeles, CA 90035

310/275-5453

HOURS: MON-SAT: 10-6:30 SUN: 11-5
CREDIT CARDS: AE, DISC, MC, V

Are you searching for the right athletic shoe for every member of your family? Sports Spectacular has over 400 models on display. Brand names include Nike, New Balance, Avia, Converse, Reebok, Fila, Ellesse and more. While you are there, check out their athletic clothing and team outfitters department for men, women and children. Prices here are discounted 20% off retail, and there's always a close out table. Parking in rear and municipal parking is across the street.

TOP TO TOP
2313 Wilshire Blvd.
Santa Monica, CA 90403

310/829-7030

HOURS: MON-SAT: 10-8 SUN: 11-6
CREDIT CARDS: AE, MC, V

Here's a place you may want to try for athletic shoes of any kind. You can expect a wide variety of styles for your entire family with a discount of 15 to 25% off retail. Nike, New Balance, Reebok, L.A. Gear and even Keds are just a few of the many different brand names represented at Top To Top. Be sure to get your name on their mailing list, so you will be notified of their special sales. These salespeople know about shoes and the proper fit, so you're in good hands.
Additional Locations:
Marina del Rey–4724-1/4 Admiralty Way, 310/821-6111

CLOTHING & ACCESSORIES

– MEN'S SHOES –

MR. BURKE'S SHOES
6424 Hollywood Blvd.
Los Angeles, CA 90028
213/462-3419
HOURS: MON-SAT: 10-7 SUN: 12-5
CREDIT CARDS: AE, MC, V

You will find only the finest in men's fashionable shoes and boots from all over the world at Mr. Burke's Shoes. Some brand names you'll find are Franco, Pirelli, Freeman, Giorgio, Brutine, Le Jazz, and Nunn Bush. They have 2,000 styles in total and a special sale rack which guaranties a pair of shoes for $25.00 and two for $45.00.

– MEN'S & WOMEN'S SHOES –

ADLER SHOES
860 S. Los Angeles St.
Los Angeles, CA 90014
213/689-1469
HOURS: 10-5:30 SEVEN DAYS A WEEK
CREDIT CARDS: AE, MC, V

There are more than 20,000 pairs of women's and men's shoes in each Adler Shoes store, and you'll always save 10 to 40% below department store prices. They have handbags and hosiery, too. Each week there are specials where you can save 40 to 70%, and there are two big sales every year. All styles are current in just about every major brand you can name. You'll find Candies, Westies, Jacques Cohen, Romance, Zodiac, Ciao, Nike, Adidas, Bass, Nunn Bush, Bill Blass, Puma, and dozens more. Adler Shoes provides great service, too. They will place special orders for you and still give you discount prices. Everything is bought direct from the manufacturer, so you save big bucks. Women's sizes are 5 thru 10, men's sizes are 6 thru 14, all widths. If you find another store selling a nonsale shoe for less, Adler will beat it.

Additional Locations: 15 other stores throughout S. CA

CLOTHING & ACCESSORIES

HENRY'S SHOE FETISH
18055 Chatsworth St.
Granada Hills, CA 91344
818/360-2010
HOURS: TUES-SAT: 10-6 SUN: 12-4
CREDIT CARDS: DISC, MC, V

If you're on a strict budget and looking for a good pair of shoes, go to Henry's Shoe Fetish where the most expensive pair is $38. You'll find a selection of 5,000 pairs of shoes from which to choose. Men's shoes range from $28 to $38 and women's from $18 to $38. Women can find brand names such as Evan Picone, Liz Claiborne, 9 West, Bandolino, Nina, and Caressa. Men will find shoes made by London Fog, Bally, Nunn Bush, and Florsheim. Their inventory is always changing.

MAYA SHOES
6523 Hollywood Blvd.
Hollywood, CA 90028
213/460-6435
HOURS: MON-SAT: 10-8 SUN: 12-6
CREDIT CARDS: AE, MC, V

You can save as much as 70% on shoes for men and women. They import most of their merchandise from European countries such as Italy, Spain, France and Morocco. Their buyers are in Europe five or six times a year purchasing the newest styles in dressy and casual shoes and boots.

PILLER'S OF EAGLE ROCK
1800 Colorado Blvd.
Los Angeles, CA 90041
213/257-8166
HOURS: FRI-SAT: 10-5:30 SUN: 12-5
CREDIT CARDS: MC, V

Would you like to find a good deal on men's or women's clothing? How about 50% off the retail price of nationally advertised brands just for a start? During the year they have sales on merchandise with prices up to 90% off retail. No hole-in-the-wall, Piller's of Eagle Rock has nearly 25,000 square feet of merchandise on display. In the shoe department, you'll find about 25,000 pairs of brand names like Bruno Magli, Bally, Johnson and Murphy, Izod, and many more. You'll find first rate quality in a variety of styles and sizes. Dressing rooms are provided, so you can be sure of the fit. Piller's has been in business since 1949, so you know they're reliable.

CLOTHING & ACCESSORIES

– WOMEN'S SHOES –

FOOTSTEPS
12518 Riverside Dr.
North Hollywood, CA 91607
818/509-9092

HOURS: MON, FRI: 10-7   TUES, THUR: 10-8   SAT: 10-6
CREDIT CARDS: AE, MC, V

Better ladies' shoes and bags, from names like Bruno Valenti, Castori, Cities, Jazz, Sacha of London and others are Footsteps specialties. You can also find clothing and jewelry for completing an outfit. By the way, they carry sizes 5 to 10 in shoes in this one stop shop for women. With the 20 to 25% off retail prices, you may want to buy two pairs at a time.

HONEY'S SHOES**
6000 Reseda Blvd., Unit G
Tarzana, CA 91356
818/343-3958

HOURS: MON-SAT: 10-5:30
CREDIT CARDS: MC, V

Here's another store that has been added to what is affectionately known as "The Alley in the Valley." Honey's Shoes, strictly for women, features medium to high-end brand names discounted 25 to 50% off retail. Shoes lovers will find brands such as Caressa, Impo, Onex, Joyce, Bruno Magli, Ferragamo and others. Be sure to take in your BUYING RETAIL IS STUPID coupon for an extra 10% savings.

LADIES SHOES PLUS
11911 Carson
Hawaiian Gardens, CA 90716
310/865-1684

HOURS: MON-SAT: 10-6   SUN: 11-5
CREDIT CARDS: MC, V

This no nonsense store has women's shoes in sizes 4B to 12W priced up to 80% off retail. Brand names change on a constant basis; those they have had in the past include Hush Puppies, Cobbies, Life Stride, Naturalizer, Joyce, Selby and Calico. If you happen to wear narrow sizes, you are definitely in luck. They buy close-outs and there are always tons of narrow sizes. Of course, they have regular sizes too and there are always at least 5000 pairs of shoes in stock.

CLOTHING & ACCESSORIES

ROY STEP SHOES**
#46 The City Shopping Center
Orange, CA 92646
714/634-0631

HOURS: MON-FRI: 10-9   SAT: 10-6   SUN: 12-5
CREDIT CARDS: MC, V

If your budget is a tight fit, this is the place to shop. All women's shoes—sizes from the narrowest to the widest—can be found in this 4500 square foot store. They carry over 1,400 different pairs of shoes, with brand-names such as Naturalizer, Penaljo, Cobbies and Brownsabout. Roy Step buys manufacturer close-outs and passes the savings on to the customer. They've been in business over 25 years at this location. You'll save 50% to 75% off retail when you shop here, that's because all shoes are $15.97! Yes, not one shoe, but a pair! So if you wear an unusual size, or find the assortment in most shoe stores lacking, then Roy Step Shoes is the solution. Even with their great prices, you can still use your BUYING RETAIL IS STUPID coupon for an extra 10% off.

SHOES BY SHIRLEY
17037 Ventura Blvd.
Encino, CA 91316
818/788-1195

HOURS: TUES-SAT: 10-5
CREDIT CARDS: MC, V

Shoes By Shirley has 1,400 square feet of women's handbags and shoes. They have famous brands including Amalfi, Jasmine, Impo, Aerosole, Cobbies, Joyce and Rockport all priced at $29.99. Most sizes of medium width are stocked and they specialize in narrows up to size 12 (no wide widths). If you have something special in mind they'll do their best to find it for you. What can $10 buy these days? At Shoes by Shirley there's always a $10 corner offering regularly stocked items. The Boutique Corner features t-shirts, shorts, slacks and sweaters at discount prices. Shoes by Shirley gives cash refunds and there's free parking in back of the store.

TIFFANY DESIGNER SHOES
8220 Santa Monica Blvd.
West Hollywood, CA 90046
213/654-3462

HOURS: MON-SAT: 10-7   SUN: 12-6
CREDIT CARDS: AE, MC, V

They have so many women's shoes here (5,000 styles) that they divided themselves into two adjoining stores, one for casual and one for dressy.

CLOTHING & ACCESSORIES

You save about 50 to 70% on everything here. They carry brand names, too, like Charles Jourdan, Dior, Cassidy, Yves St. Laurent, and many more. You'll find styles, sizes, designs and colors to please everyone's taste. Tiffany also carries handbags to coordinate with their shoes, and great service is another plus for shopping at Tiffany Designer Shoes.

– WORK SHOES –

SURPLUS CITY RETAIL CO.**
11796 Sheldon St.
Sun Valley, CA 91352
818/768-2888
HOURS: MON-SAT: 9-6
CREDIT CARDS: MC, V

Surplus City Retail Company has the largest supply of surplus clothing in Los Angeles for 10 to 30% below list. Call to find out about the sales they have every month on 501 jeans. If you buy a pair of work boots at Surplus City, use your BUYING RETAIL IS STUPID coupon for an additional 25% discount. The coupon is good on nonsale work boot only.

WORK BOOT WAREHOUSE**
21608 Sherman Way
Canoga Park, CA 91303
818/703-8498
HOURS: MON-FRI: 9:30-6:30 SAT: 9-6 SUN: 11-5
CREDIT CARDS: AE, MC, OPT, V

Work Boot Warehouse has over 3,000 pairs of shoes in stock for just about any line of work or sport that comes to mind. Prices run approximately 10 to 45% off retail on brand names such as Wolverine (including steel-toed tennis shoes), Hi-Tech, Northlake, Carolina, Thorogood, Gorilla, Danner, Chippewa, Dr. Martens, Wesco and many others. Prices start at $35 for construction boots and go up to $300 for custom boots. You'll also find well-made boots from White. If their standard sizes don't fit you, they'll make you a pair at no extra charge. Another plus with White is, no matter how beat up the boots are, you can have your shoes completely rebuilt at half the price you paid originally. Motorcycle boots by H & H are at least 20% below most retailers. There are always close-outs with even lower prices located in front of the store. You'll save $10 on a pair of boots by using your BUYING RETAIL IS STUPID coupon. The coupon is not redeemable for boots on sale or rubber boots.
Additional Locations: Sunday Only
Saugus-2234 Soledad Canyon Rd. (Speedway)
Ventura-4826 Telephone Rd. (Pacific 101 Drive-In Theater)

∞ SPECIAL SALES ∞

CALIFORNIA MART MANUFACTURERS' SAT. SALE
CA Mart Exhibit Hall–Los Angeles St. @ Olympic Blvd.
Los Angeles, CA 90015
213/623-5876
HOURS: HOURS VARY–CALL FOR INFORMATION
CREDIT CARDS: CASH ONLY

We think everyone has heard of the California Mart, but the majority of the public is unaware of how to get in. In general, they are not open to the public, but once a month or so, they allow the public in for a small entrance fee. The buys at these special sales are absolutely incredible! You'll have access to 175 brand names, 300 lines of apparel and all kinds of accessories. Most items are either excess stock or samples, and everything is priced at cost, no mark-ups. As home to all major clothing manufacturers and their sales reps, available space must be continually made for the arrival of new lines. The last time we were at this sale, we bought some jeans with leather inserts tagged at $160, but we paid only $30. Just one visit will make you a true believer in our BUYING RETAIL IS STUPID philosophy! Hours vary, so call the phone number listed above to find out about their next sale, or keep an eye out for their ads in major newspapers. Don't forget to take plenty of cash with you because they don't accept checks or credit cards.

COUNTRY ELEGANCE
10144 Riverside Dr.
Toluca Lake, CA 91602
818/985-8968
HOURS: 10-4 FIRST SATURDAY OF DECEMBER
CREDIT CARDS: CASH ONLY

Once a year Country Elegance—famous for their romantically inspired bridal gowns and special occasion dresses—has an unbelievable parking lot sale. You can save up to 70% off retail on dresses that usually run hundreds of dollars. The sale consists mostly of overruns and excess inventory from their factory that sells to several thousand boutiques around the country. Wear a bathing suit or leotard for trying on outfits because there aren't any dressing rooms. You can use your MasterCard or Visa, but you'll save an extra 4% when you use cash.

CLOTHING & ACCESSORIES

TOWN FAIR BAZAAR
317 S. Crocker St.
Los Angeles, CA 90013
213/626-4611

HOURS: 9-3 2ND SATURDAY OF EACH MONTH
CREDIT CARDS: CASH OR CHECKS ONLY

If you love great bargains and want to feel great about spending money at the same, shop at the Town Fair Bazaar. Everything you spend goes to the City of Hope. You'll find brand new merchandise that has been donated by grocery, drug, department, hardware and furniture stores throughout the area. The bazaar is divided into 21 departments featuring unbelievable prices. Don't be surprised to see a $300 lamp for $50 or a pair of L.A. Gear high-tops on sale for $10. The bazaar, which has been operating for more than 60 years, is a make-shift discount department store set up in a huge warehouse owned by the City of Hope. Expect to save lots and lots of money, but be prepared for a crowd. Call for details.

ST. JOHN KNITS, INC.
17422 Derian Ave.
Irvine, CA 92713
714/863-1171

HOURS: OPEN TO THE PUBLIC ONCE A YEAR
CREDIT CARDS: NOT ACCEPTED

If you're a devotee of St. John Knits you'll be happy to know that once a year they open their doors to the public. The sale features items from their classic apparel collection. There are quite a few restrictions to this sale, but the savings are well worth the trouble. In October call or write for information about this special sale that usually occurs towards the end of November. By the way, men are not allowed at the sale because there is open dressing.

∞ SWIMWEAR ∞

BLUE MOON
608 Main St.
Ventura, CA 93001
805/643-2553

HOURS: MON-SAT: 10-6 SUN: 12-4
CREDIT CARDS: MC, V

Blue Moon carries a wide variety of women's and junior clothing at great prices, usually wholesale or below. You will also find a wide range of accessories available to complete your outfit. Blue Moon carries sizes from 1 to 16 and occasionally they carry large sizes. They have lots of free parking; three dressing rooms and a very relaxed atmosphere. This is a great place to buy swimwear; bikini's and one-piece suits are $9.99 all summer long.

Additional Locations:
Goleta–5122 Holister Ave., 805/967-0610

KIRKPATRICK SALES CORP.
8592 Washington Blvd.
Culver City, CA 90232
310/839-6455, 213/870-3912

HOURS: MON-SAT: 10-6
CREDIT CARDS: MC, V

You can find great buys on swimwear, beachwear and sportswear for women, juniors and men at Kirkpatrick Sales. Depending on the time of year, you'll find 7,000 to 10,000 swimsuits from which to choose. Jag, Serena, Too Hot Brazil, Daffy, and Jantzen are just a few of the many brand names carried here. There are 12 large mirrored dressing rooms in back of the store for privacy, and two of them are large enough for a stroller or wheelchair. In fact, the entire store is wheelchair accessible. Instead of paying retail, the 25 to 70% you save can be spent on your cruise! Call them for their extended hours March through September.

THE OUTLET
6015 Bandini Blvd.
City of Commerce, CA 90040
213/724-4693

HOURS: MON-FRI: 9-5 SAT: 9-4
CREDIT CARDS: MC, V

The Outlet carries ladies sportswear, swimwear, men's sportswear, swimwear, and junior and children's swimwear. They carry all the famous manufacturers found in your better department stores and have over 20,000 items for sale at 50 to 75% off the retail price. They have plenty of dressing rooms for you to try on those great buys. Over 400 customers shop here a day, so their merchandise turnover means a good selection for you.

Additional Locations:
La Verne–2416 Foothill Blvd., 714/593-6415
Northridge–9040 Balboa Blvd., 818/894-3422
Riverside–5232 Arlington Ave., 714/688-1660
Roland Heights–19722 Colina Rd., 714/598-3802

CLOTHING & ACCESSORIES

TIME-OFF APPAREL
6022 Reseda Blvd.
Tarzana, CA 91356
818/344-2825
HOURS: MON-SAT: 10-6
CREDIT CARDS: MC, V

Ladies, you will find resort and casual sportswear at Time-Off Apparel, but the real draw is their enormous stock of over 4,000 swimsuits all year round! Whether you're looking for a size 3 or size 20, they have a perfect swimsuit for you. Cole, La Blanca, and Roxanne are a few of the names you can look forward to buying at savings of 50–80% off retail.

∞ UNIFORMS ∞

SAM COOK UNIFORMS
2727 S. Flower St.
Los Angeles, CA 90007
213/748-4800
HOURS: MON-FRI: 9-5 SAT: 9-1
CREDIT CARDS: MC, V

Uniforms of all kind—police, waiters, chefs, security guards, mailmen, food servers, and many different varieties of industrial garb are available here. Over 3,000 individual items are in their inventory including such brand names as Dickies, Wrangler, and shoes from Rocky and Thoro-Good. They also have a nice selection of blazers, shirts and sportswear. Here's a place to go to get dressed for work or leisure. Savings run about 15% off retail at Sam Cook Uniforms.

GLAMOUR UNIFORM SHOP**
4951 W. Sunset Blvd.
Hollywood, CA 90027
213/666-2122
HOURS: MON-FRI: 10-6 SAT: 10-5
CREDIT CARDS: AE, DISC, MC, V

Whether you are buying a uniform just for yourself or for all your employees, you can save 20 to 50% here. You can find uniforms for nurses, doctors, waitresses, beauticians, barbers and chefs. The uniforms come in sizes 3 to 56. Glamour Uniform will even give you a greater discount on group orders. Save an additional 10% when you use your BUYING RETAIL IS STUPID coupon on nonsale items only.

Additional Locations:
Los Angeles–Owl Uniform, 984 W. Vernon, 213/233-1830

CLOTHING & ACCESSORIES

LOS ANGELES UNIFORM EXCHANGE
5239 Melrose Ave.
Los Angeles, CA 90038
213/469-3965

HOURS: MON-FRI: 9-6 SAT: 9-5
CREDIT CARDS: MC, V

A lot of foreign items here: Army uniforms, British drill pants, British, American, French army shorts. They carry a wide variety of military items, including Army field jackets and Navy pea coats. You can also buy flight suits, coveralls, jackets, military insignia patches and accessories. With a tailor shop on the premises, you can have your uniform tailored right there. Parking is available, and they insist their prices are the cheapest in town!

UNIFORM DEPOT
18552 Sherman Way
Reseda, CA 91335
818/343-7554

HOURS: MON-FRI: 9:30-5 SAT: 11-3
CREDIT CARDS: MC, V

If you're in need of uniforms and you haven't shopped here, you've missed a good bet! Uniform Depot carries one of the largest selection of uniforms in the area. Whether you want coveralls, shop smocks, lab coats, nurses uniforms, tuxedo shirts, or aprons, they have it. In the past they custom designed uniforms for Charlie Browns, Bobbie McGees, and some for Disneyland, so they definitely know what they're doing! Their regular prices are 10–30% below other stores, plus additional discounts on their specials will save you even more money. They've been around since 1948, and at this location since January of 1981.

∞ VINTAGE CLOTHING ∞

AARDVARK'S ODD ARK
7579 Melrose Ave.
Los Angeles, CA 90046
213/655-6759

HOURS: MON-SAT: 11-9 SUN: 11-7
CREDIT CARDS: MC, V

Find your way to Aardvark's Odd Ark when you want to find the "unique in antique" or used clothing. This place is an adventure! You can find discarded treasures for a couple of dollars or spend a lot more on a rare antique item. When in need of certain styles of clothing for their plays,

CLOTHING & ACCESSORIES

some theater groups head straight for Aardvark's. It's a great place to browse away the hours, and their sales folks will be happy to help you find a special item if you'd like.
Additional Locations:
Canoga Park–21434 Sherman Way, 818/999-3211
Venice–85 Market St., 310/392-2996

BAB'S** (AT RERUN'S)
11626 Ventura Blvd.
Studio City, CA 91604
818/506-4399

HOURS: MON-FRI: 11:30-7 SAT: 11-6
CREDIT CARDS: MC, V

Bab's specializes in one of a kind vintage clothing and accessories. They have everything you can imagine from the 1920s to the 1970s. Bab's features such items as vintage fabrics, cowboy boots, leather jackets, hats, tuxedos, 1940s ties, costume jewelry and perfume bottles. They also carry over 100 Halloween costumes So if you and your lady want to attend the ball, clad as a flapper and Al Capone, you'll want to check out Bab's. Don't forget to use your BUYING RETAIL IS STUPID discount coupon for an additional 10% off your purchase!

GRUBB & GRUBB'S GENERAL STORE
18523 Sherman Way
Reseda, CA 91335
818/996-7030

HOURS: MON-SAT: 9:30-5:30
CREDIT CARDS: AE, MC, V

This is a one stop shop for vintage clothing and antiques. They have an extensive line of clothing for men and women, costume jewelry, vintage shoes, purses and hats.

OZZIE DOTS
3908 W. Sunset Blvd.
Los Angeles, CA 90029
213/663-2867

HOURS: MON-SAT: 11-6 SUN: 12-5
CREDIT CARDS: MC, V

Ozzie Dots has a large selection of 50s and 60s items—Go-Go boots, Hawaiian shirts, motorcycle jackets, inexpensive sterling silver jewelry and hats. Daniel Hazen says his $1 rack of old Levi jeans and jackets is world famous! They have a 1/2 price sale at the end of each month.

∞ Western Apparel ∞

BOOT HILL SQUARE DANCE APPAREL**
7610 Balboa Blvd.
Van Nuys, CA 91406
818/901-9544

HOURS: MON-FRI: 11-6 SAT: 10-5 SUN: 10-4
CREDIT CARDS: MC, V

Grab you're partner and do-si-do on over to Boot Hill Square Dance Apparel where they dress men and women from head to toe for a good old fashion square dance. Their large store has a tremendous selection of such brands as H.B.C. Western Wear, Karman, Mesquite, Coast Shoes, Promenaders, Jeri Bee and others. Dress sizes run from 4 to 20. Be the one to stand out in the crowd with a custom designed, one-of-a-kind outfit! Check out their accessories and petticoats, too! Their prices are 20 to 50% off retail, and you can use your BUYING RETAIL IS STUPID coupon to save an additional 5%. A layaway plan is also available.

CAROL'S COUNTRY CORNER
21932 Schoenborn
Canoga Park, CA 91304
818/347-1207

HOURS: MON-TUES, THUR-FRI: 11-6 WED: 11-8 SAT: 10-5
CREDIT CARDS: MC, V

Swing your partner and two step down to Carol's Country Corner for the best in western and square dance apparel. They offer quality at discount prices on items from the least expensive to the most exclusive. Save 10–30% on shoes, jewelry and belts. Carol can design a custom piece made especially for you. For unadvertised specials and additional discounts for all callers and groups, give Carol's Country Corner a twirl.

PARIS GO
8432 Sunset Blvd.
Los Angeles, CA 90069
213/650-8295

HOURS: MON-SAT: 11-7 SUN: 12-4
CREDIT CARDS: AE, MC, V

Looking for western wear, boots, shirts, and the accessories that go with them? Paris Go has it all. Justin, Tony Lama, and Larry Mahan are just a few of the brands they carry. Don't be surprised by the French accent. Simon and Pierre have been at this location for more than 14 years with discounted prices.

CLOTHING & ACCESSORIES

∞ WOMEN'S APPAREL ∞

7TH AVENUE WEST
71-842 Highway 111
Rancho Mirage, CA 92270
619/340-6555

HOURS: MON-SAT: 9:30-5 SUN: 11-4
CREDIT CARDS: MC, V

Their concept is simple. They sell current New York designer fashions at 20 to 50% below department and specialty store prices. All merchandise is first quality, with new shipments arriving daily. Brand names include: Suzelle, R.G. Arnold, Oscar de la Renta, Adolfo, Needleworks, Semplice, Vivanti, Ultrasport, Saint Germain, Pierre Cardin and Stephanie, to name a few. Their motto is, "We've redesigned designer prices."

BACKDOOR BOUTIQUE
14331 Chambers Rd.
Tustin, CA 92680
714/544-9360

HOURS: THUR-FRI: 12-4 SAT: 10-4
CREDIT CARDS: CASH OR CHECKS ONLY

If you are into natural fabrics, this factory outlet is a good source for sportswear and separates made of 100% cotton. They carry a variety of dresses, jackets, tops, and bottoms in sizes 6 to 18. We know their hours are limited, but at savings of 40 to 80%, we can't complain. Sometimes leftover fabric and notions are for sale, too.

BLACK & WHITE WHOLESALERS
1250 S. Broadway
Los Angeles, CA 90015
213/746-5841

HOURS: MON-SAT: 10-5
CREDIT CARDS: MC, V

At Black & White Wholesalers you'll see the same designer made garments found in major departments stores hung on warehouse pipe racks, and there is one large group dressing room. Because nothing is tagged, you must ask about pricing. Although this can be a bit frustrating at times, saving 40–60% off retail is definitely worth the small inconvenience. This is a favorite haunt for style and quality at truly bargain basement prices. Make sure you get on their mailing list so you can get in on their annual sales.

CLOTHING & ACCESSORIES

BLUE MOON
608 Main St.
Ventura, CA 93001
805/643-2553

HOURS: MON-SAT: 10-6   SUN: 12-4
CREDIT CARDS: MC, V

Blue Moon carries a wide variety of women's and junior clothing at great prices, usually wholesale or below. You'll also find a wide range of accessories available to complete your outfit. Sizes run from 1 to 16 and occasionally they carry large sizes. They have three dressing rooms and a very relaxed atmosphere. This is a great place to buy swimwear priced at $9.99 all summer long.
Additional Locations:
Goleta-5122 Holister Ave., 805/967-0610

CONTEMPO CASUALS OUTLET
1507 S. Riverside Ave
Rialto, CA 92376

714-877-0560

HOURS: MON-FRI: 10-9   SAT: 10-6   SUN: 12-5
CREDIT CARDS: MC, V

Here's a place where you could probably walk out with an entire wardrobe and spend only $50 Contempo Casuals Outlet has weekly specials with $1, $3 and $5 racks of their trendy clothing consisting of sportswear, swimsuits and formal wear. Some items on the $1 rack are valued at $50. All jewelry is $1. Check out their regular merchandise at 50 to 75% off retail on brand names such as Betsy Johnson and Guess.
Additional Locations:
Huntington Beach–18557 Main St., 714/841-0869

DESIGNER LABELS FOR LESS
4750 Admiralty Way
Marina del Rey, CA 90292
310/827-5115

HOURS: MON-SAT: 10-6   SUN: 12-5
CREDIT CARDS: DISC, MC, V

One of our favorite places to purchase Carole Little clothes at 40-80% off retail is at Designer Labels For Less. In fact, during one of their blow-out sales we bought a Carole Little silk dress for $10. Other brand names you'll find are Dior, Gloria Vanderbilt, Leslie Fay, and more. Call for locations with discounted men's clothes. All merchandise is first quality.
Additional Locations: 20 other stores throughout S. CA

CLOTHING & ACCESSORIES

ROBERT ELLIS**
12524 Ventura Blvd.
Studio City, CA 91604
818/769-9666

HOURS: MON-WED, FRI-SAT: 9:30-6 THUR: 9:30-8
CREDIT CARDS: AE, MC, V

If you want to look like a million dollars but just don't want to spend the money, then Robert Ellis (formerly called Poor Snob) is for you. They carry the "look," not necessarily the label. Designer styles without designer prices is what you'll encounter here. Get your famous designer look-alike for $800 instead of $7,000 to $10,000. While this boutique isn't inexpensive, it may just be one of the best values in BUYING RETAIL IS STUPID. The collection you'll find at Robert Ellis reflects their philosophy of, "The best dressed women know that style means everything, and labels don't matter." For sophisticated clothing you really must come here! You'll save an additional 10% if you remember to use your BUYING RETAIL IS STUPID discount coupon.

FANTASTIC DESIGNER ROOM
860 S. Los Angeles St., Suite 220
Los Angeles, CA 90014
213/627-4536

HOURS: MON-FRI: 9:30-5 SAT: 9-9 SUN: 11-5
CREDIT CARDS: AE, DISC, MC, V

Only top designer clothing is found here! You can get Norma Kamali, plus Beverly Hills Polo, Lanvin, Pierre Balmain, and Leon Max for 40 to 80% less than retail department store prices! They are located in the garment district in downtown Los Angeles.

THE GREAT GATSBY**
14437 Ventura Blvd., Sherman Oaks Town Center
Sherman Oaks, CA 91403
818/789-7701

HOURS: MON-SAT: 10-6
CREDIT CARDS: AE, MC, V

Want that cosmopolitan European look? Then you should stop by The Great Gatsby where you can find better women's fashions from such places as France, Belgium and Italy. Most of their chic looks are done in 100% fine cotton. They also have unique accessories. Even with fluctuations in the dollar, you'll save 20 to 40% off retail. Use your BUYING RETAIL IS STUPID coupon and save an additional 10% on your purchase.
Additional Locations:
Sherman Oaks–Gatsby Sportswear, 14622 Ventura Blvd., 818/986-6182

CLOTHING & ACCESSORIES

HARPER'S LADIES WHOLESALE CLOTHING
15616 Ventura Blvd.
Encino, CA 91316
818/789-5837

HOURS: MON-SAT: 10-6
CREDIT CARDS: MC, V

Because the prices are so low here (you can save 50 to 70%), we can't mention any brand names. In sizes 2 to 20, women will find dresses, suits, pants, tops, sweaters, knits, and more. For super bargains, watch for Harper's special sales held during the year. A woman with good fashion sense can completely outfit herself at Harper's.
Additional Locations:
Culver City–8588 W. Washington Blvd., 310/839-8507)
Thousand Oaks–1625 Thousand Oaks Blvd., 805/495-8344
Woodland Hills–22766 Ventura Blvd., 818/347-3633

JUDY'S OUTLET
19411 Victory Blvd.
Reseda, CA 91335
818/344-2044

HOURS: MON-FRI: 10-9   SAT: 10-6   SUN: 11-6
CREDIT CARDS: MC, V

Judy's is the organization responsible for starting warehouse sales featuring unbelievable prices. They still have those great warehouse sales, but having so many stores has made it necessary for them to open up Judy's Outlet Stores. All items found in Judy's chain stores can be found here at savings of 30–70% off retail. All items are first quality, no seconds. Whatever you do, when you go in don't forget to get on their mailing list. This is the only way to be notified of Judy's semi-annual warehouse sales. Their Los Angeles outlet is located in the Cooper Building.
Additional Locations:
Los Angeles–860 S. Los Angeles St., 213/627-9173

LILA'S GOURMET BASKET
31938 San Luis Rey
Cathedral City, CA 92234

619/325-7383

HOURS: MON-SAT: 9:30-5:00   SUN: 11-3
CREDIT CARDS: DISC, MC, V

Yes, even in the Palm Springs area you can find some good bargains. The name of this store might make your mouth water, but you won't find any gourmet foods here. Lila's Gourmet Basket is a charming store that discounts their merchandise 15–20% off retail. You can always find something glamorous to wear in their women's clothing department. If you're feeling generous, you can buy a surprise for someone special from their many unusual gift items located around the store. Lila's also offers sensational gift wrapping.

LOEHMANN'S
6220 W. 3rd St.
Los Angeles, CA 90017

213/933-5675

HOURS: MON-FRI: 9:30-9   SAT: 9:30-7   SUN: 12-6
CREDIT CARDS: DISC, MC, V

Professional shoppers have been shopping at Loehmann's since the 1930s for dresses, blouses, skirts, slacks, suits, evening wear, coats, jackets, and fashion accessories. They guarantee savings of at least 33% over department store prices, 20% less than discount stores, and savings on fashion accessories run even higher. After an item has been in the store for about eight weeks, the price is marked down, and then continues to be marked down every two weeks until the item is sold. When all is said and done, your savings actually average about 45 to 50% off retail. Whenever you need something extra special to wear, Loehmann's Back Room is the first place you should visit. This is where they keep their finer designer clothing for day and evening wear. You'll be pleased to know that Loehmann's is not only a great place to shop, they also appreciate their customers. To make certain their prices stay low for their loyal clientele, Loehmann's goes to the trouble of generating about 35 comparison shopping reports every month. Look for their special sale on furs held every January in selected stores.

Additional Locations: 7 other stores throughout S.CA

M. FREDERIC & CO. OUTLET STORE
2251 S. Sepulveda Blvd.
West Los Angeles, CA 90069

310/478-4240

HOURS: MON-SAT: 10-6   SUN: 11:30-5
CREDIT CARDS: MC, V

You can buy all your favorite junior labels at 40% off retail. They carry a large assortment of career and casual separates. Enhance your wardrobe from M. Frederic's huge selection of sweaters and accessories at 20 to 50% off retail. They have free parking at all locations.

CLOTHING & ACCESSORIES

LEON MAX FACTORY OUTLET
3535 S. Broadway
Los Angeles, CA 90013
213/234-0510

HOURS: MON-FRI: 10-6 SAT: 10-4
CREDIT CARDS: MC, V

Ladies, here's the store for you. Leon Max used to sell his designs through Bullocks and Nordstrom; he now has two retail stores in Brentwood and Santa Monica. Fortunately for BUYING RETAIL IS STUPID readers, he has a factory outlet where you will find terrific buys. You can buy an entire silk outfit for around $100. Silk blouses that retail for $250 can be purchased for $90. From casual to formal wear, for the missy to the matronly, you can find all styles at less than wholesale. They also have markdowns once a month on already discounted clothing.

MS. FASHIONS**
3877 Pacific Coast Hwy.
Torrance, CA 90505
310/373-4622

HOURS: MON-SAT: 10:30-5:30
CREDIT CARDS: MC, V

If your looking for variety, Ms. Fashions is the place to shop! This store offers a surprising 50 to 70% discount below retail on pants, dresses, blouses, sweaters, and evening wear. Their inventory is constantly changing, so you always have a huge selection. They also carry earrings, belts, hosiery, scarves, hats, and unique costume jewelry. A dressmaker is on the premises so alterations are no problem. Ms. Fashions is truly a one-stop fashion outlet for ladies; best of all you can use a BUYING RETAIL IS STUPID coupon to save an extra 5% when you shop here!

MS. FITS
310 Vista Del Mar
Redondo Beach, CA 90277
310/378-6998

HOURS: MON-SAT: 10-5:30
CREDIT CARDS: MC, V

Ms. Fits is a cute, personal boutique. This store carries casual wear, dresses, and other really fun clothing. Their clothes are "IN", very trendy, new-to-the-scene. You can save 30–50% off retail prices when you shop here.

CLOTHING & ACCESSORIES

MY FAIR LADY**
6000 Reseda Blvd., Unit O
Tarzana, CA 91356
818/881-1651
HOURS: MON-SAT: 10-5
CREDIT CARDS: MC, V

My Fair Lady carries name brand women's sweaters, knits, cottons, dresses, and designer pantsuits at 40 to 70% below retail prices. Owner Jonathan Rick says, "We're not fancy, just top lines at the greatest bargains going." Their Blow-out Room has super mark-downs up to 90% off retail!. A mailer is sent out four times a year, so you'll want to get on their mailing list. Last but not least, you can save an additional 10% when you use your BUYING RETAIL IS STUPID coupon. (Coupon not valid on items from Blow-out Room or parking lot sales.)

QUALITY DRESS SHOP
212 E. Ninth St.
Los Angeles, CA 90015
213/623-9167
HOURS: MON-FRI: 9:30-4:30
CREDIT CARDS: AE, MC, OPT, V

This small boutique offers quality knit dresses and suits at 25 to 50% off retail. Brand names include Sideffects, LA Suits, Kasper Suits, Three Flaggs, Willy's, Laura, Miss Joan and Leslie Fay. Although they have discounted prices, customers receive the same special attention as found in expensive boutiques. You can put your ensembles together yourself or with their professional assistance.

SARA DESIGNERS OUTLET**
18562 Sherman Way
Reseda, CA 91335
818/609-1200
HOURS: MON-FRI: 10:30-6:30 SAT: 10:30-5
CREDIT CARDS: MC, V

Although we can't name names, Sara Designers Outlet has the same brands found in many high-end department stores at 40 to 80% below retail. They concentrate on career and after-five apparel with a European flair. The clothing is very well made and most are completely lined. The staff will help you put chic ensembles together, along with adding final touches from their selection of accessories. Sizes run 3 to 16 and there are four private dressing rooms. For extra savings, use your BUYING RETAIL IS STUPID coupon, good for 10% off your purchase.

CLOTHING & ACCESSORIES

SEE ME COLOR**
625 E. Cochran St.
Simi Valley, CA 93065
805/527-9573
HOURS: MON-FRI: 9-5 SAT: 9-12
CREDIT CARDS: CASH OR CHECKS ONLY

This is a factory outlet filled with overruns priced at or under $11. You'll find the hottest styles in either 100% cotton or stretch clothing made of a cotton/lycra blend. Women's and junior styles are available in small, medium and large. They have leggings, tops, shorts and stretch pants at 20 to 50% below retail. Costume jewelry and accessories are also available at a discount. Don't forget to use your BUYING RETAIL IS STUPID coupon for savings of an extra 10%.

SEYMOUR FASHIONS**
7040 Darby Ave.
Reseda, CA 91335
818/705-1911
HOURS: MON-FRI: 9:30-5 SAT: 10-4
CREDIT CARDS: MC, V

If you'd like to save money and customize your own wardrobe at the same time, then Seymour Fashions is your kind of place. Just about everything in the store is made to be mixed and matched. Most of the tops are appliqued, and there's a large assortment of bottoms (shorts, pants, leggings, pocket pants and three styles of skirts) made from the same fabric used in the appliques. Not only can you mix and match, but you can actually have anything you see in the store made in one of many available fabrics. If you find a top and can't find a bottom to match the applique, they'll make one for you at no extra charge. As the manufacturer, they are able to do all alterations on the premises, sometimes while you wait. The clothing here is not only versatile but also very well made. Don't be surprised to meet women who have flown in from various parts of California to update their expandable wardrobe. Take your BUYING RETAIL IS STUPID coupon for an extra 10% discount.

SUSIE'S DEALS**
17060-A Valley Blvd.
Fontana, CA 92335
714/823-5695
HOURS: MON-FRI: 10-9 SAT: 10-7 SUN: 11-6
CREDIT CARDS: MC, V

How's this for a bargain? Nothing in the store is over $20 and it's true! You'll find the latest in styles for the younger set with name brands such

CLOTHING & ACCESSORIES

as Judy Knapp, Yes, Cherokee, No Excuses, Mirrors and many others. They have lots of accessories which are priced individually or sold in twos or threes for more savings. If you present your BUYING RETAIL IS STUPID coupon you'll receive an extra 10% discount.
Additional Locations: Over 70 stores throughout S. CA

UNCLE JER'S
4451 Sunset Blvd.
Los Angeles, CA 90027
213/662-6710
HOURS: MON-FRI: 11-7 SAT: 10-6 SUN: 12-5
CREDIT CARDS: V, MC

Located at the Sunset and Hollywood Boulevard junction, Jerry Morley and Helen Sloan's Uncle Jer's offers savings of 20 to 50% on clothing items by OK Sam, Surya Imports, Bila, What's Happening?, Solange and many others. A one-stop shopping place, you can buy a frock for auntie, an unusual boutique item for mom, a plaything for junior or junior miss, and greeting cards for all. You will find their folk and ethnic items a great source for unusual gifts. They are proud to state that most of their clothing is made of natural fibers. Uncle Jer's donates 10% of their profits to the Alliance for Survival and also supports many anti-nuclear and environmental organizations.

THE WILD PRICE BOUTIQUE
3680 Wilshire Blvd.
Los Angeles, CA 90010
213/388-4823
HOURS: MON-SAT: 10-6
CREDIT CARDS: AE, DISC, MC, V

Rayons, silks, lace, cotton and cotton knits are the fabrics used for the fine quality clothing you'll find at the Wild Price Boutique. Their casual and exciting styles are sold at wholesale prices and below. During special sales, savings can run as much as 80% off retail. These are the outlet stores for high fashion retail chains and manufacturers. Though most of their merchandise is for women (size 3–14), some unisex clothing is also carried. You can truly find some wild prices at the Wild Price Boutique. Their Los Angeles store is located in the USC University Village Shopping Center.

Additional Locations:
Los Angeles–3319 S. Hoover, 213/747-3148
Venice–218-B Main St., 310/396-4195

COMPUTERS

∞ Hardware & Software ∞

ABM ART TYPE BUSINESS MACHINES
15420 Devonshire St.
Mission Hills, CA 91345
818/893-8066
HOURS: MON-FRI: 9-6 SAT: 9-3
CREDIT CARDS: MC, V

It takes longer to say their name than it does to get a good deal on all types of office equipment. ABM has copiers, fax machines, typewriters, word processing calculators and supplies. Andrew Katz guarantees the lowest prices around, and they handle most name brands such as IBM, T/A Adler-Royal, Sharp, Brother, and Panasonic. You'll also find IBM compatible computers at 40-50% off retail. ABM has friendly knowledgeable service.

COMP USA
9380 Warner Ave. (@ 405 Fwy.)
Fountain Valley, CA 92708
714/965-1169
HOURS: MON-FRI: 10-9 SAT: 9-6 SUN: 12-5
CREDIT CARDS: MC, V

Formerly Soft Warehouse, Comp USA is a computer superstore and they are user friendly! At 30 to 80% below retail, they make friends easily. These people really want to save their customers money. That's why there is no membership fee. This is a complete warehouse stocked with computers, software, printers, drives, monitors, modems, accessories and everything else needed to allow you and your computer to live happily ever after. Would you like a few brand names? Okay, we'll name just a few. You'll find ALR, Toshiba, Panasonic, Packard Bell, Macintosh, Epson, NEC, Mitsubishi, Everex, Sony and Fuji.
Additional Locations:
City of Industry–18575 E. Gale Ave., 818/913-3360
Culver City–11441 Jefferson Blvd., 310/390-9993
Torrance–21303-B Hawthorne Blvd., 310/540-0593
San Diego–5630 Kearny Mesa Rd., 619/560-4300

COMPUTERS

COMPUTER PALACE
22401 Ventura Blvd.
Woodland Hills, CA 91364
818/347-3430

HOURS: MON-SAT: 9-7
CREDIT CARDS: AE, MC, V

Computer Palace carries a wide range of IBM compatible products and will guarantee the best prices. Friendly and patient salespeople will give you excellent service and can help arrange financing.

Additional Locations:
Beverly Hills–8504 W. 3rd St., 310/659-1500
Glendale–1029 E. Broadway, 818/241-2551
Glendora–1435 E. Alosta, 818/335-4033
W. Los Angeles–11909 W. Pico Blvd., 310/478-4321
Rancho Cucamonga–9798 Foothill Blvd., 714/944-4009

COMSOFT
8125 San Fernando Rd.
Sun Valley, CA 91352
818/768-5017

HOURS: MON-FRI: 10-6 SAT: 10-5
CREDIT CARDS: ALL MAJOR

If you are hard pressed to come up with a birthday present for your 14 year old, Comsoft carries one of the largest selections of Atari and Commodore software. They also carry IBM compatibles at 20 to 50% below retail.

DATA TECHNOLOGY
632 S. Victory Blvd.
Burbank, CA 91502
818/569-4929

HOURS: MON-FRI: 10-6 SAT: 11-4
CREDIT CARDS: CASH OR CHECKS ONLY

Data Technology will not be undersold on their computer equipment, and they will also give you a free loaner when you bring in your computer for repairs. Their brand names include IBM, Compaq, Toshiba, NEC, Zenith, Advance, Every, Acer, Advance Logic Research, Seiko, Sharp and software too numerous to list. Make sure to check them out on their prices and service.

COMPUTERS

EGGHEAD DISCOUNT SOFTWARE
4264 Lincoln Blvd.
Marina del Rey, CA 90292
310/823-2727
HOURS: MON-SAT: 10-7 SUN: 12-5
CREDIT CARDS: AE, DISC, MC, V

Looking for good service and the best deal in computers? Egghead Discount Software says they will match and beat by one dollar any retail price on products from another store and do it with a smile. Their regular prices on software will give you savings of up to 50% off retail on brand names such as Microsoft, Lotus, Claris, Hayes, AST and Ashton Tate. There are 200 stores nationwide, so you're always near enough to get advice from an Egghead store's experienced staff. For even greater savings of up to 90% off retail, check out the clearance center in West Los Angeles (310/473-8115). The merchandise at the clearance center consists of manufacturer close-outs, overstocks and discontinued items from 185 Egghead stores around the United States and Canada. This store also receives products from their corporate sales division which handles more than 25,000 different computer products. As a result, you'll see items here that aren't available in regular Eggheads.

Additional Locations: 31 other stores in S.CA–Call 800-EGGHEAD

PERSONAL SUPPORT COMPUTERS
10431 Santa Monica Blvd.
West Los Angeles, CA 90015
310/474-1633
HOURS: MON-SAT: 10-6 SUN: 11-5
CREDIT CARDS: MC, V

Personal Support Computers has the highest rating in Los Angeles for service and support. They guarantee lowest package prices and will train you on the use of your computer purchases. As their name states, "support" is their middle name. They are recognized as the largest Macintosh retailer in the United States and carry a large selection of computer accessories and software. You will also find many IBM compatibles, Hewlett Packard printers and other brands such as Epson, NEC and Hyundai. Their large service department is open seven days a week, with five certified technicians and an inventory of 150,000 spare parts. Get on their mailing list, so they can inform you of their super blowouts. You can't go wrong here. They have been in business for ten years and sell, lease, and service their products. The owners, Dr. Peter Huber and Debbi Reid, have received considerable publicity on their successful operation.

∞ Repair & Maintenance ∞

COMPLETE COMPUTER CURE
14950 Ventura Blvd.
Sherman Oaks, CA 91403
800/462-4438
HOURS: MON-FRI: 8-6   SAT: 10-4
CREDIT CARDS: AE, DISC, MC, V

If your computer should come down with a dreaded cold or flu, or even a virus, give these folks a call because they have the cure. They will pick up and deliver your computer for free; they even have loaners and offer maintenance contracts as well. So, for fast turn-around at a low cost (about 20% less than others), they will repair and do maintenance on all personal computers, terminals, printers and drives.
Additional Locations:
Placentia–610 S. Jefferson, 714/996-0174
Torrance–411 Amapola, 310/787-3200

DEPARTMENT & WAREHOUSE STORES

ADRAY'S
6609 Van Nuys Blvd.
Van Nuys, CA 91405
818/908-1500

HOURS: MON-FRI: 10-7   SAT-SUN: 10-6
CREDIT CARDS: MC, V

You will save about 40% on almost everything at Adray's. They are the discount headquarters for major brands of TVs, VCRs, cameras, stereos, computers, appliances, jewelry, cosmetics, housewares, sporting goods, furniture and just about anything else that comes to mind. If you are looking to make a major purchase, we suggest that you do your homework about the product you are interested in before going to Adray's. Shopping here is much different than in a retail department store, but once you see their prices, adapting won't be a problem.

Additional Locations:
Canoga Park–8351 Topanga Canyon Blvd., 818/348-2600
Los Angeles–5575 Wilshire Blvd., 213/935-8191
Torrance–4140 Pacific Coast Hwy., 310/378-6777
Ventura–6040 Telegraph Rd., 805/654-0699
W. Los Angeles–11201 W. Pico, 310/479-0797

COSTCO
21300 Roscoe Blvd.
Canoga Park, CA 91304
818/884-8969

HOURS: MON-FRI: 12-8:30 SAT: 9:30-6 SUN: 11-5
CREDIT CARDS: CASH, CHECKS OR COSTCO CREDIT CARD

Costco is truly for people who love to save money, lots of money. Each of their membership wholesale distribution centers operates in a 100,000 square foot warehouse. They carry quality name brands at substantially lower prices than other discount sources. Whether you need clothing, large and small appliances, books, furniture, groceries, toys, hardware, tires, jewelry—you name it, they've got it. Costco consistently has great brands, products and value. You can even same money on your prescriptions because most locations have pharmacies. So, for those of you who really want to save big bucks, call for information on how to become a member.

Additional Locations: 14 other stores throughout S. CA

DEPARTMENT/WAREHOUSE STORES

FEDCO
3535 S. La Cienega Blvd.
Los Angeles, CA 90016
310/837-4481

HOURS: MON-FRI: 10-8   SAT-SUN: 10-6
CREDIT CARDS: CASH, CHECKS OR FEDCHARGE

Fedco is the only member-owned, nonprofit mutual benefit corporation of its kind in California, and it must be doing something right, because it's been an unqualified success since 1949. Unlike other membership operations, Fedco charges a one-time fee of $10 to join and the membership lasts for your lifetime. At Fedco you do not need to buy in bulk to get the best deal. Fedco also accepts manufacturer's cents-off coupons. You'll find guaranteed lowest prices on TVs, camcorders, VCRs, major appliances, and tires. Fedco also carries a complete selection of family clothing, jewelry, beauty aids, housewares, toys and much more. Each location has a grocery and produce market, fresh bakery and butcher shop. Members will also find prescription pharmacies and optical centers.

Additional Locations: 8 other stores in S. CA

HARTMAN JEWELRY & GIFTS**
2535 S. Fairfax Ave.
Culver City, CA 90232
213/938-3211

HOURS: MON-SAT: 10-6
CREDIT CARDS: AE, MC, V

Come in, phone or send in your order. Hartman has quality name brand merchandise, personalized service, and low low prices. There are over 4,500 products on hand for immediate delivery—jewelry, watches, appliances, portable electronics, cameras, crystal, microwave ovens and so much more. They will be happy to send you their frequent newsletters with new specials, sale items, and even bigger savings. Make sure you ask about their preferred customers $10.00 lifetime membership card which saves you an additional 10% on all merchandise. The Hartman family has been providing their customers with great service since 1922. Not only can you expect savings of 50% off retail, they will accept your BUYING RETAIL IS STUPID coupon for an additional 10% discount off your purchase.

DEPARTMENT/WAREHOUSE STORES

J. C. PENNEY CATALOGUE OUTLET STORE
6651 Fallbrook Ave.
Canoga Park, CA 91607
818/883-3660
HOURS: MON-FRI: 10-9 SAT: 10-7 SUN: 10-6
CREDIT CARDS: AE, J.C. PENNY, MC, V

This is where J.C. Penney's sells overstocked or discontinued items featured in their catalogues. You'll find this enormous store literally packed with first quality merchandise. Choose from clothing for the entire family, toys, furniture, stereos, linens and more. We even spotted some exercise equipment. In addition to the selection, you'll love the 50% savings off retail on most items. Because they want to move this merchandise in a hurry (new merchandise arrives weekly), original prices are slashed dramatically before being put on the floor. You'll find higher savings at the special sales they hold during the the year. So, if you're a faithful J.C. Penney shopper, now you know where to go for terrific deals on their merchandise.

THE LIQUIDATION CLUB**
19032 S. Vermont Ave.
Gardena, CA 90248
310/715-6500
HOURS: SAT-WED: 11-6 THUR-FRI: 11-8
CREDIT CARDS: MC, V

BUYING RETAIL IS STUPID shoppers unite! The Liquidation Club, which operates through membership only, is extending a FREE MEMBERSHIP to all owners of this book, and this is definitely a place you want to check out. Not only do they have the lowest prices on most major department store brand names, but you'll save an additional 10% using your BUYING RETAIL IS STUPID coupon. Brand names include Liz Claiborne, Anne Klein, Bill Blass, Ralph Lauren, Bally, Georgio Armani, Perry Ellis, London Fog, Oshkosh, and more. You'll find over 50,000 items of clothing for the entire family, housewares, bedding, accessories, gift items and much more at savings of 60 to 85% off retail. New merchandise accounts for 75% of their inventory, and the remaining 25% of their merchandise is slightly damaged (such as a garment label being removed). Stock changes daily, so make sure to put The Liquidation Club on your shopping check list. Remember to use the coupon in back of the book for your free membership and 10% additional discount!

DEPARTMENT/WAREHOUSE STORES

MR. PRICE
5500 Wilshire Blvd.
Los Angeles, CA 90036
213/934-2266
HOURS: MON-FRI: 10-6:30 SAT: 10-6
CREDIT CARDS: AE, DISC, MC, V

Mr. Price is a shopper's paradise, jammed to the rafters with small appliances of every description. You will find every brand name you can think of when you take yourself shopping in this 20,000 square foot showroom for television sets, VCRs, stereos, china, crystal, camera equipment, and an assortment of wonderful gift items too numerous to name. Their prices are 30 to 60% below retail, and they have been in the same location since 1984.

Additional Locations:
Los Angeles–2480 S. Sepulveda Blvd., 310/445-5500

PACE MEMBERSHIP WAREHOUSE
6345 Variel Ave.
Woodland Hills, CA 91367
818/710-8480
HOURS: MON-FRI: 11-9 SAT: 9-6:30 SUN: 10-5
CREDIT CARDS: DISC

"Honey, don't buy that here. We'll get it the next time we go to Pace." More and more people are taking on this money-saving attitude. After all, why would you pay $4.50 for an item weighing 12 ounces when you can get the same item at Pace Club in 36 ounces for less than $4.50? BUYING RETAIL IS STUPID you know! With Pace, consumers don't have to wait for special sales to save money. They always have everyday low prices, up to 80% off retail, on a vast selection of top-quality, brand name merchandise. With over 100,000 square feet in each location, you'll find everything needed for your home or business. They have everything from bakery items, groceries and produce, to clothing, hardware, furniture, tires, electronics and jewelry. They have a consistent inventory, but that doesn't mean you won't find some surprises on every visit. The buyers for Pace Club are always on the hunt for great deals to pass on to their appreciative members. By the way, membership is $25 a year and if you don't save that much the first time you shop here, you didn't buy anything!

Additional Locations: 15 other stores throughout S. CA

DEPARTMENT/WAREHOUSE STORES

PRICE CLUB
8810 Tampa Ave.
Northridge, CA 91324
818/775-1322
HOURS: MON-FRI: 11-8:30   SAT: 9:30-6   SUN: 11-5
CREDIT CARDS: CASH OR CHECKS ONLY

Though it can be dangerous, one of our favorite things to do is wander around Price Club. How can shopping be dangerous? With over 100,000 square feet of everything imaginable—groceries, computers, televisions, VCRs, stereo equipment, clothing, office supplies, furniture, appliances, housewares, hardware, books (you name it and it's there)—the danger of spending much more than you had planned lurks along every aisle. At Price Club, the prices are so fantastic you many end up buying things you don't actually need. So before you go shopping, make out out a list of things you need in order to avoid impulse buying, unless of course impulse buying is your thing. Also, if you have never been to Price Club, make sure you schedule enough time so that you can leisurely walk this enormous warehouse and not have to rush through the place (you might miss something). With savings up to 80% off retail, you will recoup the annual membership fee very quickly. All of the salespeople are friendly and helpful, and their return policy is quite good.

Additional Locations: 17 other locations throughout S. CA

SEARS OUTLET STORE
2245 Tapo St.
Simi Valley, CA 93063
805/581-1214
HOURS: MON-FRI: 10-9   SAT: 9-7   SUN: 10-6
CREDIT CARDS: DISC, SEARS

Just about everything found at your neighborhood Sears store can be found here at huge savings of 20 to 70% off the original retail prices. Merchandise from their stores and catalogues is sent to the surplus stores to make room for new stock. Because so much of their merchandise is seasonal, you'll find something new on every visit. It's pretty much self-service in the various departments that include clothing, appliances, housewares, linens, sporting goods, carpeting, and other various goods. Inventory changes constantly, so when you see something you want, buy it! It might not be there tomorrow.

Additional Locations: 7 other stores throughout S. CA

DEPARTMENT/WAREHOUSE STORES

SMART & FINAL
10113 Venice Blvd.
West Los Angeles, CA 90034
310/559-1722

HOURS: MON-SAT: 7-8 SUN: 10-4
CREDIT CARDS: CASH OR CHECKS ONLY

Smart & Final is a pioneer when it comes to offering warehouse prices. You can save on groceries, frozen and deli items, janitorial supplies, coffee supplies, paper products and much more. You get warehouse prices without having to pay a membership fee. Brand names include Carnation, M & M's, Nestle, Proctor & Gamble, Heinz, Best Foods, Hormel and many more. Smart & Final caters mostly to food service businesses, schools, clubs and offices, but you don't have to own a business to take advantage of the low prices. In many cases, warehouse stores change brands and merchandise according to the best deals that are available. That isn't the case at Smart & Final. You can rely on finding the same products on a regular basis.

Additional Locations: 80 other stores throughout S. CA

DISCOUNT "SHOPPING CENTERS"

CITADEL OUTLET COLLECTION
5675 E. Telegraph Rd.
City of Commerce, CA 90040
213/888-1220

HOURS: MON-SAT; 9-8 SUN: 10-6
CREDIT CARDS: AE, MC, V

This is the first factory outlet center to be opened in Los Angeles. Currently it has 44 outlet stores including Eddie Bauer, Gap, Gitano, Perry Ellis, Ann Taylor, Benetton, Joan & David, Full Size Fashions, Star Baby, Corning Revere, Politix and more. Prices are discounted at about 10 to 80% off retail. If shopping make you hungry or thirsty you can "wet your whistle" at Johnny Rockets, Subway Sandwich, Taipan Express or Sbarro (Italian food). There is also an expresso stand in the middle of the center. As a point of interest, Citadel Outlet Collection sits on the site of an old tire factory. The restored facade—a replica of an Assyrian castle—was built in 1930 and was once used as a backdrop in the movie Ben Hur.

COOPER BUILDING
860 S. Los Angeles St.
Los Angeles, CA 90014
213/622-1139

HOURS: MON-SAT: 9:30-5:30 SUN: 11-5
CREDIT CARDS: CASH OR CHECKS ONLY*

This place is incredible! The Cooper Building is a "Tall Mall" 11 stories high with 8 selling floors (400,000 square feet) all bulging with exciting merchandise in the heart of the wholesale garment district. You'll find quite a collection of outlet stores representing various manufacturers, famous retail stores and discount stores. You always save 25 to 75% off retail prices every day of the week. Quality and value prevail in over 70 stores featuring current designer and brand-name fashions for men, women and children of leather fashions, shoes, handbags, fashion accessories, lingerie and home fashions, all under one roof. Why spend twice the amount on prestigious labels carried in expensive department stores when you can save a bundle buying the identical item here? *Some vendors accept credit cards.

Additional Locations: 70 stores at one location

DISCOUNT "SHOPPING CENTERS"

DESERT HILLS FACTORY STORES
48650 Seminole Rd.
Cabazon, CA 92230
714/849-6641

HOURS: MON-SUN: 9-8
CREDIT CARDS: ALL MAJOR

While taking a pleasure drive to Palm Springs make sure you stop at Desert Hills Factory Outlet Stores where you'll save 30-70% on everything from designer fashions to national brand housewares. There are 52 renowned manufacturers such as Patagonia, Royal Doulton, Joan & David, Donna Karan, Anne Klein, Alpert Nipon, Guess, Oneida, Gorham and many more in their own outlet stores.

FACTORY MERCHANTS OUTLET STORES
2837 Lenwood Rd.
Barstow, CA 92311
619/253-7342

HOURS: MON-SAT: 10-9 SUN: 10-6
CREDIT CARDS: VARIES WITH VENDOR

If brand name factory outlets are your favorite sources for discount shopping, you'll find an oasis at Factory Merchants Outlet Stores. Savings run 20–70% off retail. Some of the stores featuring various styles of apparel are Anne Klein, Benetton, Polo London Fog, Oshkosh, Barbizon, Evan Picone, Gitano, Polly Flinders, G.H. Bass and Banister Shoes. Oneida, Royal Doulton and Lenox also have stores. You'll find other outlets selling luggage, toys, light fixtures, greeting cards and paper products and perfume. Your friends might think you're crazy driving to Barstow to go shopping, but after they've seen your purchases and have heard what you paid, they'll want to hitch a ride on your next trip .

INDOOR SWAPMEET OF STANTON
10401 Beach Blvd.
Stanton, CA 90680
714/527-1234

HOURS: MON, WED-SAT: 10-7 SUN: 10-6 (CLOSED TUESDAY)
CREDIT CARDS: VARIES WITH VENDOR

You'll find over 170 vendors selling everything from haircuts to fresh roasted coffee beans. Some of the brand names carried include Reebok, Panasonic, Levi, Jordache, Kenwood, Guess, and Bugle Boy. As you can see by the small sampling of brand names, you are in for a shopping treat. This two story, air conditioned 42,000 square foot building was designed especially for swapmeets and they have thought of everything. Even the aisles were made extra wide to accommodate wheelchairs.

ORANGE COUNTY MARKETPLACE
88 Fair Dr. (Orange County Fairgrounds)
Costa Mesa, CA 92626
714/723-6616

HOURS: SAT-SUN: 7-4
CREDIT CARDS: VARIES WITH VENDOR

This happens to be one of the best swapmeets around. What impresses us most is the quality and variety of merchandise. Of course you'll still find the same things found at most swapmeets, but the selection of new products prevail. Some of the items we've purchased here include dried and silk flowers, jewelry, shoes (Sperry Topsiders and K-Swiss to be exact), salon hair products, real plants, camping equipment, baskets of all shapes and sizes, handbags, backpacks, sheets, and the list goes on and on. There's a large refreshment center and there are quite a few food vendors scattered about. Do wear comfortable shoes because there's a lot of ground to cover.

PLAZA CONTINENTAL FACTORY STORES
3700 E. Inland Empire Blvd.
Ontario, CA 91764
714/980-6231

HOURS: MON-SAT: 10-9 SUN: 10-6
CREDIT CARDS: ALL MAJOR

Nowadays you can take a mini-vacation outside of Los Angeles and almost always pass a complex of factory outlet stores. Plaza Continental Factory Stores has 20 outlets featuring such stores as Book Warehouse, Corning Revere, Converse, Prestige Fragrance & Cosmetics, Gitano, Adolfo II, and Aileen. There are also three full-service restaurants on site so you'll be able to take a break from shopping.

SAN DIEGO FACTORY OUTLET CENTER
4498 B Camino da la Plaza
San Ysidro, CA 91941
619/690-2999

HOURS: MON-FRI: 10-8 SAT: 10-7 SUN: 10-6
CREDIT CARDS: ALL MAJOR

You'll find a real variety among the 33 factory outlet stores found here. Need some jeans, stop by Levi's outlet, sneakers—Nike outlet, cosmetics—Revlon outlet, shirts—Van Huesen outlet, cookware—Corning Revere outlet, glassware—Libby Glass outlet, tools and appliances—Black & Decker outlet. There is also a food court to satisfy hungry shoppers.

DISCOUNT "SHOPPING CENTERS"

SANTA FE SPRINGS SWAPMEET
13963 Alondra Blvd.
Santa Fe Springs, CA 90670
310/921-9996

HOURS: WED-THUR, SAT-SUN: 7-3:30
CREDIT CARDS: VARIES WITH VENDOR

Santa Fe Springs Swapmeet has a little bit of everything. There are over 800 vendors selling a vast array of merchandise from antiques to clothing at discount prices. Spend a little and get a lot while shopping at the Santa Fe Springs Swapmeet. There's an entrance fee of 50¢ on Wednesday, 75¢ on weekends and it's FREE on Thursday.

VALLEY INDOOR SWAPMEET**
14650 Parthenia St.
Van Nuys, CA 91402
818/892-0183

HOURS: FRI-SUN: 10-6
CREDIT CARDS: VARIES WITH VENDOR

As the name implies, the Valley Indoor Swap Meet is located inside; it's air conditioned during the summer and protected from the elements during the winter. This makes shopping a definite pleasure. Each location features a huge array of top-quality goods such as clothes, jewelry, plants, art, antiques and more. Vendors sell merchandise for 20 to 50% off retail. If you bring along your BUYING RETAIL IS STUPID discount coupon, you'll get FREE admission on any Friday, at either of their locations!

Additional Locations: Canoga Park–6701 Variel Ave., 818/340-9120

ELECTRONICS

∞ ENTERTAINMENT & COMMUNICATION ∞

ABC PREMIUMS
7266 Beverly Blvd.
Los Angeles, CA 90036
213/938-2724

HOURS: MON-FRI: 10-7   SAT: 10-7   SUN: 11-5
CREDIT CARDS: MC, V ($10 MINIMUM PURCHASE)

This discount house has been delighting knowledgeable shoppers in the Los Angeles area for more than 10 years with very low prices on all the top name brands in televisions, stereos, video sets, household items, appliances and so much more. It's worth a visit because you will find plenty of bargains, and they guarantee the lowest prices.

AHEAD STEREO
7426 Beverly Blvd.
Los Angeles, CA 90036
213/931-8873

HOURS: MON-FRI: 11-7   SAT: 10-6
CREDIT CARDS: MC, V

Here are discount prices for home stereo systems with personalized service, in a store that stocks everything. Their inventory includes names such as Technics, Kenwood, ADCOM, and lots more. "We dare you to beat our prices," they say. You'll appreciate the full service provided by the nice sales staff. All of this, and they guarantee the best price, too.

BEL AIR CAMERA, AUDIO & VIDEO
1025 Westwood Blvd.
Los Angeles, CA 90024
310/208-5150

HOURS: MON-FRI: 9-6   SAT: 9:30-6
CREDIT CARDS: MC, V

Bel Air is one of the largest camera, audio, and video stores on the West Coast. They offer cameras and camera accessories, video cameras, audio components, tape recorders, televisions, enlargers and more. Two or three times a year, they have a large Expo & Sale where representatives from over 40 companies show their products. Shows are usually in May or December, but you can get the above items daily at 10% above their

ELECTRONICS

cost. They have Nikon, Minolta, Pentax, Vivitar, Panasonic, Olympus, Sony, Speedotron, Hasselblad and others. Feel free to write a check or charge your purchases at Bel Air, but you'll save more paying with cash.

DISCOUNT SALES
2253 S. Sepulveda Blvd.
West Los Angeles, CA 90064
310/473-5015
HOURS: MON-FRI: 10-7   SAT: 10-6   SUN: 11-5
CREDIT CARDS: MC, V

Discount Sales has to be visited to be believed. You pay prices that are generally just 8 to 10% above cost and you get top brands in microwave ovens, ceiling fans, stereos, television sets, VCRs and camcorders. They buy in huge quantities for all eight of their stores and sell in volume. Announcements are sent out to their customers when they have clearance sales on floor stock, so be sure to get on their mailing list.
Additional Locations: 7 other stores throughout S. CA

HOLLYTRON
4641 W. Santa Monica Blvd.
Los Angeles, CA 90029
213/668-1800
HOURS: MON-FRI: 11-9   SAT: 10-9   SUN: 11-8
CREDIT CARDS: MC, V

You will find a visit to Hollytron to be worthwhile because of their low prices on brand-name televisions, radios, and cameras. There are two technicians on staff to service and repair things, often while you wait.
Additional Locations:
Westminster–6741 Westminster Ave., 714/895-0075

INTERSPACE ELECTRONICS, INC.
10854 Washington Blvd.
Culver City, CA 90232
310/836-6018
HOURS: MON-FRI: 10-5   SAT: 10-3
CREDIT CARDS: MC, V

At Interspace Electronics you can save from 20 to 50% off retail prices on communications equipment, citizen band radios, scanners, auto alarms, flashlights, regular and cordless telephones, answering machines, and even radar detectors. While we haven't begun to name everything they carry, we're sure you get the idea.

L. A. TRONICS
17921 Ventura Blvd.
Encino, CA 91316
818/344-4104

HOURS: MON-FRI: 10-9 SAT-SUN: 10-6
CREDIT CARDS: AE, MC, V

L. A. Tronics has a wide variety of major brand consumer electronics. The overall concept is "guaranteed lowest price." They will meet or beat any price in Los Angeles County, subject to verification. Paying basically 10% over cost, you can get TVs, radios, VCRs, stereos, cameras, small appliances, mobile phones, batteries, and even beauty appliances.
Additional Locations:
Huntington Beach–9901 Adams Ave. (@ Brookhurst), 714/964-4400
Pasadena–3660 E. Foothill (@ Rosemead), 818/577-4444
Torrance–22724 Hawthorne Blvd., 310/373-2020)
West Hills–6751 Fallbrook Ave. (@Vanowen), 818/716-8111
West Los Angeles–12121 Pico Blvd. (@ Bundy), 310/820-8444

MIKO PHOTO-AUDIO-VIDEO CENTER
1259 3rd Street Promenade
Santa Monica, CA 90401
310/393-9371

HOURS: MON-THUR: 9-6 FRI: 9-7 SAT: 9-6 SUN: 12-4
CREDIT CARDS: AE, DISC, MC, V

Miko Photo-Audio-Video Center prides itself in its high repeat customer business, so you know they are doing something right. They have everything for your home entertainment needs. They also have cordless telephones, answeri ng machines, and video editing equipment.
Additional Locations:
Manhattan Beach–3200 Sepulveda Blvd., 310/546-5491
Santa Monica–1259 Santa Monica Place Mall, 310/395-8185

NATIONAL STEREO
6672 Hollywood Blvd.
Los Angeles, CA 90028
213/463-0772

HOURS: 10:30-8 SEVEN DAYS A WEEK
CREDIT CARDS: AE, DC, MC, V

National Stereo will meet or beat any price in town. This store is filled to the brim with a vast selection of television sets, radios, watches, the Sony Walkman, and so much more. They carry all brand names at tremendous savings. You'll like the friendly, courteous service they give their customers, too.

ELECTRONICS

OLYMPIC ELECTRONICS
6310 Hollywood Blvd.
Hollywood, CA 90028
213/467-4752

HOURS: 10-9 SEVEN DAYS A WEEK
CREDIT CARDS: MC, V

Olympic Electronics is right on the corner of Hollywood and Vine. They promise the lowest prices in the area on portable radios, cameras, and stereos for the home or car. They've got a store full of electronic wonders from all the major manufacturers, and most are priced at just 5 to 10% over cost. They are wholesale to the public, so shop here and save.

ROGERSOUND LABS
8381 Canoga Ave.
Canoga Park, CA 91304
818/882-4600

HOURS: 10-10 SEVEN DAYS A WEEK
CREDIT CARDS: AE, MC, V

Rogersound Labs carries speaker systems, audio-video components, car stereos, television sets, and much more. Their prices on such brand names as Sony, Kenwood, Yamaha, Mitsubishi, and JVC are discounted prices. You can count on finding a helpful, professional staff at any of the Rogersound Labs. By the way, the salespeople at Rogersound Labs don't work on commission. Also at the Canoga Park location is their outlet store where you'll find discontinued items at greater discounts.
Additional Locations: 10 other stores throughout S. CA

SHELLY'S STEREO HI-FI CENTER
1520 Wilshire Blvd.
Santa Monica, CA 90403
310/451-0040

HOURS: MON-WED, SAT: 10-6 THUR-FRI: 10-8
CREDIT CARDS: AE, DISC, MC, V

Owner Robert Coyle has been in business since 1964 and can save you money on quality, brand-name stereo components, plus you get old-fashioned home service for custom wiring. Shelly's has some used equipment, accepts trade-ins, and also has an excellent service department. They guarantee the best prices on their merchandise.

ELECTRONICS

SPEAKER CITY
10615 Vanowen St.
Burbank, CA 91505
818/508-1908

HOURS: MON-SAT: 10-6:30
CREDIT CARDS: MC, V OR CASH ONLY (NO CHECKS)

We have discovered a virtual candy store for speaker enthusiasts and audiophiles, filled with speakers for the home and complete sound systems for vehicles, at savings of at least 50%! All components needed to build speakers from scratch, and also complete kits for speaker systems can be found here. They do "X-overs" too. One of the great things about Speaker City is you know exactly what you are buying. The price of a speaker already built is no longer a mystery because lining the walls are the individual components that went into the speaker, along with the cost of each item. Though they only carry speakers for the home (no stereos), they do stock complete sound systems for your car (no installations). Customized speaker systems are available for both home and vehicles. Name brands include, Focal, Dynaudio, Vifa, Peerless and Pyle. If you need any technical advice, talk to Wally Noss. He's not only an expert on sound systems, he's also a professional musician.

∞ PARTS, SUPPLIES & EQUIPMENT ∞

ALL ELECTRONICS CORP.
905 S. Vermont Ave.
Los Angeles, CA 90006
213/380-8000

HOURS: MON-FRI: 9-5 SAT: 9-4
CREDIT CARDS: DISC, MC, V

This is a big surplus outlet for electronic parts and supplies. If you are handy with that sort of thing and know your way around semiconductors, relays, speakers, and transformers, you can save from 25 to 75% off retail prices on all of your purchases! As they have been in business since 1968, the folks at All Electronics Corp. know everything and have everything in their stores.

Additional Locations:
Van Nuys–6228 Sepulveda Blvd., 818/997-1806

ELECTRONICS

AMERICAN ELECTRONICS SUPPLY
1200 N. Vine St.
Hollywood, CA 90038
213/464-1144

HOURS: MON-FRI: 8:30-5:30 SAT: 8:30-5
CREDIT CARDS: MC, V

A one-of-a-kind operation! American Electronics Supply covers nearly a city block with 60 parking places available for your convenience. Known throughout the nation as the "Supermarket of Electronics", they are relied upon by both business and industry for those hard-to-get items. We won't even try listing the contents of this huge place, but rest assured, they have everything electrical that you could possibly need. Some brand names are Sony, Macintosh, RCA, Zenith, Panasonic, NAD, Revox, Teac, Electro-Voice, Bogen, Sunheiser, AKG, Neumann, University Sound plus many others. Go in; get what you want at only 20 to 40% above cost. Should you end up not buying anything, you can make your trip worthwhile by registering for a free drawing. We almost forgot to tell you about another service they offer. Are you in search of a few props for the concert scene in the latest movie you're producing? Must you have several closed circuit televisions added temporarily to your security system when Charles and Di visit next month? You can rest easy. They rent just about anything to do with electronics. For rental rates and availability, the phone number is 213/466-4321.

ASMARA OVERSEAS SHIPPERS
5568 Sepulveda Blvd.
Culver City, CA 90230
310/398-0080

HOURS: MON-FRI: 9-6 SAT: 10-6
CREDIT CARDS: MC, V

Going overseas? If you are, you should consider stopping into Asmara Overseas Shippers to make sure you have the right kind of electrical plug for your hair dryer, or the correct A/C adaptor for your camcorder's rechargeable battery-pack. If you're taking your phone with you, Asmara can sell you the right adapter(s) for the countries you will be visiting. Asmara specializes in 220 volt export products such as PAL-SCCAM TVs, VCRs, dishwashers, microwaves, food processors, juicers, coffee-makers and travel converters. With the exchange rate the way it is, you can save 50% of the cost you would pay overseas! So buy it here and take it with you. They carry such brand names as Sony, Panasonic, Frigidaire, Dirt Devil, Kenwood, Toshiba and many more.

FILAMENT PRO-AUDIO
143 E. Arrow Hwy.
San Dimas, CA 91773
714/592-2848

HOURS: MON-FRI: 9-7 SAT: 10-5
CREDIT CARDS: AE, MC, OPT, V

You won't find any musical instruments here. What you will find are over 200 lines of the best sound and lighting equipment for musicians and disc jockeys. Savings run about 35 to 40% off retail on items like P.A. speakers, amplifiers, mixers, studio monitors, recorders, and cables. In business since 1968, most of the merchandise in their 3,800 square foot showroom is for rent. They keep their inventory to a minimum, but it only takes two to three days for special orders. Brand names include J.B.L., Shure, Fostex, Numark, Soundcraft, Rane, Ampex and others.

ITC ELECTRONICS**
2772 W. Olympic Blvd.
Los Angeles, CA 90006
213/388-0621

HOURS: MON-SAT: 9-6
CREDIT CARDS: MC, V

ITC Electronics is a full line authorized distributor of electronic supplies, computer accessories, auto sound products and electronic test equipment. They also carry close-outs and special purchases. You can expect to save anywhere from 10 to 60% off retail on such brand names as Sansui, Pyle auto speakers, Fluke, Sony headphones, and Pioneer. Special pricing is available for quantity purchases and don't forget to use your BUYING RETAIL IS STUPID coupon for an extra 5% discount.
Additional Locations:
Chatsworth–9229 De Soto, 818/700-0900
Oxnard–2320 Vineyard Ave., 805/983-4115)
Torrance–20368 Hawthorne Blvd., 310/370-6211)

RADIOLAND/INGLEWOOD ELECTRONICS
4701 W. Century Blvd.
Inglewood, CA 90304
310/671-7761

HOURS: MON-FRI: 9:30-6 SAT: 9-5 SUN: 12-4
CREDIT CARDS: AE, V

Radioland/Inglewood Electronics offers discount prices on name brands every day, and you save 25 to 50% on radio and television tubes, transistors, antennas, cable TV accessories, car stereos and CB radios. They also carry radios, phonograph needles, and most other electronic parts.

ELECTRONICS

SANDY'S ELECTRONIC SUPPLY
21305 Saticoy St.
Canoga Park, CA 91303
818/346-8353

HOURS: MON-FRI: 8-6 SAT: 9-6
CREDIT CARDS: MC, V

Want to fix your own television or radio? Go to Sandy's, one of the largest outlets in the San Fernando Valley, for all your electronic needs. They have a full line of over 1,000 different items and you'll save 20 to 50% on things like connectors, surge protectors, cables and battery back-ups. Electronic test equipment is also available.
Additional Locations:
N. Hollywood–6770 Coldwater Canyon, 818/765-8585

FOOD & BEVERAGE

∞ Bakery Goods ∞

ABC DONUTS
1528 W. Olympic Blvd.
Los Angeles, CA 90015
213/381-2328
HOURS: 24 HOURS SEVEN DAYS A WEEK
CREDIT CARDS: CASH ONLY

Just imagine, these are the people who produced and delivered 1,200 dozen donuts to the Rose Parade! So if you're having a huge party, or the local Brownie troop is coming over for donuts, don't worry; these are the people who can handle the job. Call in your order of one dozen or dozens of dozens the day before and receive wholesale pricing! They'll even deliver with a minimum order. They are also open for over-the-counter sales but at a little higher price. Christmas and New Years are the only days they are closed.

OLD COUNTRY BAKERY
4324 W. Magnolia
Burbank, CA 91505
818/841-2832
HOURS: MON-SAT: 9-5:30
CREDIT CARDS: CASH OR CHECKS ONLY

A tradition of its own, Old Country has been around for over half a century baking breads, pastries, cakes and cookies in their Kosher bakery. Everything is freshly baked, and the ones that didn't come out looking picture perfect are sold at 50% off retail, however, they taste just fine. Seniors, make sure you ask about your additional 10% savings.

Additional Locations: 9 other stores throughout S. CA

FOOD & BEVERAGE

∞ Dietetic & Bulk Foods ∞

ZOMMY'S
19836 Ventura Blvd.
Woodland Hills, CA 91364
818/346-1653
HOURS: MON-SAT: 8:30-9 SUN: 10-7
CREDIT CARDS: CASH OR CHECKS ONLY

Zommy's is one of our favorite places to shop. If you want healthy but tasty food, this is the place. They specialize in low fat, low calorie, gourmet "healthful" foods of high quality. Aside from the bakery goods and frozen desserts, just about everything is sold in bulk. There are bins filled with everything from numerous varieties of dry soup mixes, flour, legumes, spices, granola, pasta, and rice, to old fashioned candies, jelly bellys, dried fruit without sulfate, and nuts (raw, roasted, unsalted). When you see what the bulk goods cost, you'll never want to pay pre-packaged prices ever again! To give you an idea of what we mean, we bought some sugar-free taffy at 75% less per pound than what we'd paid at a local candy store. Their slogan is, "Home of the Guilt Free Sundae." We're talking about an 8 ounce hot fudge sundae with less than 80 calories. With 3,000 square feet of merchandise, they have the largest selection of sugar free, lo-cal items in the Los Angeles area. Another plus is the special attention paid to diabetics. Baked or prepared daily on the premises, their diabetic line is sugar and salt free, and very low in oil. Aside from being low in calories, their diabetic line is also kosher. Also in stock are unsalted snacks, no oil Mandel Bread, Meusalis, and freshly baked muffins with NO cholesterol, NO eggs, NO animal fats and kosher, too! Health conscious, "how to" recipes are available throughout the store. For those of you with special dietary needs, Zommy's will make special orders of delicious cakes and desserts.
Additional Locations:
Northridge–9153 Reseda Blvd., 818/349-1252

FOOD & BEVERAGE

∞ DINING DISCOUNTS ∞

ENTERTAINMENT PUBLICATIONS
818/222-4233 or 310/5595

If you enjoy dining out and saving money at the same time, Entertainment Publications has discount books featuring hundreds of two-for-one or discount offers for all types of restaurants from fine food to fast food. Many of the restaurants also offer a solo option allowing discounts when dining alone. In addition to restaurants, there are discounts on many other forms of entertainment such as theaters, hotels, bowling, special and sporting events, and various services. The Entertainment books are published yearly and are priced $30 to $40. Books are available for San Fernando/Ventura, West Los Angeles/Downtown Los Angeles, Orange County, San Gabriel/Pomona Valley, South Bay/Long Beach, San Diego, and the Inland Empire/Desert Communities.

∞ HEALTH FOODS & VITAMINS ∞

DISCOUNT HEALTH FOODS
14427-1/2 Ventura Blvd.
Sherman Oaks, CA 91423

818/995-7684

HOURS: MON-SAT: 9-8 SUN: 10-7
CREDIT CARDS: MC, V

For all of you health conscious people, which includes almost everyone living in California, you must stop by Discount Health Foods and see their display of supplements, 230 feet wide and 6 feet high. They also carry organic produce, vitamins, herbs, homeopathics and a full line of cosmetics. Savings go up to 50% off retail.

NATURE MART
2080 Hillhurst Ave.
Los Angeles, CA 90027

213/660-0052

HOURS: MON-SAT: 9-10 SUN: 9-9
CREDIT CARDS: MC, V

Fresh carrot juice and a good vegie burger always makes one feel wholesome. That's why we're happy to tell you about Nature Mart. Shop for all your vitamins, produce, grains, nuts and cosmetics at discounted prices, and then take a break at their health food restaurant. Seniors receive an additional 10% off their regular low prices.

FOOD & BEVERAGE

∞ MARKETS ∞

GRAND CENTRAL PUBLIC MARKET
317 S. Broadway
Los Angeles, CA 90013
213/624-2378
HOURS: MON-SAT: 9-6 SUN: 10-5
CREDIT CARDS: CASH ONLY*

A visit to the historic Grand Central Public Market is a shopping and cultural experience at an international level. You'll find 58 vendors (in about 80,000 square feet) providing a multitude of foods and services. Along with 9 snack bars, you'll see people selling fresh produce (99¢ will buy 8 lbs. of tomatoes, 5 lbs. of bananas or 3 lbs. of grapes), eggs, dried fruits, health foods, natural juices, nuts, bakeries, delicatessens (American, Italian, Latin American and European), poultry, seafood and hard-to-find spices and herbs. You can buy choice cuts of beef, veal and lamb as well as ethnic delicacies such as beef cheeks, brains, pig snouts and lamb heads. We said this was an experience, didn't we? The basement has a complete grocery store and the kids can watch tortillas being made at a tortilla factory located on the main floor. Other stalls provide fresh flowers, toys, sundries, fresh flowers, haircuts, and jewelry repair. Don't worry if English isn't your native tongue. More than 20 languages are spoken here including Arabic, Chinese, Japanese, Korean, Portuguese, Spanish, Tagalog, Yiddish and of course, English. Savings run about 10–40% off what you'd pay at your local grocery store. You'll need to take your own shopping bags because right now they don't have shopping carts. Porters are available for assistance if you buy in large quantities. In early 1993 they'll have an 11 story parking structure, but until then, parking is available across the street and adjacent to the market. You'll receive validation for one hour of free parking with a minimum purchase of $15. The Grand Central Public Market, opened in 1917, has never closed, not even during the Great Depression. Many of the vendors have been here for more than 40 years continuing a sense of family, tradition, quality and low prices. Wear comfortable shoes and don't forget your shopping bags.
*Some vendors accept checks.

SOUTHLAND FARMERS' MARKET ASSOCIATION
1010 S. Flower St., Room 402
Los Angeles, CA 90015
213/749-9551
HOURS: OPEN 1 DAY PER WEEK
CREDIT CARDS: CASH OR CHECKS ONLY

Markets range in size from 15 to 70 farmers and all products are sold directly by the producer, catcher or collector. Shoppers save from 20 to 30% over local markets on items including fresh fruits, fresh vegetables, nuts, eggs, honey, fish, live plants, beefalo products, dried fruits, juices, olives, dates, sprouts. The markets are open one day a week. Contact the Southland Farmers' Market Association at 213/749-9551 for hours and information regarding the market nearest you.

Additional Locations: 10 markets in S. CA–Call 213/749-9551

TRADER JOE'S
7304 Santa Monica Blvd.
West Hollywood, CA 90046
213/851-9772
HOURS: 9-9 SEVEN DAYS A WEEK
CREDIT CARDS: MC, V

If you've never visited a Trader Joe's store you're in for a treat. Trader Joe's carries a crazy combination of private and national brands of food, wine and beer at exceptionally low prices. Trader Joe's products contain no artificial colors or flavors and no additives. Many products are from Europe, South America and the Far East—so it's always an adventure shopping here. They have everyday low prices on their merchandise of unique grocery products, dried fruit, nuts, cheeses, entrees and fresh salads, dairy products, chocolates, snacks, juices, frozen foods and domestic and imported wines and beers. Get on their mailing list so you can receive free four times a year their Fearless Flyer, which is a 20 page combination of Mad Magazine and Consumer Report, with stories on over 100 products. We're sure once you visit a Trader Joe's you'll be hooked!

Additional Locations: 35 other stores throughout S. CA

∞ MEAT & SEAFOOD ∞

CAVIARTERIA INC.
247 N. Beverly Dr.
Beverly Hills, CA 90210
310/285-9773
HOURS: MON-SAT: 9-6
CREDIT CARDS: AE, MC, V

What a great name for this store! You'll find fresh and vacuum-packed caviar guaranteed to satisfy any gourmet's pallet—Beluga Malassol, American sturgeon, white fish, salmon, Caspian Beluga, Sevruga, and Imperial Beluga just to name a few—at 20 to 60% off retail prices.

HOMARUS INC.**
9340 W. Pico Blvd.
Los Angeles, CA 90035
310/273-3004
HOURS: MON-SAT: 10-5
CREDIT CARDS: MC, V

Does the thought of a toasted bagel with cream cheese, onion, capers and smoked salmon make your mouth water? Whether you're buying a slice of gravlax or several pounds, you'll save 20 to 50% off retail at Homarus. They produce everything they sell and don't use any artificial colors, additives or preservatives. In other words, everything is 100% natural. You can also save your hard earned cash on smoked trout fillets, ahi, and Norwegian salmon. Other items include chubs, white fish, cod, sturgeon, herring and caviar. They even have—believe it or not—salmon pastrami. Wait! We know you're in a hurry, but before you leave the house, cut out your BUYING RETAIL IS STUPID coupon for an extra 10% discount.

PACIFIC AMERICAN FISH CO., INC.
838 E. 6th St.
Los Angeles, CA 90021
213/623-3433
HOURS: MON-FRI: 6AM-2PM   SAT: 6AM-1PM
CREDIT CARDS: CASH ONLY

You can buy direct from one of the largest fish distributors in Southern California. Pacific American Fish Company will sell you any type of frozen or fresh fish at 10 to 25% less than supermarkets. Varieties in stock include shark, mahi mahi, orange roughy, salmon, catfish, tuna, swordfish, all sizes of shrimp, whitefish, lobsters, clams, oysters, and more. If you have a special recipe calling for some type of unusual seafood they don't usually carry, they'll do their best to locate it for you. When buying fish, you generally must buy it whole, but don't worry, a filleting service is available. The filleted price is normally 15 to 20% higher, depending on the weight loss, but you pay only for the weight of the fillets. Shopping at Pacific American Fish Co. is the easy way to catch fish!

WESTERN EXCHANGE MEAT MARKET
544 W. Arbor Vita
Inglewood, CA 90301

213/678-1872

HOURS: MON-SAT: 9-6

CREDIT CARDS: MC, V

The more you buy, the more you save, so go in with a friend or friends because there are discounts on pounds purchased. Western Exchange is your freezer order specialists selling sides of beef, hind quarters, large deli selections and fresh seafood. In business since 1956, they will fill your freezer with whatever you choose or cater a party from 10 to 500 people with personalized service.

∞ MEXICAN FOODS & PRODUCTS ∞

DOS BANDERAS
3721 E. Slauson Ave.
Maywood, CA 90270

213/589-3311

HOURS: MON-FRI: 6-2:30

CREDIT CARDS: CASH OR CHECKS ONLY

In business since the early 1980s, this family owned and operated manufacturer offers wholesale prices to the public. They specialize in handmade tamales. Yes, we said handmade. They have five different kinds—beef, pork, chicken, green chili and cheese, and sweet tamales. Other quality Mexican food is also available. All of their products are USDA inspected. You can call your order in 24 hours a day, and if no one is available you can leave your order on their machine. Buy by the case for even greater discounts.

FOOD & BEVERAGE

MONTERREY FOOD PRODUCTS
3939 Brooklyn Ave.
Los Angeles, CA 90033

213/263-2143

HOURS: MON-FRI: 8-5
CREDIT CARDS: CASH ONLY

This large warehouse of wholesale groceries and restaurant supplies specializes in Mexican foods. Even though it's a giant warehouse, 8,000 square feet, they pride themselves in personal attention to each customer. There are over 40 varieties of spices available by the pound, dry chiles, tamale steamers, Mexican grinding stones, and they can make up custom blends of spices for that special dish. They will even mail the merchandise to you. This place is a must for the Mexican gourmet!

∞ NUTS & CANDY ∞

THE CANDY FACTORY**
12510 Magnolia Blvd.
North Hollywood, CA 91607

818/766-8220

HOURS: TUES-SAT: 10-5
CREDIT CARDS: MC, V

The Candy Factory has one of the most complete inventories of candy making supplies and molds anywhere. Candy is sold by one pound packages or in bulk by the 40 and 47 pound case. They also have candy making classes and will do custom candy. You'll even find "x-rated" molds in a discreet location of the store. Name brands carried here include Merckens, Nestles, and Guittard. The Candy Factory is also a factory outlet for Sheftel's Original Products. Savings run 40% off retail on goodies like chocolate covered potato chips and pretzels. Mark your calendar for the special sales they hold in July. Take in your BUYING RETAIL IS STUPID coupon for an additional 10% discount.

CANDY STORE**
707 W. 17th St.
Long Beach, CA 90813

310/436-5106

HOURS: MON-SAT: 9-5
CREDIT CARDS: MC, V

The Candy Store carries all kinds of candy and gift items at savings of 20 to 50%. They take pride in saying that their candies are the "best in the

FOOD & BEVERAGE

U.S.A." They have sugar-free and salt-free candies, also. Name brands include Miss Saylors, Jelly Bellys and Chocolate Roses. Chocolate prices start at $2.50 a pound. Pricing for candy starts at $1.95 a pound and is sold by the piece or in unlimited pounds. Satisfy your sweet tooth and get a "sweet" deal at the same time by using your BUYING RETAIL IS STUPID coupon for an additional 10% discount!

CHRISTOPHER'S NUT CO.
14333 Calvert St.
Van Nuys, CA 91401
818/787-6303
HOURS: MON-FRI: 7-5 SAT: 9-4
CREDIT CARDS: CASH AND CHECKS ONLY

Having a party? Even if you just need something to munch on, stop by Christopher's Nut Company where you purchase all kinds of nuts, dried fruit, sugarless and regular candy, all at 35 to 55% below retail. Savings are even higher if you buy in bulk. One pound of macadamia nuts costs $6.95 here, while you might pay $12 to $14 elsewhere. They are the largest distributor for major brand nuts in Los Angeles. Some brands you might recognize are Blue Diamond, Mauna Loa and Dole. They only deal with top of the line products. You can save even more when buying in bulk. They also carry spices.

GUST PECOULAS & CO.
746 Towne Ave.
Los Angeles, CA 90021
213/627-2008
HOURS: MON-FRI: 7-4:30
CREDIT CARDS: CASH OR CHECKS ONLY

Who can resist nuts that are fresh roasted daily? A person could actually go nuts trying to make a selection from all the nuts, seeds, candy, trail mix, dried fruit, glazed fruit, chocolate coated nuts and more. If you make your own candy, you can buy several varieties of chocolate. Buy it in 10 pound blocks and you'll save even more money. Gust Picoulas & Co. has been around since 1907. Not only will you be saving 10 to 25% below retail, you will be dealing with a company that really knows their nuts.

FOOD & BEVERAGE

NUTS TO YOU
644 E. 9th St.
Los Angeles, CA 90015
213/627-8855
HOURS: MON-SAT: 8-5
CREDIT CARDS: MC, V

If you go nuts over nuts like we do, then you can really save money when you buy your nuts from Nuts To You. When we sit down to watch a football game or some other sporting event, the cashews and pecans just seem to disappear. You'll save 20 to 50% off retail prices, but you have to buy 5 pounds at a time. The good news is you can buy an assortment to get to the 5 pound minimum. Even better news is that all their nuts are roasted right on the premises. You can grind your own peanut butter, and they also have a large selection of dried fruit.

SILVER ROSES NUTS
4621 Pacific Blvd.
Vernon, CA 90058
213/581-8283
HOURS: MON-FRI: 8-4
CREDIT CARDS: CASH OR CHECKS ONLY

Imagine, 48,000 square feet of NUTS! We're referring to the kind you eat! They wholesale 20 different varieties of nuts, cashews, almonds, peanuts and sunflower seeds to name a few. Custom roasting can be requested, and they'll also ship anywhere in the world. These folks are "nutty" enough to sell their merchandise at 30% below retail.

∞ SPIRITS ∞

LIQUOR BANK & DELI
3600 Stocker
Los Angeles, CA 90008
213/296-7467
HOURS: SUN-THUR: 7-MIDNIGHT FRI-SAT: 7.-2 A.M.
CREDIT CARDS: MC, V

Looking for that special bottle of wine after 10 p.m. and hungry too? The Liquor Bank and Deli is the place for you! They have great prices on liquor and party catering. Their special kosher-style deli platters are perfect for a Saturday night poker game. Stop in weekly as there is always something on special besides the prices.

LOS ANGELES WINE CO.
4935 McConnell Ave., Unit #8
Los Angeles, CA 90066
310/306-WINE (9463)
HOURS: MON-SAT: 10-6 SUN: 12-5
CREDIT CARDS: MC, V

Los Angeles Wine Co. has cinder block walls and cement floors, but what they lack in ambiance is more than made up for in low prices. Not only will you find an incredible selection, you'll find it at 35 to 50% off retail prices! All wine is personally tasted prior to making it into their inventory. The staff is very knowledgeable, so don't hesitate to ask questions. Oenologists will appreciate the fact that these folks are the largest, single-store volume purveyor of fine wines in the state of California. Brand names include Jordan, Silver Oak, Beringer, Fetzer, Mondavi, Grgich Hills, Jadot, Kendall-Jackson and many more. They also produce a monthly newsletter announcing new items in their inventory and special purchases. Whether you are looking for a private reserve Cabernet, a vintage Port, or a wine opener, you'll find it at the right price at the Los Angeles Wine Co.

Additional Locations:
Palm Desert–72-608 El Paseo (@ Hwy. 111), #2, 619/346-1763

TOPLINE WINE & SPIRIT CO.
4718 San Fernando Rd.
Glendale, CA 91204
818/500-9670
HOURS: MON-SAT: 10-6 SUN: 12-5
CREDIT CARDS: MC, V

Do you enjoy a glass of wine or two with your evening meal? Topline Wine & Spirit Co. carries all of your favorite brand names priced at 6% above their cost. For example, Korbel Natural champagne (made in California) is $4 less here than at a discount supermarket chain. Other champagnes at low low prices include Mumm Cordon Rouge, Moet White Star, Cristal, Perrier-Jouet, and Ayala & Co. Topline also carries a wonderful selection from California wineries such as Kendall-Jackson, B.V., Opus I, Grgich Hills, Jordan, Beringer Silverado, Robert Mondavi, Sterling and many others.

FOOD & BEVERAGE

TWENTY TWENTY WINE
2020 Cotner Ave.
Los Angeles, CA 90025
310/447-2020

HOURS: MON-SAT: 10:30-6:30
CREDIT CARDS: MC, V

What's a discount wine and wine accessories company doing with a name like Twenty Twenty? Their address and their telephone are both 2020, naturally. It's also natural that you will find brand name beer, wines, wine lockers and accessories at the lowest prices possible. Twenty Twenty carries such brands as Mumms, Dom Perignon, Mouton, Roederer, Cheval Blanc and Heitz. So at your next party, when you announce, "Crystal for all!," it won't break your pocketbook! Ralph Woe says his wine lockers are the most economical in the city, at 50% savings or more! The people are friendly and knowledgeable, the surroundings warm and comfortable.

WINE CLUB
2110 E. McFadden
Santa Ana, CA 92705
800/966-5432   714/835-6485

HOURS: MON-SAT: 9-7 SUN: 12-5
CREDIT CARDS: MC, V

Wine Club has a selection of a fine wine boutique with warehouse prices. They sell all your favorite wines at 12% above cost. You'll find wine from companies such as Grgich Hills, Caymus, Chateau Mouton Rothschild, Sterling, Kenwood, Robert Mondavi, Jordan, Dom Perignon and Mumms. Get on their mailing list to receive a monthly newsletter filled with information and special purchases. You can shop at the store or have orders shipped to your home.

THE WINE HOUSE
2311 Cotner
West Los Angeles, CA 90064
310/479-3731

HOURS: MON-SAT: 10-7 SUN: 12-6
CREDIT CARDS: MC, V

You can always save 10 to 50% at the Wine House. They probably have one of the most complete selections assembled here. If it's been brewed or bottled as a wine, liquor or beer, you're almost sure to find it here. Sometimes the savings go up as high as 75 to 90%. If you are interested they'll show you wine books and tell you about wine tours. True con-

FOOD & BEVERAGE

noisseurs should inquire about the wine locker rentals available for their own precious collection of private stock. Be sure to sign up for the informative newsletter. They also have free tastings.

∞ WAREHOUSES ∞

GROCERY WAREHOUSE
3443 S. Sepulveda Blvd.
West Los Angeles, CA 90034
310/390-7857

HOURS: MON-SAT: 8AM-10PM SUN: 8AM-9 PM
CREDIT CARDS: CASH OR CHECKS ONLY

You can save 10 to 15% on your groceries by shopping at Grocery Warehouse. They've been cutting out the middle man and buying directly since 1979. This, along with low overhead (the warehouses are not fancy), enables them to pass along substantial savings to consumers. You'll find name brand products on food, produce, meat, general merchandise and liquor. They provide bags for your groceries, but they'll pay you 5¢ for every grocery bag you bring from home and use. All manufacturer coupons are accepted. The stores in Westminster and Upland are open 24 hours a day, seven days a week.
Additional Locations:
Call 310/423-3595 for one of 17 stores in S. CA

SMART & FINAL
10113 Venice Blvd.
West Los Angeles, CA 90034
310/559-1722

HOURS: MON-SAT: 7-8 SUN: 10-4
CREDIT CARDS: CASH OR CHECKS ONLY

Smart & Final is a pioneer when it comes to offering warehouse prices. You can save on groceries, frozen and deli items, janitorial supplies, coffee supplies, paper products and much more. You get warehouse prices without having to pay a membership fee. Brand names include Carnation, M & M's, Nestle, Proctor & Gamble, Heinz, Best Foots, Hormel and many more. Smart & Final caters mostly to food service businesses, schools, clubs and offices, but you don't have to own a business to take advantage of the low prices. In many cases, warehouse stores change brands and merchandise according to the best deals that are available. That's not the case at Smart & Final. You can rely on finding the same products on a regular basis.
Additional Locations: 80 other stores throughout S. CA

FOOD & BEVERAGE

WAREHOUSE FOOD MART
8035 Webb Ave.
North Hollywood, CA 91605

818/767-2234

HOURS: 8-10 SEVEN DAYS A WEEK
CREDIT CARDS: MC, V

This is a full, giant-size grocery supermarket, where you can get all your groceries and meats and save 30 to 40% on your order. Check them out for everyday savings because you'll save more than a few pennies. Since their opening in March of 1984, people have been driving miles just to grocery shop at the Warehouse Food Mart.

HOME FURNISHINGS

∞ CHINA, COOKWARE & SILVER ∞

AAA ETERNAL STAINLESS STEEL CORP.**
430 S. San Bernardino Rd.
Covina, CA 91723
818/331-7204
HOURS: MON-FRI: 9-5
CREDIT CARDS: AE, MC, V

They carry a wide variety of household and kitchenware stainless steel products, including such items as waterless cookware and china. There are between 100 to 200 different items from which to choose. Depending on the item, you can expect to save 20 to 50% below retail. Regal Products are among the many name brands represented in their inventory. Special close out items are offered at prices below the standard discounts. For any large scale buying, you can arrange to have sales people come to you. Under their lifetime guarantee policy, they will replace any defective item for the rest of your life. Make sure to use your BUYING RETAIL IS STUPID coupon and save an additional 10% on your next purchase.

ALMOST & PERFECT ENGLISH CHINA
14519 Ventura Blvd.
Sherman Oaks, CA 91403
818/905-6650
HOURS: MON-FRI: 10-5:30 SAT: 10-5 SUN: 12-4
CREDIT CARDS: MC, V

Don't let the name fool you. The Lalique, Waterford and Baccarat crystal is first quality and you save 15 to 20% off retail prices. You can save up to 80% on the English bone china because the firsts and seconds are mixed together. Frankly, the seconds are of excellent quality, and most have unnoticeable flaws. During their January and July sales, crystal is discounted an additional 5% and some china an additional 15%! Stock is on open shelves so you can pick what you want. You don't have to pay for entire place settings thus saving even more money by purchasing only the items you need. You will find Royal Doulton, Wedgewood, Toby Mugs, Coalport, and lots more. They will special order any out-of-stock item.

HOME FURNISHINGS

AVERY RESTAURANT SUPPLY
905 E. Second St.
Los Angeles, CA 90012
213/624-7832
HOURS: MON-FRI: 8-5   SAT: 8-1
CREDIT CARDS: MC, V

If you've ever been to a restaurant and saw an item you wished you could take home, chances are very good you'll find it here. Avery Restaurant Supply is a one-stop supermarket for professional chefs that is open to the public. With 30,000 square feet of showroom, the store carries absolutely everything needed for restaurants from salt shakers to glass-door refrigerators. Discounts start at about 20% below retail and usually run higher. For convenience, the store is organized into sections with aisles filled with things such as baking needs, stock pots or large serving pieces seen on restaurant buffet tables. In front of the store are sets of dishes; although you might recognize some of the patterns, there is a difference between the dishes found here and those you find in a department store. Because these dishes are made for restaurant use, they are much more durable and they are much less fragile than the ones made for home use. Consequently, they don't chip as easily. You won't find any cutesy gadgets at Avery. What you will find are high-quality durable, labor-saving functional tools of the trade that aren't usually found in gourmet shops or department stores. Give yourself plenty of time when you visit Avery because there is so much to take in. If you are passionate about cooking, you'll find this to be a chef's wonderland.

DANSK FACTORY OUTLET
2550 N. Palm Canyon Dr. (Loehmann's Plaza)
Palm Springs, CA 92662
619/320-3304
HOURS: MON-SAT: 9:30-5:30   SUN: 11-5
CREDIT CARDS: MC, V

Are you a lover of the Dansk products? The elegant simplicity of Dansk always makes a perfect wedding or anniversary gift. Now you can pay factory direct prices at their factory outlet located in Palm Springs. You will find quite a selection of merchandise in various colors and patterns.

THE DISH FACTORY
310 S. Los Angeles St.
Los Angeles, CA 90013
213/687-9500
HOURS: MON-FRI: 8:30-5 SAT: 9-4
CREDIT CARDS: MC, V (NO CHECKS)

If you have kids you should probably have dishes made for restaurants. To the unassuming eye it looks the same as "normal" dishes but in fact they're much more durable and hold up better to chipping (an absolute necessity for restaurants). You'll find stacks and stacks of dishes here in lots of bright solid colors and familiar patterns. The Dish Factory gets discontinued patterns and seconds and overruns from large manufacturers. Unfortunately, we can't name names but we can tell you that much of what you see can be found in many restaurants around town. In addition to restaurant china they also carry glasses, plastic dishes and flatware.
Additional Locations:
Colton–400 E. Valley Blvd., 714/370-4040

ENGLISH CHINA HOUSE
22776 Ventura Blvd., Unit A
Woodland Hills, CA 91364
818/340-1129
HOURS: MON-SAT: 10-6 SUN: 11-3
CREDIT CARDS: ALL MAJOR

English China House is definitely the place to go if you're in the market for Spode or Royal Worcester fine bone china. Prices run up to 75% off retail on just about everything. How do they do it? They import seconds directly from the manufacturer that—unless your eyes are better than ours—look just fine. A huge set in the Harvard pattern with place settings for 12 was priced at just above $2300. Normally, a 65-piece set for twelve would retail for about $5,400, but the price at English China house includes more than 65 pieces. The set also comes with two covered vegetable dishes, an extra vegetable dish, two extra platters, 12 demitasse and saucers, a milk jug, two bread and butter servers, a gravy boat, 12 soup plates, a sugar pot, and both a tea pot and a coffee pot. On the second level you'll find odds and ends. It's a good way to replace a broken piece or pick up a few extra dessert plates. Some of the patterns we spotted in this room were Caesar, Mandarin Gold, Vine Harvest, Howard (all colors), Ribbons and Roses, Summer Palace, and of course, Christmas Tree. If for some reason buying seconds rubs you the wrong way, they will special order first quality china for you at 20% off retail.

HOME FURNISHINGS

LUNA GARCIA
201 San Juan Ave.
Venice, CA 90291
310/396-8026

HOURS: MON-FRI: 9-5 SAT: 9-2
CREDIT CARDS: CASH OR CHECKS ONLY

You'll find Gigante pottery by Luna Garcia at 50% less than what pricey gourmet and specialty stores around the U.S.A. and Europe charge. For the most part, the merchandise consists of seconds from the studio. This over-sized dinnerware has a matte glaze finish and is available in green, raspberry, blue, black, ochre and cobalt. In addition to dishes, you'll also find platters, large bowls, and other various serving pieces. They recently added a small rectangular planter that matches the dishes. It's suitable for a window sill, or it can be used as a centerpiece.

MIKASA FACTORY OUTLET
20642 S. Fordyce Ave.
Carson, CA 90749
310/537-9344

HOURS: MON-WED, SAT: 9-5 THUR: 9-7 FRI: 9-8 SUN: 12-5
CREDIT CARDS: MC, V

The Mikasa Factory Store isn't just for discontinued patterns. They have over 25,000 square feet of floor space, with more than 200 patterns in stock. You can buy new and discontinued patterns at 30 to 70% below retail prices. They carry china, crystal, flatware, stemware, gifts, candles, and table linens in a variety of brand names. Mikasa, Studio Nova, Home Beautiful, and Christopher Stuart are just a few of the manufacturers found here. They're close to the 710, 91, and 405 freeways. You can place special orders, and shipping is available for a nominal fee.
Additional Locations:
Palm Springs–2500 N. Palm Canyon Dr., 619/778-1080
San Diego–4410 Camino de la Paz, 619/428-2022

MUNN'S SILVER SHOP
209 W. Wilson
Glendale, CA 91203
818/241-2776, 818/241-1909

HOURS: TUES-SAT: 10-5:30
CREDIT CARDS: MC, V

What we have here is silver flatware, plated flatware, and silver hollowware at an unbelievable 15% over cost. They are a franchise dealer of Gorham, International Kirk-Stieff, Lunt, Reed & Barton, Towle, and

Wallace. If you already know what you want, go in and have them order it for you. This is also a great place for hard-to-find replacements of discontinued patterns.

POTTERY RANCH, INC.
248 W. Huntington Dr.
Monrovia, CA 91016
818/358-1215

HOURS: MON-SAT: 9-6 SUN: 10-6
CREDIT CARDS: MC, V

You'll find everything you need for your table at the Pottery Ranch in Monrovia. Dinnerware, gardenware, glassware, baskets, silk and dried flowers, and ceramic giftware are all sold here at discounts averaging 20% or more. They have a bridal registry, and specials are run all year. Brand names carried include Mikasa, Noritake, Houtake, and Sango. They're nice people with good buys.

∞ DECORATOR ITEMS ∞

THE 2NDS SHOP**
1975 S. Sepulveda Blvd.
Los Angeles, CA 90025
310/477-7229

HOURS: MON-FRI: 10-5 SAT: 9-5
CREDIT CARDS: MC, V

You'll find outstanding buys at The 2nds Shop which carries all seconds from the manufacturer of Los Angeles Pottery. There is always a vast array of glazed ceramics for your home and kitchen. Most merchandise is priced at or below wholesale, with even bigger savings in the Bargain Room. They have a potpourri of decorator merchandise. Perfect for gift giving, these various items are made of brass, silver, glass, wood, crystal, and more. Some of the items are duplicates that were on display at the LA Mart. For even greater savings make use of your 15% BUYING RETAIL IS STUPID coupon.

HOME FURNISHINGS

CHAMPAGNE TASTE
4352 S. Sepulveda Blvd.
Culver City, CA 90230
310/572-6037

HOURS: MON-SAT: 10-5
CREDIT CARDS: DISC, MC, V

Champagne Taste carries a potpourri of crystal, glassware, oven accessories, collector's dolls, vases, baskets and pewter figures in their 4,000 square foot store. You'll find you can do your shopping here for nearly any occasion. The nice part about it is you can show off your champagne taste even though you're paying beer-budget prices. Prices range from 25%-75% of what department store's charge retail. During November and December they are open on Sunday 11 a.m. to 4 p.m.

CRAFTERS OUTLET
6445 Desoto Ave.
Woodland Hills, CA 91367
818/347-2900

HOURS: MON-SAT: 10-7 SUN: 11-5
CREDIT CARDS: MC, V

If you love handmade crafts but don't have the time to make them, stop by Crafters Outlet where there are over 300 crafter booths. You'll save 30-60% off retail prices when you buy direct from Crafters Outlet, and the variety is endless. For the holidays, you'll love the choices of handmade wreaths. Or how about imagining you live on a farm by purchasing a barnyard wood animal for your front lawn. Other handmade items you'll find are wood toys, rag dolls, dried flower arrangements, hand-painted children and women's clothes, quilts, jewelry, gift baskets, hair accessories and much more.

EUROGIFT**
848 La Cienega Blvd., Suite 201 (Cienega Center)
Los Angeles, CA 90069
310/652-8850

HOURS: THUR-SAT: 10-6
CREDIT CARDS: MC, V

Do you love Lalique and Baccarat but hate the prices? Eurogift has these brands and more priced at a minimum of 20% below retail. You'll see classic pieces from Lalique such as a Champs Elysse centerpiece or Bacchantes vase. If you've been looking for Baccarat's Neptune vase, you'll see them in three sizes and in three colors (clear, cobalt blue and amethyst). For those of you looking for something on which to display special pieces, Eurogift carries acrylic bases like those you see in jewelry

- 216 -

store windows. The bases come in a large variety of sizes and are available either in clear or black with clear or frosted edges. Crystal isn't the only thing you'll find here. They also discount Mont Blanc and Waterman pens. The staff is always on the lookout for super deals and they spend a lot of time scouting in Europe. This means you not only get terrific prices, but you are in for a surprise every time you visit the store. You'll receive an extra 5% discount when you use your BUYING RETAIL IS STUPID coupon. The coupon is limited to in-stock, nonsale items only.

FAUX ART**
7201 Melrose Ave., Suite E
Los Angeles, CA 90069
213/930-0441
HOURS: FRI: 2-6 SAT: 1-5:30
CREDIT CARDS: AE, MC, V

When you have a particular decorating item in mind, do you go from store to store in search of a color or colors to fit into your decorating scheme? You'll find Faux Art is a store full of interesting items priced 5 to 15% above cost. Instead of paying several hundred dollars at a department store for a large vase to fill a corner, you can buy one here for under $50 in any color or colors you want. They can customize the color and finish to suit your needs. Express your creativity with all kinds of bases (columns, animals, shells and wedges) with which you can create coffee, end, sofa and dining-room tables, depending on the height of the base. Animals have been standard decorating items for years and you'll find lots of them here. Chances are you may find what you're looking for already on the floor, but if you don't find the perfect color match, you can pick from their dye-lot selection of 15 colors. You can go with a single color or select two or three colors for what is called a fantasy finish. A pastel wash will give you a Southwestern look, and solid colors in a matte or gloss finish lean toward a modern look. The faux stone comes in black, gray, white or pink. This is also a great place to buy beveled or non-beveled replacement glass. You'll save an extra 10% discount when you use your BUYING RETAIL IS STUPID coupon.

Additional Locations:
Palm Springs-376 N. Palm Canyon, 619/327-0697
Studio City-12238 Ventura Blvd., 818/753-8012

HOME FURNISHINGS

THE GIFT CORNER
2575 Pacific Coast Hwy.
Torrance, CA 90505
310/539-5011

HOURS: MON-SAT: 10-6 SUN: 12-5
CREDIT CARDS: AE, MC, V

For a unique selection of better quality collectibles and giftware, try The Gift Corner. You will see such brand names as Waterford, Goebel and Baccarat, all at 10 to 20% savings. They also have a great selection of dolls such as Effanbee at 40% off retail. Later in the year, The Gift Corner turns itself into a Christmas store full of wonderful gift ideas to go under the tree. Make sure to call them in February and August to find out about their sidewalk sales for even greater savings.

THE GLASS GARAGE
414 N. Robertson Blvd.
Los Angeles, CA 90048
310/659-5228

HOURS: MON-SAT: 10:30-6:30 SUN: 12-6
CREDIT CARDS: MC, V

The Glass Garage is a low-price interior decorator outlet which is open to the public. They offer a variety of crystal vases, in every size and color, to suit any color scheme. There is a wide selection of silk flowers and a resident silk floral designer who can arrange your flowers just the way you'd like. They stock an impressive collection of barware, stemware, candles, oil lamps and other decorator items. Shoppers can expect to save 30-70% on favorite brands such as Mikasa, Colony, Toscany, Sven Jensen and Krosno. Baccarat is also offered at lower than usual prices.

ISLAND PRODUCTS DISTRIBUTING
3311 W. MacArthur Blvd.
Santa Ana, CA 92704
714/540-6597

HOURS: MON-FRI: 9:30-5
CREDIT CARDS: CASH OR CHECKS ONLY

Get ready for a real treat. Eli Coloma, owner of Island Products, has handmade rattan from the Philippines and China, plus lots of rustic baskets too. You can shop in his 13,000 square foot warehouse in Santa Ana, which is open to the public, but the best buys to be had are found at the Orange County Swapmeet on weekends. Eli says when you get there to ask anyone who works there, "Where's the crazy Filipino?" Eli offers an early bird special at the swapmeet. From 7-9:30 a.m. you get an additional 15% off his regular 35-50% below retail prices. From 10-11 a.m.

you get an additional 10% discount. However, there's one hitch! If you don't remember to ask for the discount before you pay for the merchandise, it's sorry Charlie! As an added bonus, no matter what time it is at the swapmeet, if you are pregnant and showing or wearing "color-of-the-day" pants (this includes men), Eli will give you an additional 15% discount but you have to bring it up before money changes hands. No one said this would be easy. Island Products also extends a 15% discount to those of you in the military. You can also find Island Products at the swapmeet held at Golden West College in Huntington Beach.

MAINLY SECONDS–POTTERY, PLANTS & THINGS
12144 Magnolia Blvd.
North Hollywood, CA 91607
818/985-4499

HOURS: MON-FRI: 9-9 SAT-SUN: 9-6
CREDIT CARDS: MC, V

If you're looking for those room accessories that make your house a home, that displays your personality, then this is where you need to shop. Mainly Seconds carries pottery (clay, stoneware, ceramic), baskets, indoor plants, plant foods, potting soils, cacti, silk flowers, vases, dried flowers, macrame, and wrought iron at 40–60% below retail. Each of their locations has over 6,000 square feet always stuffed with goodies.
Additional Locations:
Buena Park–4562 Beach Blvd., 714/994-0540
Costa Mesa–1785 Newport Blvd., 714/548-7710

MIJANOU'S SILK DESIGNS**
718 E. Imperial Hwy.
Brea, CA 92621
714/990-3601

HOURS: MON-SAT: 9-6
CREDIT CARDS: MC, V

Mijanou's is a place that specializes in silk designs. They buy in quantity and pass the savings on to their very satisfied customers. Everything you need in silk greenery, trees, and flowers can be found here for only 15% above cost. They also carry floral supplies, vases, baskets, and brass. If you are a lover of silk arrangements, you'll find them here. Should you want to design your own arrangement, free consultation is available. In addition, Mijanou's makes certain they not only have a great selection of variety and color, but also take pride in stocking the unusual. Make certain you take your BUYING RETAIL IS STUPID coupon with you for an additional 5% discount.

HOME FURNISHINGS

POTTERY AND FLORAL WORLD**
3352 San Fernando Rd.
Los Angeles, CA 90065
213/254-5281

HOURS: 8:30-7 SEVEN DAYS A WEEK
CREDIT CARDS: MC, V

Pottery and Floral World has one of the West Coast's largest selections of pots, pottery, dried and silk flowers, and all the accessories that go along with them. Macrame supplies, gourmet ware, baskets and wrought iron products can also be found here. They are both a factory outlet and a direct importer, so you can expect discounts of 20 to 50% off retail prices found elsewhere. Close-outs occur weekly, so you always find a changing inventory. If you're looking for Christmas decorations, they carry a complete line. You'll get an additional 10% off your purchase price when you use your BUYING RETAIL IS STUPID Coupon.

SILK WAREHOUSE**
7651 Sepulveda Blvd.
Van Nuys, CA 91405
818/988-5970

HOURS: MON-SAT: 10-6   SUN: 10-5
CREDIT CARDS: MC, V

Savings run 20 to 40% off retail at Silk Warehouse on single stems or ready-made trees and arrangements. With 20,000 square feet of silk flowers and foliage, you can design away to your heart's content. For a minimal fee they offer classes on flower arranging. After completion of a class, you'll receive a card for a 15% discount on silk flowers and supplies. There is always a sales corner filled with super discounted items too. Take in your BUYING RETAIL IS STUPID coupon and you'll receive an extra 20% discount on nonsale items only.

VALLEY CLOCK SERVICE**
5608 Van Nuys Blvd.
Van Nuys, CA 91401
818/785-8511

HOURS: MON-SAT: 9-5
CREDIT CARDS: AE, DISC, MC, V

If it's time for a new clock, Valley Clock Service has a large selection priced 20 to 50% off retail every day of the year. Brand names include Howard Miller, Black Forest Cuckoos, Baldwin, Seiko, Bulova, Ansonia, Schatz, San Francisco, Heritage Heirlooms and many more. In business since since 1954, the owner is the third generation of clockmakers in the family. They offer factory authorized service for all manufacturers with free exchanges, delivery, set-up and a three year guarantee of grandfather clocks. If you have a favorite clock that isn't working, you can use your BUYING RETAIL IS STUPID coupon for a 10% discount on repairs.

WORLD OF PLANTS AND GIFTS**
2485 Lincoln Blvd.
Venice, CA 90291
310/823-3883

HOURS: MON-FRI: 9-7 SAT-SUN: 9-6
CREDIT CARDS: AE, DISC, MC, V

Beautiful fresh cut flowers, indoor plants, trees, baskets, macrame, pottery, flowering plants, plant stands and framed prints, are all available at discount prices. Their plants are purchased directly from growers in San Diego, so they can offer the best prices and a wide selection. If you use your BUYING RETAIL IS STUPID coupon with your purchase, your discount blossoms an additional 10%.

∞ **FURNITURE** ∞

– BEDROOM –

A-1 FURNITURE OUTLET**
6002 S. Broadway
Los Angeles, CA 90003
213/758-3963

HOURS: BY APPOINTMENT ONLY, MON-FRI: 10:30-5
CREDIT CARDS: CASH OR CHECKS ONLY

On their showroom floor are at least 100 bedroom sets, and 100 mattress and box spring sets. On top of that, they also carry living room furniture, dining room sets, dinette sets, occasional tables and much more. Many different brands are represented and they encourage customers to first check prices elsewhere. After you've decided what you want, take the brand name and model number to A-1 Furniture Outlet where you can get values as low as 10% over cost. They're open to the public by appointment only, so remember to check out the other stores before giving them a call. Remember to use your BUYING RETAIL IS STUPID coupon and you'll receive an additional 10% discount.

HOME FURNISHINGS

ALL BED & MATTRESS**
5711 Sepulveda Blvd.
Van Nuys, CA 91411
818/989-5006
HOURS: MON-SAT: 10-5   SUN: 12-5
CREDIT CARDS: AE, DISC, MC, V

All Bed & Mattress carries a vast selection of brass beds, daybeds, mattresses, and white iron beds. Because they are the manufacturer, they are able to do custom orders, refinish all brass items and do repairs in just two weeks or less! In addition to their own brand you'll find such names here as Elliotts Designs, Diamond, Restonic and Flamingo. Prices run 30-40% off retail. You can use your new mattress to hide the money you save because All Bed & Mattress will take an additional 10% off the purchase price when you present your BUYING RETAIL IS STUPID coupon.
Additional Locations: Agoura–29025 Canwood, 818/706-1202

ALPERT'S BEDROOM CITY WAREHOUSE**
7631 Canoga Ave.
Canoga Park, CA 91304
818/888-5060
HOURS: MON-FRI: 10-8   SAT: 10-6   SUN: 11-5
CREDIT CARDS: AE, DISC, MC, V

Alpert's has been selling at discount prices since 1962. They stock a large selection of bedroom furniture, specializing in solid oak products, wall units, waterbeds, flotation units, four poster beds, canopy beds, innerspring mattresses; also, contemporary lacquer upholstered beds, futons, air beds, foam beds, and youth furniture such as chest beds, and bunk beds. Everyday discounts range from 18–55% off original prices with a 30 day price guarantee. Major brands include Simmons, Beautyrest, Sealy, Somma, Sunbeam (waterbed heaters) and many others. The Canoga Park store covers 13,000 square feet of every type of sleeping surface imaginable. (Their two other locations aren't quite as large, but you'll still find a terrific selection.) With such large inventories, most items are available for delivery within 24 hours. You'll save an additional 5% when you use your BUYING RETAIL IS STUPID coupon.
Additional Locations:
Oxnard–1741-B East Ventura Blvd., 805/988-1340
Thousand Oaks–1460 Moorpark, 805/497-4529

HOME FURNISHINGS

BED BROKER**
300 E. Orangethorpe
Placentia, CA 92670
714/993-9953

HOURS: MON-FRI: 10-8 SAT: 10-6 SUN: 12-5
CREDIT CARDS: DISC, MC, V

Having almost 8,000 square feet of showroom, with a warehouse on the premises, makes them the largest bedroom furniture store in Orange County. Over 50 mattresses are on display with 22 different manufacturers from which to choose. They have 60 white iron and brass beds displayed and a selection of over 600. There are over 45 day beds and bunk beds with more than 400 from which to choose. Most major brands are available, including Sealy, Aireloom, Stearns & Foster, Concorde, Lady Americana, Tempo and many more. The Bed Broker offers savings of 50 to 70% off list price and guarantees lowest prices. They advertise "never undersold" and emphasize quality and courtesy as much as price. Don't forget to use your BUYING RETAIL IS STUPID coupon for an additional 5% savings.

BEDS UNLIMITED**
21505 Sherman Way
Canoga Park, CA 91303
818/702-9999

HOURS: 10-6 SEVEN DAYS A WEEK
CREDIT CARDS: DISC, MC, V

Beds Unlimited, in business since 1984, features beds, daybeds futons and frames at 40-60% off retail. They buy in huge quantities and pass the savings on to their customers. The showroom is a block wide and features brands such as Serta, Spring Air, Corsican, Swan Brass, Raymond Oak, Tempo and Americana. Their electric beds by Spring Air and Sleeper Lounge are discounted 20%. If you mention you found them in BUYING RETAIL IS STUPID you will receive free delivery and set-up on any bed purchased. You'll also receive a free decorator pillow when you buy any day bed comforter set. And if that isn't enough, you can use your BUYING RETAIL IS STUPID coupon for an extra 5% discount.

BRASS BEDS DIRECT
4866 W. Jefferson Blvd.
Los Angeles, CA 90016
213/737-6865

HOURS: MON-SAT: 10-5
CREDIT CARDS: AE, DISC, MC, V

Brass Bed Direct offers the highest quality of brass beds and accessories available at 65% off retail prices. Call and inquire about specific items. Layaway and financing plans are available.

ELECTROPEDIC ADJUSTABLE BEDS
15600 Roscoe Blvd.
Van Nuys, CA 91406
818/909-0077

HOURS: MON-SAT: 10-4 SUN: 12-4
CREDIT CARDS: AE, MC, V

When one of our husbands unfortunately threw his back out while playing paddle tennis, we decided an electric bed was one of the answers for a quick recovery. And it was. Electropedic Adjustable Beds is a factory outlet and sells these comfortable beds at savings of 40 to 50% off retail. The beds are available in twin, full, queen, king, dual queen, and dual king.

F B WATERBEDS
6311 Laurel Canyon Blvd.
North Hollywood, CA 91606
818/763-5586

HOURS: MON-FRI: 11:30-7:30 SAT: 11:30-7 SUN: 11-6
CREDIT CARDS: AE, MC, V

Looking for a change from your standard sleeping mattress? F B Waterbeds says, "Shop us last.you'll be glad you did." They claim to have the best prices on waterbeds, airbeds and floatation beds, along with a complete selection of frames, heaters, linens, bedroom furniture and all accessories at 40 to 70% off. They also run terrific specials on their demos. Financing is available.

MATTRESS OUTLET
38747 Sierra Hwy.
Palmdale, CA 93550
805/267-6332

HOURS: MON-FRI: 11-6   SAT: 10-5   SUN: 12-5
CREDIT CARDS: AE, MC, V

You can save 30-50% buying your new mattress here. As a manufacturer, you can order a custom mattress and actually watch them make it. Delivery is free anywhere in Los Angeles county, and it's possible you can sleep on your new ready-made mattress the same day you buy it. Children get free balloons on weekends and if you mention BUYING RETAIL IS STUPID you'll receive a free t-shirt.

MATTRESS WAREHOUSE**
4825 W. Rosecrans
Hawthorne, CA 90250
310/675-5400

HOURS: MON-FRI: 10-6   SAT: 10-5
CREDIT CARDS: MC, V

The Mattress Warehouse carries name brand mattresses and box springs in all sizes. They also carry bed frames, brass beds, headboards, and mattress covers. All of this at 40–50% off retail! They have quality merchandise and pass on the manufacturer's warranty. Look for extra savings on factory overruns and cancellations on beds with department store labels. If your purchase totals $250 or more you'll get a free bed frame and free delivery by using your BUYING RETAIL IS STUPID coupon.

RICHARD PRATT'S MATTRESS WAREHOUSE
18717 Parthenia St.
Northridge, CA 91324
818/349-8118

HOURS: MON-FRI: 9-8   SAT-SUN: 9-6
CREDIT CARDS: MC, V

Why pay department store prices when you can buy at Richard Pratt's? They carry King Koil, Aireloom, Serta, Sealy, Englander, and more. You can get all sizes and models, from twin sized to California king. Buying up what others can't sell results in savings for their customers of 30 to 70% off retail. You're likely recognize department store labels on many of their beds. Also to be found are barely used mattresses bought from stores that offer a trial period to their customers. These beds were either too hard, too soft or too something and were returned. We'll bet the store owners hate seeing Goldilocks pulling up to their store front.

HOME FURNISHINGS

RTC MATTRESS WAREHOUSE
5142 Clareton Dr., Unit 140
Agoura, CA 91301
818/991-5868

HOURS: MON-FRI: 10-6 SAT: 10-6 SUN: 11-5
CREDIT CARDS: DISC, MC, V

You'll save 15 to 40% off retail prices when you shop at RTC Mattress Warehouse for Simmons, Beautyrest, Maxipedic, Bassett, or Stearns & Foster. Savings are even higher on mismatched mattress sets The motto here is, "Who cares if the covers don't match?" They offer same-day, local delivery and will even haul your old mattress away. All sizes of mattress sets are available, plus trundle beds, roll-aways and bed frames.
Additional Locations:
San Marcos–947 Rancheros Dr., 619/746-7447

SIT'N SLEEP
3880 & 3824 Culver Center
Culver City, CA 90230
310/842-6850

HOURS: MON, FRI: 10-8 TUES-THUR, SAT: 10-6 SUN: 11-5
CREDIT CARDS: AE, MC, V

You'll find 20 to 40% savings off manufacturer list prices here. Sit'n Sleep carries name-brand mattress sets in all sizes and firmnesses. They stock the largest selection of futons and futon frames in Los Angeles, at guaranteed best prices. Sofa beds, platform beds, oak wall units, bedroom sets and more, are available. They offer a 30 day price guarantee and a 30 night sleep trial. The 500 mattresses they have in stock means, "Buy it today and try it tonight." You'll also enjoy the pleasant staff.

UNDERWOOD MATTRESS FACTORY
16310 Hawthorne Blvd.
Lawndale, CA 90260
310/370-1918

HOURS: MON-TUES & FRI: 9-5 WED-THUR: 9-7 SAT: 10-5
CREDIT CARDS: ALL MAJOR

Underwood Mattress Factory has been manufacturing mattresses and box springs since 1952. They carry only their own brand of quality mattress sets and savings run 30 to 40% off comparable brands. The factory, where they also do repairs and rebuild beds, is located behind the showroom. If you've been searching high and low for an odd-sized mattress for your antique bed frame, this is where to go. Underwood Mattress Factory can customize a mattress set no matter how large or small.

HOME FURNISHINGS

VALLEY MATTRESS & BUNK BED CENTER**
15015 Keswick
Van Nuys, CA 91405
818/765-6451, 213/873-4004

HOURS: MON-FRI: 9-7 SAT: 9-5 SUN: 12-5
CREDIT CARDS: DISC, MC, V

With a motto like "Comfort is our most important product," you know you'll be taken care of at Valley Mattress & Bunk Bed Center. Selling at "warehouse to you" prices, they have a large selection of space saving children's bedroom furniture and over 50 bunk beds on display in their 5,000 square foot store. Some of their more unusual styles are hard-to-find space-savers, trundle bunks that sleep three, chest bunks that include 9 drawers of storage, and study centers with a loft bed, desk and chest. Try out their space shuttle and fire engine bunks. Make sure to bring in your BUYING RETAIL IS STUPID coupon for an additional 5% discount.

WHOLESALE MATTRESS DISTRIBUTOR
44738 Sierra Hwy.
Lancaster, CA 93534
805/948-9906

HOURS: MON-FRI: 10-6 SAT: 10-5 SUN: 12-4
CREDIT CARDS: MC, V

Whatever type of bed you need is available here at 20 to 50% off retail. They have mattresses, corner groups, electric beds as well as headboards and footboards in iron and brass. Brand names include Sealy, Serta, and Americana Brass Beds. They have a price guarantee; if you find the same item advertised for less, they'll refund the difference. Delivery is available and they'll haul away your old mattress at the same time.

WOODEN SHIPS WATERBED DISCOUNT WAREHOUSE
2933 University Ave.
Riverside, CA 92507
714/781-8112

HOURS: MON-SAT: 9-6
CREDIT CARDS: AE, DISC, MC, V

Bargain hunters paradise is the nickname they give to Wooden Ships Waterbed Discount Warehouse. Riverside's oldest waterbed store features factory close-outs and damaged goods at huge savings from their retail store. A waterbed priced at $499 (a 10-30% discount) at their retail store sold for $250 here. With about 10,000 square feet of beds, furniture and accessories, shoppers have a large variety from which to choose.
Additional Locations:
Palm Springs–2777 N. Palm Canyon Dr., 619/778-1313

WOODEN SHIPS WATERBEDS
10181 Indiana Ave.
Riverside, CA 92503
714/359-3131
HOURS: MON-FRI: 10-8 SAT: 10-6 SUN: 12-5
CREDIT CARDS: AE, DISC, MC, V

This is the retail outlet for Wooden Ships Waterbed Discount Factory Warehouse. Here you'll find downright honest salespeople who tell you like it is and won't try to sell you something you don't need. Wooden Ships wants their clients to be satisfied for life and makes sure they are. A customer, trying to decide whether to replace their waterbed at a cost of several hundred dollars or to repair it, was advised by a Wooden Ships salesperson to patch it at a cost of $10.00. They work on a lower profit margin than most waterbed stores, so you'll save 10 to 30% on your purchases. You'll find excellent buys on their waterbed accessories, too. All military people get an added 10% discount on nonsale items.

– HOME –

ADCO
818/340-9910
HOURS: BY APPOINTMENT ONLY
CREDIT CARDS: CASH OR CHECKS ONLY

Jean Chapman works on an extremely low mark-up which enables you to buy furniture, mattresses and window coverings for less than cost-plus-10%. They work completely from catalogues at ADCO (since 1955) and will even give price quotes over the phone. After you have made a decision regarding the product you want, call them with the manufacturer's name, model number of the item, and any other pertinent information. A 25% deposit is required and you can pick up the merchandise when it arrives or make arrangements for delivery.

AL'S DISCOUNT FURNITURE**
4900 Lankershim Blvd.
North Hollywood, CA 91601
818/766-4289 213/877-4783
HOURS: MON-FRI: 9-9 SAT: 9-6 SUN: 10-6
CREDIT CARDS: AE, DISC, MC, V

Al's has been in business since 1962 selling every kind of furniture and bedding for the home; top name brands included are Sealy Posturepedic, Berkline, Basset, Schweiger, Lea, Somma, Ashley, and many more. Al's claims the reason for their success and longevity is that they sell quality furniture at the lowest price in Southern California and give "full service." As a direct result of their selling philosophy, they report that over 70% of their customers are repeat or referral. Be sure to use your BUYING RETAIL IS STUPID coupon, and you'll save an additional 5%. They're awfully nice people, and knowledgeable too!

ALL IN 1 HOME FURNISHINGS**
382 N. Allen Ave.
Pasadena, CA 91106
818/795-1143   213/681-1476

HOURS: TUES-FRI: 10-6   SAT: 10-5
CREDIT CARDS: MC, V

If you already know what you want in the way of home furnishings then catalogue purchasing is a great way to save money. All in 1 Home Furnishings sells everything you need in the way of furniture at about 35% below retail. Window coverings are discounted 50-75% and wall coverings 30%. Brand names include Stanley, Lane, Sealy, Serta, Universal, Parkview and many more. All you have to do is give them the brand name and model number of the item you want. If you pay by cash or check you can use your BUYING RETAIL IS STUPID coupon for an extra 5% discount.
Additional Locations:
Lomita–2041A Pacific Coast Hwy., 310/539-4002

ANGELUS HOME CENTER
3650 E. Olympic Blvd.
Los Angeles, CA 90023
213/268-5171

HOURS: WED-SUN: 10-6
CREDIT CARDS: MC, V

In June of 1991, Angelus Furniture Warehouse closed their business after 63 years of service to the community. The recession hit the entire furniture industry unusually hard and Angelus was no exception. Now they are back as Angelus Home Center, offering larger discounts than before. They have reopened their business on a more modest scale and are activating new plans for their giant 385,000 square foot warehouse, which will include an entire complex of discount stores. The complex will be ready to open around April of 1993 In the meantime, they have relocated Angelus Home Center to the second floor and are still offering top quality name brand furnishings at discount prices.

BYRNE HOME FURNISHINGS
3516 W. Magnolia Blvd.
Burbank, CA 91505
818/845-0808

HOURS: MON-SAT: 9-5
CREDIT CARDS: MC, V

Located in Burbank, Byrne Home Furnishings' showroom is 7,000 square feet of displays in room like settings. Feast your eyes on many beautiful and unique decorator items including antiques, mirrors, clocks, lamps and many samples from the various manufacturers that are available at a 25-40% savings below retail prices. Thomasville, Century, Henredon, Aireloom, Simmons, Stiffel, Lane, and Stanley are a few of the many quality brand names they carry. Find out about their floor sample sale held in the month of January.

COLORMART FURNITURE
1207 N. Western Ave.
Hollywood, CA 90029
213/464-3397

HOURS: MON-SAT: 8-6 SUN: 10-6
CREDIT CARDS: MC, V

Dealing in upholstered furniture they manufacture themselves, Colormart has prices that are easily affordable. You can save up to 80% off retail. Customers get a variety of styles and fabrics to choose from in sofas, sofa beds, playpens and/or conversations pits, and side or occasional chairs. Their other stores are called Sofa U Love.

Additional Locations:
City of Industry–17733 Gale Ave., 818/913-1172
Glendale–333 W. Broadway, 818/545-7293
Lawndale–4537 W. Artesia, 310/370-9100
Los Angeles–5823 W. Pico Blvd., 213/936-1050
Sherman Oaks–14082 Ventura Blvd., 818/990-9721

CONSUMERS GUILD, INC.
17034 Devonshire St.
Northridge, CA 91325
818/363-3900

HOURS: MON-SAT: 10-5 SUN: 12-5
CREDIT CARDS: MC, V

Consumers Guild in Northridge has been specializing in catalogue discount sales for more than 20 years. With low overhead, no fancy showroom, no warehousing, fewer salespersons and less advertising, they are able to pass on discounts of 20 to 50% off retail to their customers on such quality brand names of furniture as Bassett, Lane, Henredon, Simmons, Sealy, Stanley, Universal and almost 200 additional manufacturers. In addition to furniture, they carry lamps and window treatments. Delivery and installation are also available.

CORY'S FURNITURE SHOWCASE**
2975 Cochran St., Unit C
Simi Valley, CA 93065
805/584-9042

HOURS: MON, FRI: 10-8   TUES-THUR, SAT: 10-6   SUN: 11-5
CREDIT CARDS: MC, V

Are you about ready for a new sofa or dining room table? You'll find brand names such as Bassett, Keller, Kincaid and many others discounted 40 to 50% off retail prices. Located in the Target shopping center, you'll find plenty of furniture for every room in your house. If you don't see anything on the floor to your liking, you can look through their catalogues. For purchases of $500 or more, you'll receive an additional $50 discount when you use your BUYING RETAIL IS STUPID coupon.

NAT DIAMOND EMPIRE FURNITURE**
4431 W. Adams
Los Angeles, CA 90011
213/732-8128

HOURS: MON, FRI: 10-7   TUES-THUR: 9:45-6:30   SAT: 9:30-6
CREDIT CARDS: AE, DISC, MC, V

This store has been in business over 50 years selling furniture and appliances at 20 to 50% below retail prices. They carry a huge inventory of General Electric appliances which include refrigerators, freezers, stoves, washers, dryers, and more. Nat Diamond Empire Furniture also carry the latest furniture trends and styles. You'll save an additional 10% off their already terrific prices by using your BUYING RETAIL IS STUPID coupon.

ELEGANCE FURNITURE
19404 Business Center Dr.
Northridge, CA 91324
818/993-4416

HOURS: TUES-FRI: 10:30-7   SAT: 10:30-5   SUN: 12-5
CREDIT CARDS: MC, V

Are you in a redecorating, throw-out-the-old-bring-in-the-new kind of mood? Yes? Then Elegance Furniture is the place to go. Grab your checkbook (it's okay, they take checks) and rush over while the force is still with you. They have Thomasville, Hare, Lane, and Burlington to name a few at 20–25% off retail.

EUROSTYLE FURNITURE
19511-1/2 Business Center Dr.
Northridge, CA 91324
818/993-5772

HOURS: MON-SAT; 10-6 SUN: 11-5
CREDIT CARDS: MC, V

If you love ornately designed European furniture, have we got a deal for you. Eurostyle imports all of their merchandise from Italy and sells it directly to the public at up to 50% off retail. And, discounts run higher if you buy several pieces. You can customize your furniture by selecting from one of many wood finishes and nearly 300 fabrics. Customers are important to Eurostyle, and you'll always find one of the owners on the floor. Appointments are available after business hours and if it's more convenient they will come to your home for a free consultation.

MARK FRIEDMAN FURNITURE
1437 4th St.
Santa Monica, CA 90404
310/393-2338

HOURS: MON, THUR-SAT: 11-5 TUES-WED: 11-7
CREDIT CARDS: CASH ONLY

This store has home furnishings for every room in the house. They carry every style including contemporary, traditional, country and classic. You can get bedrooms, living rooms, dining rooms, mattresses sets, dinettes, carpeting, lamps, wall hangings, curios, leather, and occasional items. They have all famous national brand names at 10% above cost. And for even greater savings check out their floor sample sales.

FURNITURE TRENDS
2585 Cochran St.
Simi Valley, CA 93065
805/584-0116

HOURS: MON-FRI: 10-7 SAT: 10-6 SUN: 12-6
CREDIT CARDS: AE, MC, OPT, V

Furniture Trends is known for "Upscale Furniture...Downscale Prices." See their large collection of fine country, traditional, contemporary, and southwestern styles. With 20–50% savings on popular brand names such as Lifestyle, Universal, Hooker, Karen Lawrence, T & T Leather, Vargas and P.A.M.A., you'll get lots of value for your money. They also have outstanding values in dining room, living room and bedroom sets.

HOME FURNISHINGS

EDDIE GOLD FURNITURE, INC.
4935 McConnell Ave., Bldg. 3
Los Angeles, CA 90666
213/870-3050

HOURS: TUES-FRI: 9-5 SAT: 11-5
CREDIT CARDS: DISC, MC, V

It may take you a while, but when shopping here, eventually you'll notice that there aren't any pushy salespeople hanging around. What you will find hanging around is quality furniture for your entire home. Brand names include Bernhardt, Lane, Sealy, Universal and others at about 40% below retail; and, if you happen to get in on one of their floor sample sales, savings can run as high as 70% off retail. Not many stores in today's marketplace can say they've been in business for three generations, but this one can. This family owned business has kept their customers happy with low prices for over 40 years.

GOOCHEY'S FURNISHINGS & LIGHTING
14241 Ventura Blvd., #104
Sherman Oaks, CA 91423
818/986-4772, 213/872-1113

HOURS: MON-FRI: 10-6 SAT. AND EVENINGS BY APPOINTMENT
CREDIT CARDS: CASH OR CHECKS ONLY

Goochey's Furnishings & Lighting can help you decorate your entire home or office. They carry wallpaper, carpeting, furniture, light fixtures, draperies, blinds and even art for your empty walls. You'll save at least 30% off retail on all your decorating needs at this one-stop shop.

IKEA
17621 E. Gale Ave.
City of Industry, CA 91748
818/912-7867

HOURS: MON-FRI: 11-9 SAT: 10-8 SUN: 11-6
CREDIT CARDS: MC, V

Because IKEA has over 100 stores in 25 countries, their huge worldwide buying volume translates into low manufacturing costs which they pass along to the consumer. By designing all of their products themselves in Sweden, they are able to reduce costs even further and offer the lowest everyday prices, while still keeping design and quality high. When you visit an IKEA store, you'll find 12,000 unique items and coordinated home furnishings—all at affordable prices. There are over 70 coordinated room settings offering hundreds of home decorating ideas. They

HOME FURNISHINGS

have 12 shops in their marketplace with thousands of accessories—offering everything from cookware to lighting, rugs and plants. IKEA has a supervised play area for children, a Swedish style restaurant that offers baby food and child-size meals, a baby changing room with free diapers, and strollers to push around the little ones while you're shopping. All in all, IKEA offers everything you need to turn your house into a home. With four football fields of home furnishings to choose from, you better make sure you wear comfortable shoes.

Additional Locations:
Burbank–600 N. San Fernando Blvd., 818/842-4532
Fontana–17284 Slover Ave., 714/832-1444
Tustin–2982 El Camino Real Blvd., 714/838-7867

JEROLD'S FINE HOME FURNISHINGS
13441 Sherman Way
North Hollywood, CA 91605
818/788-8825

HOURS: TUES-FRI: 9-5 SAT: 10-5 SUN: 12-5
CREDIT CARDS: DISC, MC, V

Whether you're furnishing your entire home or making an office out of one of your bedrooms, you'll save 30 to 50% off retail at Jerold's Fine Home Furnishings. You can select your furniture from at least 100 different manufacturers represented in their 12,000 square foot showroom. If you don't see what you want on the floor, let your fingers do the walking through tons of furniture catalogues. Brand names include Barcalounger, Bassett, Bernhardt, Boyd, Broyhill, Century, Drexel, Henredon, Hickory White, Stanley, Thomasville and more. They also have bedding, brass beds, patio furniture, mirrors, lamps, office furniture and mini-blinds and verticals. Accessories are plentiful, too.

LEON'S FURNITURE
5700 Lankershim Blvd.
North Hollywood, CA 91601
818/506-6881

HOURS: MON-SAT: 10-8 SUN: 12-5
CREDIT CARDS: MC, V

From coffee tables and corner groups, to bunkbeds, playpens, sofas and rollaways, they have it here. You can save as much as 50% on all types and styles of furniture. You'll find Broyhill, Bassett and many other major brands.

HOME FURNISHINGS

METZLER'S HOME FURNISHINGS
22637 Ventura Blvd.
Woodland Hills, CA 91364
818/346-4610
HOURS: TUES-FRI: 10-6   SAT: 10-5
CREDIT CARDS: MC, V

This store offers the creme de la creme in home furnishings for the San Fernando Valley at 20 to 50% off retail prices. They offer decorating service, and top quality merchandise at their 4,000 square foot showroom in Woodland Hills. You can also buy carpeting, draperies, wallpaper, shutters, and blinds. Metzler's Home Furnishings has excellent service, and you must get on their mailing list for their Spring and Fall sales.

ROBERT'S INTERIORS
4935 McConnell Ave., Suite 10
Los Angeles, CA 90066
310/822-3028
HOURS: TUES-FRI: 9-5   SAT: 11-5
CREDIT CARDS: MC, V

Robert's Interiors has name brand furniture priced at least 40% off retail. You'll save even more buying floor samples from their 4,500 square foot showroom. Special orders are no problem because over 100 factory sources are available from more than 100 catalogues for your selection. Just a few of the brands found here are Lane, Hickory, Platt, Bernhardt, Lexington, Cal Style and Stanley.

ROSCOE FURNITURE LIQUIDATORS**
21612 Sherman Way
Canoga Park, CA 91303
818/719-0220
HOURS: SUN-MON, FRI: 10-6   TUES-THUR: 10-8
CREDIT CARDS: MC, V

"Quality at Discount" is the theme at Roscoe Furniture Liquidators, and that's just what you'll find. Their prices range from 50 to 70% below major department stores and 20 to 30% below other discount furniture stores. In their 20,000 square foot store, you'll find savings on all types of furniture, bedding, lamps, decorator items, and tables featuring brand names such as Universal, BP John, Sterns & Foster, Klausner, Kincaid, Lane Recliners and Douglas. Financing is also available. Make sure to use your BUYING RETAIL IS STUPID coupon for an extra 5% discount.

HOME FURNISHINGS

SITTING PRETTY INC.
7115 Darby
Reseda, CA 91335
818/881-3114

HOURS: MON-SAT: 10-6 SUN: 12-5
CREDIT CARDS: DISC, MC, V

Sitting Pretty offers factory discounts on bars, bar stools, dinettes, game sets and chairs. They have over 18,000 square feet of beautiful merchandise in decorator designs. Expect to save 25% off retail prices on brand names like Cal Style, Cardinal, Dino, Studio K, and many more.

– INFANTS & CHILDREN –

BABY MOTIVES
8362 W. Third St.
Los Angeles, CA 90048
213/658-6015

HOURS: MON-SAT: 10-5
CREDIT CARDS: MC, V

Baby Motives specializes in infant and children's furniture and bedding. Whether you are looking for a stroller, car seat, crib or highchair, you'll find them at 20% to 50% off retail prices. Baby Motives carries brand names such as Childcraft, Nojo, Carters, Gund and McLaren. They have weekly unadvertised specials. and can special order from catalogues so you can coordinate the wallpaper and the bedding.

BABY TOYTOWN, INC.
16800 E. Gale Ave.
Industry, CA 91745
818/333-6440

HOURS: MON-FRI: 10-6 SAT: 10-6 SUN: 11-5
CREDIT CARDS: DISC, MC, V

These stores carry everything you may need for a baby up until they are six or seven years old. They have such items as cribs, strollers, chests, lamps, mobiles, toys, bottles, teen furniture, and more. Major brands, including Simmons, Bassett, Lullabye, and Childcraft, are available at 20% above COST. Major sales take place each year, where customers are willing to wait two hours just to come in the door.

Additional Locations:
Reseda–18719 Sherman Way, 818/881-4441
Rosemead–8930 E. Valley Blvd., 818/288-6220
Upland–1414 W. 7th St., 714/981-4438

CAROUSEL BABY FURNITURE
1726 E. Colorado Blvd.
Pasadena, CA 91106
213/684-0457

HOURS: MON-THUR, SAT: 9-6   FRI: 9:30-9
CREDIT CARDS: MC, V

Roll those dice. Baby needs a new pair of shoes. If not, then a new car seat might be in order. You won't have to take any gambles at Carousel Baby Furniture. They have everything you need—strollers, playpens, mattresses, clothing, layettes and many other furniture items. For brand new mommies, there are breast pumps, diapers, and bassinets. You'll find bunkbeds, mirrors, headboards, books, lamps, replacement pads and parts. They have wicker items too! When buying your Simmons, Childcraft, or Aprica you can expect to pay up to 50% off retail prices.

ENCINO DISCOUNT PATIO & BABY FURNITURE
17563 Ventura Blvd.
Encino, CA 91316
818/986-1074

HOURS: MON-FRI: 9-6   SAT: 9-5   SUN: 11-4
CREDIT CARDS: MC, V

Looking for that perfect outdoor swing for your baby while you're entertaining guests at your backyard garden party? Encino Discount Patio and Baby Furniture has it all. Patio and baby furniture and accessories. They carry Innova, California Umbrella, Homecrest, Pacific Sun, O.W. Lee, Kettler in patio furniture and Childcraft, Century, NoJo, Lambs and Ivy, and Creative Playthings for baby furniture. Owner Mackie Singer says her customers tell them that they have the best selection and prices (30 to 50% off retail) and have been coming back to the store since 1939.

KIDS FURNITURE WAREHOUSE**
2270 Honolulu Ave.
Montrose, CA 91020
818/957-7622

HOURS: MON-SAT: 10-6
CREDIT CARDS: MC, V

Instead of buying new bedroom furniture for your children every few years, wouldn't it be great to have furniture that grows right along with them? Well, that's exactly the premise behind the merchandise found at Kids Furniture Warehouse. Most of the furniture is made of solid Swedish pine and is easily adjusted to different configurations. Savings run about 10 to 30% below retail, and if you use your BUYING RETAIL

IS STUPID coupon you'll save an additional 10% on your purchase. The store in Woodland Hills is open 10-5 on Sundays.
Additional Locations:
Woodland Hills: 22837 Ventura Blvd., 818/703-1522

SID'S DISCOUNT BABY FURNITURE
8338 Lincoln Blvd.
Los Angeles, CA 90045
310/670-5550

HOURS: MON-THUR: 10-6 FRI: 10-7:30 SAT: 10-6
CREDIT CARDS: MC, V

Sid's is an institution where you can find everything in baby furniture and clothing for infants. There are all the necessities, of course, like strollers and car seats. Sid's carries all major brands like Simmons, Lullabye, Childcraft, Bassett, Pride and Babyline. They offer free layaway, free shower registry, a most knowledgeable staff and big savings! Families have been shopping for their baby needs at Sid's since 1951.

THE STORK SHOP
1868 S. La Cienega Blvd.
Los Angeles, CA 90035
310/839-2403

HOURS: MON-SAT: 10-5:30
CREDIT CARDS: MC, V

The Stork Shop promises a fun visit. They have everything you could possibly want in furniture and clothes for your baby. In fact, they also carry over 50,000 garments for boys and girls up to age 14. Their layettes are beautiful and you'll love the many designer styles of furniture items and accessories. You'll save 20 to 50% off retail prices on most of your purchases too!

– LEATHER –

LEATHER FACTORY
11970 Wilshire Blvd.
West Los Angeles, CA 90025
310/820-8477

HOURS: MON-FRI: 10-8 SAT: 10-6 SUN: 12-6
CREDIT CARDS: AE, DISC, MC, V

Save 40 to 60% when you buy factory direct! The Leather Factory manufactures their own products and sells them out of their showrooms throughout California. They have more than 50 different styles of leather sofas and loveseats, sleepers, chairs, ottomans, recliners and office furniture. Everything is made to order, and you have a choice of over 100 colors. They also carry lamps, tables and accessories. Best of all, you get a lifetime warranty on the frame, springs and construction. Financing is available with 24 months to pay, or you can go with their 90 day financing which is interest free.

Additional Locations: 23 other stores throughout S. CA

– RATTAN & WICKER –

RATTAN DEPOT
10588-1/2 W. Pico Blvd.
Los Angeles, CA 90064
310/839-9003

HOURS: MON-SAT: 10-6 SUN: 12-5
CREDIT CARDS: MC, V

Rattan Depot carries rattan and wicker for the living room, dining room, and bedroom. Their prices are 20 to 50% below retail department store prices. You'll find a good selection, and they are very helpful in assisting you with your decorating decisions.

RATTAN DISTRIBUTION WAREHOUSE
8010 Wheatland Ave., Unit I
Sun Valley, CA 91352
818/504-0119

HOURS: TUES-SUN: 10-4
CREDIT CARDS: CASH OR CHECKS ONLY

Have you ever wondered why the rattan furniture purchased by interior decorators look so much better than what you are able to find? Rattan Distribution Warehouse, selling only to decorators, not stores, is the reason. Open to the public only on Friday, Saturday, and Sunday, this 4,000 square foot outlet is a direct importer of the finest rattan from the Philippines. Everything they carry is 100% rattan, and even in the places you can't see, no wood is used. They carry very high quality rattan furniture for the living room and dining room and also have bar stools, and wall units. The custom sets they sell will allow you more decorating control than you thought possible. You have the option of not only selecting the stain for the rattan, you also have the option of using one of their fabrics or supplying your own for the upholstery work. Prices are 40 to 50% below retail and you can save even more on floor samples. Delivery on custom orders takes 2 to 3 weeks.

WICKER MART
36 W. Main St.
Alhambra, CA 91801
818/576-1313, 818/281-4711
HOURS: MON-FRI: 10-5 SAT: 10-6
CREDIT CARDS: MC, V

If you want wicker furniture, custom rattan furniture, cane planters, cane seat repairs and accessories, come to Wicker Mart and save 20 to 50% off retail and enjoy their extensive selection. Custom upholstery and a layaway plan is also available. For even higher discounts, keep your eyes open for their summer sales.

– UNFINISHED –

FROCH'S WOODCRAFT SHOP, INC.
6659 Topanga Canyon Blvd.
Canoga Park, CA 91303
818/883-4730
HOURS: AE, MC, V
CREDIT CARDS: MON-THUR: 9-6 FRI: 9-5 SAT: 9-6

Froch's Woodcrafts Shop manufactures their unfinished furniture in the San Fernando Valley with their own craftsmen. This allows for the fantastic savings of 50% off retail. You'll find a wide assortment of all types of home furnishings, from dining room tables and chairs to huge wardrobes and dressers. You can remodel your kitchen with cabinetry available in different styles and sizes. If you are ready to revamp your closets, Froch's has various units you can mix and match to suit your own particular needs. Everything is all wood and of the finest quality, so you won't be able to find any particle board at Froch's.
Additional Locations:
Panorama City–7945 Van Nuys Blvd., 818/787-3682

WOODY'S UN-FINISHED FURNITURE
1222 Commerce Center Dr.
Lancaster, CA 93534
805/945-0551
HOURS: 10-9 SEVEN DAYS A WEEK
CREDIT CARDS: ALL MAJOR

You can save 40 to 50% off retail furniture prices by applying the finish yourself. Woody's carries only solid wood furniture (absolutely no particle board) in pine, oak and ash. If you've never finished furniture before you can take advantage of their free classes. They have furniture

for every room in your house such as dining room tables and chairs, entertainment centers, buffets, corner nooks, barstools, appliance carts, bunk beds, computer and office furniture, desks and shelves of all sizes. Brand names include Whittier, Rods, Master Craft, Maco, Athol and Union City.
Additional Locations:
Palmdale–20th St. East, 805/265-7410

– USED FURNITURE –

BUDGET RENTS FURNITURE AND SALES**
6051 Telegraph Rd.
Los Angeles, CA 90040
213/720-5020

HOURS: MON-FRI: 9-5:30 SAT: 10-5
CREDIT CARDS: MC, V

This is where you buy home and office furniture that was previously available for rent at one of their stores. The furniture is well made and, depending on the condition of the item, is priced 30 to 90% off retail. Whether you need a sofa, dinette set, television, or office partitions, you will find it all here. New shipments arrive several times a week and next day delivery is available. Remember to use your BUYING RETAIL IS STUPID coupon for an extra 10% discount.

∞ LAMPS & LIGHT FIXTURES ∞

BEVERLY HILLS FAN CO. FACTORY OUTLET
6033 De Soto
Woodland Hills, CA 91367
818/992-5562

HOURS: TUES-FRI: 11-6 SAT: 10-6
CREDIT CARDS: MC, V

Ceiling fans are great for moving the air around in your house. You can get them here at savings of at least 50% off retail. The fans come with three or five blades 42 or 52-inches in size. All of their well-made fans have three speeds and reversible motors. Although the fans are displayed with lights, most of them don't come with light kits. You can buy them separately here, but on our visit the selection wasn't very large. The fans (discontinued models or overruns) are available in high-tech and traditional styles.

HOME FURNISHINGS

CASTLE CHANDELIERS & LIGHTING CO.
7045 Topanga Canyon Blvd.
Canoga Park, CA 91303
818/340-0681

HOURS: MON/WED/FRI: 10- 9   TUES/THUR: 10-7   SAT: 9:30-6
         SUN: 11-5
CREDIT CARDS: AE, DISC, MC, V

If it has to do with lighting fixtures, Castle has it all. They stock lamps, fans, chandeliers, track lights, exterior lighting, shades, and more. Products they haven't manufactured themselves are imported from Europe. All merchandise is offered at factory-direct prices. With the biggest showroom in Southern California, you are bound to find what you are looking for with over 1,000 of the finest lamps from which to choose.

Additional Locations: 7 other stores throughout S. CA

RAY FERRA'S IRON & ANTIQUE ACCENTS
342 N. La Brea Ave.
Los Angeles, CA 90036
213/934-3953

HOURS: TUES-FRI: 10-5   SAT: 10-3
CREDIT CARDS: MC, V

If you've been looking for replacement glass for an old antique lamp, then Ray Ferra can come to your rescue. If the problem isn't replacement glass, he also does rewiring for most lamps, ceiling fixtures, and crystal chandeliers. Commercial and residential lighting are also specialties. If you're looking to find more of an antique look, you'll find Ray Ferra carries reproduction and original Tiffany lamps, handles, and many hard to find lighting items. He's been providing excellent service since 1967, and you can save 20% or more off retail prices, even if you could find it elsewhere. You'll find ample parking in back of the store.

GOOCHEY'S FURNISHINGS & LIGHTING
14241 Ventura Blvd., #104
Sherman Oaks, CA 91423
818/986-4772, 213/872-1113

HOURS: MON-FRI: 10-6
CREDIT CARDS: CASH OR CHECKS ONLY

Goochey's Furnishings & Lighting can help you decorate your entire home or office. They carry wallpaper, carpeting, furniture, light fixtures, draperies, blinds and even art for your empty walls. You'll save at least 30% off retail on all your decorating needs at this one-stop shop. Saturday and evening hours are by appointment only.

HANSEN WHOLESALE FAN CO.
11239 183rd St.
Cerritos, CA 90101
310/ 865-6376, 818/883-7511

HOURS: MON-FRI: 9-5
CREDIT CARDS: CASH OR CHECKS ONLY

Hansen Wholesale Fan Co. has get rock bottom prices on ceiling fans and light fixtures. All you have to do is step up to their order desk and place your order. Working only with catalogues, they'll process your order for Casablanca and Hunter fans and light fixtures. Sometimes they will have the item you want in stock, but normally an order takes two to four weeks. The money you save will be well worth the wait.

LAMPMART
5821 S. Main St.
Los Angeles, CA 90003
213/234-5320

HOURS: MON-FRI: 9-5:30 SAT: 9-3
CREDIT CARDS: MC, V

One of the largest lamp and lighting fixture inventories in the greater Los Angeles area can be found here. Their prices are 33% below retail on lamps, lampshades, chandeliers, fans, and mirrors. If you've got a lamp that needs to be fixed, they can do it right on the premises, or if you need your fixtures installed, they can handle that too. Not only does Lampmart offer terrific pricing, they also carry top name brands.

MC NALLY ELECTRIC
10792 Los Alamitos Blvd.
Los Alamitos, CA 90720
310/598-9438, 714/761-0692

HOURS: MON-FRI: 9-5
CREDIT CARDS: DISC, MC, V

Whatever your lighting needs, McNally Electric can satisfy them. Table and floor lamps, fluorescents, incandescents, HID, low voltage, track or recess lighting, indoor or outdoor you'll find them here at 20 to 50% savings. Whether your needs are commercial, residential, or office, their trained sales personnel will help you with your purchase. They also carry all the "stuff" that goes behind the light fixture such as switches, pipe, breakers, fuses, and PVC. If you have a favorite lamp that needs repair, bring it in. We can't begin to list all of the brand names they carry, but some of the names are Tivoli, Fredrick Ranond, Hilite, Nutone, Plantation, Melissa, Angelo, Dinico, and Halo Lighting.

∞ LINENS ∞

BED BATH & BEYOND
19836 Ventura Blvd.
Woodland Hills, CA 91364
818/702-9301

HOURS: MON-FRI: 9:30-9 SAT-SUN: 9:30-6
CREDIT CARDS: MC, V

With their prices, Bed Bath & Beyond says, "We make you laugh at white sale prices." Their large stores are filled with giant selections of sheets, towels, bedspreads, comforters, pillows, kitchenware, dinnerware, cookware, gift items, toss pillows, shower curtains, everything! You'll find Martex, Fieldcrest, Wamsutta, Nettlecreek and Mikasa, just to name a few, and the prices are way below usual department store sale prices.

Additional Locations:
Huntington Beach–18641 Main St. (5 Points Plaza), 714/842-0068
Redondo Beach–1611 Hawthorne Blvd., 310/370-1225
San Diego–5644 Mission Center Rd., 619/295-9888)
Studio City–12555 Ventura Blvd., 818/980-0260
W. Los Angeles–11801 W. Olympic Blvd., 310/478-5767

BEDSPREAD CREATIONS**
14054 E. Firestone Blvd.
Santa Fe Springs, CA 90670
310/802-7938

HOURS: MON-FRI: 9-6 SAT: 10-5
CREDIT CARDS: AE, DISC, MC, V

As the manufacturer for their own stores, Bedspread Creations is able to offer wholesale prices to people lucky enough to know about them. They have about 3,500 square feet with more than 1,000 bedspreads in stock. With over 2,000 different fabrics to choose from, they will make anything you want, even if you wish to furnish your own fabric. They carry comforters, pillows, mini and vertical blinds, and all the other items necessary to make them a one-stop bedroom decorating center. Name brands include Bedspread Creations, Pacific Designs, India Ink, Laurel Wood, and many others. You'll save an additional 5% with your BUYING RETAIL IS STUPID coupon. Deals don't get much better than this.

HOME FURNISHINGS

BEDSPREAD WAREHOUSE
6949 Topanga Canyon Blvd.
Canoga Park, CA 91303
818/887-4347

HOURS: MON-SAT: 10-6
CREDIT CARDS: MC, V

Bedspread Warehouse offers a wide variety of bedspreads, comforters, pillows, day bed sets, and bath accessories at 20 to 60% off retail. You'll find a full line of quality merchandise with brand names such as Dakota, India Ink, and Croscille. Stressing customer service, their experts will provide assistance in helping you to color coordinate your rooms in style.

CALICO CORNERS
3830 Foothill Blvd.
Pasadena, CA 91107
818/792-4328

HOURS: MON: 10-7 TUES-SAT: 10-6 SUN: 12-5
CREDIT CARDS: MC, V

Wouldn't you love to own a quilted bedspread? Well, you can at 30 to 60% above cost when you shop at Calico Corners. They carry designer fabrics, slipcovers, tablecloths, feather and down pillows. Upholstery fabrics and books on upholstering are for sale, plus books on slipcovers and windows. They have tape for making Roman and Austrian shades, and pleating tape for making curtains. Get on their mailing list so you'll know about their really big sales.

COUNTRY LINENS**
18 Fashion Square
Sherman Oaks, CA 91423
818/995-7417

HOURS: MON-FRI: 10-9 SAT: 10-7 SUN: 11-6
CREDIT CARDS: AE, DISC, MC, V

Not only will you find a large selection of top of the line bed and bath accessories at 20% below department store prices, they also specialize in monogramming and creating custom bedding. Country Linens knows how to take care of their customers with complimentary gift wrapping and friendly service. You'll find a large selection of imported soaps and toiletries, and items such as vanity benches and vanity mirrors. Their selection is so good that the movie studios frequently come in to shop. Save an extra 10% when you use your BUYING RETAIL IS STUPID coupon.

HOME FURNISHINGS

EVER-RICH BEDDING**
22135 Sherman Way
Canoga Park, CA 91303
818/999-2184
HOURS: MON-SAT: 10:30-5:30
CREDIT CARDS: MC, V

Trying to keep cool in the summer and warm in the winter? Stop by Ever-Rich Bedding, and check out their goose down comforters and pillows. They have designer toss pillows, bedspreads, daybed sets, waterbed and regular sheets, and complete comforter sets. Some of the brand names you'll find are Crown Craft, Purofied Down, Max Rawicz Designs and Hollander Home Fashions. If your purchase is over $100, they will take off an additional 10% when you use your BUYING RETAIL IS STUPID discount coupon. (Down items not included in discount.)

AL GREENWOOD BEDSPREAD KING
2750 E. Pacific Coast Hwy.
Long Beach, CA 90804
310/498-9277
HOURS: MON-THUR, SAT: 10-5:30 FRI: 10-7 SUN: 12-5
CREDIT CARDS: MC, V

When a man calls himself the Bedspread King, you know you are going to find one of the country's largest selections of bedspreads. Well, it's true. In addition to an incredible selection of bedspreads at savings 20 to 50% off retail, Al Greenwood also carries a large variety of custom drapes in matching fabrics. You can match your drapes and take them home with you, and get this, with no waiting! Make or create your own accessories to match your new bedspread. Just have them cut the length you need of matching fabric, and you are on your way.
Additional Locations:
South Gate–8468 State St., 213/566-9393

THE LINEN CLUB
100 Citadel Dr., #136
City of Commerce, CA 90040
213/721-2444
HOURS: MON-SAT: 9-8 SUN: 10-6
CREDIT CARDS: AE, MC, V

Victor, the owner of The Linen Club, guarantees not to be undersold. If you're looking for bedspreads, comforters, sheets, or towels, look no further. The store is filled with linens, including most designer names such as Wamsutta, Cannon, Fieldcrest, Martex, Laura Ashley and more, at savings of 35–70% off retail. They also have accessories for your pow-

der room. If you need a warm comforter for your Aunt Tilley in Montana, you can phone your order in and have it shipped just in time for her birthday. They've been satisfying their customers since the late 1970s, so they must be doing something right.
Additional Locations:
Los Angeles–The Linen Room, 860 S. Los Angeles, 213/627-3333

MR. SATIN, INC.
2236 S. Barrington Ave.
Los Angeles, CA 90064
213/879-3353

HOURS: MON-FRI: 8:30-4 SAT: 12-5
CREDIT CARDS: CASH OR CHECKS ONLY

This factory outlet specializes in satin sheets, comforters, shams, dust ruffles, boudoir pillows, and dust covers. You can save 30–70% off retail shopping here. They also carry seconds. Feel like a King or Queen when you sleep between satin sheets without paying regal prices!

∞ RUGS ∞

EMBASSY AUCTIONEER, INC.
18517 Ventura Blvd.
Tarzana, CA 91356
818/996-9244

HOURS: MON-FRI: 9:30-5
CREDIT CARDS: AE, MC, V

Take a ride on a flying carpet. This store has quite a selection of handmade Persian and Oriental rugs. Take one home and wait for the magic to happen. If there's no magic, then you'll just have to settle for the envy of your friends. Their handmade rugs come from countries such as China, India, Iran, Afghanistan, Romania, Pakistan, and Turkey.

ORIENTAL RUG EXCHANGE**
339 N. La Cienega Blvd.
Los Angeles, CA 90048
310/657-1100

HOURS: MON-SAT: 10-6 SUN: BY APPOINTMENT ONLY
CREDIT CARDS: AE, DISC, MC, V

In business since 1972, Oriental Rug Exchange carries over 7,000 handmade rugs from all around the world. They carry modern, and antique rugs from China, Persia, India, Pakistan, Russia, and many other countries. You'll also find intricate tapestries and needlepoint. Walk through

HOME FURNISHINGS

their large 5,000 square foot showroom and a huge warehouse near by. This store is truly an exchange because they buy or trade in used rugs. Need your rug repaired or cleaned? The Oriental Rug Exchange offers expert service on any handmade rug. They will also appraise your rugs. Jacob Shabtai guarantees the best price in town, 50–75% below retail prices, and he'll accept your BUYING RETAIL IS STUPID coupon for additional savings of 5%.

WESTPORT CARPET INDUSTRIES
18314–6 Oxnard St.
Tarzana, CA 91356
818/344-3291

HOURS: MON-FRI: 8-05   SAT: 9-4
CREDIT CARDS: MC, V

If you're in the market for new carpeting or flooring of any sort, you can save big dollars at Westport Carpet. This is where interior designers, architects and contractors shop. Have you ever seen a beautiful rug in a model home or a hotel lobby and thought that you'd love to have one, but done a little differently? Westport has one section with sample books of area rugs that you design yourself. There are a multitude of patterns from which to choose—e.g., a very simple bordered sculpted rug to one with an intricate floral design. The best part is that you get to pick the color and texture combinations. For those of us that are less adventurous, Westport has a selection of area rugs that are already made. With literally thousands of domestic and imported carpet samples, this is a great place to buy carpeting also.

∞ UPHOLSTERY SERVICE ∞

VALLEY UPHOLSTERING
18165 Napa St., Unit 8
Northridge, CA 91324
818/349-4336

HOURS: MON-FRI; 8-5
CREDIT CARDS: CASH OR CHECKS ONLY

Until recently, Valley Upholstering has been a labor wholesaler to hotels and major department stores. The public can save about 50% off retail on upholstering services. You can use your own fabrics or select brand name fabrics from one of their sample books from Waverly, Schumacher, Bar-row, Robert Allen, Endura and many more.

JEWELRY

BES INTERNATIONAL JEWELRY
607 S. Hill St., #334
Los Angeles, CA 90014

213/626-1075

HOURS: MON-FRI: 9:30-5 SAT: 10-3
CREDIT CARDS: MC, V

Here's a complete line of jewelry at wholesale prices. You will save at least 50% in their glittering showroom filled with 14 and 18 karat gold! Owner Evelyn LeVine has bracelets, necklaces, chains, rings, engagement sets, earrings, and more. Custom designing is available, and repairs are done while you wait. In fact, if you are bored with some of your old jewelry lying around, let Bes redesign or remount it for you in a new style. They've been in business since 1977, so you can rely on them.

CALIFORNIA JEWELSMITHS
250 S. Beverly Dr.
Beverly Hills, CA 90212

213/272-5364

HOURS: MON-SAT: 9:30-5:00
CREDIT CARDS: MC, V

California Jewelsmiths has been in business since the 1940s and has maintained two and three generations of clients strictly by word of mouth. They don't advertise about the great savings, usually 30% off retail, on their fine diamond jewelry, bracelets, necklaces, rings, precious and semi precious stones, charms, pendants, chains and watches. Check them out when shopping for a dependable jewelry store. Repair work for jewelry and watches is done on the premises.

CLAYDON'S JEWELERS
2772 Artesia Blvd.
Redondo Beach, CA 90278

310/542-0501

HOURS: TUES, THUR, FRI: 10-6 WED: 10-7 SAT: 10-4:30
CREDIT CARDS: AE, MC, V

We found Claydon's Jewelers from a woman's letter saying she was their new customer for life. Why? She saved $500 there on a diamond and didn't write to us about it until she had done some apples-to-apples comparison shopping. Claydon's can do everything for you from custom designing a piece of jewelry using rare gemstones in unusual shapes, to repairing silver and pewter items such as candle holders, tea sets, or frames. All this is done on their premises. They also do watch repairs, string pearls and engrave your merchandise. Always wanting to do just a little more for their customers, Claydon's will schedule special appointments during and after their normal business hours. Now we'd say that this is a one stop jewelry shop.

COLLECTOR'S EYE
21435 Sherman Way
Canoga Park, CA 91303
818/347-9343
HOURS: MON-SAT: 10-6
CREDIT CARDS: AE, MC, V

This is definitely one of our favorites. Walking into the Collector's Eye is like walking through a rainbow and finding the pot of gold. All of their elegantly displayed vintage jewelry is arranged by colors and/or style. You might find an antique vanity draped in pearl brooches, bracelets, earrings, chokers, necklaces, rings and ropes. Another display might consist of 75 various styles in shades of blue or perhaps, sterling silver. The antique jewelry, real and costume, is from the early 1800s up through the early 1960s and all at 50% to 70% below retail. You can literally spend hours browsing through this oasis of jewelry acquired from estate sales, swapmeets and retirement homes. The Collector's Eye does jewelry repair and will also buy your vintage jewelry. A definite stop when in the San Fernando Valley!

DARVA JEWELERS
18410 Ventura Blvd.
Tarzana, CA 91356
818/881-GOLD
HOURS: MON-FRI: 9:30-5:30 SAT: 10-5
CREDIT CARDS: MC, V

Darva Jewelers offers quality jewelry at 25 to 60% below retail and watches at 30 to 40% off retail. Their motto is service, and they offer a money back guarantee if not satisfied within 14 days. They even will add a 5% discount for each can of food you bring in (up to a 25% discount) during their Annual Sale to help the Homeless. Make sure to call and find out when the sale is, not only to save money, but to help the homeless. Appraisals and repairs done on the premises.

DESIGNER JEWELRY MART
18456 Clark St.
Tarzana, CA 91356

818/345-0535

HOURS: TUES-SAT: 10-6
CREDIT CARDS: DISC, MC, V

The owner of Designer Jewelry Mart, Nick Dembowich, is the reason people enjoy shopping here for jewelry and watches. Nick runs his business with a philosophy that is rare in today's world. He believes in making a lifetime happy customer, not a quick sale. Nick carries most anything you need and if he doesn't have it, he will get it for you. Diamonds are bought direct resulting in higher savings for his customers. Prices on jewelry run approximately 10% above cost, and you can save up to 50% on Seiko watches. Custom designing and repairs are also available.

THE DIAMOND MINE
1060 Hamner Ave.
Norco, CA 91760

714/735-7447

HOURS: MON-FRI: 9:30-5:30
CREDIT CARDS: AE, DISC, MC, V

Why not save yourself at least 50% below mall jewelry store prices by checking out The Diamond Mine? You can buy on sight or design what you want in 14K and 18K gold. In addition, they carry loose diamonds and gemstones, and they do their own castings. If you are longing for a solid gold watch in 14K or 18K gold, with or without diamonds, head for the Diamond Mine. Though owner Dan Shevitski doesn't keep expensive watches like this in stock, he'll get one for you for only 10% over what he is charged for the watch. Knowing that the same item costing $100 at retail jewelry stores, will cost only $40 at The Diamond Mine, why would anyone want to pay $100?

ENCINO JEWELRY EXCHANGE
17143 Ventura Blvd.
Encino, CA 91316
818/990-8944
HOURS: MON-SAT: 10-5:30
CREDIT CARDS: AE, MC, V

First the freebies: free jewelry cleaning, free verbal appraisals and free parking. The Encino Jewelry Exchange has a large selection of watches like Seiko, Citizen, Omega, and others at 50% off retail prices. Their collection of 14K and 18K gold jewelry is priced 50 to 70% less than you'd pay at department stores or chain jewelry stores. Jewelry and watch repair is done on the premises. Many jobs can be done while you wait.

GERALD'S FINE JEWELRY**
23622 Calabasas Rd., #111
Calabasas, CA 91302
818/591-2651
HOURS: TUES-THUR: 9-6 FRI-SAT: 9-5
CREDIT CARDS: MC, V

Prices here are generally 30 to 50% off the sale prices of most retail establishments. As a manufacturer for smaller jewelry stores, they are able to offer the public lower-than-low prices on high quality jewelry. All gold jewelry is sold by weight, and this includes intricate pieces, too. (Although some retailers may want you to believe differently, in most cases, after a mold is made the same process is used for making both simple and intricate jewelry.) Custom work is a specialty, and they can duplicate just about anything. With such low prices, you might think service is nonexistent, but unless you're spending bundles of money at a jewelry store on Rodeo, you won't find better service. Gerald's is a comfortable store—not too big, not too small, but just right. Whether you're spending $50 or $50,000, one-on-one service is given to every customer for as long as necessary, and there is no high pressure selling. Because customers are never rushed, a waiting room is provided complete with television, refreshments and reading material. Repair work and restoration is available, and if it makes you feel more comfortable, you can even sit next to the jeweler while he works on your jewelry. In addition to everything else, Gerald's offers a money back guarantee on all merchandise. Before you head out to Gerald's Fine Jewelry, don't forget to cut out your BUYING RETAIL IS STUPID coupon for an extra 10% discount.

GRAFSTEIN & CO.
1851 E. First St.
Santa Ana, CA 92705
714/835-6100
HOURS: BY APPOINTMENT ONLY MON-FRI: 10-5
CREDIT CARDS: AE, MC, V

Grafstein's has been in business over 50 years selling upscale watches, diamonds, precious gemstone rings, bracelets, earrings, pendants and other fine jewelry. They carry the top-of-the-line names in watches such as Rolex, Cartier, Piaget, Ebel, Patek Philippe, Corum and Concord. Discounts range from 20% to 65% depending on model availability. There motto is the 11th commandment—"thou shalt not pay retail." They carry new merchandise and estate pieces. Their multi-million dollar inventory must be seen to be appreciated.

ALEX LAZAR JEWELERS, INC.**
3648 Central Ave.
Riverside, CA 92506
714/683-1149
HOURS: MON-FRI: 10-6 SAT: 10-2
CREDIT CARDS: CASH OR CHECKS ONLY

So you've set the wedding date, and you're in search of that perfect diamond for his and her rings. Consider stopping by Alex Lazar Jewelers and selecting those perfect rings or loose stones. You'll find everything in the store at about 20% below retail, and loose stones are an even better buy at 40% below retail. They also have wedding rings and other fine jewelry. Appraisals are given with purchase so you know exactly what you are getting. These folks have been in Riverside since 1964 and they know their stuff! Use your BUYING RETAIL IS STUPID coupon and you'll receive another "jewel" of an additional 5% discount!

LORD OF THE RINGS**
607 S. Hill St., Suite 807
Los Angeles, CA 90014
213/488-9157

HOURS: BY APPOINTMENT ONLY
CREDIT CARDS: AE, DISC, MC, V

Lord of the Rings offers all types of fine jewelry, precious stones, diamonds, engagement rings and wedding bands to the public at wholesale prices. In addition, owner/gemologist David Barzilay offers a free mini-class on "everything you always wanted to know about diamonds but were afraid to ask." Generally, your savings will run about 33 to 50% below retail. They are open six days a week and some evenings if requested. Please call them to set up an appointment. They will also accept your BUYING RETAIL IS STUPID coupon for an additional 5% discount on your purchase.

MAGIC JEWELRY
17654 Ventura Blvd.
Encino, CA 91316
818/501-3137

HOURS: TUES-FRI: 10-4 SAT: 10-5
CREDIT CARDS: MC, V

If you're looking for unusual gold chains or broaches in 14k or 18k gold, then Magic Jewelry is the place for you! A $100 chain found elsewhere, costs $40 here. In business for over 20 years in downtown L.A.; the Valley store was opened in 1990. Most of their jewelry is imported from Italy. They also carry estate pieces, rings and earrings. There is plenty of parking, and repair work is done on the premises, usually while you wait.

MAYA
7452 Melrose Ave.
Los Angeles, CA 90046
213/655-2708

HOURS: MON-THUR: 11-7 FRI: 11-9 SAT: 11-8 SUN: 12-6
CREDIT CARDS: AE, DISC, MC, V

Maya says she has the greatest earring show on earth. With over 4,000 pairs to choose from, she may be correct. Earrings in gold, silver, enamel, copper, and brass, whatever you're looking for, you can find it here. This unique store also carries some clothing items, necklaces, and other gift items. You'll always save about 20%, and Maya will usually have some specials to entice you.

JOHN MOYEN'S JEWELLERY CONNECTION**
31149 Via Colinas, #609
Westlake Village, CA 91362
818/707-1230, 805/494-8114
HOURS: MON–SAT: 10–6
CREDIT CARDS: AE, DISC, MC, OPT, V

It's hard to top jewelry as a gift. If you're tired of shopping in run-of-the-mill jewelry stores, John Moyen's Jewellery Connection will be a welcome breath of fresh air. Not only will you find many very unusual pieces, high quality and low prices (about 40-60% off retail) go hand-in-hand here. Should you find a particular ring but would prefer, for example, the center stone to be a ruby instead of a sapphire, switching stones is no problem. Of course, the price will be adjusted up or down, depending on the type and quality of the stone you choose. When shopping here, you know exactly what you are buying because it's all listed separately on the tag. (They even separate the weight of round and baguette diamonds.) If you travel a lot you'll appreciate their section of travel jewelry featuring cubic zirconias and synthetics set 14K gold. It looks like the real thing, but it won't break your heart if it gets lost or stolen. The staff here goes the distance for their customers. On a recent visit, a gentleman came in needing a pin for his watchband. Less than five minutes later he was out the door with his watchband fixed at no charge. John Moyen started as a wholesaler in the industry in the early 1960s and recently opened his doors to the public. John says, "Shopping here is always better than a sale–guaranteed." You can save an extra 10% off your purchase if you remember your BUYING RETAIL IS STUPID coupon. The coupon can be used for everything except loose stones.

RUBINFELD-KENNEDY ESTATE JEWELRY**
607 S. Hill St.
Los Angeles, CA 90014
213/627-8116
HOURS BY APPOINTMENT ONLY: MON-FRI: 10-5 SAT: 10-2
CREDIT CARDS: ALL MAJOR

If you appreciate the fine craftsmanship of antique jewelry, you should definitely give Rubinfeld-Kennedy a call. They carry a large selection of estate jewelry from just about every famous maker in the world. If you drool over showcases filled with antique jewelry at special sales held by high-end department stores, but cringe at the prices, you'll be ecstatic with the prices and selection found here. You can also save big money on fine jewelry and loose stones. The owners are perfectionists and insist on carrying only the very best. To assure the best for their customers, Rubinfeld and Kennedy work by appointment only. When you pay them a visit, make sure to take your BUYING RETAIL IS STUPID coupon for an extra 10% discount.

SHANES JEWELRY STORE
1065 Broxton Ave.
Los Angeles, CA 90024
310/208-8404
HOURS: 10:30-6 SEVEN DAYS A WEEK
CREDIT CARDS: AE, DISC, MC, V

This business offers their customers a complete jewelry service. Not only do they carry an incredibly large stock of 14K gold and diamond jewelry at all times, they also supply the following services: special orders, jewelry designing, jewelry repair, and a very convenient layaway plan. Any alterations a customer may want, on any piece of merchandise, can be done quickly and professionally. Shanes also has sapphires, rubies, emeralds, opals, and sterling silver at wholesale prices. They offer 50% off on gold and diamond jewelry.

ST. VINCENT JEWELRY CENTER
650 S. Hill St.
Los Angeles, CA 90014
213/629-2124
HOURS: MON-SAT: 10-6
CREDIT CARDS: VARIES WITH EACH VENDOR

St. Vincent Jewelry Center, the single largest jewelry exchange in the world, is home to over 400 wholesalers and manufacturers. This is the place to go for jewelry of any kind, we don't care what you want—it's here! Opened in 1982, the individual jewelry stores offer you factory-direct prices at savings of 40 to 70% below retail. Would you like a gold chain, a bracelet or maybe a diamond watch? Perhaps you have a coronation to attend and need a matched set (in diamonds and rubies) that includes a tiara, choker, pair of earrings, bracelet and ring to complement your new Ungaro gown. Whatever you need or desire is here to fit any budget. You can spend $25 or $1,500,000. True jewelry lovers will think they've hit buried treasure. Aside from ready-made jewelry, you'll find businesses specializing in custom work, loose stones, repair, restoration, and you'll also find gold, precious metal and jewelry buyers. It's hard to believe that this fabulous selection is all under one roof. They're located on 7th and S. Hill. Call to get a free directory listing all stores.

STEVEN & CO. JEWELERS
437 N. Bedford Dr.
Beverly Hills, CA 90210
310/274-8336

HOURS: MON-FRI: 10-5:30
CREDIT CARDS: AE, MC, V

Dreams turn into reality here. Steven & Co. has jewelry with diamonds, emeralds, rubies, sapphires and pearls at 10 to 20% above cost, as well as watches, clocks, and gold jewelry. They carry such brand names as Rolex, Cartier, Ebel, Movado and others. Expert repairing of watches and jewelry, custom designing, redesigning and ear piercing is available. Estate jewelry is bought, sold and appraised, and they purchase and appraise estates. Free parking at 461 Bedford. Get on their private mailing list for special sales. Private appointments are also available.

WATCH CONNECTION**
3033 S. Bristol
Costa Mesa, CA 92626
714/432-8200

HOURS: MON-FRI: 11-5:30 SAT: 11-5
CREDIT CARDS: ALL MAJOR

The Watch Connection carries one of the largest selections of fine wristwatches (at least 2,500) we've ever seen. Discounts average about 25% off suggested retail prices on brand names such as Citizen, Concord, Corum, Longines, Movado, Omega, Piaget, Rado, Seiko and many others. In addition to wristwatches, along with batteries and watch bands, they also offer complete watch repair. This family-owned business was started in the early 1970s. When you use your BUYING RETAIL IS STUPID coupon you'll get an extra 10% discount.

M. WEINSTEIN INC.
9454 Wilshire Blvd.
Beverly Hills, CA 90212
310/276-0696

HOURS: MON-FRI: 10-4:30
CREDIT CARDS: MC, V

Previously in Los Angeles, Mr. Weinstein has been in the jewelry business for over 60 years. He offers his clientele new and used jewelry at all different price levels, so don't let the Beverly Hills address intimidate you. You'll discover exceptional values on everything from a simple chain to fabulous estate pieces. If you want to start from scratch, they also carries loose diamonds and gemstones. Satisfaction is guaranteed.

JEWELRY

∞ Diamond Purchasing Information ∞

DYNAMIC TANGIBLES CORPORATION**
643 S. Olive St.
Los Angeles, CA 90014
213/627-4042
CREDIT CARDS: AE, MC, V

Dynamic Tangibles is offering the readers of BUYING RETAIL IS STUPID something very special. They sell a 20 minute video tape that teaches all you need to know about diamonds. Now you can become an expert and walk into a jewelry store with confidence. The video tape retails for $79.95, however with your BUYING RETAIL IS STUPID discount coupon, your price is $15.95. The speaker is a graduate gemologist, and a former instructor at the world famous GIA (Gemological Institute of America). The savings on the purchase of one diamond will more than pay for the cost of the video and then some.

MEDICAL NEEDS

∞ Drug Stores & Pharmacies ∞

CONSUMER DISCOUNT DRUGS
6542 Hollywood Blvd.
Hollywood, CA 90028
213/461-3606
HOURS: MON-SAT: 9-9 SUN: 10-6
CREDIT CARDS: DISC, MC, V

You can save an average of 30% off the retail price on most items in this fully stocked drug store. Consumer Discount Drugs carries everything from vitamins and brand name cosmetics, to health and beauty aids. Every week, they feature at least 10-20 special sale items, so check those out for extra savings!

P X DRUGS NO. 2**
6318 Van Nuys Blvd.
Van Nuys, CA 91406
818/785-0441
HOURS: MON: 8:30-6:30 TUES-FRI: 8:30-8 SAT: 9-1
CREDIT CARDS: MC, V

Everything you buy in this drug store is discounted. Prescriptions, hair and skin care products, greeting cards, cosmetics, health aids and food items such as soft drinks, ice cream and lots of munchies. P X Drugs honors most insurance plans in their pharmacy. Presentation of your BUYING RETAIL IS STUPID coupon will get you an additional 10% discount on anything in the store but prescriptions.

SUPER-RITE DRUGS INC.
14425 Burbank Blvd.
Van Nuys, CA 91401
818/787-2552
HOURS: MON-FRI: 9-6 SAT: 9-3
CREDIT CARDS: MC, V

With the high cost of medication, it's wise to shop around for the best price. Super-Rite Drugs will guarantee the lowest price on any prescription with verification of pricing from another pharmacy. While waiting for your prescription, free coffee and cookies are offered as a special

MEDICAL NEEDS

touch. You can also browse around the store examining their low prices on vitamins, health and beauty aids, cosmetics and greeting cards. Super-Rite ships prescriptions anywhere in the United States.

∞ SUPPLIES & EQUIPMENT ∞

ANDERS ORTHOPEDICS & PROSTHETICS
1825 N. Western Ave.
Los Angeles, CA 90027
213/461-4279
HOURS: MON-FRI: 9-5
CREDIT CARDS: CASH OR CHECKS ONLY

From braces to wheelchairs, Anders carries everything in orthopedic and prosthetics lines. They have more than 25 years of experience so you will receive knowledgeable, professional service plus savings of 30 to 50% off retail. They also have corsets, trusses, orthopedic shoes, surgical stockings, crutches, and many other necessary items. Just ask for Johnny Anders.

ELECTROPEDIC ADJUSTABLE BEDS
15600 Roscoe Blvd.
Van Nuys, CA 91406
818/909-0077
HOURS: MON-SAT: 10-4   SUN: 12-4
CREDIT CARDS: AE, MC, V

When one of our husbands unfortunately threw his back out while playing paddle tennis, we decided an electric bed was one of the answers for a quick recovery. And it was. Electropedic Adjustable Beds is a factory outlet and sells these comfortable beds at savings of 40 to 50% off retail. The beds are available in twin, full, queen, king, dual queen, and dual king.

MEDICAL NEEDS

QUICKMED SUPPLIES INC.
3421 San Fernando Rd., #H
Los Angeles, CA 90065
800/336-3660, 213/259-1000

HOURS: MON-FRI: 9-5
CREDIT CARDS: CASH OR CHECKS ONLY

Quickmed Supplies is your one-stop shop for all medical supplies such as wheelchairs, orthopedic goods, portable commodes, gauze, bandaids, and cotton. They carry back supports, canes, knee braces, and other related products. This is a discount warehouse where you can save 20 to 30% off retail prices. If it's portable, you'll find everything related to medical recuperation at Quickmed Supplies.

∞ USED EQUIPMENT ∞

GALAXY SALON EQUIPMENT MFG. CO.
5411 Sheila St.
Los Angeles, CA 90040
213/728-3980

HOURS: MON-FRI: 10-5
CREDIT CARDS: MC, V

Galaxy Salon Equipment is at your service with factory direct prices on hospital and physician supply equipment. If new equipment isn't in your budget, you can save even more on their used equipment. Savings run up to 50% off retail.

KAGAN SURPLUS SALES**
8050 Webb Ave.
North Hollywood, CA 91605
818/768-1422

HOURS: MON-THUR: 8:45-5:45 FRI: 8:30-5:15 SAT: 10-4:30
CREDIT CARDS: CASH OR CHECKS ONLY

Kagan Surplus Sales specializes in used office furniture, hospital furniture, home care items, and material handling equipment. This 4,000 square foot warehouse offers items that have been completely refurbished (repaired, painted and recovered if necessary). Savings range from 50 to 90% off what you would pay normally if these items were brand new. The price is the only way to tell that the wheelchairs (always a large

MEDICAL NEEDS

selection) and Geri-chairs are used. In addition, Kagan Surplus Sales carries desks, credenzas, chairs, file cabinets, shelving, casters, carts, lockers, storage cabinets, medical, lab and x-ray equipment. Don't forget to use your BUYING RETAIL IS STUPID coupon for additional savings. You'll save 5% if your purchase is under $100, and 10% if your purchase is over $100.

MUSIC & MOVIES

∞ CDs, Records, Tapes & Videos ∞

ARON'S RECORD SHOP
1150 N. Highland
Hollywood, CA 90038
213/469-4700
HOURS: MON-SAT: 10-10 SUN: 11-8
CREDIT CARDS: AE, DISC, MC, V

You'll always save 10 to 20% off new items such as cassettes, laser disks, CDs and LPs. Aron's Record Shop has everything in current releases, plus a wide selection of Japanese and European imports, audiophile pressings, and small local labels. They put out at least 1,000 used records each day, at special discount prices. Blank audio and video tapes are offered at big savings. Check out the buys on video games, soundtracks and Broadway shows. Bring in your old albums, CDs, tapes and laser discs for trade value towards the purchase of new merchandise.

CD BANZAI!
8250 W. 3rd St.
Los Angeles, CA 90048
213/653-0800
HOURS: MON-THUR: 12-8 FRI-SAT: 12-10 SUN: 12-6
CREDIT CARDS: AE, MC, V

For everything in CDs, visit CD Banzai! New CD selections at savings of 10 to 20% include rock, jazz, classical, movie sound tracts, show tunes, reggae, collector items and world beat music. What they don't have in stock will be researched and special-ordered for you. They also carry hundreds of used CDs with good up-to-date titles. Joining their yearly membership program offers you further discounts and many other benefits. Trade-ins are accepted. They are very customer service oriented and additional discounts are given on all new CDs if you pay in cash.

MUSIC & MOVIES

DISC-CONNECTION RECORDS & COMPACT DISCS
10970 W. Pico Blvd.
West Los Angeles, CA 90054
310/208-7211

HOURS: MON-THUR, SAT: 11-7 FRI: 11-9
CREDIT CARDS: AE, MC, V

Eighty thousand albums in one room. Find me a sales clerk, quickly. Of course, with that many records, you'll always find what you want, especially since they specialize in hard-to-find movie soundtracks and Broadway show tunes or original cast albums. At only 6% above cost, you'll want to replace all the records where you've worn out the grooves over the years. They also carry cassettes (blank and prerecorded), CDs and records, plus tape cleaning paraphernalia, books and record collecting magazines. But that's not all, ladies and gents, they have a large stock of comedy and personality albums. Here's a switch. This store gives you money! Bring in your unwanted LPs or cassettes, and they'll pay you cash or give you credit towards purchases.

MOBY DISC
1835 Newport Blvd.
Costa Mesa, CA 92627
714/897-2799

HOURS: MON-SUN: 10-10
CREDIT CARDS: DISC, MC, V

Moby Disc sells new and used CDs. All used merchandise is priced as follows: CDs $1.99 to $8.99; CD singles 49¢ to $3.99; cassettes/LPs 25¢ to $4.99. If you have any CDs, cassettes or LPs that are unwanted, trade them in for credit against your purchase. You can also get cash for your trade-in. If your looking for Stevie Wonder's Greatest Hits, Eric Clapton or Cream, you'll find them here at a "whale" of a savings.
Additional Locations: 6 other stores throughout S. CA

MUSIC EXCHANGE**
210 W. Colorado St.
Glendale, CA 91204
818/240-6539

HOURS: MON-FRI: 12-10 SAT: 11-10 SUN: 12-9
CREDIT CARDS: MC, V

Are the prices of new CDs putting a pinch in your music budget? You can buy recycled CDs here for 99¢ to $10. Used CDs make up about a third of the store and are alphabetized in bins according to subject, not artist. Before making your purchase, you can listen to any used CD over headsets on one of their eight CD players. If you have a few CDs lying around that you no longer listen to, take them to Music Exchange for cash or credit. They also take used cassettes. (Used cassettes sell for 99¢ to $3.99.) All new releases are carried, and the top 30 hits are always on sale. They'll beat any advertised price. All you have to do is show them the ad. Everything in the store is sold with satisfaction guaranteed. If you are unhappy with your purchase you get your money back by presenting your sales receipt. This goes for new items as well as recycled. Special orders are no problem—with their computer system, they can see if what you're looking for is already in stock, new or used. They want their customers to be happy. If you use your BUYING RETAIL IS STUPID coupon, you'll receive an extra 20% discount on used CDs or cassettes.

PENNY LANE
62 Windward Ave.
Venice, CA 90291
310/399-4631

HOURS: 10-7 SEVEN DAYS A WEEK
CREDIT CARDS: AE, MC, V

With new music groups popping up more and more every day, one truly needs to be educated in all the current sounds. Penny Lane is a place that keeps you updated in rock, heavy metal and rap. New and used records, tapes and CDs are bought and sold. Bored with some of your old sounds? Take them to Penny Lane's and trade them in for store credit. Make sure you check out their 99¢ section of tapes and records.

RECORD SURPLUS
11609 Pico Blvd.
West Los Angeles, CA 90064
310/478-4217

HOURS: MON-THUR: 11-9 FRI-SAT: 11-10 SUN: 11-7
CREDIT CARDS: MC, V

Record Surplus (A.K.A. The Last Record Store) has used records and tapes starting at 92¢ and CDs at $1.85. They have all styles and categories of music—rock, jazz, soul, classical, movie soundtracks, and collectibles—guaranteed to tickle anybody's fancy. You can also get cash for your old LPs, CDs, cassettes and videos. Every store provides listening stations for customers to use prior to making purchases. Customer satisfaction is guaranteed.

Additional Locations:
Costa Mesa–2300 Harbor Blvd., 714/546-3711
Sherman Oaks–4620 Van Nuys Blvd., 818/501-1022
West Hollywood–8913 Sunset Blvd., 310/659-9994

MUSIC & MOVIES

ROCKET J'S RECORDS
18758 Ventura Blvd.
Tarzana, CA 91356
818/881-2844
HOURS: MON-SAT: 11-8
CREDIT CARDS: AE, MC, V

Looking for a rare or out of print LP? Rocket J's has a vast inventory of these, both new and used! They also carry new and used CDs and cassettes. The price of new CDs is just $1 over their cost, and everything else is discounted as well. Whether the item you purchase is new or used, Rocket J's gives you a 100% guarantee of satisfaction!

SECOND TIME AROUND RECORDS**
7704 Melrose Ave.
Los Angeles, CA 90046
213/852-1982
HOURS: MON-SAT: 11-9 SUN: 12-7
CREDIT CARDS: AE, MC, V

Love isn't the only thing better the second time around. Go to Second Time Around Records and you'll see what we mean. Shoppers will find new and used records, CDs, tapes, videos and used stereo equipment. Because they love a challenge, they'll hunt down any record you want. Elvis and Beatles lovers will find collectibles among their memorabilia. Used records start at 99¢. Don't forget to bring your BUYING RETAIL IS STUPID coupon to receive an extra 5% discount. They also have stores in Orange County (Discount Records) and San Diego (Record Heaven).
Additional Locations: 6 other stores throughout S. CA

SUPER POPS RECORD DETECTIVE**
1242 3rd St., #102
Santa Monica, CA 90401
310/395-1344
HOURS: MON: 1-5 TUES: 2-5 FRI-SAT: 1-6 SUN: 1-5
CREDIT CARDS: CASH OR CHECKS ONLY

You'll find used CDs and tapes here, but the focus is on rare LPs. The hours are limited because the primary business is searching for out-of-print records or CDs, which is done free of charge. All you have to do is give them a call (or leave a message on the answering machine) and they will do their best to find the long lost album of your dreams. Prices start at $1 for records and go up depending on the age and condition. CDs and imports start at $6. You'll receive a 10% discount on your purchase when you present your BUYING RETAIL IS STUPID coupon.

TOWER RECORDS
8801 Sunset Blvd.
West Los Angeles, CA 90069
310/657-7300
HOURS: 9 AM-MIDNIGHT SEVEN DAYS A WEEK
CREDIT CARDS: AE, MC, V

Tower has the largest selection of records in the western United States, and they have every conceivable tape and cassette you can mention. Usu-ally, tapes and records are $1–$3 off list price, but there are big savings on everything. They have a separate building on Sunset just for classical selections and another for videos. They sell cases and accessories too. Oh, there is something else you should know. Unless an urge hits you in the wee hours of the morning, Tower Records is open 365 days a year for immediate music gratification.
Additional Locations: 10 other stores throughout S. CA

∞ CONCERTS & PLAYS ∞

HOLLYWOOD BOWL
2301 N. Highland Ave.
Hollywood, CA 90068
213/850-2000
HOURS: TUES, THUR, FRIDAY - CALL FIRST
CREDIT CARDS: FREE

For those of us who really enjoy great music and really appreciate the simple pleasures in life, keep your ears tuned for the FREE Hollywood Bowl performance rehearsals that take place during July through September. They usually rehearse Tuesdays, Thursdays and Fridays between 9:00 a.m. and 11:00 a.m., but be sure to call first to check on the season's schedule.

"ON THE HOUSE"
P.O. Box 5215
Santa Monica, CA 90409
310/392-7588
HOURS: TUES: 1-5 WED-FRI: 11-5
CREDIT CARDS: CHECKS ONLY

Once in a while, you'll hear about something that seems "to good to be true," but that's not the case with "On The House." It is a theatre membership club where members pay annual dues of $125.00 for two people, to receive 12 months of free tickets to every event their service offers (25 to 40 events each week). You could literally attend a different performance every night of the week if time allowed. "On The House" doesn't advertise, so members just pass the good news along to friends. You will enjoy everything from live theatre, small theatres, large theatres, movie screenings at major motion picture studios, nightclub shows and dance events. There's a special reservation number, and a private 24-hour hot line announcing what shows are available.

∞ MOVIES ∞

ODYSSEY VIDEO
11910 Wilshire Blvd.
Los Angeles, CA 90025
310/477-2523

HOURS: 9-12 SEVEN DAYS A WEEK
CREDIT CARDS: AE, MC, V

If you've felt like it's been an odyssey lately finding that special movie you've wanted to see, then look no more! The Odyssey carries over 10,000 movies. You won't believe the prices. They have the lowest prices in town! Tuesday and Wednesday their movies are 99¢ per day. They charge $2.50 on the other days. Musicals, westerns, children's films, and selected new releases are 99¢ everyday. It takes no Herculean effort to get there, so you can cocoon the whole weekend.

– MOVIE THEATER –

SUPER SAVER CINEMAS
12343 Seal Beach Blvd.
Seal Beach, CA 90740
310/594-9411

HOURS: CALL THEATER FOR SCHEDULE
CREDIT CARDS: CASH ONLY

Imagine, going to the movies for only $1.50. No, we aren't in a time warp. No matter what time of day it is or what first run movie is playing, that's what you pay at Super Saver Cinema. So, if you are a movie buff who still enjoys the sights, sounds and smells of a real movie theater, this is the place for you. Their are seven theaters at the Seal Beach location and eight theaters at the Pomona location.
Additional Locations:
Pomona–1460 E. Hills Ave., 714/620-1036

MUSICAL INSTRUMENTS

∞ Music Stores ∞

ABEL'S MUSIC
5456 Centinela Ave.
Mar Vista, CA 90066
310/827-7837
HOURS: BY APPOINTMENT ONLY, MON-SUN: 11-5
CREDIT CARDS: CASH OR CHECKS ONLY

James Abel, owner of Abel's Music offers you Steinway at cost to 25% above cost. They carry everything from spinets to grands. So if you're ready to accompany Itzhak Perlman, or if your goal is just to get through your exercises without missing a note, they've got you covered. There are always 15 grand pianos, and up to 20 vertical pianos on hand at any given time. The assortment available ranges from beginner practice pianos to concert grands. Other brand names carried are Baldwin, Kawai, Yamaha and Hanil. They also have electronic keyboards and synthesizers. Abel's has recently added musical instruments to the inventory. New instruments are 25-50% off retail and you'll save 70-80% on used instruments. Financing and credit are available. As part of his excellent customer service, Mr. Abel offers free delivery and tuning. Buy one of their used pianos or wait for one of their special sales offered three to four times a year. Remember to call for an appointment.

ACE MUSIC
1714 Wilshire Blvd.
Santa Monica, CA 90403
310/828-5688
HOURS: MON-SAT: 10-6
CREDIT CARDS: MC, V

Finally, a store that quotes discount prices over the telephone without hemming and hawing. Just tell those customers what they want to hear. That may be because this store has had continuous ownership since 1964, guaranteeing interest in the customer after the sale. They have brand name musical instruments like Fender, Gibson, Martin and Guild, and all makes and models of electric and acoustic guitars, amps, pianos, synthesizers, plus PA equipment. Service is provided on all products they sell. They offer a special in-store warranty beyond what the manufacturers offer. You can expect to save 20 to 50% off retail prices.

MUSICAL INSTRUMENTS

AMENDOLA MUSIC, INC.
1692 Centinela Ave.
Inglewood, CA 90302
310/645-2420
HOURS: MON-FRI: 11-7 SAT: 10-5:30
CREDIT CARDS: AE, MC, V

At Amendola Music, you can save up to 50% off the manufacturer's retail price on musical instruments, amplification systems, professional sound systems, recording equipment and other accessories. They carry such names as Fender, Gibson, Guild, Ovation, JBL, Yamaha, Ibanez, Tama, Ludwig, Rogers, Zildjian, Paiste, Shure, Armstrong, Bach, Elmer, and more. They also have a complete repair center. Says Mr. Amendola, "We discount anything, anytime!" Financing is also available.

BETNUM MUSIC
403 N. Larchmont Blvd.
Los Angeles, CA 90004
213/464-7468
HOURS: MON-SAT: 10:30-6 SUN: 12-4
CREDIT CARDS: AE, DISC, MC, V

Betnum carries over 1,000 instruments, with one of the largest selections around of winds and horns. They consider themselves the number one saxophone dealer on the West Coast. In addition to band and orchestra instruments, they also have guitars, synthesizers, amps and electronic pianos, in most name brands. Savings range from 20% to 30% off retail on new instruments. Rentals are available and you can also have repair work done at Betnum Music. Since they've been in business since the early 1960s, I guess they are entitled to "toot" their own horn.

GOODMAN MUSIC
1676 W. Lincoln Ave.
Anaheim, CA 92801
714/520-4500
HOURS: MON-FRI: 10-7 SAT: 10-6 SUN: 12-5
CREDIT CARDS: ALL MAJOR

You'll find Goodman Music has discounted prices on a large selection of keyboards and professional audio and sound gear—including direct-to-disk and digital multitrack recording equipment—P.A. systems and micro-phones. They also carry a full line of digital pianos, home keyboards and synthesizers. Brand names include Apple, Atari, Claris, Digidesign, Roland, Yamaha, Korg, Peavey, Son, Techics, Casio and

Lexicon. Make sure you put your name on their mailing list. During special sales savings can run up to 80% off retail.
Additional Locations:
Long Beach–4145 Viking Way, 310/429-9795 (closed on Sundays)
Los Angeles–780 S. La Brea Ave., 213/937-2177
North Hollywood–4227 Lankershim Blvd., 818/760-4430
Sherman Oaks–4631 Van Nuys Blvd., 818/784-6900
West Covina–544 N. Azusa Ave., 818/967-5767

THE GUITAR STORE
496 E. Holt Ave.
Pomona, CA 91767
714/623-6448

HOURS: MON-FRI: 11-7 SAT: 11-6
CREDIT CARDS: MC, V

This discount music store, offering up to 50% off retail prices, is a dream come true for professional bands. They have 10,000 square feet stocked with a full line of guitars, amplifiers, drums, sound systems, keyboards, recording equipment, stage lighting and accessories. With their seven departments staffed by experts, you'll get straight answers to your questions. Some of the brands carried are Yamaha, Roland, JBL, Tama, Fender, Gallen Krueger and Ibanez. They handle both new and used items. Trade-ins are accepted, and they buy used equipment. Financing is available.

HOUSE OF DRUMS AND GUITARS
17046 Devonshire St.
Northridge, CA 91325
818/360-7100

HOURS: MON-SAT: 11-7 SUN: 12-3
CREDIT CARDS: AE, DISC, MC, V

The House of Drums and Guitars carries drums, guitars, PA systems, keyboards, synthesizers and recording equipment at savings of 20 to 50% off retail price. During the year they hold special clinics for musicians. One of their clinics for drummers featured "the 8 year old wunderkid," Jacob Armen, who performed and shared techniques. Major brands such as Fender and Ovation guitars, Yamaha keyboards, and Ludwig drums are always in stock. They are the Valley's largest Peavy distributor, and lessons are also available at a nominal charge.

MUSICAL INSTRUMENTS

NADINES MUSIC
18136 Sherman Way
Reseda, CA 91355
818/881-1411

HOURS: MON-FRI: 11-7   SAT: 10-6
CREDIT CARDS: ALL MAJOR

Nadines has been in the valley for 17 years, selling guitars, amps, keyboards, multi-track tape recorders, acoustic drums, microphones, PA systems, speakers, computers and software at 20% below retail prices. They carry such brand-names as Fender, Gibson, Roland, Korg, Guild, Atari, Casio, Electro-Voice and JBL. There is no high-pressure salesmanship; the people are all friendly, knowledgeable, and really want to help. Great prices and good service, what more could you want?
Additional Locations:
Hollywood–6251 Santa Monica Blvd., 213/464-7550

SIGHTSINGER MUSIC
3203 S. Harbor Blvd.
Santa Ana, CA 92704
714/540-1441

HOURS: MON-FRI: 10-7   SAT: 10-6
CREDIT CARDS: AE, DISC, MC, V

Looking for 20 to 50% off on the best in electronic keyboards, synthesizers, music computers, music software, guitars (acoustic and electric), amplifiers, PA systems, drums or accessories? At Sightsinger Music you'll find name brands like Roland, Yamaha, Korg, Fender, Guild, Martin, Takamine, Ovation, JBL, Ricken Backer, Sunn, Marshall, Ampeg and Atari. They have one of the largest selections in musical gear along with a very service oriented and knowledgeable staff. Satisfied musicians have been buying equipment at Sightsinger Music since 1964.
Additional Locations:
Orange–804 N. Tustin Ave., 714/639-3940

WEST L.A. MUSIC
11345 Santa Monica Blvd.
Los Angeles, CA 90025
310/477-1945, 818/905-7020

HOURS: MON-FRI: 11-7   SAT: 10-6
CREDIT CARDS: AE, MC, V

This is THE music store where you can find everything in professional audio equipment, everything in musical instruments, and everyone who is anyone in the music or recording industry. The recording stars aren't on Hollywood Boulevard or Sunset. They're at West L.A. Music, buying the equipment they need for their studios, their band members, their tours. West L.A. Music will beat any deal you can get anywhere else, and they have guitars, drums, speakers, microphones and stands, keyboards, synthesizers, computers and music software, recording equipment and all accessories. They are usually the first in town to get the newest items, and they have frequent special sales, so check them out often if music is your beat. You'll find helpful,and knowledgeable sales people to assist you in every department.

WOODLOWE MUSIC CENTER
21410 Ventura Blvd.
Woodland Hills, CA 91364
818/883-0050
HOURS: MON-FRI: 10-8   SAT: 10-6
CREDIT CARDS: MC, V

Woodlowe Music Center offers a terrific range of merchandise and service, at 20 to 40% off retail prices. In addition to selling quality instruments such as guitars, drums, clarinets, flutes, violins, trumpets and any other type of musical instrument, they have one of the finest teaching staffs in the San Fernando Valley. Amplifiers, sheet music and books are also available. They have provided fantastic service since 1965 along with instruments, lessons and repairs.

∞ PIANOS, ORGANS & KEYBOARDS ∞

HOLLYWOOD PIANO RENTAL CO.
1647 N. Highland Ave.
Hollywood, CA 90028
213/462-2329
HOURS: MON-FRI: 9-5:30   SAT: 9-4   SUN: 12-5
CREDIT CARDS: MC, V

Family owned since 1928, Hollywood Piano Rental offers savings of 10 to 20% on all types of pianos and organs for home or professional needs. They have about 2,000 pianos for rent which makes them one of the largest private collectors of pianos in the world. They also sell both new and used pianos in all styles. In-house financing is available for your purchases.
Additional Locations:
Burbank–933 W. Olive Ave., 818/848-0222

MUSICAL INSTRUMENTS

KEYBOARD CONCEPTS INC.
5600 Van Nuys Blvd.
Van Nuys, CA 91401
818/787-0201
HOURS: MON-SAT: 10-6 SUN: 12-5
CREDIT CARDS: ALL MAJOR

Keyboard Concepts has over 100 new and used acoustic and digital pianos and home keyboards on display. You'll save 30-50% off retail on such brand names as Kawai, Yamaha, Steinway, Baldwin, Technics, Korg and more. Need to rent instead of purchase—Keyboard Concepts can solve the problem. With each purchase of a new keyboard they offer free lessons. Owners Dennis and Jeff are committed to servicing their customers—so give them a call.

KEYBOARD EXCHANGE
30613 Canwood St.
Agoura, CA 91301
818/889-9780
HOURS: MON-SAT: 10-6 SUN: 12-5
CREDIT CARDS: AE, DISC, MC, V

For the past 10 years Keyboard Exchange has been serving the community with exclusive, factory-direct pianos and electronic keyboards made by Baldwin, Kawai, Young Chang. Whether you are in search of a grand piano or a spinet, you'll find that their prices average 25 to 50% off the retail prices charged in most stores. Lessons, repair work and financing are also available.

KEYBOARD LIQUIDATORS
6600 Telegraph Rd.
Commerce, CA 90018
213/724-2828
HOURS: MON-SAT: 10-6
CREDIT CARDS: MC, V

Pianos and organs are the only game in town here, and you'll save 30 to 50% on high quality instruments at wholesale prices. There are spinets and there are grands. If they don't have it, they'll order it for you. Pianos start at $200 and organs at about $400. You know you've got plenty to choose from with styles that include pianos that would retail for as much as $20,000. They carry brands such as Baldwin, Yamaha, Kawai, Hammond, Samick, Kimball, Story & Clark and have been in business since 1915. They also handle churches and recording studios.

Their work is primarily by appointment, and 75% of all their business comes from word-of-mouth because they specialize in satisfied customers. You can save even more on their used pianos and organs, and also at their special sales held twice a year.

THE LITTLE PIANO SHOP
26111 Bouquet Canyon Rd.
Santa Clarita, CA 91350
805/254-9710

HOURS: MON-FRI: 10-6   SAT: 10-5   SUN: BY APPOINTMENT ONLY
CREDIT CARDS: MC, V

You will definitely feel Boris Bernards' love for the piano as you walk into his store, The Little Piano Shop. He has been selling new and used pianos since 1961. They are a factory authorized dealer for Wurlitzer and Yamaha. And yes, Mr. Bernards will even give BUYING RETAIL IS STUPID readers a gift, valued at $30 to $60, when a new piano is purchased.

MERRILL'S MUSIC**
1428 4th St.
Santa Monica, CA 90401
310/393-0344

HOURS: MON-FRI: 10-7   SAT: 10-6   SUN: 12-5
CREDIT CARDS: ALL MAJOR

Merrill's Music is the place to go for keyboards of any type. Discounts run 20 to 50% off retail on all major brands such as Yamaha, Kawai, Technics, Casio and others. If within 60 days of purchasing an item from Merrill's you see it for less money, you can get a refund on the difference. Rentals start at $10 for acoustic pianos and $15 for electronic keyboards. Should you buy from Merrill's and later decide to trade up, you get the full price credited to your new purchase. This trade-in policy is good for one full year on electronic keyboards and is good for five years on acoustic keyboards. For the best deals, check out their used keyboards. The price is usually lower than what you'd pay a private party and includes a full 10 year parts and labor warranty, delivery and tuning in your home. They accept trade-ins on keyboards and professional audio equipment of any kind. They don't take trade-ins of organs, accordions or Kazoos. Also, they have a "music software bar," and they don't carry drums or guitars. You'll save an extra 10% discount when you use your BUYING RETAIL IS STUPID coupon.

∞ REPAIR ∞

UNITED BAND INSTRUMENT CO.
3833 W. Avenue 43
Los Angeles, CA 90041
213/257-7514

HOURS: TUES-SAT: 10-5
CREDIT CARDS: CASH OR CHECKS ONLY

If you have a woodwind or brass instrument in need of repair take it to United Band Instrument Co. They have been in business since 1954 and know their stuff! Repairs cost about 30% less than you'd pay elsewhere. When it comes to repairing a favorite instrument, we can definitely say that good deals are blowing in the wind, or brass, or woodwind.

OFFICE & BUSINESS NEEDS

∞ ONE-STOP SUPPLIERS ∞

A 'N B STATIONERY
12338 Ventura Blvd.
Studio City, CA 91604
818/760-0244

HOURS: MON-FRI: 9-5:30 SAT: 10-5
CREDIT CARDS: AE, MC, V

This is a small, personal store but their stock and service are large. A 'N B Stationery carries a complete line of office supplies, office furniture, accounting and computer supplies, and even greeting cards. You will discover all major brands and all at a 20 to 50% savings. Call to find out about A 'N B Stationery's quarterly sales for even bigger discounts.

BUDGET OFFICE PRODUCTS
19553 Parthenia St.
Northridge, CA 91324
818/993-3211 or 213/873-4545

HOURS: MON-FRI: 9-5:30 SAT: 10-4
CREDIT CARDS: MC, V

This company has a friendly, knowledgeable staff headed by Barbara Bakley, and they offer immediate free delivery of office supplies, furniture, equipment and printing. You'll find everything at Budget Office Products is discounted from 10 to 80% and they guarantee meeting or beating the competition with ad proof within 30 days of purchase. You may place your order by phone.

DISCOUNT DESK CENTER
21035 Sherman Way
Canoga Park, CA 91303
818/883-2112, 800/227-8571

HOURS: MC, V
CREDIT CARDS: MON-FRI: 9-6 SAT: 10-5

At Discount Desk Center you can save 40% off list price on most items, and they have a full catalogue of desks, chairs, credenzas, sofas, bookshelves, cabinets, and a lot more. Each year, they purchase millions of

dollars worth of desks, so they get great savings which they can afford to pass on to you. Their warehouse is on the premises and there is 10,000 square feet of showroom space. Ask to be put on their mailing list.
Additional Locations:
Burbank–633 San Fernando, 818/244-7723, 800/350-2112
Ventura–4071 E. Main St., 805/656-3375, 800/310-3375

MEYER'S OFFICE PRODUCTS
1952 S. Main St.
Los Angeles, CA 90007
213/749-7138

HOURS: MON-FRI: 8-5

CREDIT CARDS: AE, MC, V

Meyer's Office Products has been serving the Southern California business community for over 40 years with discount prices and quality personalized service. Their store is located just south of the Los Angeles Convention Center. On display are many styles of desks, chairs, files, computer furniture, data supplies, and general office supplies. Over 15,000 items are available in one day from their catalogues. Everything you need is discounted 10–50% below retail. Ken Meyer and his staff specialize in personal service and offer expert product knowledge.

MODERN SERVICE OFFICE SUPPLY CO., INC.
1345 East 16th St.
Los Angeles, CA 90021
213/748-4171, 800/672-6767

HOURS: MON-FRI: 7:30-5:30

CREDIT CARDS: AE, MC, V

This store offers you business necessities such as fax machines, copier supplies, typewriter ribbons, micro computer supplies, calculators, office furniture, writing instruments, word and data processing supplies, and computer furniture. You can save 20 to 80% off retail prices when you shop here. Modern Service Office Supply Company offers free delivery in California, Arizona, Utah and Nevada with a minimum order.

OFFICE & BUSINESS NEEDS

OFFICE DEPOT
15385 Oxnard St.
Van Nuys, CA 91411
818/988-2582

HOURS: MON-FRI: 8-7   SAT: 9-5
CREDIT CARDS: CASH OR CHECKS ONLY

The Office Depot is a warehouse store with low prices, and you don't have to sacrifice service for savings. Their knowledgeable sales staff will assist you or answer any questions you have about office supplies, equipment or furniture at this one-stop shop. They offer discount prices on thousands of best selling, top-quality, brand name office products in their huge, no frills warehouse stores.
Additional Locations: 20 other stores throughout S. CA

OFFICE SUPPLY CO.
6141 Kester Ave.
Van Nuys, CA 91411
818/786-1660

HOURS: MON-FRI: 8:30-5:30
CREDIT CARDS: MC, V

The Office Supply Company has been doing business for over 35 years. You can save a lot of money if you are furnishing a new office or restocking your present one. Save up to 50% on office furniture and at least 10% or more on office supplies. With all those years of experience, you know you'll get professional help here.

STAPLES
1962 Barranca Rd.
Irvine, CA 92714
714/250-3133

HOURS: MON-FRI: 7-9 P.M.   SAT: 9-6   SUN: 11-5
CREDIT CARDS: ALL MAJOR

You'll find everything you need in the way of brand name office supplies, equipment and furniture at 20–70% off retail. If you find a lower price, they'll match it. Membership is free and nonmembers pay an additional 5% above posted prices. Delivery is free for orders larger than $150. This doesn't include furniture delivery. You can call 800/333-3330 for next-day delivery or same-day pick-up at the store. Hours for this service are 8:30 a.m. to 5 p.m. Monday through Friday.
Additional Locations: 24 other stores throughout S. CA

∞ BUSINESS MACHINES ∞

ABM ART TYPE BUSINESS MACHINES
15420 Devonshire St.
Mission Hills, CA 91345
818/893-8066
HOURS: MON-FRI: 9-6 SAT: 9-3
CREDIT CARDS: MC, V

It takes longer to say their name than it does to get a good deal on all types of office equipment. ABM has copiers, fax machines, typewriters, word processing calculators and supplies. Andrew Katz guarantees the lowest prices around, and they handle most name brands such as IBM, T/A Adler-Royal, Sharp, Brother, and Panasonic. You'll also find IBM compatible computers at 40–50% off retail. ABM has friendly knowledgeable service.

CITY TYPEWRITER OF WESTWOOD
10917 W. Pico Blvd.
West Los Angeles, CA 90064
310/478-7282
HOURS: MON-FRI: 8:30-5:30 SAT: 9-5
CREDIT CARDS: MC, V

Do you have a problem trying to work your new answering machine, word processor, typewriter, Fax machine or calculator? Then make your next investment at City Typewriter of Westwood where you'll find such brand names as Smith Corona, Sanyo, Sony, Norelco and Brother. Their prices are very low, and they will give you lessons on how to operate every machine you purchase. These days, even typewriters and calculators have so many different options you need some instructions other than those printed in the manual. City Typewriter does repairs on the premises and is an authorized center for Smith Corona.

COMMERCIAL TYPEWRITER CO.
18344 Oxnard St., #109
Tarzana, CA 91356
818/344-1495
HOURS: MON-FRI: 8:30-5
CREDIT CARDS: DISC, MC, V

If you are a person that prefers dealing with experience, Commercial Typewriter has been serving Los Angeles since 1911. Today they offer typewriters at savings of 40% below retail prices. Choose from IBM,

Olympia, Olivetti, SCM, and others. You know you'll get a good deal, as Commercial Typewriter also offers big savings on calculators, computers, and copiers. They also have maintenance agreements, and they have an excellent service department.

DISCOUNT OFFICE MACHINES
11351 Santa Monica Blvd.
Los Angeles, CA 90025
310/477-6091
HOURS: MON-FRI: 9:30-6 SAT: 10-5
CREDIT CARDS: MC, V

You can save up to 50% on typewriters, answering machines, cash registers, dictating machines, calculators, copy machines, and more. Discount Office Machines carries Canon, IBM, Sanyo, Olympia, Sharp, Texas Instruments, and provide in-house service.

∞ USED FURNITURE & EQUIPMENT ∞

A B E CORPORATION
3400 N. Peck Rd.
El Monte, CA 91732
818/443-4223
HOURS: MON-FRI: 8-6 SAT: 9-5
CREDIT CARDS: MC, V

A.B.E. is a 30 year old corporation that specializes in purchasing, recycling, and selling high quality, pre-owned office furniture and equipment. They buy from savings and loans and other failed businesses so they can pass on huge savings (up to 90%.) They have three locations that sell wholesale to dealers and retail to the public. There is a multi-million dollar inventory to choose from in their 40,000 square foot showroom which is one of the largest in California; however, they have another 80,000 square feet of warehouse and a fleet of trucks for pick-up and delivery. They boast being the largest company specializing in recycled office furniture; from what we can tell, there is no disagreement.
Additional Locations:
Rosemead–2542 San Gabriel Blvd., 818/280-7823
Whittier–2865 Pellissier Pl., 310/692-0514

OFFICE & BUSINESS NEEDS

ACE USED OFFICE FURNITURE WAREHOUSE**
843 Ventura Blvd.
Oxnard, CA 93030
805/981-0290

HOURS: MON-FRI: 9-5 SAT: 9-3:30
CREDIT CARDS: CASH OR CHECKS ONLY

This 4,000 square foot warehouse is full of name-brand office furniture. Because the merchandise is used, savings run 50-90% off original retail prices. You'll find desks, chairs, filing cabinets, bookcases, refurbished panel systems, conference tables, reception desks and just about anything else found in any office. They also repair and refinish furniture, plus they will custom build items to your specifications. Brands include Anderson, Hayworth, Hon, Steelcase, Kimball, Harpers and many more. You can save an extra 5% on your purchase when you present your BUYING RETAIL IS STUPID discount coupon.

AMERICAN SURPLUS TRADERS**
18643 Parthenia St.
Northridge, CA 91324
818/993-5355

HOURS: MON-FRI: 8:30-5:30 SAT: 10:30-3:30
CREDIT CARDS: MC, V

They specialize in Holga office furniture and have 6,000 square feet of desks, secretarial chairs, executive chairs, file cabinets, lateral files, cabinets, shelf files, bookcases, and computer furniture. You'll find new furniture, which are factory seconds, used furniture, and industrial shelving. You can anticipate saving 15 to 60% off retail, but if you use your BUYING RETAIL IS STUPID coupon, you'll save an additional 10%!

BUDGET RENTS FURNITURE AND SALES**
6051 Telegraph Rd.
Los Angeles, CA 90040
213/720-5020

HOURS: MON-FRI: 9-5:30 SAT: 10-5
CREDIT CARDS: MC, V

This is where you buy home and office furniture that was previously available for rent at one of their stores. The furniture is well made and, depending on the condition of the item, is priced 30 to 90% off retail. Whether you need a sofa or office partitions, you'll find it all here. New shipments arrive several times a week and next day delivery is available. Remember to use your BUYING RETAIL IS STUPID coupon for an extra 10% discount.

OFFICE & BUSINESS NEEDS

KAGAN SURPLUS SALES**
8050 Webb Ave.
North Hollywood, CA 91605
818/768-1422

HOURS: MON-THUR: 8:45-5:45 FRI: 8:30-5:15 SAT: 10-4:30
CREDIT CARDS: CASH OR CHECKS ONLY

Kagan Surplus Sales specializes in used office furniture, and home car equipment. This 4,000 square foot warehouse has items that have been completely refurbished if necessary. Savings range from 50–90% off what you would pay normally if these items were brand new. The price is the only way you can tell their wheelchairs and Geri-chairs are used. In addition, Kagan carries desks, credenzas, chairs, file cabinets, shelving, casters, carts, lockers and cabinets. Don't forget to use your BUYING RETAIL IS STUPID coupon for additional savings. You'll save 5% if your purchase is under $100, and 10% if your purchase is over $100.

∞ SERVICES ∞

– PRINTING –

BUDGET PRINTING
6019 Sunset Blvd.
Hollywood, CA 90028
213/467-6048

HOURS: MON-FRI: 9:30-6
CREDIT CARDS: CASH OR CHECKS ONLY

In a bind because you needed something yesterday? Here's the place to get money-saving prices and rush services on all types of printing and typesetting. Budget Printing also has one day service on business cards and will handle all your photocopying needs. So stay within your budget, Budget Printing that is!

WHOLESALE PRINTING FACTORY 1**
17523 Ventura Blvd.
Encino, CA 91436
818/789-1055

HOURS: MON-FRI: 8:30-5:30
CREDIT CARDS: CASH OR CHECKS ONLY

The Wholesale Printing Factory will handle all of your printing and copying needs. They offer one day service on most items, and you will save 20% off the prices most other printers charge. A fax service is available for that document that just has to get there fast! Not only do you save on printing, you will save an additional 5% when you present your BUYING RETAIL IS STUPID coupon.

– SECRETARIAL –

AUTOMATED OFFICE SERVICES
10616 Bothwell Rd.
Chatsworth, CA 91311
818/368-4261
HOURS: MON-SAT: 8-5
CREDIT CARDS: CASH OR CHECKS ONLY

Automated Office Services offers complete secretarial services mandatory in today's business world. They can provide you with business letters, mailings, financial reports, resumes, and form letters at very competitive prices. One day service is available and they have the capability of "desk top publishing". In business since 1981, they are customer oriented and easy to deal with. If you need a secretary, but really don't want to hire one, then Automated Office Services may be the answer for you!

OPTICAL SERVICES

DR. M. FRIEDMAN AND ASSOCIATES**
10724 Washington Blvd.
Culver City, CA 90232
213/870-2848, 310/559-0500

HOURS: MON-TUES, THUR-FRI: 9:30-6:30   WED: 9:30-7   SAT: 9-5
CREDIT CARDS: AE, DISC, MC, V

Computerized eye exams. Hmmm, that sounds interesting. Well, there are also three doctors and ten assistants to give you traditional eye exams for $29. Contact lenses are available plus glasses with consumer discount frames or designer, high-fashion frames. Prices start at $39 for a standard single vision lens and frame. Bausch & Lomb soft spin contacts are $89, including eye examination. Services are 30% less than other offices, and they have a laboratory on the premises. After buying your first pair of glasses, standard vision lens are free with the purchase of two, three or more eyeglass frames. Dr. Friedman offers a money back guarantee on all merchandise. Presenting your BUYING RETAIL IS STUPID for an additional savings of 5% on eye glasses or contact lens.

DR. THOMAS KUTROSKY**
5308 Lankershim Blvd.
North Hollywood, CA 91601
818/769-2020

HOURS: MON-SAT: 9-6
CREDIT CARDS: AE, MC, V

You can get lenses, frames, and contacts from Dr. Tom at discount prices. While his storefront is not as large as some, his discounts are bigger than most. You'll save 25% and receive personalized service at the same time at Dr. Tom's office. Your BUYING RETAIL IS STUPID coupon will give you additional 5% discount, so don't leave it at home.

OPTICAL SERVICES

FOR EYES OPTICAL OF CALIFORNIA, INC.
18724 Ventura Blvd.
Tarzana, CA 91356
818/705-4020

HOURS: MON-FRI: 10-7:30 SAT: 10-5
CREDIT CARDS: DISC, MC, V

This full-service optical company sells prescription, sun, sport and other eyewear in its own stores coast-to-coast. It was started in the early 1970s by two opticians who decided to save the public money. As a result, you can now visit any For Eyes and save 25 to 50% on all prescription and nonprescription glasses. Each pair is custom made but the stores maintain a "one price" policy of $49 for regular line frames and lenses. A second pair purchased at the same time is $30. There are no added charges for plastic lenses, tinted lenses or oversized lenses. You can select such designer names as Anne Klein, Pierre Cardin, Oscar de la Renta and Gloria Vanderbilt. We have good news for moms and dads. A guarantee is provided for one year against breakage on children's glasses! Eye examinations are not available at most locations.

Additional Locations: 6 other stores throughout S. CA

FRAME-N-LENS
7914 Sunset Blvd.
Los Angeles, CA 90046
213/851-2068

HOURS: MON-FRI: 10-7 SAT: 10-6
CREDIT CARDS: DISC, MC, V

You should know about these convenient, price worthy stores if you're in the market for eyeglasses. Frame-N-Lens will make you two pair of single vision glasses for $63 and two pair of bifocals for $81. With over 400 frames to choose from, there are styles sure to please everyone. Designer frames are also available at additional cost. And, they do eyeglass repairs and adjustments, too.

Additional Locations: Over 120 stores–Call 800-GLASSES

PAPER & PARTY SUPPLIES

∞ BOXES ∞

BOX CITY**
16159 Sherman Way
Van Nuys, CA 91406
818/901-0336
HOURS: MON-SAT: 9-6 SUN: 10-3
CREDIT CARDS: AE, DISC, MC, V

If you need a box of any kind, this is definitely your kind of place—gift boxes, mailing boxes, shipping boxes and moving boxes. Whatever kind of box you need they have, plus all necessary supplies for shipping and moving. Not only do they have every kind of box imaginable, but you can expect to save big bucks! We can't mention any names, but Box City is 30% lower than a well known do-it-yourself moving business that most of us have used in the past and wait, it gets better! Not only does Box City charge 50% less for their boxes than your major moving companies, but the owner will accept a 10% BUYING RETAIL IS STUPID coupon! So, if you need a box, go to Box City.
Additional Locations:
Sun Valley–11101 Sherman Way, 818/982-5675
Valencia–23403 Lyons Ave., 805/254-1178
Van Nuys–16113 Sherman Way, 818/901-0336
W. Los Angeles–10775 W. Pico Blvd., 213/474-5144)

∞ COSTUMES ∞

BAB'S (AT RERUN'S)**
11626 Ventura Blvd.
Studio City, CA 91604
818/506-4399
HOURS: MON-FRI: 11:30-7 SAT: 11-6
CREDIT CARDS: MC, V

Bab's specializes in one of a kind vintage clothing and accessories. They have everything you can imagine from the 1920s to the 1970s. You'll find carry 100 Halloween costumes, and rentals are available on most items. So if you and your lady want to attend the masquerade ball, clad as a flapper and Al Capone, you'll want to check out Bab's. Don't forget your BUYING RETAIL IS STUPID coupon for an extra 10% discount.

CENTER THEATRE COSTUME SHOP
3301 E. 14th St.
Los Angeles, CA 90023
213/267-1230
HOURS: MON-FRI: 10-5 (EXTENDED HOURS IN OCTOBER)
CREDIT CARDS: MC, V

Ever get an invitation to a costume party or Halloween party and dream about wearing a costume like they wear in the movies? Well dream no more! The Center Theatre Costume Shop has over 40,000 theatrical and masquerade costumes from which to choose. If you don't like the selection, they can design a costume just for you. They are open all year, so let your imagination be your guide. Go ahead and knock'em dead at the next special event you get invited to.

PARTY CORNER DISCOUNT CENTER**
11422 Laurel Canyon Blvd.
Mission Hills, CA 91345
818/365-6909
HOURS: MON-SAT: 10-6 SUN: 11-4
CREDIT CARDS: MC, V

Can't think of anything to wear as a costume for that come-as-you-are party? You'll find it at Party Corner Discount Center and much more. They rent and sell costumes, along with accessories, wigs, and masks. When you use your BUYING RETAIL IS STUPID coupon you'll save 10% more on your purchase. They have an inventory of over 1,000 costumes at Party Corner, so you can definitely appear at your party in style!

∞ PAPER & PARTY SUPPLIES ∞

ALIN PAPER COMPANY
4929 Woodruff Ave.
Lakewood, CA 90713
310/925-5501
HOURS: MON-FRI: 9-9 SAT: 9-6 SUN: 11-5
CREDIT CARDS: MC, V

This store is the greatest! Whatever you need for your next celebration can be found at Alin Paper Company at only 10–40% above their cost. They carry a complete line of supplies for banquets, parties, weddings, and receptions, including invitations (regular, religious, Spanish, Morman, Jewish). You'll find supplies for anniversaries, luaus, Bar Mitzvahs, Quince Anos, and more. Have a wedding coming up in the future? Select your invitations from over 20 sample books, all of which are avail-

able at full priced competitors, and save up to 30%. They have a great selection of wrapping paper. Buy as much or as little as you need.
Additional Locations:
Downey–12270 Paramount Blvd., 310/862-1661
Riverside–5188 Arlington Ave., 714/354-9680

INDIVIDUAL PAPER PRODUCTS
5333 Downy Rd.
Vernon, CA 90058
213/583-4121

HOURS: MON-FRI: 7-5
CREDIT CARDS: CASH OR CHECKS ONLY

This store is family owned and has been in business since 1926. This is a no frills warehouse where you can save big bucks on paper, plastic and aluminum products. If you don't care what is imprinted on the paper plates, napkins and cups, you will save even more than the usual 25 to 50% off retail because they buy the overruns from manufacturers. Get on their mailing list so you'll be in on their special sales.

PARTY CORNER DISCOUNT CENTER**
11422 Laurel Canyon Blvd.
Mission Hills, CA 91345
818/365-6909

HOURS: MON-SAT: 10-6 SUN: 11-4
CREDIT CARDS: MC, V

Party planning is a cinch with Party Corner's large selection of party supplies which includes decorations, wedding invitations, crepe paper, garlands and decorations for cars. They'll blow your balloons up for you or you can rent a helium tank and do it yourself. Expect to find discounts in the neighborhood of 10–20% off retail prices. When you use your BUYING RETAIL IS STUPID coupon you'll receive a 10% discount.

PARTY KING
6038 Reseda Blvd.
Tarzana, CA 91356
818/343-3343

HOURS: MON-FRI: 8:30-8 SAT: 8:30-6 SUN: 9-5
CREDIT CARDS: MC, V

This 4,000 square foot store has a huge selection of party supplies for every occasion and theme. They have over 150 designer patterns and fashion colors including an incredible selection of juvenile ensembles, decorations and favors. Party King offers 25% off retail prices on wed-

PAPER & PARTY SUPPLIES

ding invitations, Bar Mitzvah invitations, and 20% off all greeting cards. They've been in business since 1979 and can offer you expert advice.

PARTY WORLD
19450 Business Center Dr.
Northridge, CA 91324
818/993-3033

HOURS: MON-THUR: 10-6 FRI: 10-7 SAT: 9:30-5:30 SUN: 12-5
CREDIT CARDS: MC, V

There are 10 Party World stores in Southern California. Each store is a one-stop center for all your party needs. Save 10 to 70% on everything from invitations, to helium tanks and balloons. If you are going to have a party for your child, they have over 27 patterns available. To give your next bash a personal touch, make sure to inquire about their custom imprinting service. Whether you are having a party for 2 or 2,000, Party World has it all.
Additional Locations: 9 other stores throughout S. CA

WILBURN'S DISCOUNT PARTY CENTER
8730 Santa Fe
South Gate, CA 90280
213/569-7169

HOURS: MON-FRI: 9-5 SAT: 9-6
CREDIT CARDS: DISC, MC, V

Discounts of 10 to 25% on paper and plastic items, and 30% below retail on printed invitations are the tail end of the story at Wilburn's, where they can service any kind of party from 8 to 800 from start (printed invitation) to finish (plastic garbage bags). They can usually fill your order from available stock. A complete and varied assortment of favors and decorations includes such items as pinatas, and glass wedding cake decorations. Among their unique birthday ensembles for children you'll find a complete line of Mickey Mouse and Batman goodies. You can also get punch concentrate and snow-cone base available in 13 flavors for children's parties. Table coverings come in all colors of the rainbow and are available in all shapes and sizes.
Additional Locations:
Whittier–12555 Telegraph Rd., 310/944-8044

PETS & ANIMAL SUPPLIES

ALLAN'S AQUARIUM AND PET SHOP
845 Lincoln Blvd.
Venice, CA 90291
310/399-5464

HOURS: MON-FRI: 11-8 SAT-SUN: 10-6

CREDIT CARDS: AE, DISC, MC, V

Allan's Aquarium and Pet Shop has two complete floors of merchandise filled with aquariums, goldfish, tropical fish, salt water fish, aquarium plants, live crickets, tarantulas, chameleons, birds of all kinds, guinea pigs, chicks and ducks. Rodents are bought and sold. They also carry dog and cat foods, animal traps, cages, dog houses, and scratching posts.

B & A HAY CO.
7615 Archibald
Corona, CA 91720
714/272-9050

HOURS: MON-FRI: 6-2

CREDIT CARDS: CASH OR CHECKS ONLY

Selling their products wholesale, this place is for the rancher or horse breeder that buys hay by the trailer load, B & A's minimum order. A trailer load weighs approximately 12–13 tons! They sell varieties of hay/alfalfa and oat hay in various grades. Expect to save $1–2 per bail depending on the variety and grade. Remember, they deal by the trailer load only, so get together with your neighbors to get in on this great deal. Make hay while the sun shines!

BIRDS PLUS
14041 Burbank Blvd.
Van Nuys, CA 91401
818/901-1187

HOURS: MON-FRI: 10-7 SAT-SUN: 10-6

CREDIT CARDS: MC, V

Birds Plus specializes in exotic birds, cages and supplies at savings of 20 to 40% off the prices charged in retail pet stores. They carry all your favorite name brand pet products. Whether you're feeding a parakeet or a pelican, they can help you with any of your bird needs or problems. They offer boarding and consulting on breeding, and groom for free. Call to find out about their special sales held during the year.

PETS & ANIMAL SUPPLIES

BRACKEN BIRD FARM
10797 New Jersey St.
Redlands, CA 92373

714/792-5735

HOURS: MON, WED-SUN: 9-5 (CLOSED ON TUESDAY)
CREDIT CARDS: MC, V
(CHECKS ACCEPTED ONLY FOR $100 OR LESS ON WEEKENDS)

For all of you bird lovers out there, we have found a place where many pet store owners buy their stock. The Bracken Bird Farm is an acre filled with hundreds of birds from which to choose. You'll find macaws, cockatoos, finches, and parakeets. Love birds run $25 to $70 ($45 to $200 in pet stores), cockatiels are $30 to $50 ($48 to $100), and gray cheek parrots are $135 ($249). They have hand fed, baby parrots, and they even have toucans! Bracken's also carries all necessary bird supplies. If you are looking for a bird for one of your children, it would be well worth the drive. The beautiful grounds in this pastoral setting feature a walk-thru aviary, a Texas long horn steer, turtles, and a duck pond. Also residing in the pond is the Bracken Bird Farm mascot, a yellow albino frog. While the frog is not for sale, you can save 25 to 50% below retail on your bird selection.

THE BUZZARD HOUSE
11052 Limonite Ave.
Mira Loma, CA 91752

714/736-0197

HOURS: MON-FRI: 10-7   SAT: 10-6   SUN: 10-5
CREDIT CARDS: MC, V

Don't you love the name of this place? Open seven days a week, The Buzzard House has a complete selection of pet supplies at discount prices; you can save 10–25% off the retail prices of other pet stores. They buy in large quantities and pass on the savings. If you're in need of dog food, bird food, bird supplies or nonprescription medicinal items, this is the place to go. You'll also appreciate the devoted animal lovers working at The Buzzard House.

PETS & ANIMAL SUPPLIES

CONSOLIDATED PET FOODS**
1840 14th St.
Santa Monica, CA 90404
310/393-9393   800/479-4977

HOURS: MON-FRI: 8-5 SAT: 9-12:30
CREDIT CARDS: CASH OR CHECKS ONLY

You can save approximately 15% off retail buying food for the furry members of your family at Consolidated Pet Foods. Brand names include Nature's Recipe, Science Diet, Eukanuba, Iams, Nutro Max. They also have their own line of food—regular and specially formulated foods for animals on special diets—made with only natural ingredients. As we all know, time is money, and you'll save both with free deliveries from Consolidated Pet Foods. Their delivery area is bordered by Oxnard, Ontario and San Clemente. If you give them a call, they'll deliver a free sample of pet food the next time they're in your area. You'll receive a 15% discount on your first order when you use your BUYING RETAIL IS STUPID coupon.

DISCOUNT PET FOOD
17641 Vanowen St.
Van Nuys, CA 91406
818/996-2066

HOURS: MON: 10-7 TUES-FRI: 10-6 SAT: 10-5
CREDIT CARDS: MC, V

At Discount Pet Food you can buy the four-legged loved one in your life just about all brand name products. This huge store is filled with food and all kinds of supplies for furry friends priced 20 to 50% below retail. Canned foods for cats and dogs are sold at case prices. Whether you buy one can or a case, the price per can is the same. Dog biscuits are sold in bulk and brand names include Milk Bone, Natures Recipe, Bonz, Triumph, Old Mother Hubbard, Breeders Choice and Iams. Rawhide is a good way to keep your pooches chewing on something of your choosing—not theirs—and you have 28 varieties to choose from. They even have cow hooves for the same purpose. You can also get products for rabbits, hamsters, rats, guinea pigs, horses, turtles, chickens, ferrets, chinchillas, hermit crabs and tropical fish. Bird food is available for parrots, parakeets, cockatiels, large hookbills, pigeons, doves, canaries and finches.

DISCOUNT TROPICAL FISH
561 W. La Habra Blvd.
La Habra, CA 90631
310/691-2037

HOURS: MON-FRI: 10-9 SAT-SUN: 10-8
CREDIT CARDS: DISC, MC, V

If it's fresh water or salt water fish you're wanting for your tank or outdoor pond, make sure to stop at Discount Tropical Fish. They carry all kinds of fish, and carry both dry and living foods. You will find basic tropical fish like guppies, neons and black mollies, to fancy gold fish, koi (Japanese carp), African chiclid, live coral, sea anemone and invertebrates. Their tanks run 10% over their cost, fish are discounted 10 to 15%, and all dry goods are discounted 25%. If you have been longing for a koi pond in your backyard, Discount Tropical Fish can make recommendations for having one built.

ELLIOT'S PET EMPORIUM
6370 Brockton
Riverside, CA 92506
714/787-0241

HOURS: MON-FRI: 9-9 SAT: 9-7 SUN: 10-7
CREDIT CARDS: MC, V

This is one of the world's largest pet stores with over 25,000 pet items at discount prices. Because they buy in huge volume they pass the savings on to their customers. Every Wednesday they offer an additional 10% discount on everything in the store including items already on sale. Among the brands they carry are: Science Diet, Iams, Nutro and Pro Plan. Senior citizens always receive an additional 10% discount.

FOR PET'S SAKE PET SHOP
3671 Thousand Oaks Blvd.
Westlake Village, CA 91362
805/496-3430

HOURS: MON-SAT: 10-6
CREDIT CARDS: MC, V

This is one pet shop you'll really enjoy. The animals at For Pet's Sake are known to be the healthiest in the area. They carry birds, kittens, reptiles, small animals and fish. They also have pet supplies, beds, houses and books on animal care. The store is very clean, and all their skin and flea products are guaranteed The sales people are knowledgeable and can answer almost any question you might have. For Pet's Sake has built quite a reputation by solving dog and cat disorders naturally, without drugs!

NORM'S FEED STORE
11708 South East End Ave.
Chino, CA 91710
714/628-7016

HOURS: MON-SAT: 8-6   SUN: 8:30-12

CREDIT CARDS: CASH OR CHECKS ONLY

When was the last time you walked into a store and really felt that the management was there to help you? Norm's Feed Store is that kind of place. You'll find very friendly salespeople, knowledgeable about the food your dog and cat eat. They have pet and vet supplies, and you can even pick up hay, straw and alfalfa cubes. Delivery is available for large orders.

PEDLEY VETERINARY SUPPLY INC.
8978 Limonite Ave.
Riverside, CA 92509
714/685-3511

HOURS: MON-SAT: 9-5

CREDIT CARDS: MC, V

Do-it-yourself vaccinations for your dogs, cats, horses and even some available for your goat! Purchasing a dog's vaccination, for example, can save you quite a bit of money. A parvo vaccination for your dog can run from $15 to $25 when administered by your vet. Do it yourself and it costs only $2.50. Most of the vaccinations are ready to go in a syringe, and antibiotics are also available. While not vets, the animal lovers employed at Pedley's are very knowledgeable about your pet's needs. They also carry medical supplies, vitamins, plus most pet supplies.

PETS & ANIMAL SUPPLIES

RED BARN FEED & SADDLERY INC.**
18601 Oxnard St.
Tarzana, CA 91356
818/345-2510
HOURS: MON-FRI: 9-6   SAT: 9-5   SUN: 11-4
CREDIT CARDS: MC, V

This enormous store has one of the largest inventories of pet products in the Los Angeles area. They carry Kal Kan, Purina, Friskie, Carnation, Iams, Breeder's Choice, Quaker, Nutro, Science Diet, and many other brand names. You can save 20 to 40% off retail prices. There are always in-store specials and if you live in the Los Angeles area, keep an eye out for discount coupons in local newspapers. They also carry foods and supplies for your pet chicken, rabbit, horse, goat, ostrich or elephant. All employees are animal owners and can answer any questions based on personal experience. They are also very involved with local animal organizations. If you need firewood, hay (sold by weight, not by bale), tack, cages or nursery supplies, Red Barn Feed and Saddlery has it all. You'll save an additional 5% by using your BUYING RETAIL IS STUPID coupon.

PHOTOGRAPHY

ABC CAMERA-PHOTO-VIDEO
10224 Mason St.
Chatsworth, CA 91311

818/709-1931

HOURS: MON-FRI: 10-6 SAT: 10-4
CREDIT CARDS: MC, V

ABC Camera-Photo-Video is truly your one-stop shop for any type of photography. Whether you are a beginner, amateur or professional, all your needs will be met. They sell, buy, take trade-ins, rent and repair (on the premises) all equipment and are an authorized dealer for major brands such as Nikon, Minolta, Pentax, Canon, and Ricoh. You can have your passport pictures done as well as rush custom film developing in color or in black and white. ABC averages 10% over cost on their prices and they have once-a-month special sales. For photographic needs, it's as simple as A–B–C.

BEL AIR CAMERA, AUDIO & VIDEO
1025 Westwood Blvd.
Los Angeles, CA 90024

310/208-5150

HOURS: MON-FRI: 9-6 SAT: 9:30-6
CREDIT CARDS: MC, V

Bel Air is one of the largest camera, audio, and video stores on the West Coast. They offer cameras and camera accessories, video cameras and recorders, audio components, tape recorders, televisions, enlargers and more. Two or three times a year, they have a large Expo & Sale where they invite representatives from over 40 companies to show their products. Shows are usually in May or December, but you can get the above items daily at 10% above their cost and sometimes at cost. They have Nikon, Minolta, Pentax, Vivitar, Olympus, Panasonic, Sony, Speedotron, Hasselblad and others. Feel free to write a check or charge your purchases at Bel Air, but these people give special discounts if you pay in cash.

CAMERA CITY
12236 W. Pico Blvd.
Los Angeles, CA 90064
310/477-8833

HOURS: MON-FRI: 9:30-6 SAT: 9:30-5
CREDIT CARDS: AE, DISC, MC, V

Camera City has been at their present location since 1969 with prices discounted at 20 to 50% below what you'd pay at other camera stores. In photo equipment, they carry camera lenses, flashes, cases and tripods. Their video equipment includes cameras, recorders and lenses. Both departments offer rentals and repairs on Canon, Nikon, Ricoh, Sharp, Vivitar, Kiron, Kodak and Polaroid. Camera City is happy to say that they service what they sell.

FRANK'S HIGHLAND PARK CAMERA
5715 N. Figueroa St.
Los Angeles, CA 90042
213/255-0123

HOURS: MON-SAT: 9-6
CREDIT CARDS: AE, MC, V

The Vacek family has been selling all types of cameras in their 10,000 square foot store since 1969. Their bargain tables offer even greater savings than their standard 6% over wholesale pricing. You can also find everything you need for your darkroom including paper, chemicals and equipment. If you would like to trade in your camera or pick up a used one, see Frank's Highland Park Camera.

HOOPER CAMERA AND VIDEO CENTERS**
5059 Lankershim Blvd.
North Hollywood, CA 91601
818/762-2846

HOURS: MON-SAT: 9-6
CREDIT CARDS: MC, V

If it takes a picture, you can buy it at cost plus 5 to 10% at Hooper Camera and Video Centers. Merchandise other than cameras are sold at 10 to 35% off retail prices. This is the largest chain of photographic stores in the combined areas of San Fernando Valley and Conejo Valley. They carry everything you need in photographic equipment and supplies, at

prices you can't beat. They carry all the major brands, and have special sales during the year. Six of their stores have in-house labs for custom, economy, and one hour photo finishing. You'll find helpful, knowledgeable salespeople to assist you. Take your BUYING RETAIL IS STUPID coupon with you for an additional 5% off on your purchase.
Additional Locations: 8 other stores throughout S. CA

LLOYD'S CAMERA SURPLUS
1612 N. Cahuenga Blvd.
Hollywood, CA 90028
213/467-7956

HOURS: MON-FRI: 9-5
CREDIT CARDS: MC, V

Owner Lloyd Berman says, "We may be the largest dealer in the U.S. on 8mm and 16mm movie cameras." In business since 1954, LLoyd's carries a large supply of cameras, tape recorders, and film. You'll find top name brands at savings of about 25% off retail. Rentals are available, and the people are super nice and helpful.

MIKO PHOTO-AUDIO-VIDEO CENTER
1259 3rd Street Promenade
Santa Monica, CA 90401
310/393-9371

HOURS: MON-THUR: 9-6 FRI: 9-7 SAT: 9-6 SUN: 12-4
CREDIT CARDS: AE, DISC, MC, V

Miko Photo-Audio-Video Center prides itself in its high repeat customer business, so you know they are doing something right. They have everything for your home entertainment center, video cameras, portable audio systems, stereos, electric games and more. In addition to their camera equipment and supplies, you can have your film processed there, too. They also have cordless telephones, answering machines, and video editing equipment.

Additional Locations:
Manhattan Beach–3200 Sepulveda Blvd., 310/546-5491
Santa Monica–1259 Santa Monica Place Mall, 310/395-8185

PHOTOGRAPHY SUPPLIES & EQUIPMENT

SIMON'S DISCOUNT CAMERA STORE
720 N. Vermont Ave.
Los Angeles, CA 90029
213/665-8825

HOURS: MON-SAT: 9-6
CREDIT CARDS: MC, V

Simon says, "See us first." He'll sell you top-brand cameras like Nikon and Canon at the best discount prices around. In fact, their cameras and supplies are usually marked at only 5 to 10% above cost, so you know you will be finding good bargains here. Simon's also rents and services cameras. Now take a minute to focus on these bargains at Simon's. One hour photo enlargement service is also available. Their low pricing is based on cash and carry, so your purchase will be 3% higher if you use your credit card.

VALLEY 1-HOUR PHOTO
7576 Winnetka Ave.
Canoga Park, CA 91306
818/998-6572

HOURS: MON-FRI: 9:30-7 SAT: 10-5
CREDIT CARDS: MC, V

No kidding! If you need a passport picture immediately and you can't possibly wait, this is the place to go. Valley 1-Hour Photo gets them processed right away and the cost is two for $6.99. In addition to processing your film right on the premises, you can get your keys made or duplicated while you wait. You'll find that Valley 1-Hour Photo beats retail prices by at least 15%.

PLANTS, LAWN & GARDEN

∞ Lawnmowers ∞

LEE LAWNMOWER**
1345 S. Bristol
Santa Ana, CA 92704
714/546-6334
HOURS: MON-SAT: 7-6 SUN: 9-3
CREDIT CARDS: MC, V

If you are looking for great service and buys, find your way to Lee Lawnmower, in business since 1960. You can usually get same day service if something goes wrong with your gas, electric or diesel lawnmower. Lee Lawnmower guarantees that nobody can beat their prices or especially their service. In addition to lawnmowers, you can also find blowers, edgers, hedge trimmers, weed-eaters and of course most parts and supplies. They carry Astron, Briggs & Stratton, Echo, Homelite, Snapper, Toro and Power Trim to name just a few of their brand names. If you can't find what you are looking for, just ask. Should you find something you absolutely have to have and can't afford to pay cash, ask about their own credit financing with no interest. Take your BUYING RETAIL IS STUPID coupon with you for an additional discount of 10%.

∞ Nurseries ∞

AMERICAN WHOLESALE NURSERIES
23915 San Fernando Rd.
Newhall, CA 91321
805/259-2900, 818/368-8591
HOURS: MON-FRI: 6-5 SAT-SUN: 8-5
CREDIT CARDS: MC, V

Wow! They have approximately 30 acres filled with 500,000 plants. If that isn't enough to wow you, you also have 500 varieties from which to choose. They are the largest Snapper lawn equipment supplier in the San Fernando Valley. Discounts are at 50% off retail. Many other name brands are available. Also, come with your truck and fill up on bulk soil blends. They buy their plants direct from growers, so they pass the sav-

PLANTS, LAWN & GARDEN

ings on to you. Any flowering plants you see are grown by American Wholesale Nurseries. You may want to enroll in the Golden Eagle Garden Club that offers bimonthly newsletters, seminars, and additional discounts to members on top of the regular discounts. Membership is free; it's just part of the service offered by American Wholesale Nurseries.
Additional Locations:
Simi Valley–5000 Bennett Rd., 805/582-2800

BEVERLY GARDEN CENTER
316 N. La Cienega Blvd.
Los Angeles, CA 90048
310/652-2583
HOURS: 10-7 SEVEN DAYS A WEEK
CREDIT CARDS: MC, V

You are in for a big surprise at the Beverly Garden Center. As you enter, you'll discover a greenhouse behind the storefront filled with a terrific selection of in-door plants. As these plants are purchased direct from the growers, you can save 20 to 50% of regular nursery prices. The savings are the same on the great selection of baskets, hampers and accessories. Call to find out about their special sales held during the year.

DIRT CHEAP PLANT CO.
488 E. 17th. St. (Corner of 17th & Irvine)
Costa Mesa, CA 92677
714/645-4553
HOURS: MON-SAT: 9-7 SUN: 10-6
CREDIT CARDS: MC, V

Dirt Cheap Plant Company is just that. Assorted house plants from four-inch pots to giant jungle monsters in the four to nine-foot range are for sale at dirt cheap prices. Check out their outrageous selection of baskets and other plant related items too. All products and plants are first quality, greenhouse fresh and at savings of 40 to 60% off retail. They are always running specials of some sort, so give them a call to see what's happening. Well what are you waiting for? Get those green thumbs moving!

NURSERY LIQUIDATORS
1500 S. State College Blvd.
Anaheim, CA 92806
714/533-4065

HOURS: MON-TUES, THUR-SUN: 10-4:30
CREDIT CARDS: MC, V ($20 MINIMUM PURCHASE)

Nursery Liquidators has been around for 26 years selling plants and trees at prices you wouldn't believe. Save as much as 50% off the prices of other nurseries. They have over two million plants and trees for your selection. They grow about 70% of their own inventory, so they are able to pass on significant savings to you. They carry very few house plants. If you're doing some landscaping, this is the place to shop.

VALLEY SOD FARMS
16405 Chase St.
Sepulveda, CA 91343
818/892-7258

HOURS: MON-SAT: 7:30-5
CREDIT CARDS: MC, V

Blue grass, blue rye, fescue, dichondra, hybrid Bermuda and St. Augustine—no, we're not talking about race horses. These are all the different types of grass sod you can buy at the only sod farm in the San Fernando Valley. They'll deliver anywhere in the area, and if you are out of the area, they can make delivery arrangements with some of their affiliates. So, if you're looking for grass sod or even some ground cover, check them out. Savings for the average yard will run 40 to 60% below most nursery prices.

WORLD OF PLANTS AND GIFTS**
2845 Lincoln Blvd.
Venice, CA 90291
310/823-3883

HOURS: MON-FRI: 9-7 SAT-SUN: 9-6
CREDIT CARDS: AE, DISC, MC, V

Indoor plants, trees, baskets, pottery, macrame, flowering plants and plant stands, are all available at World of Plants and Gifts for discount prices. Their plants are purchased directly from growers in San Diego, so they can offer their customers the best prices around. If you use your BUYING RETAIL IS STUPID coupon your discount blossoms an additional 10%!

∞ POTS, PLANTERS & FOUNTAINS ∞

FOUNTAINS BY SANTI
18888 Van Buren Blvd.
Riverside, CA 92504
714/780-0622
HOURS: MON-TUES: 9-4 WED-SUN: 9-5
CREDIT CARDS: MC, V

This is definitely not your run of the mill operation. Descendents of one of the most influential painters from the Italian Renaissance, Raphael, the Santi family has quite a few generations behind them of knowledge and expertise in handcrafted artworks. You will at last be able to find the perfect fountain for your courtyard or patio. In addition, they have Spanish, Italian and Oriental pottery, bird baths and bench sets. Because the manufacturing is done on right on the premises, they have more of selection than most. Look to save 15% on your purchases here.

MAINLY SECONDS–POTTERY, PLANTS & THINGS
12144 Magnolia Blvd.
North Hollywood, CA 91607
818/985-4499
HOURS: MON-FRI: 9-9 SAT-SUN: 9-6
CREDIT CARDS: MC, V

Mainly Seconds carries all sizes of ceramic, plastic and clay pottery, baskets, indoor and outdoor plants, cactus, plant foods, potting soils, cacti, silk flowers, vases, dried flowers, macrame, and wrought iron at 40 to 60% below retail. Each of their locations has over 6,000 square feet always stuffed with goodies.
Additional Locations:
Buena Park–4562 Beach Blvd., 714/994-0540
Costa Mesa–1785 Newport Blvd., 714/548-7710

POTTERY AND FLORAL WORLD**
3352 San Fernando Rd.
Los Angeles, CA 90065
213/254-5281
HOURS: 8:30-7 SEVEN DAYS A WEEK
CREDIT CARDS: MC, V

Pottery and Floral World has one of the West Coast's largest selections of pots, pottery, dried and silk flowers, and all the accessories that go along with them. They have macrame supplies, gourmet ware, baskets and wrought iron. Being both a factory outlet and a direct importer, you can expect discounts of 20 to 50% off retail prices found elsewhere. Close-outs occur weekly, so shoppers can always count on seeing different items from visit to visit. You'll receive an extra 10% off your purchase when you use your BUYING RETAIL IS STUPID coupon.

POTTERY ETC.**
7403 Canoga Ave.
Canoga Park, CA 91303
818/704-0741

HOURS: MON-FRI: 8-6 SAT: 9-6 SUN: 10-5*
CREDIT CARDS: MC, V (PURCHASES OVER $25 ONLY)

This is the place to go for an enormous selection of unusual and standard pottery in just about every size imaginable. Prices run 5 to 50% off retail on pottery from Tuscany and the northern clay areas of Italy. They also have pottery from Mexico and Texas. Animal lovers will find planters in all kinds of animal shapes (cats, lambs, rabbits, cows, pigs, swans, ducks, etc.). If you're in search of unique items, take a look at one of their catalogues. You'll find all kinds of pottery, statues, pedestals and fountains that can be special-ordered from Italy. Special orders require a 50% deposit, and delivery takes about four months. Family owned and operated, you'll find it a pleasure shopping here. You'll receive a 5% discount and a free 2-1/2 inch clay pot when you use your BUYING RETAIL IS STUPID coupon. *Winter hours are 8 a.m. to 4:30 p.m., seven days a week.

POTTERY MANUFACTURING & DISTRIBUTING
18881 S. Hoover St.
Gardena, CA 90248
310/323-7754

HOURS: MON-SAT: 8:30-4:30
CREDIT CARDS: MC, V

Pottery Manufacturing & Distributing is a wholesale outlet with over an acre of red clay pots. They are also a factory outlet for their manufacturing plant located in Gardena. You can save 50% off retail on factory seconds. They carry pots ranging from 4 inches up to 180 pounds. You'll also find imported Italian stoneware, "poly-planters," and cactus potting soil.

PLANTS, LAWN & GARDEN

THE POTTERY STORE
10761 Venice Blvd.
Los Angeles, CA 90034
310/558-3124
HOURS: MON-SUN: 9-5:30 (9-6 APRIL–OCT)
CREDIT CARDS: MC, V

The Pottery Store has one of the largest inventories of indoor and outdoor decorator vases, pots, and planters in Los Angeles. The styles range from Italian terra cotta to California red clay, ceramic and stoneware. The Pottery Store also carries a large selection of plants, trees and budding flowers. Whether you are decorating your home, office or restaurant, you'll find what you need here at a discount usually 20% to 50% below retail.

SIG'S POTTERY & NURSERY
17825 Devonshire St.
Northridge, CA 91325
818/368-5171
HOURS: MON-SAT: 9-6 SUN: 9:30-6
CREDIT CARDS: MC, V

Sig's has seconds of glazed ceramic and red clay pots priced at 50 to 75% off retail. They also have first quality pots at 20% off retail. You'll find a large selection (half an acre to be exact) of pottery consisting of Mexican, American, Italian, Asian, stoneware and plastic pottery. Plants for your new pots (indoor, outdoor and cactus) are discounted 15–20%. They also have about 75 cement fountains and birdbaths. If you don't see what you want, just ask. Special orders are no problem at Sig's.

POOL & PATIO

∞ BARBECUES ∞

BARBECUES GALORE
18922 Ventura Blvd.
Tarzana, CA 91356
818/345-7314
HOURS: MON-SAT: 9:30-5:30   SUN: 11-5
CREDIT CARDS: AE, MC, V

Just thinking about a Saturday afternoon barbecue makes our mouth water. Barbecues Galore has approximately 200 barbecues on display (gas, electric and charcoal), along with smokers, accessories, fireplaces and fireplace accessories. Some brand names carried include Ducane, Charbroil, Arkla, Amberlight, and Weber. For those chefs that enjoy experimenting, they stock the unusual, as well as products from other countries. Their knowledgeable staff will be able to answer all of your questions regarding your particular needs. In addition to offering assembly and delivery on all products, Barbecues Galore discounts everything in the store 20–50% off retail. For even higher savings, watch for their special sales held each week.
Additional Locations: 14 other stores throughout S. CA

HALF PRICE STORES INC.
6367 Van Nuys Blvd.
Van Nuys, CA 91401
818/780-6844
HOURS: MON-FRI: 10-6:30   SAT: 10-6
CREDIT CARDS: MC, V

Local consumers have known about exploratory shopping at the Half Price Stores since 1967. Depending on the items purchased, you can save from 10 to 70% shopping here. There are watches, toothpaste, paper products, cleaning aids, and much more. We could go on and on trying to list the thousands of things on the shelves. In back of the store you'll discover gas and electric barbecues. There are at least 10 units on display representing brand names such as Amerilight, Broilmaster, Char-Broil and Patio. Barbecue accessories and replacement parts are also stocked.

POOL & PATIO

WOODLAND HILLS FIREPLACE SHOP**
21140 Ventura Blvd.
Woodland Hills, CA 91364
818/999-2174
HOURS: MON-SAT: 9–6 SUN: 12–3
CREDIT CARDS: AE, MC, V

If it's too hot, get out of the kitchen. What better way to do that than by barbecuing? If you don't have a barbecue, or if the one you have now has seen better days, this is the place to shop. The sign painted on the window of the store says, "Guaranteed Lowest Prices," and it's true! Savings usually run 35 to 40% off suggested retail prices, and you'll find the prices to be 15 to 20% lower than their discount competitors. Brand names include such as Charmglow, Ducane, Fire Magic, Arkla, Weber and Broilmaster. During the season, there are always at least 18 models of free-standing barbecues on display, plus another six built-in models. If your existing barbecue is collecting dust because of missing or worn-out parts, replacements also are available. In addition to barbecues, the shop carries tools and accessories for outdoor cooking. Everything is available promptly as their huge warehouse is only minutes from the store. By the way, they also have the same terrific prices on fireplaces and related accessories. Contractors and customers alike drive in from all over Southern California to take advantage of their low prices. During September they have an inventory sale with all barbecues priced at 5% above cost. You can get an additional 10% discount by using your BUYING RETAIL IS STUPID discount coupon. The coupon is redeemable on nonsale items only.

∞ Patio Furniture ∞

ABC POOL & PATIO**
24449 Hawthorne Blvd.
Torrance, CA 90505
310/373-0935
HOURS: MON-FRI: 10-6 SAT: 9-5 SUN: 11-5
CREDIT CARDS: MC, V

Established in 1958, ABC now has 10,000 square feet of furniture for patios, barbecues, fireplace accessories, pool and spa supplies and gifts. Tropitone furniture and Ducane barbecues are among the various brand names represented. You can expect to save 35% off retail prices on patio furniture. You'll save 10–15% on barbecues and other items. Don't miss their bargain room located upstairs, and special sales on the Fourth of July and Labor Day. Be sure to use your BUYING RETAIL IS STUPID coupon to save an additional 5%.

BERKS
2520 Santa Monica Blvd.
Santa Monica, CA 90404
310/828-7447
HOURS: MON-SAT: 9-6 SUN: 10-5
CREDIT CARDS: MC, V

If you are looking for a complete selection of outdoor and casual indoor furniture, and you'd like to pocket savings of 20 to 60%, then shop at Berks. They've been selling everything you need to furnish your patio or porch since the 1950s. You can purchase things like tables, chaise lounges, and umbrellas by makers such as Brown Jordan, Samsonite, Kenneth James and others. Customers always find variety of styles and colors, and Berks offers immediate, free delivery. If you find it advertised cheaper anywhere else, show it to them; if they have it in stock they will meet it or beat it. Check out their special sales during the year for extra savings.

POOL & PATIO

COTTAGE SHOPS
7922 W. 3rd St.
Los Angeles, CA 90048
213/658-6066

HOURS: MON-SAT: 9:30-6 SUN: 11-5
CREDIT CARDS: AE, MC, V

This discount store, in business since the late 1940s, has a complete selection of pool and patio furniture, lounges, umbrellas, and much more. A division of Scotty's Casual Furniture, the Cottage Shops will save you about 20% and more off retail on most items and they really stand behind what they sell. Brand names include Tropitone, Allibert, and Barlow Tyrie Teak. Delivery and layaway services are available, and they can refurbish your old pool and patio furniture. You'll find free parking in back of the store and a free catalogue is available.

DEFOREST'S PATIO AND FIRESIDE
22105 Ventura Blvd.
Woodland Hills, CA 91364
818/348-5040

HOURS: MON-SAT: 9-6 SUN: 11-5
CREDIT CARDS: DISC, MC, V

Love relaxing in your backyard sipping on ice tea, but don't have any outdoor furniture to sit on? Deforest's Patio and Fireside can take care of all your needs so you can have fun in your backyard. They carry quality, name-brand patio furniture such as Brown Jordan, Tropitone, Woodard, Samsonite, Grosfillex and much more, including umbrellas, cushions and accessories—all at discounts of 20–40% off retail. Round out the entire outdoor experience by purchasing one of their discounted barbecues. And if you're not an outdoor person but love a romantic fire in your fireplace, you'll be able to purchase and assortment of fireplace tool sets, wood baskets, screens, custom glass doors at 20–30% off list.

ENCINO DISCOUNT PATIO & BABY FURNITURE
17563 Ventura Blvd.
Encino, CA 91316
818/986-1074

HOURS: MON-FRI: 9-6 SAT: 9-5 SUN: 11-4
CREDIT CARDS: MC, V

Looking for that perfect outdoor swing for your baby while you're entertaining guests at your backyard garden party? Encino Discount Patio and Baby Furniture has it all. Patio and baby furniture and accessories. They carry Innova, California Umbrella, Homecrest, Pacific Sun, O.W. Lee, Kettler in patio furniture. Owner Mackie Singer says her customers tell them that they have the best selection and prices (30–50% off retail) and have been coming back to the store since 1939.

FISHBECK'S
150 S. Raymond Ave.
Pasadena, CA 91105
818/796-9255

HOURS: MON-SAT: 9-6 SUN: 10-5
CREDIT CARDS: MC, V

Depending on the item, you can save between 20 and 50% on outdoor furniture at Fishbeck's. They've been selling to people "in the know" at a discount since 1899. Brand names include Brown Jordan, Winston, Grosfillex, United Outdoor, Woodard, Tropitone, Medowcraft, O.W. Lee, Primavera and U.S. Cedar. To give you an idea of the selection found here, the showroom covers 20,000 square feet, with an additional 15,000 square feet of patio displays outside.

WOODLAND CASUAL
19855 Ventura Blvd.
Woodland Hills, CA 91364
818/348-6000

HOURS: MON-SAT: 10-6 SUN: 12-5
CREDIT CARDS: MC, V

Well here it is, the largest selection of patio furniture in the San Fernando Valley. There are four entire floors of wicker, rattan, sofa sets, bedroom furniture and entertainment centers to choose from. You can expect to find such brands as Tropitone, Grosfillex, Thypon Wicker and Pacific Rattan to name a few. With a purchase of $500 or more they'll even deliver. You can look forward to saving 30% off retail on most items.

POOL & PATIO

∞ Pool Supplies & Spas ∞

J. B. SEBRELL CO.
301 S. San Pedro St.
Los Angeles, CA 90013
213/625-2648
HOURS: MON-FRI: 9-5:30 SAT: 9-5 SUN: 10-3
CREDIT CARDS: MC, V

Swimming pool equipment and supplies, all marked at savings of 20 to 50% below list price, are available for you at J. B. Sebrell. They have everything—heaters, pumps, ladders, chemicals, skimmers, diving boards, redwood tubs, spas, toy accessories—plus equipment for spas, fish ponds, fountains, even above ground pools. They accept trade-ins, buy and sell used equipment, and do repairs. Ask for their free catalogue and shop by phone. They've been in business since 1938 and you'll save money on everything you see in their huge inventory.

SPA BROKER
6518 Van Nuys Blvd.
Van Nuys, CA 91406
818/782-9000
HOURS: MON-FRI: 9-5 SAT: 10-4 SUN: 11-4
CREDIT CARDS: MC, V

Dave English has been selling spas before they were the "in" thing. You can view 60 spas and gazebos on display at their 10,000 square foot store in Van Nuys where you'll find brand names including Pageant, Hydro-Swirl, Swim Spas and more. Shopping here will result in savings of $300 to $700 per spa. Keep in touch with Spa Broker to find out when they are offering even greater savings with their special sales. Financing is available.

SAFES & VAULTS

1ST SECURITY SAFE CO.
900 S. Hill St.
Los Angeles, CA 90015
213/627-0422
HOURS: MON-FRI: 10-5 SAT: 10-4
CREDIT CARDS: CASH OR CHECKS ONLY

You will save so much money using this book, you're going to need a safe to keep it in. 1st Security Safe Company specializes in jewelry safes, floor safes, and wall safes at 10–30% below retail. Not only do they sell safes, they install and service their products as well. Arrangements can be made if you'd like to finance your purchase.

IN-A-FLOOR SAFE COMPANY**
Los Angeles, CA 90015
213/749-2448
HOURS: MON-FRI: 9-6 BY APPOINTMENT ONLY
CREDIT CARDS: CASH OR CHECKS ONLY

In business since 1935, In-A-Floor Safe Company is the originator of in-floor safes, receiving a patent in 1932. Because the company is family owned and operated, you can expect to receive service not always available in today's world. You pick the combination yourself. In addition to the in-floor safes at up to 40% off retail, you can also get fire safes and media/data safes. Low cost installation is available, and they also service all brands of safes. In-A-Floor Safe will take 10% off your purchase with your BUYING RETAIL IS STUPID coupon. Ask for Carl when you call to book an appointment.

SAFES & VAULTS

RAP DISCOUNT SAFE CO.
21407 Vanowen St.
Canoga Park, CA 91303
818/884-3370
HOURS: MON-FRI: 8-9   SAT: 8-5   SUN: 9-5
CREDIT CARDS: AE, DISC, MC, V

If you need to lock things up and keep them safe, Rap Discount Safe Company is the place for you. Whether it's commercial or residential, wall or floor, sunken or free standing, you'll find safes at 20 to 50% off retail at Rap. Their safes range from small ones to hold your prize pistol to large, fireproof safes for all your important documents and valuables. With over 50 varieties in stock, they have one of the largest inventories of safes in the San Fernando Valley.

SERVICES

∞ FLOWERS & BALLOONS ∞

BALLOON FACTORY
8766 Holloway Dr.
Los Angeles, CA   90069
213/225-5666, 800/BALLOON
HOURS: MON-SAT: 8-6   SAT: 8-4   SUN: 10-2
CREDIT CARDS: AE, MC, V

What a great way to liven up that special occasion with balloons! These folks aren't filled with hot air either. They describe themselves as "LA's most innovative and affordable balloonists." With brilliant balloon bouquets, in over 50 selections for all occasions, arches, centerpieces, sculptures and more, this place can really add a "lift" to your next party. They also have unique gifts, stuffed toys, popcorn, champagne, fun candies and cards. If you are a do-it-yourselfer you can rent a tank and fill your own balloons. In the surrounding Los Angeles area, the Balloon Factory will come to your party and decorate. For savings of 20 to 30% off retail, call 213-BALLOON or 1-800-BALLOON.

KIM-E'S FLOWERS**
818/885-6957
HOURS: BY APPOINTMENT ONLY
CREDIT CARDS: CASH OR CHECKS ONLY

With 15 years experience in the floral industry, Michael and Kim Holtzer will definitely put the cherry on the top of your next affair with exceptional floral arrangements at discounted prices. They personally come to your home or office and help select the perfect arrangements to be used for weddings, banquets or parties. When the floral arrangements are completed, they will then make sure the arrangements are displayed to your satisfaction. Their specialties are preparing arrangements for weddings from bridal bouquet, table centerpieces, and ceremony arrangements, to stands along the aisle. Their prices average about 50% off retail. Don't forget, you can to use your BUYING RETAIL IS STUPID coupon and receive even greater savings of 10%.

SERVICES

MID-VALLEY FLOWER EXCHANGE**
22746 Oxnard St.
Woodland Hills, CA 91367
818/989-0075
HOURS: THUR-SUN: 9-5
CREDIT CARDS: MC, OPT, V

Do you love fresh cut flowers? At Mid-Valley Flower Exchange you buy fresh cut flowers in bunches of 10 stems with prices from $3.00 up to $9.50 per bunch depending on the type of flowers. Shopping at Mid-Valley will save you 50-200% off florist and supermarket prices. And if you're planning a party, $50 will fill about seven vases with these beautiful flowers. Make sure to bring your BUYING RETAIL IS STUPID coupon for an additional 10% discount and a free bouquet of flowers.

SHE'S FLOWERS
971 N. Hills St.
Los Angeles, CA 90012
213/620-1619
HOURS: MON-SAT: 7:30-6
CREDIT CARDS: AE, MC, V

Save up to 50% on flowers and plants for all occasions. She's Flowers grows many of their own flowers and imports others directly; then She's Flowers wholesales them to the public. You can also buy silk flowers, dried flowers, trees, baskets, even balloons for weddings, birthdays, and holidays. They deliver, and you can charge your purchase by phone.

SOMETHING SPECIAL
14303 Ventura Blvd.
Sherman Oaks, CA 91423
818/905-8664
HOURS: MON-SAT: 9-7 SUN: 10-5
CREDIT CARDS: CASH ONLY FOR SATURDAY SPECIALS

Now you can fill your rooms with fragrant flowers before your guests arrive for dinner Saturday night. Something Special has discounted prices all week, but Saturday is the day you really save money. Single stemmed flowers priced during the week at $4 ($6 retail) are sold in bunches of 10 for $12.50. You can buy flowers such as roses, gladiolus, calla lilies, tulips, orchids, iris and many others. If it's dark when your guests arrive, you can tell them the flowers are from your garden. We won't tell, if you won't.

∞ HOME REPAIR & MAINTENANCE ∞

END RESULT
818/784-1572
HOURS: 9-9 SEVEN DAYS A WEEK

Do you need some work done on or in your home? End Result has been referring people to trustworthy tradesmen—with down to earth prices—since 1979. Whether you need a roofing contractor or a handy man, End Result will refer you to someone thoroughly screened and reliable. They have nearly 10,000 satisfied clients including some of the biggest names in Hollywood. There is no charge to the customer for this service.
Additional Locations:
Orange County Referral Service: 714/546-6008

∞ LEGAL SERVICES ∞

A-WILSON DIVORCE CLINIC
3860 Crenshaw Blvd., Suite 201
Los Angeles, CA 90008
213/290-2268
HOURS: MON-FRI: 9-5
CREDIT CARDS: MC, V OR CASH (NO CHECKS)

If you are a person seeking help in filing for an uncontested divorce, A-Wilson's Divorce Clinic says they can save you up to 75% of standard legal fees. They provide the typing, filing and serving of papers. They can also provide advice in the areas of child support problems, restraining orders, collections and bankruptcy. Your first consultation is free.

DIVORCE CENTERS OF CALIFORNIA
6399 Wilshire Blvd., #909
Los Angeles, CA 90048
213/462-3405
HOURS: MON-FRI: 9-5:30
CREDIT CARDS: CASH ONLY

They have offices statewide, but Lois Isenberg at this office can help you in divorce matters and name changes. It's like do-it-yourself with assistance, and prices start as low as $75. You know that's quite a savings if you've ever had to pay an attorney's retainer fee. They've been in business since 1974, and this is a cash operation. In some cases arrangements can be made for payments.
Additional Locations: 6 other offices throughout S. CA

SERVICES

DO-IT-YOURSELF L.A.W. (LEGAL ACTION WORKSHOP)
4515 Van Nuys Blvd.
Sherman Oaks, CA 91403
818/995-4224

HOURS: MON-FRI: 9-5
CREDIT CARDS: MC, V

Why pay a fortune for standard legal services with complete low cost legal services available? You can get a divorce, file a bankruptcy, change your name, start a corporation, and more. There is attorney assistance.
Additional Locations: 6 other offices throughout S. CA

∞ LIFE INSURANCE ∞

WHOLESALE INSURANCE SERVICES
1116-A 8th St, Suite 203
Manhattan Beach, CA 90266
310/352-2600

HOURS: BY APPOINTMENT ONLY
CREDIT CARDS: CASH OR CHECKS ONLY

When someone says, "I can get it wholesale," one doesn't usually think they are talking about insurance! John Avery says, "Times are changing, even in the insurance industry." John swears he can save you $20,000 or more on a typical $200,000 life insurance policy. All his wholesale policies are from A and A+ rated companies so you're getting the highest quality at the lowest cost. If this sounds good to you, call and compare. See if you can't find better places for that high insurance premium money.

∞ LOCKSMITH ∞

MARC'S DISCOUNT LOCK & KEY
1503 S. Holt
Los Angeles, CA 90035
310/274-9644

HOURS: 24 HOURS-SEVEN DAYS A WEEK
CREDIT CARDS: CASH OR CHECKS ONLY

If you've ever locked yourself out of your house or your car, you'll love this one! Marc handles all jobs, large or small. Allow the phone to ring at least 12 times; someone will always be there. That's good news when you have an emergency, and you save 25% over other locksmiths.

∞ Party Coordinating Service ∞

THE CANDY FACTORY**
12510 Magnolia Blvd.
North Hollywood, CA 91607
818/766-8310
HOURS: TUES-SAT: 10-5
CREDIT CARDS: MC, V

The Candy Factory can create a fun and unforgettable birthday party for your little ones. Everything—birthday cake, punch, party favors, games—is included, plus the kids get to actually make their own chocolate candy. The party lasts for two hours and each child takes home about a pound of chocolates in a box personalized with the birthday boy or girl's name. The parties are held at their factory, so you won't end up with chocolate everywhere. The cost is $15 per child, with a minimum of 15 children per party. You'll receive 10% discount with your BUYING RETAIL IS STUPID coupon.

WITH KIDS IN MIND**
12080 Ventura Pl.
Studio City, CA 91604
213/462-2211, 818/761-4011
HOURS: CALL FOR APPOINTMENT
CREDIT CARDS: MC, V

Gracie Nicols, better known as Gracie the Clown, owns and operates With Kids In Minds and specializes in children's character birthday parties and craft parties. Standard one and a half hour parties include character of choice and some games at very reasonable rates. Characters include: Bart Simpson, Little Mermaid, Peter Pan, Ninja Turtles, Batman and more. Save an additional $20 on a one and a half hour character party with your BUYING RETAIL IS STUPID coupon (not to be used with any other offer).

SOUND ENTERTAINMENT
Canyon Country, CA
805/251-9772, 818/909-9119, 714/952-2900
HOURS: MON-SAT: 11-7
CREDIT CARDS: MC, V

Planning a wedding, Bar Mitzvah, or any party where you will want entertainment? Sound Entertainment may be just the ticket! They are professional D. J.'s that not only provide the entertainment, but also can help you plan, coordinate and emcee your party. They offer a 10% dis-

SERVICES

count on a 4 hour minimum package. You can get a discount of 25% or more if your party is longer than 4 hours. Sound Entertainment has a 24 hour booking service available. You tell them the types of music, from Big Bands to Top 40 and they will provide the fun for your guests. They travel throughout Southern California, so let the show begin.

THE WRITE PLACE
213/839-1340, 213/839-6794
HOURS: BY APPOINTMENT ONLY
CREDIT CARDS: CASH OR CHECKS ONLY

Too busy to plan your party? The Write Place will do it all—from addressing your invitations to finding the right caterers, bands, photographers, even writing your "thank you" notes at savings of 10 to 20%. Calligraphy is their specialty.

∞ PHOTOGRAPHERS ∞

FACES N' PLACES PHOTOS
44910 18th St. West
Lancaster, CA 93534
805/942-5361
HOURS: MON-FRI: 10-6 SAT: 10-4
CREDIT CARDS: CASH OR CHECKS ONLY

Wesley and Rosemary Jones have an alternative to the usually expensive family or wedding photographic sessions. Their complete package will average under $500 with a guarantee of satisfaction or no charge above the $150 deposit. They specialize in the intimate, family oriented, or modestly organized wedding. Their emphasis is on spontaneous, impromptu shots that bring back the fondest memories of the happy occasion. What started out as a hobby has turned into growing business. The Jones' are flexible, easy to work with, and pride themselves on listening to their customer's needs.

LYNN PHILLIPS PHOTOGRAPHY
213/739-0208
HOURS: BY APPOINTMENT ONLY
CREDIT CARDS: CASH OR CHECKS ONLY

Lynn Phillips specializes in photography for all special occasions as well as portraits, fashion composites and candid shots taken during parties. Her prices are about 25–40% lower than most studios. And, you, not the studio, own the negatives. This gives you the freedom to have your prints and enlargements done anywhere of your choice.

∞ Used Mobile Home Sales ∞

MOBILE HOME MANAGEMENT
10712 Sepulveda Blvd.
Mission Hills, CA 91345
818/361-7364
HOURS: MON-SUN: 9-6
CREDIT CARDS: CASH OR CHECKS ONLY

If you've been looking for a mobile home or want to trade up, then this may be the place for you. The team at Mobile Home Management are in-park resale specialists. If you're from out of town, they can put you immediately in a park. Financing and insurance are available. You can save around 20% on brand names such as Home Systems, National Pre-built, Baron Homes, and Hallmark. You can save even more on their bank repossessions, and they take trade-ins.

∞ Video Transfers ∞

E V S PRODUCTIONS**
18356 Oxnard St.
Tarzana, CA 91356
818/996-5810
HOURS: MON-FRI:8-6
CREDIT CARDS: MC, V

E.V.S. Productions is the place to go for video duplication and film-to-video transfers. When they do a film-to-videotape transfer, everything is done by hand on the premises. All video tape is time base corrected. They do PAL-SCCAM transfers and customers are welcome to view the tape before transferring, by appointment. The film viewing is free as well as any consulting necessary, whatever the customer needs. They use Fuji and Panasonic film and equipment. Most of all, the people at E.V.S. Productions are very professional. Be sure to take along your BUYING RETAIL IS STUPID coupon for a 10% discount off their already discounted prices.

SERVICES

∞ WEIGHT LOSS PROGRAM ∞

NUTRI/SYSTEM
22653 Ventura Blvd.
Woodland Hills, CA 91364
800/321-THIN
HOURS: VARY FROM CENTER TO CENTER
CREDIT CARDS: ALL MAJOR

With the media exposure we've experienced in the last couple of years, we decided that to look good on camera shedding a few pounds was necessary. To save time, we wanted a set program with pre-prepared foods. Most importantly, we wanted a good value for our dollar. On the recommendation of a friend, we visited Nutri/System and were very impressed with their program. With Nutri/System, you stop in weekly at their centers and pick up your food for the week, meet with your counselor to discuss your progress and weigh in. The food is well-balanced with vitamins and minerals and is low in fat, cholesterol and sodium. There is a large selection of delicious foods to choose from and classes which help overcome problem eating habits. There is also an exercise plan that will help you enjoy an active lifestyle. Most meals take less than two minutes to prepare. After all, time is money. Because we are so busy, having a program that requires little or no thinking is worth its weight in gold. We were also amazed at how much there is to eat in a day. The food costs about $62–69 a week (three meals, snacks, and desserts). Enrollment fees vary depending on which program you choose. They range from introductory offers starting as low as $19 to full-service programs (which include maintenance) and on-going services. One of the programs offers a financial rebate of 50% of your program services as a reward for maintaining your weight.
Additional locations: 95 other centers throughout S. CA

SPORTS & RECREATION

∞ BICYCLES ∞

ALL PRO BICYCLES
2381 Tapo St.
Simi Valley, CA 93063
805/583-4296

HOURS: MON-FRI: 10-6 SAT: 10-5 SUN: 11-5
CREDIT CARDS: ALL MAJOR

The first week in May is bicycle week, and All Pro Bicycles is a great place to buy your new bike! All Pro carries Diamond Back, Nishike, Haro, Dyno, Klein, and Robinson bikes at prices lower than most of the competition. If you find any advertised price lower in the Santa Clarita, Conejo, San Fernando and Simi valleys than All Pro, they will refund 125% of the price difference to you. They boast the largest selection of bikes in the Simi Valley. You'll find a knowledgeable staff and experts at wheel building. They carry all the accessories you will need and have an excellent service department. Their two other stores are Chatsworth Cyclery and Joe's Cycle Center in Newhall.

Additional Locations:
Chatsworth- 21112 Devonshire St., 818/886-5404
Newhall-24727 San Fernando Rd., 805/255-7871

BIKECOLOGY–SANTA MONICA
1515 Wilshire Blvd.
Santa Monica, CA 90403
310/451-9977

HOURS: MON-WED: 10-7 THUR-FRI: 10-8 SAT: 9-6 SUN: 9-5
CREDIT CARDS: AE, DISC, MC, V

You can save as much as 25% below retail on bicycles, bicycle clothing, parts and accessories here. This big store also has special sales in the fall and after Christmas, where you can save even more. You'll find Centurion, Nishiki, and lots more here, and you can take their bicycles for a test ride. They have bicycles for ages 2 to 102, and clothing from XXS-XL. Ask for a catalogue and make sure you get on their mailing list. Their two other locations are called Super Go.

Additional Locations:
Brea–900 E. Imperial Hwy., 714/255-9977
Fountain Valley–8850 Warner, 714/842-3480

SPORTS & RECREATION

CRITERIUM CYCLE SPORT**
16927 Vanowen St.
Van Nuys, CA 91406
818/344-5444

HOURS: MON-WED, FRI: 10-6 THURS: 10-8 SAT: 9-5 SUN: 11-4
CREDIT CARDS: AE, DISC, MC, V

The folks at Criterium Cycle Sport carry new bicycles and lots of cycling accessories. This is not a self-service operation; they have professional salespeople who take the time to make sure you select the right bike for your needs. They carry all major brands such as Yakima, Nike, Giro, Trek, Giant, Univega and Cyclepro. They also provide repairs and offer customers a lifetime warranty on all bicycle purchases. You'll receive an extra 10% discount with your BUYING RETAIL IS STUPID coupon, so you can ride away with an even better deal!

I. MARTIN BICYCLES
8330 Beverly Blvd.
Los Angeles, CA 90048
213/653-6900

HOURS: MON: 10-8 TUES-FRI: 10-7 SAT: 10-7 SUN: 12-6
CREDIT CARDS: AE, MC, V

The savings vary according to your selection, but you can be sure to save money on bicycles and accessories. There are about 900 bikes on hand, making I. Martin one of the largest bicycle buyers in Southern California. The selection runs from children's bicycles to racing bicycles. You can also get cycling shoes and have your wheels serviced and repaired.

SPOKES 'N STUFF
7701 Santa Monica Blvd.
West Hollywood, CA 90046
213/650-1076

HOURS: THUR-SUN: 10:30-8:30
CREDIT CARDS: AE, V

Save about 20 to 30% on everything when it comes to bicycles. Spokes 'N Stuff has bikes by Fuji, Ross, Mongoose, Nitaka, KHS, Diamond Back, plus tricycles, adult trikes, unicycles, tandems, and Rollerblades. In business since 1972, they do repairs, ship around the world, and sell clothes and accessories for the bicycle enthusiast. If, on the spur of the moment you want to cruise the beach on a bicycle or skates, you'll find rentals at one of their beach locations.

Additional Locations: Rentals Only
Marina Del Rey–4175 Admiralty , 310/306-1763
Venice–20-1/2 Washington Blvd., 310/306-3332

- 324 -

TUAZON'S BIKE SHOP
3375 Iowa St., Suite I
Riverside, CA 92507
714/684-6255

HOURS: MON-SAT: 9:30-6
CREDIT CARDS: MC, V

More and more people are finding alternative ways to get to work, have fun on the weekends and get some exercise. As a result, the bicycle is a vehicle that is growing in popularity. At Tuazon's you'll find excellent prices (guaranteed best price) on standard, racing, mountain, and folding bicycles. They also carry bikes and scooters for children. If you think that your balance may not be as sharp as it used to be, you can buy a 3 wheeler for adults, which would definitely make getting around in your community a breeze. Repairs done on all makes.

∞ EXERCISE EQUIPMENT ∞

SPORTS AGAIN
19942 Ventura Blvd. (Winnetka Square Shopping Center)
Woodland Hills, CA 91367
818/888-9728

HOURS: MON–FRI: 10-6   SAT: 10-5   SUN: 11-3
CREDIT CARDS: MC, V

If high prices have kept you from buying a treadmill or exercise bicycle, you have no more excuses. By shopping here you can save 30–70% off retail on recycled and new sporting equipment. Much of the inventory is made up of manufacturer overruns, discontinued lines, demonstration models and retail store returns. Anything you see that is recycled is being sold on consignment. Recycled ski equipment will cost you less money to buy than it would to rent. To keep costs down, there are no guarantees or warranties with purchases. However, for safety reasons, all bicycles are checked out thoroughly by a professional bicycle mechanic prior to being put on sale. If you happen to be one of those people who bought exercise equipment with the best intentions but instead are using it to hang clothes on, then put your little-used equipment on consignment with them. For those of you who have something specific in mind, add your name to their Wish Book. When the item you want becomes available, they'll give you a call and will hold it for one week. After that, it's up for grabs.

SPORTS & RECREATION

TIFFANY'S TOYS
3280 Motor Ave.
West Los Angeles, CA 90034
310/838-TOYS (8697)

HOURS: MON-FRI: 9-7 SAT: 9-6 SUN: 10-5
CREDIT CARDS: AE, MC, OPT, V

Located in West Los Angeles, Tiffany's Toys has discounted exercise equipment featured in a state-of-the-art showroom. They carry all major brands and specialize in new and previously owned exercise equipment with savings of 20–70% off retail. You'll find treadmills, stairclimbers, exercise bicycles, multi-station gym sets, and much more. Some brand names you'll recognize are Lifecycle, Precor, Image, Soloflex, Trotter and Universal. Demonstration (floor) models are always on sale at even greater savings. Prior to making a purchase, individuals are encouraged to work out under the guidance of one of their sales associates. Immediate delivery is available because all merchandise is stocked in five giant warehouses adjacent to the showroom.

∞ GAME ROOM "TOYS" ∞

BILLIARDS & BARSTOOLS**
563 N. Central Ave.
Upland, CA 91786

714/946-1366

HOURS: MON-FRI: 10-6 SAT: 10-5 SUN: 11-5
CREDIT CARDS: V, MC

Billiards & Barstools is your one-stop shop for home recreation. Whether you are a dart thrower, poker player or billiard champion, everything you need can be found here in standard or customized form. You'll find at least 30 different styles in billiard tables made by World Leisure and Brunswick. In addition to items found in most billiard stores, you can spice up your game room with a nostalgic juke box, a slot machine, or even a carousel horse or two. If shooting pool makes you thirsty, you can chill your favorite beverages in an old Coke machine found here. How about an antique gas pump converted into a tropical fish aquarium? If you're short on space but still want a pool table, ask out their dining-pool table combination. Being factory direct, you can expect to spend 30–50% below retail and sometimes a lot less! They've been in business since 1967, so they're not behind the eight ball, and neither will you

when you use your BUYING RETAIL IS STUPID coupon for an additional 10% discount.
Additional Locations:
City of Industry–18605 E. Gale Ave., 818/810-1388
Redlands/San Bernardino–432 E. Redlands Blvd., 714/885-4669
West Covina–322 N. Azusa Ave., 818/332-5099

CROWN BILLIARDS & BAR STOOLS
2090 E. Main St.
Ventura, CA 93001
805/653-5255
HOURS: MON-FRI: 8-5:30 SAT: 9-5 SUN: 11-5
CREDIT CARDS: AE, DISC, MC, V

For savings of 20–25% below suggested retail prices on pool tables and bar stools, Crown Billiards is the place to go. They feature a large selection of name brands: Brunswick, Global, Mevcci, Adams, Walton Bars, Cal Style, Mikhail-Durafeev and Gomez to name a few. If you are looking for a pool table to match the decor of your home, they can even match your furniture with the legs on the pool table. If you don't find just the right thing you're looking for, they have lots of catalogues so you have an even wider variety of products to choose from.

EL DORADO GAMES
7031 Marcelle St.
Paramount, CA 90723
310/630-3300
HOURS: MON-SAT: 9:30-7
CREDIT CARDS: CASH OR CHECKS ONLY

If you're a pinball wizard or want to be one, then El Dorado Games is a place you must visit. You can buy your own pinball machine at low prices here. Whether for personal use or commercial use, El Dorado Games is the home for coin-operated entertainment. They have a showroom and 8,000 square feet of warehouse filled with brand names such as Williams, Bally, Nintendo, Merit and Atari. Pinball machines share the showroom with video games, foosball tables, juke boxes, and dart machines.

SPORTS & RECREATION

GOLDEN WEST BILLIARD MFG.
21260 Deering Court
Canoga Park, CA 91304

818/888-2300

HOURS: MON-TUES, THU-FRI: 8-5   WED: 8-7 SAT: 9-5 SUN: 12-5
CREDIT CARDS: MC, V

Buy factory direct and save on pool tables at Golden West. They always have at least 12–14 tables of every size and style on display with prices starting at just over $800. Prices represent savings of 15–20% off retail stores. Golden West has been in business locally since 1962. They have a big selection of lamps, racks, custom cues, oak bars and barstools, and game tables, too. You can give them a call if you have a table in need of repair. By the way, don't overlook their Brunswick antique tables.
Additional Locations:
Beverly Hills–301 S. Robertson Blvd., 310/659-9487

MURREY AND SONS
14150 S. Figueroa
Los Angeles, CA 90061

213/321-5161

HOURS: MON-FRI: 8:30-5
CREDIT CARDS: MC, V

Murrey and Sons has been in business since 1938 selling billiard tables, pool tables, and all the supplies that go along with them. Their prices are 25% below retail, and the customer can customize his or her table with over 24 different cloth covers. Murrey and Sons has one of the largest inventories in Los Angeles, so don't miss out on this one.

∞ GOLF ∞

DESERT EMPIRE GOLF CENTER
74-121 Hwy. 111
Palm Desert, CA 92260

619/568-4644

HOURS: MON-SAT: 9-5 (10-4 DURING JUNE, JULY, AUG)
CREDIT CARDS: MC, V

If you like to golf you will want to look good walking or riding the course. Here's the place to get top name-brand golf wear for both men and women at great savings of 20% to 50% off retail. Desert Empire has been in business for 14 years and has a 2,800 square foot store. You can expect personal service even though the prices are sliced, and it won't be rough to find additional savings during the summer or other seasons. You will find yourself on the right course for golf shoes, shirts, slacks, warm-ups, tops, shorts, skirts and sweaters, but don't get teed off because they carry clothing only. Desert Empire has grown through word of mouth which is the best kind of advertising.

GOLF FAIRE
17635 Vanowen
Van Nuys, CA 91604
818/343-2454

HOURS: MON-FRI: 9:30-7 SAT: 9:30-6 SUN: 10-5
CREDIT CARDS: MC, V

You may be wondering where all the golf fanatics go. Well, stop by the Golf Faire which has one of the largest selections of equipment in the Southland. These people are serious, claiming "absolutely no lower prices on all name brands." For Foot Joy and Dexter Shoes, the PGA tour clothing collection, bags, putters, videos, balls, gloves and all accessories, don't drive past the Golf Faire. They carry Pro-Line clubs and brands include, Ping, Hogan, Wilson, Lynx, Powerbilt, Titleist and Spaulding too. They offer one day repair service and regripping while-U-wait. Their second store is called Woodland Hills Discount Golf.
Additional Locations:
Woodland Hills–19836 Ventura Blvd., 818/999-4477

LUMPY'S DISCOUNT GOLF AND FASHION PLACE
67625 Hwy. 111
Cathedral City, CA 92234
619/321-2437

HOURS: MON-SAT: 9-6 SUN: 10-5
CREDIT CARDS: ALL MAJOR

Lumpy's is the largest discounter in the valley for clubs, accessories and fashion apparel. Everything they carry in stock is 10–50% below retail, and they guarantee "we will meet or beat advertised prices on golf merchandise in stock or give you the item free." They have plenty of stock on hand in brand names like Hogan, Titleist, Lynx, Foot-Joy, Miller, Spaulding, Lion, Wilson, Etonic, Yamaha, Dexter, Yonex and many more. Just for walking in the door, they'll provide a free swing analysis with their sport tech analyzer. Lumpy's has been in business since the early 1980s and they treat their customers just like neighbors.
Additional Locations:
La Quinta–Hwy. 111 & Washington, 619/346-8768

SPORTS & RECREATION

PRO GOLF DISCOUNT**
1317 Los Angeles Ave.
Simi Valley, CA 93065
805/520-9801
HOURS: MON-FRI: 9-8 SAT: 9-6 SUN: 9-5
CREDIT CARDS: MC, V

If you live in Simi Valley, Pro Golf Discount is a great place to shop for all your golf equipment needs. Pro Golf's discounts range from 20% to 50% off the retail price on brand-names such as Spalding, Footjoy, Etonic, Taylormade, Sota, Ram, Powerbilt and Maxfli. They boast the greatest selection of clubs in Simi Valley. A huge selection of left-handed golf clubs is available, and clubs are matched to individual needs. Most repairs are done in the store and satisfaction is guaranteed. Use your BUYING RETAIL IS STUPID discount coupon, and you'll receive an additional 10% discount.

SHAMROCK GOLF SHOPS
1425 N. Main St.
Santa Ana, CA 92701
714/542-4981
HOURS: MON-FRI: 11-7 SAT: 9-5
CREDIT CARDS: DISC, MC, V

Here's one for the golfers! It seems like most golfers feel they can change their game by changing their equipment. If you are this type of golfer or if you are just starting out, Shamrock Golf Shops carry brand-name golf equipment at discounts 40% below retail. They carry Calloway, Cobra, Hogan, Ping, Wilson, Taylormade, Mizuno, Titleist and Shamrock. You should call for a price on "Big Bertha," you will be surprised. The prices are shown assuming you will pay by credit card. You will save an additional 2% if you pay with cash or check. The money you save could allow you to press on the back nine!
Additional Locations:
Los Angeles-11776 W. Pico Blvd., 310/478-8627
Pasadena-1250 E. Green St., 818/793-3165

∞ Guns, Ammo & Fishing Gear ∞

ARMY-NAVY SURPLUS
11812 E. Garvey
El Monte, CA 91732
213/283-6272

HOURS: MON-FRI: 10-6:30 SAT: 9:30-6 SUN: 10-4
CREDIT CARDS: AE, DISC, MC, V

Going hunting? This store has handguns and rifles plus a complete stock of ammunition. Do you need something to wear? Levi's jeans are here, plus shoes, t-shirts, and camouflage pants. They also carry tents, tent poles, boats, tarps in poly and canvas. Everything already mentioned plus car covers and hard-to-get surplus items are all at 20 to 50% above cost.

Additional Locations:
Hollywood–6664 Hollywood Blvd., 310/463-4730
Santa Barbara–631 State St., 805/963-3868
Santa Monica–1431 Lincoln St., 310/458-4166

B & B SALES
12521 Oxnard St.
North Hollywood, CA 91606
818/985-2329

HOURS: 11-7 SEVEN DAYS A WEEK
CREDIT CARDS: MC, V

With over 12,000 guns in stock, B & B Sales claims to be the largest gun store in the United States. They have every brand of quality firearm known to man, from Colt and Smith & Wesson to Beretta and Walther, plus ammunition, reloading equipment and shooting accessories. In business since 1969, they say you'll save 20–50% off retail prices. They do expert gunsmithing, and buy and trade guns, too.

Additional Locations:
Westminster–14522 Goldenwest St., 714/892-8881

SPORTS & RECREATION

TURNER'S OUTDOORSMAN
1932 N. Tustin Ave.
Orange, CA 92667
714/974-0600

HOURS: MON-FRI: 10-9 SAT-SUN: 10-6
CREDIT CARDS: MC, V

This is the largest chain west of the Rockies specializing in hunting and fishing products. Turner's Outdoorsman carries everything you need for hunting and fishing at savings of 20 to 30% off retail prices. You will find a huge selection of handguns, rifles and shotguns along with necessary supplies. The fisherman will love the various rods, reels, tackle boxes, lures and you name it. They have been in business since 1970.
Additional Locations: 9 other stores throughout S. CA

TURNER'S OUTDOORSMAN OUTLET
12615 Colony St.
Chino, CA 91710
714/590-7225

HOURS: 10-6 SEVEN DAYS A WEEK
CREDIT CARDS: MC, V

Turner's Outdoorsman stores sell equipment and supplies for hunting and fishing at 20–30% off retail prices. This is their outlet store. You'll find 2,000 square feet of merchandise with prices at about 50% off retail. Overstock and last year's hottest items from the chain stores end up here. So, anglers, cast your lines, and hunters, set your traps, for a good deal.

∞ SPORTING GOODS & OUTERWEAR ∞

P F MCMULLIN CO.
1530 E. Edinger, #9
Santa Ana, CA 92705
714/547-7479

HOURS: MON-FRI: 10-9 SAT: 10-6 SUN: 12-5
(CLOSED MAY, JUNE, JULY)
CREDIT CARDS: MC, V

For the past 26 years P.F. McMullin Co. has been clothing families in Southern California who love to ski. What's great about this store is they can fit children starting at size 2 up to men's XX-large to help make your skiing experience a memorable one with the whole family. They have excellent choices of socks, pants, sweaters, jackets, gloves, goggles and much more, with discounts ranging from 20–50% off retail.

OLGA WARNER'S MANUFACTURER'S OUTLET
15750 Strathern
Van Nuys, CA 91406
818/994-7963

HOURS: MON–SAT: 9–5   SUN: 12–4
CREDIT CARDS: AE, MC, V

For bargains on ski wear for men and women, it's hard to beat the prices at the Van Nuys Olga Warner's Outlet. This store has a large selection of Edelweiss bibs, shells, ski pantsuits and powder jackets. Discounts start at about 30% below retail prices. If you happen to go in before the beginning of ski season, you'll find some real bargains on last year's ski clothes. On our last visit we spotted a White Stag parka that originally retailed for $200 tagged at $66.

REAL CHEAP SPORTS
36 W. Santa Clara
Ventura, CA 93001
805/648-3803

HOURS: MON-SAT: 10-6   SUN: 11-5
CREDIT CARDS: AE, MC, V

This is where you'll find Patagonia outdoor clothing. Prices start at about 30% below retail. The merchandise consists of discontinued items from the previous season and overruns and seconds from the current season. The seconds are clearly marked, and the flaws are always cosmetic, never functional. There are always at least half-dozen items on special at low low prices, and the sale items change every two weeks. In addition to ski pants, parkas, sweats, polo shirts, long underwear and other wearables, you'll also find various types of outdoor equipment such as down sleeping bags and a large variety of backpacks.

SUNSHINE SPORTS FACTORY OUTLET
20103 Saticoy St.
Canoga Park, CA 91304
818/341-5805

HOURS: MON-WED, FRI: 10-6   THUR: 10-8   SAT: 10-4   SUN: 12-4
CREDIT CARDS: CASH OR CHECKS ONLY

Skiers, campers and backpackers are going to love us for finding the Sunshine Sports Factory Outlet. Skiers will find everything they need in clothing for the slopes, along with some ski accessories. Campers, backpackers and bicyclists will find clothing and accessories, along with many other related items. They feature tents (more than 40 different models to choose from), both new and factory seconds, and a large selection of sleeping bags (over 50 different styles). Sunshine is the only store in Southern California that specializes in replacement tent poles. They can usually supply a pole (a single section or a complete set) for most styles of tents. They offer low prices all year round of 10 to 60% off retail.

WEST HOLLYWOOD ATHLETIC SUPPLY**
848 N. La Cienega Blvd., #203
Los Angeles, CA 90069
310/652-9221
HOURS: MON-SAT: 10-6
CREDIT CARDS: MC, V

If you've absolutely got to have a pair of Rollerblades, head your wheels over to West Hollywood Athletic Supply. They have the complete line, including every possible color combination, discounted 20% off retail. You'll also find all mandatory accessories needed to complete your Rollerblade ensemble. In addition, the store carries a large variety of athletic shoes—tennis, aerobic, running, cross training—for men and women. The shoes consist mainly of Reebok and Keds. They'll soon have another famous brand, but we can't name names. What we can say is that they have great commercials. Make sure to get your name on their mailing list because they have several terrific sales during the year. The store is on the second level of the building, and there's a parking lot in front. Take in your BUYING RETAIL IS STUPID coupon for a 5% discount on in-stock and nonsale items

SURPLUS

AMERICAN SURPLUS TRADERS**
18643 Parthenia St.
Northridge, CA 91324
818/993-5355
HOURS: MON-FRI: 8:30-5:30 SAT: 10:30-3:30
CREDIT CARDS: MC, V

They specialize in Holga office furniture and have 6,000 square feet of desks, secretarial chairs, executive chairs, file cabinets, lateral files, storage cabinets, shelf files, bookcases, and computer furniture. You will find new furniture, which are factory seconds, used furniture, and industrial shelving. If you're starting a new business on a low budget, this is a good place to start. You can anticipate saving 15 to 60% off retail, but if you use your BUYING RETAIL IS STUPID coupon, you'll save an additional 10%!

ARMY-NAVY SURPLUS
11812 E. Garvey
El Monte, CA 91732
213/283-6272
HOURS: MON-FRI: 10-6:30 SAT: 9:30-6 SUN: 10-4
CREDIT CARDS: AE, DISC, MC, V

Going hunting? This store has handguns and rifles plus a complete stock of ammunition. Do you need something to wear? Levi's jeans are here, plus shoes, t-shirts, and camouflage pants. They also carry tents, tent poles, boats, tarps in poly and canvas. Everything already mentioned plus car covers and hard-to-get surplus items are all at 20 to 50% above cost.

Additional Locations:
Hollywood–6664 Hollywood Blvd., 310/463-4730
Santa Barbara–631 State St., 805/963-3868
Santa Monica–1431 Lincoln St., 310/458-4166

SURPLUS

SURPLUS CITY RETAIL CO.**
11796 Sheldon St.
Sun Valley, CA 91352
818/768-2888

HOURS: MON-SAT: 9-6
CREDIT CARDS: MC, V

Surplus City Retail Company has the largest supply of surplus clothing in Los Angeles with the best prices. You will discover camping supplies, maps, knives, and camouflage uniforms, new and used, from all over the world for 10 to 30% below list. Call to find out about the sales they have every month on 501 jeans featuring the lowest prices around. If you buy a pair of work boots at Surplus City, use your BUYING RETAIL IS STUPID coupon for an additional 25% discount. The coupon is good only on boots not already on sale. Surplus isn't the only thing at Surplus City. You will see 105mm cannons and messenger bikes from WWII, a Nike missile, tanks, trailers and even an old astronaut's uniform. Unfortunately, only surplus goods are for sale.

VAN NUYS ARMY & NAVY STORE
6179 Van Nuys Blvd.
Van Nuys, CA 91401
818/781-3500

HOURS: MON-SAT: 8:30-9 SUN: 9-6
CREDIT CARDS: MC, V

You will find this to be one of the best stocked surplus stores in the area. Van Nuys Army & Navy Store is filled to the rafters with Levis, jackets, belts, caps, camping gear, sleeping bags, pea coats, sweats, thermal pants, boots, and a million other items for both men and women. You can find Coleman coolers here and motorcycle boots, Swiss army and Buck knives, Schott leather jackets, outdoor products, MA-1 and M65 field jackets come in both nylon and leather, soft packs, and duffels. Their complete military department stocks camouflage from at least six different companies. In business since 1950, Carol and Joe head the Van Nuys store and Dave oversees the one in Reseda. Both stores will meet or beat their competitors' prices. Check out the Air Force sunglasses and Halloween costumes too.

Additional Locations:
Reseda– 7116 Reseda Blvd., 818/344-0237

TOYS, DOLLS & GAMES

COMPUTER GAMES PLUS
1839 E. Chapman Ave.
Orange, CA 92667
714/639-8189

HOURS: MON-FRI: 12-6 SAT: 12-5
CREDIT CARDS: MC, V

Computer Games Plus carries computer software and video game cartridges at 25–30% off retail. Make sure to ask about their specials that feature discounts up to 90% off.

GAME CITY**
14541 Ventura Blvd.
Sherman Oaks, CA 91403
818/986-3500

HOURS: MON-SUN: 10-8
CREDIT CARDS: MC, V

Video game freaks unite! Game City is open every day of the week to satisfy the growing industry of video game lovers. They have one of the largest selections in the Southland of Nintendo, Super Nintendo, and Genesis games—new and used as well as the systems to play them on. If you already have a collection of games and want to update, they'll buy your old ones. Rentals games are available so you can try them out prior to purchase. Rentals range from $1.50–$1.99. With your BUYING RETAIL IS STUPID coupon you'll not only receive a 5% discount, but also with the paid rental of one game, a second rental is free.

TOY LIQUIDATORS**
100 Citadel Dr., Suite 144 (Citadel Outlet Collection)
City of Commerce, CA 90040
213/722-1998

HOURS: MON-SAT: 9-8 SUN: 10-6
CREDIT CARDS: DISC, MC,

Toys, toys, and more toys at 40 to 70% off retail can be found at Toy Liquidators. You can count on finding all your brand names here, including Mattel, Playschool, Tyco, and Hasboro. They also carry battery-operated toys such as Nintendo Games, Sega Games, and Game Boy. So

take in your BUYING RETAIL IS STUPID coupon to receive an extra 10% discount.
Additional Locations:
Barstow–Toys Unlimited, 2845 Lenwood Rd., 619/253-3420
Cabazon–48650 Seminole Rd., 714/849-8155
San Ysidro–444 Camino de la Plaza, 619/428-4826

TOYS "R" US
16040 Sherman Way
Van Nuys, CA 91411
818/780-5115

HOURS: MON-SAT: 9:30-9:30   SUN: 10-7
CREDIT CARDS: AE, DISC, MC, V

These stores are huge toy warehouses filled with discounted and low priced toys for youngsters of every age, plus goods and furniture for infants, books, games, bikes and tricycles, and much more. When a toy is "Hot" they're sure to have it here and at great prices. Toys "R" Us also stocks quite a bit of merchandise for babies. By the way, this place isn't just for youngsters. They have things like games, puzzles and other items for adults. Frequent sales and specials are held all year round.
Additional Locations: 38 other stores throughout S. CA

UNCLE TOM'S TOYS
2281 Honolulu Ave.
Montrose, CA 91020
818/249-1557

HOURS: MON-WED, SAT: 9:30-6   THUR-FRI: 9:30-8:30   SUN: 11-6
CREDIT CARDS: MC, V

Are your children always hitting you up for the latest toy they saw while watching cartoons on Saturday? You can buy whatever your little one's heart desires at Uncle Tom's Toys, at 10 to 60% off retail. In business since 1966, Uncle Tom's Toys has 6,000 square feet filled with fun stuff for youngsters and oldsters who are young at heart. They carry at least 200 brand names adding up to thousands of different items from which to choose. You'll find an extensive selection of Barbie everything, Playmobil play centers (doll houses, pirate ships, etc.), Little Tikes, rows of Lego sets, Illco and more. They also have an aisle filled with games from Milton Bradley and Parker Brothers. Towards the back of the store, there is a large section devoted to Breyer animal figures sold individually and in sets. Doll collectors can save 50% off retail on Suzanne Gibson dolls. Uncle Tom's Toys is a friendly place, staffed with people who enjoy playing as much as their customers do.

TRAVEL & VACATION NEEDS

∞ Luggage & Travel Accessories ∞

A V LUGGAGE AND BRIEFCASE
44230 10th St. West
Lancaster, CA 93534
805/940-1997
Hours: Mon-Sat: 10-6
Credit Cards: AE, DISC, MC, V

For those of you living in the Lancaster area, we found a luggage store that guarantee the lowest prices, usually 20% to 50% off retail. They carry brand names such as Samsonite, Delsey, Tumi and Olympia. All merchandise carries a one-year warranty, and repair work is done on the premises. Monograms and gift wrapping are free, as is UPS delivery, if needed. They have difficult to find items such as passport holders and currency exchange calculators here. Got a broken strap? Chances are A V luggage has a replacement!

H. SAVINAR LUGGAGE
4625 W. Washington Blvd.
Los Angeles, CA 90016
213/938-2501
Hours: Mon-Fri: 8-5:30 Sat: 9-5:30
Credit Cards: MC, V

This is a good example of why "BUYING RETAIL IS STUPID!" was written. Why pay retail prices when you can go to stores like H. Savinar, enjoy big savings, have a more complete selection than any department store offers, and be waited on by helpful and knowledgeable salespeople? With a selection that is incomparable, this 14,000 square foot warehouse is stocked with luggage representing every major brand. The savings range from 20 to 60% on luggage, tote bags, travel-related accessories of all kinds, briefcases, portfolios and small leather goods They also have free monogramming with purchase. The Savinar family has been in business since 1917, and at this location since 1958. Most of their salespeople have been working there for at least 10 years. Look for their special sales during the year. If you want to buy the best for less, be sure to visit H. Savinar Luggage.
Additional Locations:
Canoga Park–6931 Topanga Canyon Blvd., 818/703-1313

TRAVEL & VACATION NEEDS

LAX LUGGAGE
18711 Ventura Blvd.
Tarzana, CA 91356
818/343-4422

HOURS: MON-SAT: 10-6 SUN: 11-5
CREDIT CARDS: MC, V

Find name brand luggage here at discounted prices. At LAX Luggage you'll see sets made by Ricardo, Samsonite, Skyway, Lucas, Members Only, Adolfo, Andiamo, Turi and Lark just to name a few. They also carry attaches, briefcases, travel items and Seiko clocks. If your luggage is in need of repair, they do authorized airline luggage repair as well.
Additional Locations:
Inglewood–11010 S. La Cienega Blvd., 310/417-2307
W. Los Angeles–2233 S. Sepulveda Blvd., 310/478-2661

LUGGAGE OUTLET
17775 Main St.
Irvine, CA 92714
714/250-0774

HOURS: MON-FRI: 9-6 SAT: 10-5 SUN: 11-5
CREDIT CARDS: MC, V

Whether you're traveling overnight to San Francisco or touring Europe for a month, Luggage Outlet will help you choose the perfect luggage for your journey. They have discounted prices (20 to 50% off retail) on all name brand luggage such as Samsonite, Andiamo, Tumi, Hartman, Boyt, Lark, Skyway, Ventura, Delsey and more. And while you're at it, why not get your initials monogrammed on your new set, free of charge? The Luggage Outlet also has business cases.

TRAVEL & VACATION NEEDS

∞ TRAVEL ARRANGEMENTS & SERVICES ∞

AUTOMOBILE CLUB OF SOUTHERN CALIFORNIA
2601 S. Figueroa
Los Angeles, CA 90007
213/741-3330
HOURS: MON-FRI: 9-5
CREDIT CARDS: MC, V

The Automobile Club's 3.7 million members benefit by the organization's emergency road services; travel planning with maps, tourbooks and reservations; automotive testing and analysis; automobile buying services; auto pricing information and competitively priced auto and homeowners insurance. Most services (not insurance) are free with your annual membership. All this for a first-time membership fee of $58. Members rejoining pay only $38 each year. With just one road service tow, you'll probably recoup your investment. Your membership card entitles you to four free tows a year. When you're planning a trip, stop by any of their 79 locations in Southern California and pick up some of their excellently written tour books. They have a wealth of information, and can suggest many places to use your membership card for additional discounts or benefits while traveling.
Additional Locations: 78 other sites in S. CA

ALL REASONS TRAVEL**
18902 Ventura Blvd.
Tarzana, CA 91356
818/705-2810
HOURS: MON-FRI: 9-5:30 SAT: BY APPOINTMENT ONLY
CREDIT CARDS: AE, DC, DISC, MC, V

We all have a good reason to travel and that's to get away so we can relax! These folks specialize in trips to Hawaii, South America and Mexico. Give them a call and see if you can arrange for that fantastic, well deserved getaway. Don't forget to ask about extra savings on flights outside the United States. With your BUYING RETAIL IS STUPID coupon you can get an additional 10% discount on a cruise, so how can you resist?

TRAVEL & VACATION NEEDS

THE CRUISE COMPANY
10824 White Oak Ave.
Granada Hills, CA 91344

800/626-4006

HOURS: MON-FRI: 9-5:30
CREDIT CARDS: ALL MAJOR

Save money (20–50%) and relax while traveling on one of their many cruises on Holland America, Princess, Cunard or Carnival. Your savings can be used to increase the amount you've budgeted for shopping. Get on their mailing list to be notified about specials on upcoming cruises. This is a "no frills" operation, so you can have your "frills" on the cruise of your choice.

FLIGHT COORDINATORS
1150 Yale St.
Santa Monica, CA 90403

310/453-1396   800/366-3544

HOURS: MON-FRI: 9-5:30   SAT: 11-3
CREDIT CARDS: AE, MC, V

Offering more than 30 years experience in low cost air fare, Flight Coordinators say they can save you plenty on your overseas flights, especially if you need to fly on one day's notice. They deal mostly with overseas flights, but they do handle some domestic flights at a discount. Depending on where you're off to, you can expect to save from 5 to 50% on your airline tickets. You'll save more money if you pay by money order or cashier's check.

VARIETY & THRIFT STORES

∞ GENERAL MERCHANDISE ∞

99¢ ONLY STORE
18222 Sherman Way
Reseda, CA 91335
818/609-0990
HOURS: 9-9 SEVEN DAYS A WEEK
CREDIT CARDS: MC, V

If your lucky number is 99, then this is the store for you! Absolutely everything in the store is sold for 99¢. You can really get great bargains on things like sundries, food, glassware, paper goods, small gift items, plus much more. New merchandise arrives daily and there is never any limit on quantities purchased. Call 213/LUCKY-99 for information.
Additional Locations: 25 other stores in S. CA

BARGAIN FAIR**
7901 Beverly Blvd.
Los Angeles, CA 90048
213/655-2227
HOURS: MON-FRI: 9-7 SAT-SUN: 10-6
CREDIT CARDS: MC, V

In business since the early 1960s, Bargain Fair is an adventure in shopping. As a buyer of close-outs and discontinued merchandise, they are always turning over their inventory of household items. Selection varies from visit to visit, but normally you'll find everything from dinnerware from Japan or Germany to Revlon shampoo at 25–75% off retail. Some of the names we've seen in the past include Anchor Hocking, Mirro, Toastmaster, Canon (towels), Stuart Hall (stationery). You can save an extra 10% by using your BUYING RETAIL IS STUPID discount coupon.

VARIETY STORES

BARGAIN SAVER
5500 Hollywood Blvd.
Los Angeles, CA 90028
213/466-5383

HOURS: MON-SAT: 10:30-7   SUN: 12-6
CREDIT CARDS: MC, V

With just about absolutely everything you can imagine in this catch-all store, you've got to see it to believe it! Bargain Saver has household items, clothing, cookware, drinking glasses, jogging shoes, pillows, comforters, blankets, mattress pads, towels, toys, soap, rugs, statues, and a lot of odds and ends. Yes, we said odds and ends. Nonetheless, you can get Toastmaster and Hamilton Beach products for 20 to 50% above their cost.

HALF PRICE STORES INC.
6367 Van Nuys Blvd.
Van Nuys, CA 91401
818/780-6844

HOURS: MON-FRI: 10-6:30   SAT: 10-6
CREDIT CARDS: MC, V

Local consumers have known about exploratory shopping at the Half Price Stores since 1967. Depending on the items purchased, you can save from 10 to 70% shopping here. There are watches, jewelry, toothpaste, paper products, Christmas goods, socks, underwear, cleaning aids, towels, and much more. We could go on and on trying to list the thousands of things on the shelves. In the back room you'll discover gas and electric barbecues. There are at least ten units on display representing brand names such as Amerilight, Broilmaster, Char-Broil and Patio. Barbecue accessories and replacement parts are also stocked.

LA BREA BARGAIN CIRCUS
852 N. La Brea
Los Angeles, CA 90038
213/466-7231

HOURS: MON-SAT: 9-9   SUN: 9:30-8
CREDIT CARDS: MC, V

A grocery store and so much more! In addition to food products, La Brea Bargain Circus features knives, silver, beer and an assortment of ceramic planters and dishes. The stock changes weekly, so it's like going to a

VARIETY STORES

new store every week. They buy inventory close-outs and job lots, so the prices are terrific; the people are nice and friendly, too. With this store having over 80,000 square feet, not only do you have a large assorted selection, you have lots of area to cover. Watch for their newspaper ads for their latest specials.

SAWYERS & SAWYERS
5263 Lankershim Blvd.
North Hollywood, CA 91604
818/761-5781
HOURS: MON-SAT: 10-6
CREDIT CARDS: CASH ONLY

At Sawyers & Sawyers you're apt to find just about anything. Joe used to sell wholesale only to the studios, but he now sells to the public out of a 2,500 square foot store located in North Hollywood. The brand name merchandise is sold at 50% below name store sale prices. If you know the merchandise you want and have the model number, call Joe and he can order it for you. He can't accept coupons or credit cards because his discounts are so high! By the way, Joe will be moving in the next six months. He's keeping the same phone number, so make sure you give him a call before making the drive.

TREASURE HUNT
5029 E. Florence Ave.
Bell, CA 90201
213/773-7622
HOURS: MON-SAT: 9:30-9:00   SUN: 10:30-7:00
CREDIT CARDS: DISC, MC, V

If you like the adventure of treasure hunts, then you'll love this store. They buy close-outs, overstocks and liquidations on famous-brand clothing, food, snacks, cleaning supplies, health and beauty supplies, linens and much more with savings up to 70%. Their stock is constantly changing, so shop them often for new treasures.
Additional Locations: 6 other stores throughout S. CA

VARIETY STORES

∞ New & Used Merchandise ∞

AD-MART
9937 Commerce Ave.
Tujunga, CA 91402
818/353-1447
HOURS: MON-SAT: 9-5
CREDIT CARDS: CASH OR CHECKS ONLY

Everything you see in Ad-Mart is sold on consignment and believe us when we say, you never know what you'll find. They have clothing for the whole family, with the largest selection of men's jeans we've ever seen in a store like this. There are quite a few household items and a large bin filled with linens. Ad-Mart, a family owned business, has been serving their community since 1947. Consignments are taken Monday through Friday from 9 a.m. to 10 a.m. and again at 1 p.m. to 2p.m., and on Saturday 9 a.m. to 10 a.m. only.

AUNT FANNIE'S ATTIC
7146 Reseda Blvd.
Reseda, CA 91335
818/705-9429
HOURS: MON-FRI: 9-5 SAT: 10-4
CREDIT CARDS: MC, V

Aunt Fannie's Attic is a charity thrift shop for the National Asthma Center. Inventory—clothing, housewares and sometimes furniture—is always on the move, and they have quarterly sales to make room for incoming merchandise. There's always a rack with everything priced at $1, and believe it or not, they have a layaway plan and dressing rooms, too. Occasionally there are new items donated by manufacturers, and if you have a few items around the house you no longer use, donations are always welcome. Senior citizens receive an additional 20% discount, but only if they ask.

CINEMA GLAMOUR SHOP
343 No. La Brea
Los Angeles, CA 90036
213/933-5289

HOURS: MON-FRI: 10-4
CREDIT CARDS: CASH ONLY

Now you can wear or use things from movie stars. Cinema Glamour Shop's entire stock of merchandise is from donations made by the movie industry. Anything and everything donated to them by the industry is for sale here, so you never know what you're going to find. If you go down to the thrift shop to do some exploring, leave your checkbook and credit cards at home. This shop operates strictly on a cash basis.

COLLATERAL LOANS, INC.
18520 Sherman Way
Reseda, CA 91335
818/345-9600

HOURS: MON, WED-SAT: 9-5
CREDIT CARDS: CASH OR CHECKS ONLY

This is really a loan corporation store where all of the merchandise has been preowned but not necessarily used. You can save as much as 80% on video equipment, typewriters, jewelry, crystal, bicycles, stereos, appliances, and more. Some personal property was collateral on loans; other items have been bought outright from individuals and estates. You'll see some items still in factory-sealed cartons from IBM, Nikon, Pioneer, Martin, Zeiss and more. Ask for Sam or Scott, and be sure to inquire about their twice-yearly sales. Parking is free.

DISCOVERY SHOP
4454 Van Nuys Blvd.
Sherman Oaks, CA 91423
818/905-9141

HOURS: MON-SAT: 10-5
CREDIT CARDS: MC, V

The chain of Discovery Shops is run and operated by volunteers for the American Cancer Society. The thrift stores carry merchandise donated from generous people and retailers from all over Southern California. You'll find new and used clothing, jewelry, furniture, books, miscellaneous household items, and as in all thrift stores, a variety of odds and ends. Donations are always welcome.
Additional Locations: 7 other stores in S. CA–Call 818/956-8052

VARIETY STORES

LOAN MART, INC.
6426 Van Nuys Blvd.
Van Nuys, CA 91401
818/787-3502

HOURS: MON-SAT: 9-5
CREDIT CARDS: MC, V

Don't judge this store by its name! They don't sell loans; they sell out-of-pawn merchandise. You can get great buys on fine jewelry, cameras, lens, binoculars, guns, and art objects sold at 20 to 50% above cost. They are the largest pawn shop in the San Fernando Valley. If you have never been in a pawn shop, Loan Mart is a good place to start. You'll find them to be a unique store with some really terrific buys!

IV

DIRECTORY

OF

MAIL-ORDER

COMPANIES

CATALOGUES

We have included here, for the most part, only mail-order houses that sell at a discount. A few non-discount catalogue firms have been included because they offer unique, special merchandise and/or low prices. So send for the ones that interest you and start your collection today. You will have a lot of fun going through these interesting, informative, colorful materials. And, when your purchases start arriving in the mail, it will seem like Christmas every day.

∞ ARTS, CRAFTS, & HOBBIES ∞

– ART SUPPLIES –

CARTOON COLOUR COMPANY, INC.
9024 Lindblade St.
Culver City, CA 90230
213/838-8467
COST: FREE

Since 1947, Cartoon Colour Company has manufactured superior artists' paints for the animation industry, as well as for other fields of commercial art. You'll appreciate the low prices.

CO-OP ARTISTS' MATERIALS ATLANTA AIRBRUSH
P.O. Box 53097
Atlanta, GA 30355
800/877-1228
COST: FREE

Featured in this catalogue is everything an artist needs—brushes, easels, pens, portfolios, and much more. They rate high in customer service too.

COS-TOM PICTURE FRAMES
1031 Bay Blvd.
Chula Vista, CA 92011
800/854-6606
COST: FREE

Cos-Tom Picture Frames is your connection to hundreds of frames of all types and styles at factory direct prices. Their selection includes the popular look of the Southwest, wood tones, contemporary metal, embossed European designs, and formica frames in every color of the rainbow.

CATALOGUES

PEARL PAINT COMPANY
308 Canal St.
New York, NY 10013
800/221-6845
COST: FREE

Get your creative juices flowing and call Pearl Paint Company for any artist, graphic and craft supplies you need. They are 10 floors filled with these items at savings up to 70% off retail.

DANIEL SMITH ARTISTS MATERIALS
4130 First Ave. South
Seattle, WA 98134
800/426-6740
COST: FREE

Daniel Smith Artists Materials has a beautiful catalogue and offers savings for the artistic minded. They have a wide selection of brushes, paint, paper, and equipment. You'll also find that ordering from them is a pleasure. They are very customer service oriented.

– CRAFT SUPPLIES –

GETTINGER FEATHER CORP.
16 W. 36th St.
New York, NY 10018
212/695-9470
COST: $2.00

Be a little daring and dress up your evening wear with a feather boa from Gettinger's. You'll find every type of feather for any purpose. Want to restuff your old feather pillows? Why not buy their bedding feathers or for crafts try some of their pheasant, turkey, duck, goose, rooster, peacock, pheasant, or ostrich feathers? Gettinger's is a landmark in New York, serving the public with savings of up to 50% off retail since 1915.

ROUSSEL
1013 Mass Ave.
Arlington, MA 02174
617/643-3388
COST: FREE

Roussel offers terrific buys on supplies and equipment for making your own costume jewelry. In addition to jewelry kits and findings, you never know what you'll find in Roussel's specials and close-outs. Most items are sold by the dozen, but the prices can't be beat.

SMILEY'S YARNS
92-06 Jamaica Ave.
Woodhaven, NY 11421
718/847-2185
COST: FREE

Since 1935, Smiley's Yarns has been the ultimate yarn source for people who take their knitting seriously. For more than 50 years, they have offered first quality, name brand yarns at discounts of 40-80% off retail. Some brand names they feature are Phildar, Riviera, Bernat, Patons and more. If for any reason you aren't completely satisfied, return the yarn for an immediate refund. They offer "Only the best, always for less."

TAYLOR'S CUTAWAY & STUFF
2802 E. Washington St.
Urbana, IL 61801
COST: FREE

Looking for a new hobby? Why not try crocheting or making soft toys with patterns from Taylor's Cutaway & Stuff. They carry patterns for Raggedy Ann & Andy dolls which dates back to the 1940s as well as Little Orphan Annie. There are over 40 patterns to choose from as well as a variety of other craft supplies, all at 50 to 75% off retail.

– FABRICS & NOTIONS –

THE BUTTON SHOP
7023 Roosevelt Rd.
Berwyn, IL 60402
708/795-1234
COST: FREE

Don't let the name of this store fool you. The Button Shop, in addition to a large selection of buttons, also carries every type of basic sewing notions at 20-50% off retail.

THE FABRIC CENTER
485 Electric Ave.
Fitchburg, MA 01420
508/343-4402
COST: $2.00

The Fabric Center has been in business for 61 years. They are the country's foremost mail-order distributor of the finest home decorating fabrics available. Their years of experience has given them the expertise to bring first quality fabrics to the public at savings of 25-50% off the national average retail price. Orders are, usually shipped within 24 hours. Their 132 page catalogue contains photos of thousands of fabrics in full color.

CATALOGUES

GLOBAL VILLAGE IMPORTS
1101 S.W. Washington, #140
Portland, OR 97205
503/274-8778
COST: $3.50

Buy direct from Global Village Imports and save 20-50% off retail on their ikat fabrics from Guatemala. Ikat is an extremely complex type of weaving. First, threads are tie-died and carefully arranged into intricate patterns. The threads are then woven into fabric on large footlooms. All fabrics are 100% cotton, 36" wide and machine washable. Send $3.50 (refundable with first order) and receive a substantial swatch pack of fabrics. Choices of additional cotton and silks are available in swatch kit for $5 (also refundable). They also donate a percentage of your purchase to organizations working for peace and justice in Guatemala.

SHAMA IMPORTS INC.
P.O. Box 2900
Farmington Hills, MI 48333
313/478-7740
COST: FREE

Because of the low overhead costs and no middleman in the distribution of Shama Imports' merchandise, you can get elegant crewel fabrics at about 50% off retail prices. All fabrics are directly imported from the craftsmen of Kashmir, India and made of 100% wool and hand embroidered on a 100% hand-loomed cotton background. These fabrics are best used for upholstery, draperies, bedspreads, slipcovers, tablecloths, wall coverings and apparel. They also carry ready-made crewel fabric bedspreads, tablecloths, cushion covers and tote bags. Any merchandise not cut or damaged is returnable within 30 days for a money back guarantee.

THAI SILKS
252 State St.
Los Altos, CA 94022
800/221-SILK, 415/948-8611
COST: FREE

Lustrous, exotic silks in over 400 designs makes Thai Silks one of the leaders in supplying silk fabrics to the public. You can get an entire sample collection of all their styles and various types of silks for only $20.00 which is refunded if returned in 30 days. They also carry a selection of silk clothing. All this at 30–50% savings.

CATALOGUES

– HOBBIES –

FREE THINGS FOR KIDS TO WRITE AWAY FOR
Jetco Publications, Dept. TFK
P.O. Box 85
Livingston, NJ 07039-0085
COST: $2.00

Children will be thrilled with this catalogue filled with all kinds of free things to send away for. Replicas of historical documents, iron-ons, vegetable seeds, posters, coloring books, puppets, genuine foreign money are just a few samples of the free offers in this catalogue. Young sports fans can send for freebies from several professional football and baseball teams. Also available are many informational and how-to booklets. Parents will also find items of interest in this catalogue.

JAMESTOWN STAMP COMPANY
341–3 E. Third St.
Jamestown, NY 14701-0019
716/488-0763
COST: FREE

This catalogue offers stamps from all over the world, plus all related supplies and accessories. You'll get the best prices buying stamps in bulk, which is perfect for someone just starting a collection. They also have baseball cards, postcards and bank notes.

∞ APPLIANCES ∞

AAA-ALL FACTORY, INC.
241 Cedar
Abilene, TX 79601
915/688-1311
COST: $2.00

AAA-All Factory provides brand name vacuum cleaners such as Hoover, Panasonic, Royal, Eureka and more at substantial savings.

ABC VACUUM CLEANER WAREHOUSE
6720 Burnet Rd.
Austin, TX 78757
512/459-7643
COST: FREE

ABC Vacuum Cleaner Warehouse is known for their inventory of leading brand name vacuum cleaners with savings up to 35%. They also carry liquidated merchandise at up to 75% off retail.

SEWIN' IN VERMONT
84 Concord Ave.
St. Johnsbury, VT 05819
800/451-5124
COST: FREE

If you do your own sewing, check out Sewin' in Vermont. They carry brand name sewing machines at unbelievable prices.

SUBURBAN SEW'N SWEEP
8814 Ogden
Brookfield, IL 60513
800/642-4056
COST: FREE

Suburban Sew 'N Sweep carries the complete selection of Singer and White lines of sewing machines and sergers. All machines are new, with full factory warranty and shipped UPS. They also carry the Singer Magic presses (both dry and steam), Rowenta irons, and the Hy-Steam gravity feed irons. Savings range between 30-50%.

∞ AUTOMOTIVE PARTS & ACCESSORIES ∞

ARCTIC SHEEPSKIN OUTLET
I-94 at Hammond Exit
Hammond, WI 54015
800/428-9276
COST: FREE

If you're heading for cold country and need to keep your ears warm or just want the comfort of luxurious sheepskin as a bicycle seat cover, then Arctic Sheepskin Outlet is the place for you. Savings of 20% on hats and slippers and up to 50% on seat covers, rugs, mittens, car seats, bicycle seats, steering wheels covers and more. Children's slippers also available. A $5 shipping charge for each order covers all merchandise. Their merchandise is also guaranteed to be free of defects for one year.

J.C. WHITNEY & CO.
P.O. Box 8410
Chicago, IL 60680
312/431-6102
COST: FREE

Save up to 50% by shopping from J.C. Whitney's catalogue with a huge selection of parts and accessories for all cars, vans, pick-ups, RVs, off-road vehicles and motorcycles.

∞ BOOKS ∞

BARNES & NOBLE
126 Fifth Ave.
New York, NY 10011
800/242-6657
COST: FREE

Claiming to be the world's largest bookstore, Barnes & Noble has been selling books since 1873. Their catalogue offers a tremendous selection of hard and soft cover books at up to 75% off retail. You'll even find a few "coffee table" art books. Audio book fans will enjoy the selection of best sellers and classics on cassettes. They also have videos featuring movie classics, foreign films and documentaries. Culture vultures will appreciate videos on subjects such as opera, ballet, classical music and theater featuring the greatest artists of our time.

DAEDALUS BOOKS
Box 9132
Hyattsville, MD 20781
800/395-2665
COST: FREE

From the thousands of books offered by publishers as remainders every year, Daedalus chooses only those books which, in their judgment, are of lasting value. They believe that the quality of remainders in their catalogue demonstrates that they're not "books that didn't sell," but rather books whose publishers' stock was larger than projected future sales. Many of the finest books published every year are remaindered at some point to make room for another season's hopefuls. They feature categories such as fiction, history, poetry, children's, gardening, and the arts. Books are generally 50-90% off retail.

JESSICA'S BISCUIT
Box 301
Newtonville, WA 02160
800/878-4264
COST: $2.00

Can you imagine looking through 63 pages of delicious, scrumptious, delectable cookbooks? Within the catalogue there are over 13 pages of cookbooks featured in their "special sale selection" at 30-70% off the retail price. How about Julia Child's Menu Cookbook for $19.98 (reg. $35.90) or Wolfgang Puck Cookbook for $7.98 (reg. $19.95) and if you want to dazzle your salads try "The Ultimate Salad Dressing Book" for $5.98 (reg. $12.95). Let your tastebuds go wild!

CATALOGUES

PUBLISHERS CENTRAL BUREAU
One Champion Ave., Dept. 491
Avenel, NJ 07001-2301
800/722-9800, Ext. 491
COST: FREE

This catalogue is chocked full of books, videos, cassettes and compact discs. You'll find savings of up to 87% off retail on their enormous selection of books and audio/visual products.

U.S. GOVERNMENT BOOKS
Superintendent of Documents–U.S. Government Printing Office
Washington, DC 20402-9325
COST: FREE

Government publications for people of all ages are available through this catalogue. This is an unbelievable source for government books on all subjects. Covering everything from agriculture, military equipment and foreign policy to travel, exercise and nutritional needs, there are over 21,000 different publications available. Some items such as informational booklets are $1, and historical documents reproduced on parchment paper run $2 (great for student projects). Also listed are their locations in various states where you can browse to your heart's content.

∞ BUILDING & REMODELING ∞

ARTIC GLASS & WINDOW OUTLET
565 County Rd. T
Hammond, WI 54015
800/657-4656
COST: FREE

Unlike most large companies, the President and owner of Artic Glass & Window Outlet, Joe Bacon, is still accessible, should you have a problem or unanswered questions about windows, doors, sunrooms and skylights. Joe emphasizes fairness, fast service, quality products and the lowest prices possible. They are committed to helping people use insulated glass to promote energy efficiency and for ventilation and decoration.

HIAWATHA HOMES
P. O. Box 1148
Pacific Palisades, CA 90272
310/454-4809

Do you dream about building your own home? Hiawatha Homes is a unique mail-order company that stocks over 1,000 architect designs of single family homes. Starting at $19.00, you can get a set of books to view these designs. Then call Hiawatha Homes again to purchase the working drawings and outline specifications at a cost of $95 to $600. These plans usually cost up to $5,000 when prepared by an architect.

∞ CIGARS, PIPES & TOBACCO ∞

WALLY FRANK, LTD.
63-25 69th St.
Middle Village, NY 11379
718/326-2233
COST: FREE

Save up to 50% on a wide selection of domestic and imported cigars, pipes and tobacco. They even have a 8 3/4" long 60 ring gauge cigar that comes in a cedar wood hinged case. You can buy both name brand products and generic brands from Wally Frank. They also have gift items such as flasks, walking sticks and a selection of srimshaw collectibles.

∞ CLOTHING ∞

ARCTIC SHEEPSKIN OUTLET
I-94 at Hammond Exit
Hammond, WI 54015
800/428-9276
COST: FREE

If you're heading for cold country and need to keep your ears warm or just want the comfort of luxurious sheepskin as a bicycle seat cover, then Arctic Sheepskin Outlet is the place for you. Savings of 20% on hats and slippers and up to 50% on seat covers, rugs, mittens, car seats, bicycle seats, steering wheels covers and more. Children's slippers also available. A $5 shipping charge for each order covers all merchandise. Their merchandise is also guaranteed to be free of defects for one year.

CHADWICK'S OF BOSTON
One Chadwick Place, Box 1600
Brockton, MA 0240-1600
508/583-6600
COST: FREE

Chadwick's of Boston is known as the original off-price catalogue. They feature the latest in fashion and yet carry classic clothing as well. For the busy career woman or the equally busy woman at home, Chadwick's has a marvelous selection at affordable prices.

CATALOGUES

CHARISMA CALIFORNIA
1119 Barbara, Unit 2
Redondo Beach, CA 90277
800/TRY-HOSE
COST: FREE

If you're fed up and tired of spending too much money replacing panty hose, then call Charisma. They are the U.S. distributor for 20 denier stockings that wear durably and carry a money back guarantee. The hosiery comes in 31 colors and range in sizes from petite to queen. Hosiery is sold in dozen lots only and start at $26.95 per dozen. You'll save a bundle not having to continuously replace your nylons.

THE DEERSKIN PLACE
283 Akron Rd.
Ephrata, PA 17522
717/733-7624
COST: FREE

Choose from a wide selection of jackets, handbags, shoes, moccasins, gloves and wallets for men and women made from cowhide, sheepskin and deerskin. You can even order a coonskin cap.

DESIGNER DIRECT
Designer Circle
Salem, VA 24156-0501
800/848-2929
COST: FREE

Designer Direct brings you exclusive women's fashions you won't find elsewhere, plus A.J. Valenci footwear and elegant accessories at up to 60% below retail. Make a positive impact with their up-to-date women's fashions.

LEATHER UNLIMITED CORP.
7155 Hwy. B, Dept. BR5
Belgium, WI 53004
414/994-9464
COST: $2.00 (REFUNDABLE)

If you love the feel of leather, purchase one of the garment kits featured in Leather Unlimited's 64 page catalogue. Not only will you find a wide variety of leather kits, but you can also purchase finished leather and sheepskin products including belts, handbags, wallets, slippers, totes—even log carriers. They're also an authorized dealer for Harley-Davidson accessories. Their prices feature a 50% savings.

CATALOGUES

✓ RUBENS & MARBLE, INC.
P.O. Box 14900-S
Chicago, IL 60614
312/348-6200
COST: FREE

Since 1890 Rubens & Marble, Inc. has been supplying infant garments to hospitals all over the country. You'll save up to 60% on shirts, gowns, kimonos, sheets, stay-up stretch diapers, training panties, waterproof panties and terry bibs for sizes ranging from infant to 36 months. Most items are first quality cotton with some seconds that with small flaws.

SHOWCASE OF SAVINGS
P.O. Box 748
Rural Hall, NC 27098
919/744-1170
COST: FREE

Ladies, you'll be able to cover your legs with some of the lowest priced stockings around from Showcase of Savings. L'eggs knee highs can be purchased at only 34¢ per pair while Active Support pantyhose are $2.25. Or, try Hanes silky thigh highs for $2.75 per pair. Other stocking brands featured are Underalls and Isotoner. This 67 page catalogue also carries bras, panties, socks, and activewear for men, women and children.

SPORTSWEAR CLEARINGHOUSE
P.O. Box 317746Y2
Cincinnati, OH 45231
513/522-3511
COST: FREE

Surprise, surprise, surprise! That's what you'll receive when you order t-shirts, sweatshirts, visors and caps, socks, and shorts from Sportswear Clearinghouse. They have overruns from other manufacturers with a logo on the goods. When ordering, you can only specify the size. The rest will be a surprise when you receive the goods.

WINTER SILKS
2700 Laura Lane
Middleton, WI 53562
800/648-7455
COST: FREE

This catalogue features all kinds of clothing and accessories made of silk. You'll find silk pajamas, sweaters, blouses, lingerie and even long johns at substantially lower prices than found in retail stores. Skiers that wear only silk long underwear will be amazed at the money they save.

CATALOGUES

∞ COSMETICS & WIGS ∞

BEAUTIFUL VISIONS
810 S. Hicksville Rd.
Hicksville, NY 11855
516/349-7180
COST: FREE

Name brand cosmetics and nationally advertised fragrances at remarkable savings of up to 90% off. There are regular sizes as well as samples sizes that are great for traveling.

BEAUTY BOUTIQUE
6836 Engle Rd.
Cleveland, OH 44101-4519
216/826-1712
COST: FREE

Save up to 90% on nationally known cosmetics when you order from Beauty Boutique. You'll find products for your entire body in name brands such as Estee Lauder, Loreal, Revlon and Cutex. Fragrances and various personal products are also featured in this catalogue.

BEAUTY BY SPECTOR, INC.
Dept. OR
McKeesport, PA 15134
COST: FREE

Exciting designer styles of wigs and hairpieces up to 50% off are available from Beauty by Spector. Also featured is an extensive list of additional catalogues you can order for convenient shopping from your home.

ESSENTIAL PRODUCTS CO., INC.
90 Water St.
New York, NY 10005
212/344-4288
COST: FREE

Why pay up to $300 an ounce for designer perfumes? Beautifully packaged in their own distinctive gift box and individually gift wrapped, Naudet fragrances make wonderful gifts at huge savings. Just let them know your favorite perfume or cologne such as Joy, Giorgio, Opium or Obsession and they'll send you an ounce of a similar smelling scent for $19 or $11 for a half ounce. Men's fragrances sell for $10 for 4 ounces. If you're not satisfied with your purchase, return it within 30 days for a prompt refund. Send a large self-addressed stamped envelope to receive five scent cards free, a fragrance list, and an order form.

∞ ELECTRONICS ∞

CRUTCHFIELD
1 Crutchfield Park
Charlottesville, VA 22906
800/446-1640
COST: FREE

You won't have to wait for a special sale of consumer electronics to find a good value. Crutchfield's helps you make the smartest possible decision through catalogues filled with informative articles, comparison charts, consumer tips, diagrams and objective product descriptions. In addition, you'll receive free publications like The Car Security Specialist, Putting Together a Home Stereo System as well as a 30 day satisfaction guarantee with every order. Their 126 page catalogue carries all you'll need for stereos, security systems, VCRs, phones and computers. U.S. customers pay a $3 handling charge, regardless of order size.

S & S SOUND CITY
58 W. 45th St.
New York, NY 10036
212/575-0210
COST: FREE

S & S Sound City prides itself on giving excellent service and prices since 1975. They inventory a large stock of electronics such as TVs, video equipment, radios, telephones and even electronics for the hearing impaired with savings of up to 50% off retail.

∞ FOOD & BEVERAGE ∞

ACE SPECIALTY FOODS
P. O. Box 100
Cordele, GA 31015
800/729-8999
COST: FREE

Ace Specialty Foods offers very fancy nuts at very "un-fancy" prices. Their cashews, pecans, pistachios, macadamia nuts, dried fruit and chocolate candy are all guaranteed to be delivered fresh to your doorstep.

CATALOGUES

CAVIARTERIA INC.
29 E. 60th St.
New York, NY 10022
800/4-CAVIAR
COST: FREE

Dine like the rich and famous with Caspian Beluga and Sevruga caviar, plus American sturgeon, whitefish and salmon caviar but without the high prices. Caviarteria, established in 1950, is the largest distributor of caviar in the U.S. and features discounts from 20-60% off retail. Call for their catalogue which features a wide variety of other gourmet treats such as pates, smoked salmon and much more.

THE CHEF'S PANTRY
P.O. Box 3
Post Mills, VT 05058
800/TRY-CHEF
COST: FREE

The New York Times and food editors across the country have reviewed The Chef's Pantry catalogue and the verdict is in...sensational! One of the best selections of hard-to-find cooking and baking ingredients, such as Callebaut Belgium chocolate, Vilux vinegars and vanilla extract by Nielsen Massey, is offered in their 17 page catalogue.

FARMER TO CONSUMER DIRECTORY
Small Farm Center, University of CA
Davis, CA 95616
916/757-8910

This invaluable directory lists more than 180 certified farmers from California who sell directly from roadside stands, U-pick farms and farmers' markets. Savings run about 20-30%. Also included are Christmas tree and pumpkin farms.

WINE LINK
420 Talbert St.
Daly City, CA 94014
800/231-1171
COST: FREE

If you enjoy a glass of wine and are sensitive to the chemicals and pesticides used on the grapes, then Wine Link is for you. They import French and Italian wines made from certified organically grown grapes. This means no chemical fertilizers, no herbicides and no fungacides are used in the grape-growing process. All this and savings of 15% off retail.

WOOD'S CIDER MILL
Rd. 2, Box 477
Springfield, VT 05156
802/263-5547
COST: FREE

If you like traditions, make sure you purchase some unsweetened cider jelly and other fine apple products made by the same family on the same farm for over 100 years. They start with fresh apples and squeeze the juice on their century old cider press. The cider is then boiled over a wood fire until it is thick enough to jell, with nothing added. Let your tastebuds carry you back to the good ol' days with their cider jelly, boiled cider cider syrup and maple syrup all at very reasonable prices.

– DO-IT-YOURSELF KITS –

THE CELLAR
14411 Greenwood Ave. N.
Seattle, WA 98133
206/365-7660
COST: FREE

The Cellar has everything you need for brewing beer and making wine and liqueur at the best prices around. Their catalogue features free recipes and if you have a problem there's an expert on duty (just a phone call away) to help you Monday through Sunday.

NEW ENGLAND CHEESEMAKING SUPPLY CO., INC.
85 Main St.
Ashfield, MA 01330
413/628-3808
COST: FREE

If you're a health nut or just want to experiment with something new, try making your own cheese. It's less expensive, less fattening, lower in cholesterol and has no preservatives—can't beat that! Bob and Ricki Carrol have been offering home dairying supplies for over 13 years. If you're lucky, you might be able to attend one of their workshops during their National Cheese Workshop Tours. (Tours are listed in their catalogue.) Cheesemaking kits range in prices from $12.95 for a Mascarpone kit (a delicious fresh Italian cheese made from cream) to $189.95 for the Wheeler Cheese Press handcrafted in England and made from hardwood and stainless steel made to last a lifetime.

– HEALTH FOODS & VITAMINS –

JAFFE BROS. INC.
P.O. Box 636
Valley Center, CA 92082
619/749-1133
COST: FREE

If you're one of the many who like to eat healthy foods, then order Jaffe Bros.' 16 page catalogue featuring organically or naturally grown dried fruits, nuts, seeds, beans, wholewheat pastas, oils, honey and more. They keep prices down by selling a minimum of 5 pounds on most items or 3 jars of such items as organic low-salt sauerkraut or apple butter.

VITAMIN CO-OP
44-823 Guadalupe Dr.
Indian Wells, CA 92210
619/341-1070
COST: FREE

Save 30% and more on special formulas, vitamins, and health and beauty aids. They also have an extensive list of hard to find items.

VITAMIN POWER, INC.
39 Saint Mary's Pl.
Freeport, NY 11520
800/645-6567
COST: FREE

Vitamin Power is in the business of promoting health. They sell products that help people relax, sleep, control weight, build strength and increase energy. You'll find their healthcare and specialty products that cannot be found in mass merchandise stores or discount chains.

∞ GENERAL MERCHANDISE ∞

DAMARK INTERNATIONAL
6707 Shingle Creek Pkwy.
Minneapolis, MN 55430
800/729-9000
COST: FREE

Damark International specializes in manufacturer close-outs and some of their prices are out of this world. A Sharp Copier/Fax machine with a suggested retail price of $2,295.00 was $499.99! They call this the "Great Deal" catalogue because you can get famous name products below dealer cost. They carry a very wide selection of merchandise such as appliances, sports equipment, electronics, furniture, giftware and leather accessories. Your first catalogue is free, but if you don't order something they won't automatically send you another.

∞ HOME FURNISHINGS ∞

– DECORATOR ITEMS & DISHES –

A COOK'S WARES
211 37th St.
Beaver Falls, PA 15010
412/846-9490
COST: $2.00

Tired of looking for new accessories for your Cuisinart? In "A Cook's Wares" catalogue you'll find almost every type of blade and accessory for any type of Cuisinart appliance. Byron and Gail Bitar, owners for the past 10 years, are constantly seeking only the finest cookware and utensils at 20-40% off retail. The 46 page catalogue features cutlery such as Henckels, appliances such as direct infusion coffee makers, expresso makers, pasta machines, Rosti bowls, cookbooks and condiments, bakeware, porcelains, pepper mills and "Try Me" specials.

BARRONS
22790 Heslip Dr.
Novi, MI 48050
800/538-6340
COST: FREE

Fifteen years in business, Barrons provides you with the finest giftware, collectibles, crystal, dinnerware and flatware. They have the largest in-stock selection in the United States. Brand names include Hummel, Royal Doulton, Lenox and many more.

BEVERLY BREMER SILVER SHOP
3164 Peachtree Rd. NE
Atlanta, GA 30305
404/261-4009
COST: FREE

Missing a piece of your sterling silver flatware? Beverly Bremer Silver Shop keeps over a thousand patterns of new and beautiful-as-new sterling in stock so they can help you locate exotic as well as practical flatware items for your collection. They also have new and antique silver gift items. Contact them if you are interested in selling your sterling silver.

CATALOGUES

BUSCHEMEYER'S SILVER EXCHANGE
515 S. 4th Ave.
Louisville, KY 40202
502/587-7342
COST: FREE

This is a source for approximately 1,400 different active, inactive and obsolete sterling and silverplate patterns. They will be glad to find your pattern and quote prices. Send for brochures listing active sterling silver or silverplate patterns which are available from Buschemeyer's Silver Exchange at discount prices.

THE CHEF'S CATALOGUE
3215 Commercial Ave.
Northbrook, IL 60062-1900
708/480-8305
COST: FREE

This catalogue is filled with products for indoor and outdoor cooking. You'll find items for basic food preparation and specialized equipment for unusual or complicated recipes. This catalogue has range and oven cook-ware in a variety of shapes, sizes and materials, barbecues (indoor, out-door, large and small) and accessories, ice cream makers and many other culinary necessities. There are also lots of kitchen gadgets chefs won't be able to live without.

COLONIAL GARDEN KITCHENS AND HOME
P. O. Box 66
Hanover, PA 17333-0066
COST: FREE

If you enjoy unique, cleverly designed products that in many cases aren't available in any store, this catalogue is full of interesting and unusual products that can make cooking and entertaining easier.

MIDAS CHINA & SILVER
5050 Nicholson Lane
Rockville, MD 20852
800/368-3153
COST: FREE

Pass on the memories of fine china and sterling flatware from Midas China & Silver. Your children and grandchildren will enjoy receiving items from their elegant selection. Only the finest merchandise is in this catalogue at savings up to 60%.

PLEXI-CRAFT QUALITY PRODUCTS CORP.
514 W. 24th St.
New York, NY 10011
800/24-PLEXI, 212/924-3244
COST: $2.00

Buy direct from the manufacturer and save up to 50% with Plexi-craft's own line of lucite and plexiglass. Their 16 page catalogue features acrylic furnishings and accessories such as telephone and television stands, chairs, luggage racks, vanities and stools, magazine units, kitchen organizers, bathroom fixtures and much more. They also do custom work.

ROBIN IMPORTERS, INC.
510 Madison Ave.
New York, NY 10022
800/223-3373
COST: FREE

There are over 1,000 patterns of china and flatware from all major manufacturers at Robin Importers. If the pattern you specifically want is not in stock, they will special order it for you. Robin Importers also has a 30 day price guarantee.

ROSS-SIMONS
136 Lambert Lind Hwy (Rt 5)
Warwick, RI 02886
800/556-7376
COST: FREE

Whether fine jewelry or beautiful things for your home, Ross-Simons offers it priced up to 40% below fair retail. They also carry a line of Christmas collectibles.

TAPESTRY
P.O. Box 46
Hanover, PA 17333-0046
800/833-9333
COST: FREE

If you enjoy adding the final touches to a room with tasteful, yet inexpensive decorator items, you're going to love Tapestry. You'll find things like cachepots, planters with stands, nesting tables, lamps, magazine racks, storage items, screens, and chests in a variety of styles and price ranges. They also carry dishes, glasses and linens. One of our favorites was a ceramic canister set with an embossed weave design and wild red strawberries on the lids.

CATALOGUES

– FLOOR COVERINGS –

JOHNSON'S CARPETS
3239 South Dixie Hwy.
Dalton, GA 30720
800/235-1079, 404/277-2775
COST: FREE

No need to spend days looking for the perfect carpet and the best price because Johnson's Carpets manufactures carpets and sells direct to you with savings as high as 80%. Samples are available for all carpets they manufacture so you can feel the weight and select exactly the right color before placing an order.

WAREHOUSE CARPETS, INC.
Box 3233
Dalton, GA 30721
800/526-2229
COST: FREE

Save as much as 50% on brand name carpets such as Mohawk, Aladdin, Columbus, Galaxy, Masland, World, Salem, Coronet and many more.

– FURNITURE –

ADIRONDACK DESIGNS
350 Cypress St.
Fort Bragg, CA 95457
800/222-0343
COST: FREE

Purchase direct from the manufacturer of outdoor redwood furniture at savings of 30-50% off retail. They carry chairs, love seats, lounges, foot rests and much more. All furniture comes with pre-assembled and pre-drilled holes for easy assembly. Satisfaction is guaranteed or you get a full refund.

BRASS BEDS DIRECT
4866 W. Jefferson Blvd.
Los Angeles, CA 90016
800/727-6865
COST: FREE

Superb workmanship and attention to detail has kept Brass Beds Direct in business for the past 19 years with happy customers from all over the United States. They have excellent prices too.

FURNITURE BARN OF FOREST CITY, INC.
1190 Hwy. 74 Bypass
Spindale, NC 28160
704/287-7106
COST: FREE

If you like furniture from the 18th century, you can purchase some from Furniture Barn of Forest City at 40-50% off retail. They also carry current styles of showroom samples, discontinued merchandise, and imports.

SHAW FURNITURE GALLERIES
P.O. Box 576
Randelman, NC 27317
800/334-6799
COST: FREE

Shaw Furniture Galleries represents 300 major manufacturers of home furnishings with savings up to 40% off retail. This company is for people who know what they want and are looking for the best buy. They have been serving their customers since 1940.

SOBOL HOUSE OF FURNISHINGS
Richardson Blvd.
Black Mountain, NC 28711
704/669-8031
COST: FREE

Shop around and compare brand names and cost on your next furniture purchase, then call Sobol House of Furnishings. They'll save you 40 to 50% off retail prices on their selection of traditional, 18th century or modern furniture.

– LAMPS & LIGHT FIXTURES –

ALLIED LIGHTING
Drawer E
Trextertown, PA 18087
800/241-6111
COST: FREE

Elegant crystal chandeliers, Tiffany style lamps, outdoor lighting, floor lamps and more with up to 60% savings. Over 40 manufacturers are represented in their catalogue.

CATALOGUES

KING'S CHANDELIER COMPANY
Hwy. 14 Dept. BRIS
Eden, NC 27288
919/623-6188
COST: $3.50

"We love our work" is the motto at King's Chandelier Company. The King family has been collecting, designing, making and selling chandeliers for generations. Every fixture is especially made for you with crystal parts from such places as Venice, Czechoslovakia, Austria, and metal parts from the U.S.A. or Europe. They do their own designing and importing and therefore can offer top quality products at 20-50% less than similar chandeliers. For the serious minded, King's Chandelier Company will furnish you with a color VHS video cassette tape showing any of the chandeliers from all angles and specifying their dimensions. Advise them of up to six chandeliers from their catalogue you'd like them to tape. A $25 deposit is required which is refundable when you return the tape.

– LINENS –

THE COMPANY STORE
500 Company Store Rd.
La Crosse, WI 54601-4477
800/356-9367
COST: FREE

The Company Store has been in business since 1911 keeping people warm and toasty with their plush down products. Their comforters, in a variety of styles and grades, are all covered in downproof fabric with a minimum 232 thread count. You can get high quality merchandise without paying department store prices.

DOMESTICATIONS
Box 40
Hanover, PA 17333
800/782-7722
COST: $2.00

Are you a Waldo watcher? If you know what we mean, then you can have your very own Where's Waldo? sheets and matching pillow cases at $19.99 for a twin, 3-piece set. This is only one of the many selections of linens from Domestications. For those who like a romantic look, a "full" 8-piece embroidered eyelet lace trim bedroom set with a flat and fitted sheet, 2 standard pillowcases and shams, comforter, and dust ruffle is $129.99 ($300 retail). We're certain this 100 page catalogue will satisfy all your linen needs.

HARRIS LEVY, INC.
278 Grand St.
New York, NY 10002
800/221-7750, 212/226-3102
COST: FREE

Discounted up to 40%, Harris Levy will send you linens for your bed, bath and table. Their motto is, "The very best at the least."

MONTERY MILLS OUTLET STORE
1725 E. Delavan Dr.
Janesville, WI 53545
800/4 FUN-FUR
COST: FREE

Are you trying to help make this world a better place to live? Monterey Mills has manufactured deep pile fabrics for over 25 years. They currently carry a line of women's fake fur coats and jackets, as well as synthetic fur by the yard, remnants in a variety of styles, polyester stuffing, and 100% merino wool mattress pads all at savings of 50% or more below retail. You'll find this catalogue a great resource for materials used in making stuffed toys and animals, pillows, bedspreads and craft items.

– WALL & WINDOW TREATMENTS –

#1 WALLPAPER
Box 396
Ledgewood, NJ 07852
800/631-9341
COST: FREE

Leading distributor for over 90% of the wallcoverings available in the United States. Their merchandise is delivered free to your home and savings run 35–70% off retail.

AMERICAN DISCOUNT WALLCOVERINGS
1411 Fifth Ave.
Pittsburgh, PA 15219
800/777-2737
COST: FREE

You'll find over 100 brands of wallpaper, window treatments and upholstery fabrics at substantial savings of 10–50% off retail. They don't have a catalogue, but they'll send you a list with most of the brand names they carry. After you've shopped around call American Discount Wallcoverings with pattern numbers and book names.

CATALOGUES

POST WALLCOVERING DISTRIBUTORS, INC.
2065 Franklin Rd.
Bloomfield Hills, MI 48302
800/521-0650
COST: FREE

Don't worry about shipping costs for your wallcovering. Post will pick up the charges. Choose any brand from any wallpaper book then call Post for a quote. Discounts are up to 75% off retail and you pay no sales tax. They'll process your order the same day and guarantee fast delivery.

ROBINSON'S WALLCOVERINGS
222 West Spring St.
Titusville, PA 16354
814/827-1893
COST: 50¢

Walk from room to room with Robinson's catalogue in hand and visualize the beautiful new rooms you can create. Do-it-yourself decorators have been shopping Robinson's for 70 years.

SANZ INTERNATIONAL
P.O. Box 1794
High Point, NC 27261
919/882-6212
COST: FREE

When calling Sanz with the pattern name and number of your wallpaper, you will be speaking with an actual salesperson who works in their "open to the public" stores. Their stores carry over 5,000 patterns of wallpaper and border. You'll find the salespeople to be knowledgeable and helpful with information on hanging wallcoverings and estimating. They also will meet or beat any other quote. Check out their extra discounts based on quantities ordered. No shipping charges are incurred.

SILVER WALLPAPER, INC.
3001-15 Kensington Ave.
Philadelphia, PA 19134
800/426-6600, 215/426-7600
COST: FREE

Silver Wallpaper has an extensive selection of first quality wallcoverings, borders and fabrics, in virtually every pattern manufactured in the country. Call them with the name of book and pattern number to receive their discounted prices up to 66% below retail.

∞ JEWELRY ∞

✓ JAMES KAPLAN JEWELERS
40 Freeway Dr.
Cranston, RI 02920

800/343-0712

COST: FREE

Unusual gift items, elegant jewelry, and brand name china and silver has been offered by James Kaplan Jewelers for the past 35 years. Savings are approximately 20–75% off retail.

ROSS-SIMONS JEWELERS
9 Ross-Simons Dr.
Cranston, RI 02920-9848

800/556-7376

COST: FREE

This catalogue features fine jewelry priced at 40% below retail. They have traditional and contemporary styles in gold and sterling silver. Call their toll-free number for their catalogue or to place an order.

∞ LUGGAGE ∞

A TO Z LUGGAGE
4627 New Ultrecht Ave.
Brooklyn, NY 11219

800/342-5011

COST: FREE

Famous maker luggage, briefcases and leather accessories up to 50% off. Some brand names to look for are Hartmann, American Tourister, Samsonite and more.

ACE LEATHER PRODUCTS
2211 Avenue U
Brooklyn, NY 11229

800/DIAL ACE

COST: FREE

You'll love their excellent selection on name brand luggage, attache cases, handbags, travel and desk clocks and small leather goods. Ace Leather Products has been in business for 69 years.

∞ MEDICAL SUPPLIES ∞

AARP PHARMACY SERVICE
500 Montgomery Street
Alexandria, VA 22314
800/456-2277

Save up to 50% on your prescription drugs when ordering through AARP Pharmacy Service. Just call their 800 number with your prescription to check prices. To receive their discounts you must be 50 years or older and first invest $8 to join AARP if you are not already a member. The pharmacy will enroll you with your first order. Incidentally, the $8 membership fee entitles you to numerous other benefits.

PHARMAIL
P.O. Box 1466
Champlain, NY 12919
800/237-8927
COST: FREE

With hospital and medicine costs on the rise, we need to find ways to care for our health without breaking the piggy bank. Pharmail specializes in dispensing maintenance prescription drugs at highly competitive prices based on true acquisition cost and a small dispensing fee. Generic drugs, especially in large quantities, are often available at a fraction of the cost of the brand name drugs. Additional discounts are offered on large quantities and as limited-time specials. There are no age or membership requirements and shipping is free on orders of $10 or more for prescription drugs, or $25 for over the counter items. Just send in your physician's signed prescription (not a photocopy). At your request, Pharmail will call your doctor directly for a prescription. To benefit from their quantity prices, have your doctor write a prescription for several months' supply at a time. Allow two weeks for delivery (although shipment may arrive much sooner).

RITEWAY HEARING AID CO.
Box 597635
Chicago, IL 60659
312/539-6620
COST: FREE

If you have a problem hearing, it might be time to invest in one of the highest quality and current state-of-the-art hearing aids at a discounted price. Savings of up to 50% are featured on Riteway's all-in-the-ear, behind-the-ear and body hearing aids. Riteway has a 30 day trial policy which allows you to try the aid for 30 days before paying for it.

∞ MUSIC & MOVIES ∞

CABLE FILMS
P.O. Box 7171
Kansas City, MO 64113
913/362-2804
COST: FREE

Established in 1976, Cable Films features film classics. You will find films from the 30s and 40s, silents, Chaplin short features, Hitchcock and Sherlock Holmes mysteries, Bela Lugosi and more.

FORTY-FIVES
Box 358
Lemoyne, PA 17043
717/232-4391
COST: FREE

Those oldies but goodies remind me of you! Remember the tunes that made you fall in love, like April Love by Pat Boone or the ones that got you on the dance floor, like Hound Dog Man by Fabian? Forty-Fives carries over 1,500 different 45 RPM phonograph records at 50% below the cost of other record sellers. Most of their records are priced at $1 and $2 and are rated for their condition. Ratings used are M for mint, V for very good, and P for poor (i.e., scratches dominate over sound reproduction). The P records usually go for 10¢. Most of their stock is rated M or V.

KICKING MULE RECORDS, INC.
P.O. BOX 158
Alderpoint, CA 95411
800/262-5312
COST: $1.00

Even though their prices are discounted their service is not! Kicking Mule guarantees that you will be satisfied with every item purchased or return it within 14 days for a full refund. They carry compact discs, cassettes, music books, LPs and teaching tapes for guitar, banjo, dulcimer, fiddle, harp, harmonica and more. Kicking Mule specializes in acoustic music including a selection of some of the finest Christmas pieces you'll ever hear. Much of their catalogue is devoted to instrumental guitar, banjo and dulcimer music played by the cream of the acoustic performers in North America and Europe. So kick back and relax while listening to some good down home music.

CATALOGUES

RICK'S MOVIE GRAPHICS
P.O. Box 23709
Gainesville, FL 32602
800/252-0425
COST: $3.00

"Sooner or later...everybody comes to Rick's." That's if you're looking for authentic movie advertising posters—the actual posters used in movie theaters. Rick's has thousands of posters from the mid 1970s and earlier that are in good to near-mint condition as well posters from the 1980s and all current and upcoming releases. Prices starting at $12. Make sure to get on their mailing list to receive their catalogue featuring sales where you can save up to 60% off their already low prices.

SPECIAL INTEREST VIDEO
475 Oberlin Ave. South, CN2112
Lakewood, NJ 08701
800/522-0502
COST: FREE

Special Interest Video is just what they say. Offering videos you can't buy in your local video shop, you'll find titles on the Civil War, modern military aircraft, World War II and even an exclusive volume of Arthur Murray Dance Steps. Other exciting titles are Play Bridge with Omar Sharif, How to Gamble and Win, Hummingbirds Up Close and more.

∞ MUSICAL INSTRUMENTS ∞

ALAS ACCORDION-O-RAMA
16 W. 19th St.
New York, NY 10011
212/675-9089
COST: FREE

Now you can own a top brand, expertly rebuilt accordion, that has been completely reconditioned and approved by a tuning and service expert to be as good as new. And at a substantial savings.

INTERSTATE MUSIC SUPPLY
13819 W. National Ave
New Berlin, WI 53151
800/837-BAND
COST: FREE

If you're in need of any musical instrument, we're sure you'll find it at Interstate Music Supply. They've been serving schools for the past 20 years with their large inventory of band instruments and accesories. Brand names you'll find in their 160 page catalogue are Yamaha, Korg, Gibson, Ludwig, Roland and more at savings of 20-60% off retail.

SAM ASH MUSIC CORPORATION
124 Fulton Ave.
Hempstead, NY 11550
800/4 SAM-ASH, 516/485-2151
COST: FREE

For over 60 years the family owned business of Sam Ash Music has been selling musical instruments and equipment at discounted prices. They run monthly specials, deals on close-outs and have one-of-a-kind items.

SHAR PRODUCTS COMPANY
2465 S. Industrial Hwy.
Ann Arbor, MI 48104
800/248-7427
COST: FREE

Shar Products is the largest supplier of musical merchandise geared to string musicians. Celebrating 30 years in business, their 64 page catalogue offers 20-50% off retail prices.

∞ OPTICAL PRODUCTS ∞
– CONTACT LENS –

CONTACT LENS REPLACEMENT CENTER
P.O. Box 1489
Melville, NY 11747
516/491-7763
COST: FREE

Contact Lens Replacement Center guarantees the lowest price for contact lens replacement. Most orders are shipped the same day received and carry a money back guarantee if unsatisfied within 30 days.

NATIONAL CONTACT LENS CENTER
3527 Bonita Vista Dr.
Santa Rosa, CA 95404
800/326-6352
COST: FREE

Is the doctor in? You bet! National Contact Lens Center claims they are the only mail-order contact lens replacement center that has a doctor available for questions and if he/she is not in at the time of your call,

CATALOGUES

he/she WILL call you back. Their prices are 20-70% off retail, and they guarantee the lowest price. Prescriptions can be taken from the original vials if necessary, but written prescriptions are preferred. There's a money back guarantee available when lenses in their original vials are returned within 30 days.

– GLASSES & SUNGLASSES –

ELITE EYEWEAR
P.O. Box 680030
North Miami, FL 33168
800/321-1819
COST: FREE

Elite Eyewear offers high-fashion frames with prices up to 50% off retail. Elite's stock includes frames and sunglasses under the labels of Carrera, Dior, Polo, Vuarnet and more. Just order the frames and take them to a local optical store for your prescription lenses to be inserted. Every frame has a one month, 100% money-back guarantee, no questions asked. Simply return the frame in new condition, in its original packaging, and a refund will promptly be sent.

HIDALGO INC.
45 La Buena Vista
Wimberley, TX 78676
512/847-2177 (product information) 800/786-2021 (orders)
COST: FREE

Choose from over 7,000 Daniel Hunger Vintage Collection lens/frame combination sunglasses, and prescription glasses. They have eyeglass frames designed to look like old time eyeglasses, plus state-of-the-art polarized lenses from Hidalgo. Many unique styles are featured in their 71 page catalogue such as frames that won't break, made of non-allergenic rubber and great for rugged outdoor activities. Hidalgo Premier metal frames are made in the U.S.A. and are guaranteed for 5 years against manufacturing defects. All merchandise has a 30 day money-back guarantee.

SUNGLASSES U.S.A.
469 Sunrise Hwy.
Lynbrook, NY 11563
800/USA-RAYS
COST: $1.00

Now you can buy everyone's favorite sunglasses, Ray-Bans, at genuine wholesale prices. You'll pay the same price as your local optometrist pays when you order from Sunglasses U.S.A. Their catalogue offers quite a large selection of shades (75 categories on the price list) from which to choose, and they'll waive the customary $2.00 shipping and handling charge on your first order.

∞ OFFICE SUPPLIES & EQUIPMENT ∞

FIDELITY PRODUCTS
P. O. Box 155
Minneapolis, MN 55440
800/328-3034
COST: FREE

You'll find a quality selection of all office supplies, furniture, machines and equipment all at the lowest prices guaranteed. If you find a current price lower than the prices shown in their catalogue, send them a copy of the ad or catalogue page within 30 days of purchase and you'll receive a refund of the difference.

VIKING DISCOUNT OFFICE PRODUCTS
P. O. Box 61144
Los Angeles, CA 90061-0144
800/421-1222
COST: FREE

With savings up to 75% off retail on some items, you'll find some really terrific discounts on office supplies in this catalogue. Orders over $25 are delivered free anywhere in the continental United States. Most orders arrive within two days.

∞ PARTY & PAPER PRODUCTS ∞

CURRENT
The Current Building
Colorado Springs, CO 80941
COST: FREE

From stationery to wrapping paper, note cards to gifts, Current offers a unique line of fine quality products suitable for every occasion at lower than card shop prices. Their selection of items with nature and animal themes are bound to please children and adults alike. Gift wrapping perfectionists will appreciate the multitude of styles and colors available individually or in sets. The catalogue that comes out in time for Valentines Day is not to be missed.

CATALOGUES

ROCKY MOUNTAIN STATIONERY
11725 Co. Rd. 27.3
Dolores, CO 81323
303/565-8230
COST: $1 PLUS DOUBLE STAMPED SELF-ADDRESSED ENVELOPE

Rocky Mountain Stationery uses real flowers and leaves for "Nature" note cards. They are then carefully pressed and preserved to last for years. In a collection of 12, no two are alike. Buy direct from them to save 50% off retail.

∞ PET SUPPLIES ∞

R.C. STEEL
1989 Transit Way
Brockport, NY 14420
800/872-3773
COST: FREE

This catalogue offers dog equipment and kennel supplies at wholesale prices! You can order books, grates, cages, grooming supplies, toys, treats, nutritional products, training aids plus anything else found at your local pet store, but at bargain prices.

UNITED PHARMACAL CO., INC.
Box 969
St. Joseph, MO 64502
816/233-8800
COST: FREE

Since 1952 UPCO has cared about serving you and your animal's needs. They offer products at the lowest possible prices backed by guaranteed service. You'll find everything for your pet in their 160 page catalogue.

∞ PHOTOGRAPHY ∞

BI-RITE PHOTO AND ELECTRONICS
15 E. 30th St.
New York, NY 10016
800/223-1970
COST: FREE

You can save up to 60% on cameras and accessories, typewriters, video equipment, telephone systems and more.

PORTER'S CAMERA STORE, INC.
P. O. Box 628
Cedar Falls, IA 50613
800/553-2001
COST: $2.00

Whether you are a professional or an amateur photographer, you'll appreciate the savings (10-88% off retail) found in this catalogue. In addition to cameras, lenses, filters, tripods and all other necessary camera accessories, Porter's Camera Store carries everything you need in darkroom equipment and supplies. Backdrops, light meters, slide viewers, film and projectors are just a few more items carried in their extensive inventory.

∞ PLANTS, LAWN & GARDEN ∞

BURPEE–W. ATLEE BURPEE & CO.
300 Park Ave.
Warminster, PA 18991-0001
215/674-4915
COST: FREE

Neighborhood horticulturists in all parts of the country have been buying seeds, bulbs, and plants from Burpee for years. Make your garden more beautiful with flowers, roses, vines, trees and shrubs. Chefs can enhance dishes with vegetables and herbs picked fresh from the backyard. You can also order tools, supplies and specialized products for gardening.

HARRIS MORAN SEED COMPANY
1155 Harkins Rd.
Salinas, CA 93901
408/757-3651
COST: FREE

Treat yourself to the finest vegetable seeds and bedding plants from Harris Moran Seed Company. Their reasonable prices will even encourage the part time gardener into growing tomatoes in the backyard.

INDOOR GARDENING SUPPLIES
P. O. Box 40567
Detroit, MI 40567
313/668-8384
COST: FREE

Want to have country living in the city, then purchase some of these light fixtures, plant stands and accessories and get your greenhouse started in your apartment or house. Your plants will love you!

CATALOGUES

VAN BOURGONDIEN
P.O. Box A
Babylon, NY 11702
800/873-9444
COST: FREE

Familiar and unfamiliar varieties of tulips, daffodils, iris, ranunculus, crocus (including rare Crocus Sativus, source of the ultra expensive spice, saffron), hyacinths, lilies, ferns, and more are all available from Van Bourgondien in bulb or plant form. Discerning gardeners will appreciate the unusual specimens most of us have never seen or heard of before.

∞ SPORTING GOODS ∞

CAMPMOR
Box 999
Paramus, NJ 07653
800/525-4784
COST: FREE

You'll find everything needed for backpacking and camping in Campmor's catalogue at discounted prices. This catalogue is a must for outdoor lovers.

DEFENDER INDUSTRIES, INC.
P.O. Box 820
New Rochelle, NY 10802
800/NAU-T-CAL (800/628-8225)
COST: $3.50

Defender has been quietly outfitting boats and boat owners across North America for 53 years. Since they do not advertise, they have been able to keep their prices low. They also offer a guarantee. If you find a lower quote from a legitimate domestic source which has the same merchandise available for delivery, they will gladly honor the lower price. You'll find everything needed to outfit your boat in their 244 page catalogue.

E & B DISCOUNT MARINE
201 Meadow Rd.
Edison, NJ 08818-3138
800/523-2926
COST: $5.00

Boating enthusiasts will find this catalogue to be an absolute find. We found a SeaRanger ALN 200 Advanced Loran Navigator that retails for $1,395 priced at $499.99 Whether you're into boats powered by sails or high performance engines, you'll find all that you need from barbecues, fishing reels, water skis and nautical clothing to bilge pumps, anchors and engines. Helms alee!

HOLABIRD SPORTS DISCOUNTERS
9008 Yellow Brick Rd, Rossville Industrial Park
Baltimore, MD 21237
301/687-6400
COST: FREE

There are hundreds of items to choose from at guaranteed lowest prices on tennis, squash, racquetball, badminton racquets. And don't forget the balls to go with each sport as well as the proper attire from shoes to clothing. You can buy stringing machines, ball machines, tennis nets, ball hoppers, court equipment, grips, vibration dampeners, eyeguards and even sports medical supplies. We found many of their everyday prices to be lower than sale prices at sporting good stores. Brand names include Head, Prince, Wilson, Fila, Slazenger, Ektelon, Adidas, Ellesse, Etonic, Keds, K-Swiss, Tretorn, Nike, New Balance, Estusa and Lobster. Their 48 hour shipping policy can come in handy if you need something fast.

OKUN BROTHERS SHOES
356 E. South St.
Kalamazoo, MI 49007
800/433-6344
COST: FREE

Save up to 35% off retail on shoes for the entire family through this catalogue service. Okun Brothers Shoes handles brand name such as New Balance, K-Swiss, Dexter, Rocsports, Allen Edmonds, Reebok, Avia and many more. They can provide nearly every shoe size in widths from AAA to EEEE. They say, "Shop by mail, no traffic, no parking, no babysitters and no fuss!"

OVERTON'S
111 Red Banks Rd, Box 8228
Greenville, NC 27835
800/334-6541
COST: FREE

Overton's catalogue is filled with everything, and we mean everything, you can think of related to water sports. Products such as boat seats, skis and accessories, vests, running lights, electronics and navigation equipment are all available at discounted prices.

CATALOGUES

∞ TELESCOPES & BINOCULARS ∞

ASTRONOMICS/CHRISTOPHERS, LTD.
2401 Tee Circle, Suites 105/106
Norman, OK 73069
800/422-7876
COST: FREE

Are you a star gazer? Astronomics/Christophers, Ltd. specializes in quality optics for astronomy and nature study featuring brand names such as Zeiss, Leica, Swarovski, Meade, Celestron, Pentax, Nikon and more. Their prices are 5-60% off retail, ranging from $100 to $3,000 for binoculars and spotting scopes and $350 to $15,000 for telescopes. Due to their large inventory, most orders are shipped within 24 hours. You can save on shipping costs by pre-paying. A 30 day return policy is offered.

MARDIRON OPTICS
37 Holloway St.
Malden, MA 02148
617/322-8733
COST: FREE

See the action explode with a pair of binoculars from Mardiron Optics, a Steiner brand dealer. Steiner Binoculars have been used by over 40 military forces worldwide and are rugged, yet lightweight for concert goers. They also carry telescopes, astronomy equipment and accessories.

∞ TRAVEL ∞

CAMPUS TRAVEL SERVICE
P.O. Box 8355
Newport Beach, CA 92660
COST: $14.50

This is the most expensive catalogue in our book, but will probably save you the most amount of money if you like to travel. Campus Travel Service puts out a 76 page directory featuring travel accommodations in the United States and the world with costs of $12 to $24 per day. How do they do it? All rooms are located at over 700 university campuses. You'll find uncrowded sports facilities—tennis, swimming, golf, hiking, fishing, boating, theater, film festivals, art and craft shows and much more—at some of the most beautiful locations in the world and of course a bed and even breakfast. The catalogue has the phone numbers of the universities, price for single or double room, dates available, if they offer food, and the activities in their area.

V

DIRECTORY

OF

CONSUMER

INFORMATION

RESOURCES

CONSUMER INFORMATION

A TO Z BUYING GUIDE–THE BETTER BUSINESS BUREAU
Council of Better Business Bureaus
4200 Wilson Blvd.
Arlington, VA 22203
COST: $9.95

Three hundred pages which provide essential information necessary to making sound, economical purchasing decisions on hundreds of products and services. It can be obtained at local Better Business Bureaus and bookstores, or by writing directly to the Council. Also, includes information about Better Business Bureaus consumer education books, pamphlets, and other publications and services designed to help you make informed buying decisions. This is another book which will become a welcome companion.

AAA AUTO TEST–AMERICAN AUTOMOBILE ASSOCIATION
1000 AAA Dr.
Heathrow, FL 32746
COST: $9.95

AAA Auto Test (250 pages) provides you with the facts you need to walk into a dealer's showroom with the confidence of a wise and prudent shopper. It will help you make the right decision with less confusion and more peace of mind. You will be privy to the test results of 112 of the most popular foreign and domestic car models. Each vehicle's performance, comfort, convenience, workmanship and value is reported. Lists of each vehicles best and worst features are provided along with photographs of each car's exterior, interior, dashboard and cargo area. Price lists are also included. Introductory chapters deal with analyzing your needs, test driving, understanding your warranty, negotiating, maintaining your vehicle and resolving disputes. You can obtain the book at any local AAA office. It's well worth the investment.

AAA CAR BUYERS HANDBOOK
9940 Main St., Suite 200
Fairfax, VA 22031
COST: $9.95

This 122 page, concisely written book, packs a wallop which will knock your wallet for a loop. It contains everything you need to know in order to make the best possible deal in buying, leasing or financing a new or used car and selling a used car. Once you have read this manual, you will no longer feel at the mercy of any car salesman, dealer or manufacturer.

CONSUMER INFORMATION

You will feel like an expert and your next purchase will be made with confidence. For test results on 112 popular foreign and domestic vehicles, see the companion book, "AAA Auto Test."

AUTOMOBILE CLUB SOUTHERN CALIFORNIA AUTOMOTIVE INFORMATION CENTER (AIC)
P.O. Box 2890, Terminal Annex
Los Angeles, CA 90051-0890
213/741-4487
COST: FREE

If you're in the market for a new car or you want to sell one, you can order informational brochures from the Auto Club. Choose from "Buying a New Car," "Buying a Used Car," "Financing a Car," "Leasing vs. Buying," and "Selling Your Vehicle." The brochures are well-written, contain much useful information, and can save you time and money. Auto Club members need only call and they will send you any of these easy-to-understand brochures.

CONSUMER ACTION
116 New Montgomery St.
San Francisco, CA 94105
COST: $1.00

The Consumer Services Guide is a must! It includes the addresses and telephone numbers of regulatory and law enforcement government agencies, business sponsored complaint resolution offices, nonprofit information and referral organizations and agencies that offer free, or low cost legal assistance.

CONSUMER INFORMATION CENTER
Pueblo, CO 81009
COST: FREE

Hundreds of booklets free or low cost featuring information on such topics as small business, careers, cars, children, education, health, nutrition, building, buying and financing a house, exercise and weight control, money management, travel and hobbies and much more.

CONSUMER REPORTS
P.O. Box 53029
Boulder, CO 80322
800/234-1645
COST: $3.50 PER ISSUE

Consumer Reports is a magazine which reports results of field tests on a wide variety of goods and services. Published by Consumers Union, a nonprofit organization established in 1936 to provide information on goods, services, health, and personal finance to maintain and enhance the quality of life for consumers. It is a highly respected resource which consumers should make a habit of consulting prior to purchasing expensive items. Most libraries have it (including back issues) or you can subscribe to the magazine for $22.00 a year.

CONSUMER'S RESOURCE HANDBOOK
Consumer Information Center
Pueblo, CO 81009
COST: FREE

A U.S. Government publication of nearly 100 pages listing many consumer affairs contact names; also lists addresses and phone numbers of hundreds of manufacturers, and county, state and federal agencies handling a wide variety of consumer problems. A worthwhile addition to your consumer information library.

THE FRUGAL SHOPPER
P.O. Box 19367
Washington, DC 20036

Cost: $10.00

Written by consumer advocate, Ralph Nader (along with Wesley J. Smith), this 255 page book is a must for anyone who wants to become a smart shopper. It contains a wealth of information about what to look for and pitfalls to avoid regarding saving money and obtaining value on credit, insurance, professional services (doctors, lawyers, bankers, home contractors), auto repairs, food, autos and homes. Put this into your library and refer to it often.

INDEX – STORES

1ST SECURITY SAFE CO.	313
2NDS SHOP**, THE	215
3RD FAZE CLOTHING COMPANY	135
7TH AVENUE WEST	166
99¢ ONLY STORE	343
A 'N B STATIONERY	277
A APPLIANCE FACTORY	28
A B E CORPORATION	281
A J SPECIALTY BATH PRODUCTS	97
A V LUGGAGE AND BRIEFCASE	339
A-1 FURNITURE OUTLET**	221
A-WILSON DIVORCE CLINIC	317
A. A. BAKER'S PAINT & HARDWARE	95
AAA CARPET EXCHANGE	87
AAA ETERNAL STAINLESS STEEL CORP.**	211
AARDVARK'S ODD ARK	163
ABC AUTO PARTS DISTRIBUTING	54
ABC CAMERA-PHOTO-VIDEO	297
ABC DONUTS	197
ABC POOL & PATIO**	309
ABC PREMIUMS	189
ABEL'S MUSIC	269
ABLE CARPETS	87
ABM ART TYPE BUSINESS MACHINES	175, 280
ACADEMY AWARD CLOTHES, INC.	130
ACE MUSIC	269
ACE USED OFFICE FURNITURE WAREHOUSE**	282
ACRES OF BOOKS	74
ACTA FAST FRAME	30
ACTION SCREEN & DOOR**	86
AD-MART	346
ADCO	228
ADdRESS, THE	144
ADLER SHOES	154
ADRAY'S	179
AERO SHADE	102
AFFAIR OF THE HEART**	109
AHEAD STEREO	49, 189
AIR CONDITIONING EXCHANGE**	77
AL'S DISCOUNT FURNITURE**	228
ALBEE'S DISCOUNT APPLIANCES	21

INDEX – STORES

ALIN PAPER COMPANY	288
ALL BED & MATTRESS**	222
ALL ELECTRONICS CORP.	193
ALL IN 1 HOME FURNISHINGS**	229
ALL PRO BICYCLES	323
ALL REASONS TRAVEL**	341
ALL STAR GLASS	58, 86
ALL VALLEY SHOWER DOOR CO.	86
ALLAN'S AQUARIUM AND PET SHOP	291
ALLIED MODEL TRAINS	45
ALMOST & PERFECT ENGLISH CHINA	211
ALPERT'S BEDROOM CITY WAREHOUSE**	222
ALTO APPLIANCE SERVICE	27
AMENDOLA MUSIC, INC.	270
AMERICAN ELECTRONICS SUPPLY	194
AMERICAN SURPLUS TRADERS**	282, 335
AMERICAN WHOLESALE NURSERIES	301
AMORE CREATIONS	126
AMSTERDAM ART	33
ANDERS ORTHOPEDICS & PROSTHETICS	260
ANGELUS HOME CENTER	229
ANTELOPE	115
ANTIQUE CLOCK SHOP, THE	17
ANTIQUE HOUSE	17
ARMY-NAVY SURPLUS	331, 335
ARON'S RECORD SHOP	263
ART STORE, THE	33
ASMARA OVERSEAS SHIPPERS	194
ASSOCIATED AUTO BODY**	57
ASSOCIATED FOREIGN EXCHANGE, INC.	44
AUNT FANNIE'S ATTIC	346
AUTO STEREO WAREHOUSE	49
AUTOMATED OFFICE SERVICES	284
AUTOMOBILE CLUB OF SOUTHERN CALIFORNIA	61, 341
AVERY RESTAURANT SUPPLY	212
A–WAHL'S BUILDING MATERIALS	94
B & A HAY CO.	291
B & B MARINE EQUIPMENT & SERVICE, INC.	69
B & B SALES	331
BAB'S**	164, 287
BABY MOTIVES	236
BABY TOYTOWN, INC.	236
BACK ON THE RACK**	141
BACKDOOR BOUTIQUE	166
BAG LADY	116

INDEX – STORES

BAILEY'S**	143
BALL BEAUTY SUPPLIES	63
BALLOON FACTORY	315
BARBECUES GALORE	307
BARGAIN FAIR**	343
BARGAIN SAVER	344
BARRETT'S APPLIANCES	21
BATTERY DEPOT	53
BATTERY SPECIALIST CO.	53
BAY CITY APPLIANCES	22
BEAN SALES CO., HERB	22
BED BATH & BEYOND	244
BED BROKER**	223
BEDS UNLIMITED**	223
BEDSPREAD CREATIONS**	244
BEDSPREAD WAREHOUSE	245
BEL AIR CAMERA, AUDIO & VIDEO	189, 297
BERKS	309
BES INTERNATIONAL JEWELRY	249
BETNUM MUSIC	270
BEV'S CRAFTS & LACE	35
BEVERLY GARDEN CENTER	302
BEVERLY HILLS FAN CO. FACTORY OUTLET	241
BEVERLY WESTERN INTERIORS	102
BIG Y YARDAGE OUTLET	39
BIG, THE BAD & THE BEAUTIFUL**, THE	123
BIKECOLOGY–SANTA MONICA	323
BILLIARDS & BARSTOOLS**	326
BIRDS PLUS	291
BLACK & WHITE WHOLESALERS	166
BLUE CHIP DRAPERY, INC.	102
BLUE MOON	160, 167
BOB'S AUTO SUPPLY	54
BOB'S TIRE TOWN	62
BODHI TREE ANNEX	71
BOHEMIAN CRYSTAL	34
BOOK CASTLE INC	74
BOOK CITY	74
BOOK MART U.S.A.	71
BOOKANEER, THE	75
BOOKSTAR	71
BOOKSVILLE	75
BOOT HILL SQUARE DANCE APPAREL**	165
BOX CITY**	287
BRACKEN BIRD FARM	292

INDEX – STORES

BRASS BEDS DIRECT	224
BRICK CORRAL	78
BRIDAL FACTORY OUTLET**	110
BRIDE'S ALTERNATIVE, THE	110
BRITE AND SHINE, INC	103
BUDGET OFFICE PRODUCTS	277
BUDGET PRINTING	283
BUDGET RENTS FURNITURE AND SALES**	241, 282
BUILDER'S DISCOUNT	95
BUZZARD HOUSE, THE	292
BYRNE HOME FURNISHINGS	230
C & R CLOTHIERS	130
C.E.N.T.R.E. SALON	67
C.W. DESIGNS	118
CALICO CORNERS	40, 245
CALIFORNIA JEANS	112
CALIFORNIA JEWELSMITHS	249
CALIFORNIA MART MANUFACTURERS' SAT. SALE	159
CALIFORNIA SOCKS	113
CALIFORNIA WHOLESALE TILE	82
CAMERA CITY	298
CANDY FACTORY**, THE	204, 319
CANDY STORE**	204
CARLSON'S T.V. & APPLIANCES**	22
CARMEN'S VERANDA	135
CAROL'S COUNTRY CORNER	165
CAROUSEL BABY FURNITURE	237
CARPET BAZAAR	88
CARPET COLLECTION**	88
CARPET LAND MILLS	88
CARPET MANOR**	89
CARPET MARKET OUTLET	89
CASTLE CHANDELIERS & LIGHTING CO.	242
CAVIARTERIA INC	202
CD BANZAI!	263
CELLULAR WHOLESALERS**	50
CENTER THEATRE COSTUME SHOP	288
CHAMPAGNE TASTE	216
CHARADES OF CALIFORNIA	118
CHEAP FRILLS**	107
CHERIE'S SECRETS	144
CHIC LINGERIE OUTLET	126
CHRISTOPHER'S NUT CO.	205
CINEMA GLAMOUR SHOP	347
CITADEL OUTLET COLLECTION	185

INDEX – STORES

CITY TYPEWRITER OF WESTWOOD	280
CLAYDON'S JEWELERS	249
CLOTHES HEAVEN	144
COLLATERAL LOANS, INC.	347
COLLECTOR'S EYE	18, 250
COLORMART FURNITURE	230
COMMERCIAL TYPEWRITER CO.	280
COMP USA	175
COMPAGNIA DELLA MODA INC.	131
COMPLETE COMPUTER CURE	178
COMPUTER GAMES PLUS	337
COMPUTER PALACE	176
COMSOFT	176
CONSOLIDATED PET FOODS**	293
CONSUMER DISCOUNT DRUGS	259
CONSUMERS GUILD, INC.	230
CONTEMPO CASUALS OUTLET	167
CONVERSE FACTORY OUTLET	150
COOK UNIFORMS, SAM	162
COOPER & KRAMER, INC.	131
COOPER BUILDING	113, 185
CORY'S FURNITURE SHOWCASE**	231
COSMOPOLITAN BOOK SHOP	75
COSTCO	179
COTTAGE SHOPS	310
COUNTRY ELEGANCE	159
COUNTRY LINENS**	245
CRAFTERS OUTLET	216
CRAFTS PLUS**	35, 46
CREATIVE WOMAN	126
CRITERIUM CYCLE SPORT**	324
CROWN BILLIARDS & BAR STOOLS	327
CROWN BOOKS	72
CROWN DISCOUNT BEAUTY SUPPLY**	63
CRUISE COMPANY, THE	342
CRYSTAL'S LACES & GIFTS**	36
CULVER CARPET CENTER	89
D'MUNDO TILE	82
D/M YARDAGE OUTLET	40
DANSK FACTORY OUTLET	212
DARVA JEWELERS	250
DATA TECHNOLOGY	176
DAVID'S CHILDREN'S WEAR	119
DEFOREST'S PATIO AND FIRESIDE	310
DESERT HILLS FACTORY STORES	186

INDEX – STORES

DESERT EMPIRE GOLF CENTER	107, 328
DESIGNER FABRIC SHOWCASE	40
DESIGNER JEWELRY MART	251
DESIGNER LABELS FOR LESS	167
DIAMOND EMPIRE FURNITURE**, NAT	23, 231
DIAMOND MINE, THE	251
DIAMOND V INTERIORS	103
DIRT CHEAP PLANT CO.	302
DISC-CONNECTION RECORDS & COMPACT DISCS	264
DISCOUNT DESK CENTER	277
DISCOUNT FRAMES	31
DISCOUNT HEALTH FOODS	199
DISCOUNT OFFICE MACHINES	281
DISCOUNT PET FOOD	293
DISCOUNT PICTURE FRAMES	31
DISCOUNT READER BOOKSTORE	72
DISCOUNT SALES	190
DISCOUNT TILE CENTER	83
DISCOUNT TRAIN WAREHOUSE**	45
DISCOUNT TROPICAL FISH	294
DISCOUNT WALLPAPER & INTERIORS	100
DISCOVERY SHOP	347
DISH FACTORY, THE	213
DIVORCE CENTERS OF CALIFORNIA	317
DO-IT-YOURSELF L.A.W	318
DOS BANDERAS	203
DRESS UP	145
DRESSED TO KILL	138
DUTTON'S BOOKS	72
DYNAMIC TANGIBLES CORPORATION**	258
E V S PRODUCTIONS**	321
EGGHEAD DISCOUNT SOFTWARE	177
EL DORADO GAMES	327
ELECTROPEDIC ADJUSTABLE BEDS	224, 260
ELEGANCE FURNITURE	231
ELLIOT'S PET EMPORIUM	294
ELLIOTT PRECISION BLOCK CO	78
ELLIS**, ROBERT	110, 168
EMBASSY AUCTIONEER, INC	247
ENCINO DISCOUNT PATIO & BABY FURNITURE	237, 311
ENCINO JEWELRY EXCHANGE	252
ENCYCLOPEDIAS BOUGHT & SOLD	73
END RESULT	100, 317
ENGLISH CHINA HOUSE	213
ENTERTAINMENT PUBLICATIONS	199

INDEX – STORES

ESTATE HOME FURNISHINGS	18
ESTHER'S FULL FASHIONS	123
EUROGIFT**	216
EUROSTYLE FURNITURE	232
EVER-RICH BEDDING**	246
EVERYTHING FOR KIDS	140
F B WATERBEDS	224
FABRIC WAREHOUSE	41
FACES N' PLACES PHOTOS	320
FACTORY MERCHANTS OUTLET STORES	186
FAIRFAX KITCHEN CABINETS	79
FANTASTIC DESIGNER ROOM	168
FASHION WEST	116
FATOR'S APPLIANCES & PLUMBING	23, 97
FAUX ART**	217
FEDCO	180
FENCE FACTORY	93
FERGUSON'S MARINE SPECIALTIES**	47
FERRA'S IRON & ANTIQUE ACCENTS, RAY	19, 242
FILAMENT PRO-AUDIO	195
FISHBECK'S	311
FLAP HAPPY KIDS	119
FLIGHT COORDINATORS	342
FLOOR COVERING UNLIMITED	90
FLOORMART	90
FOAM MART**	41
FOOT FIESTA**	151
FOOT MART SPORTS**	151
FOOTSTEPS	156
FOR EYES OPTICAL OF CALIFORNIA, INC.	286
FOR KIDS ONLY	119
FOR PET'S SAKE PET SHOP	294
FORD DRIVING SCHOOL	60
FOUNTAINS BY SANTI	304
FRAGRANCE BOUTIQUE	63
FRAME-N-LENS	286
FRAMEX	31
FRAMING OUTLET**	32
FRANCO'S ENGINE REBUILDERS	58
FRANK'S HIGHLAND PARK CAMERA	298
FRIEDMAN AND ASSOCIATES**, DR. M.	285
FRIEDMAN FURNITURE, MARK	232
FRIEDMAN'S–THE MICROWAVE SPECIALISTS	23
FROCH'S WOODCRAFT SHOP, INC.	79, 240
FUNKY & DAMNEAR NEW	136

INDEX – STORES

FURNITURE TRENDS	232
GAINES HANDBAGS, MARLENE**	116
GALAXY OF GOWNS**	111
GALAXY SALON EQUIPMENT MFG. CO	261
GAME CITY**	337
GAYNOR'S CYCLE SALES	58
GENTLEMEN'S EXCHANGE	143
GERALD'S FINE JEWELRY**	252
GHQ OUTLET	131
GIFT CORNER, THE	218
GLAMOUR UNIFORM SHOP**	162
GLASS GARAGE, THE	218
GOLD FURNITURE, INC., EDDIE	233
GOLDEN FLEECE DESIGNS INC.**	42, 69
GOLDEN WEST BILLIARD MFG.	328
GOLF FAIRE	329
GOOCHEY'S FURNISHINGS & LIGHTING	233, 242
GOODMAN MUSIC	270
GRAFSTEIN & CO.	253
GRAND CENTRAL PUBLIC MARKET	200
GRASON'S ART CRAFTS AND FLORAL SUPPLIES	36
GREAT GATSBY**, THE	168
GREAT NAME, THE	145
GREENWOOD BEDSPREAD KING, AL	246
GREY GOOSE	32
GROCERY WAREHOUSE	209
GRUBB & GRUBB'S GENERAL STORE	19, 164
GUITAR STORE, THE	271
GUST PECOULAS & CO.	205
H & H CRAFT & FLORAL SUPPLY CO.	37
H R D DISTRIBUTORS**	136
H. LEWIS REX FINE ART**	29
H. SAVINAR LUGGAGE	339
HALF PRICE STORES INC	307, 344
HALF-PRICE HOUSE	111, 124
HANDBAG HANGUP	117
HANSEN WHOLESALE FAN CO	243
HARPER'S LADIES WHOLESALE CLOTHING	169
HARRIS & FRANK CLEARANCE CENTER	136
HARTMAN JEWELRY & GIFTS**	180
HENRY'S SHOE FETISH	155
HIAWATHA HOMES**	94
HOLLYTRON	190
HOLLYWOOD BOWL	267
HOLLYWOOD PIANO RENTAL CO	273

INDEX – STORES

HOMARUS INC.**	202
HOME COMFORT CENTER**	77
HONEY'S SHOES**	156
HOOPER CAMERA AND VIDEO CENTERS**	298
HOSIERY OUTLET, INC.**	117
HOUSE OF DRUMS AND GUITARS	271
HOWARD'S MATERNITY FACTORY, DAN	129
I. MARTIN BICYCLES	324
IKEA	233
IN-A-FLOOR SAFE COMPANY**	313
INDIVIDUAL PAPER PRODUCTS	289
INDOOR SWAPMEET OF STANTON	186
INTERIOR MOTIVES	103
INTERIOR RESOURCES	80
INTERNATIONAL CUSTOM TAILORS**	150
INTERSPACE ELECTRONICS, INC.	50, 190
ISLAND PRODUCTS DISTRIBUTING	218
ITC ELECTRONICS**	50, 195
J & Y WELDING & IRONWORKS	93
J. B. SEBRELL CO.	312
J. C. PENNEY CATALOGUE OUTLET STORE	181
JASMINE CLEANERS	149
JEAN'S STARS' APPAREL**	146
JEROLD'S FINE HOME FURNISHINGS	234
JUDY'S OUTLET	169
KAGAN SURPLUS SALES**	261, 283
KAGAN TRIM CENTER	42
KEYBOARD CONCEPTS INC.	274
KEYBOARD EXCHANGE	274
KEYBOARD LIQUIDATORS	274
KID'S CLOSET	140
KIDS CLUB OUTLET**	120
KIDS FURNITURE WAREHOUSE**	237
KIDS' ART SPACE	37
KIM-E'S FLOWERS**	315
KING RICHARD'S ANTIQUE MALL	19
KIRKPATRICK SALES CORP.	161
KITCHEN & BATH WAREHOUSE**, THE	80
KLEIN'S BEAD BOX**	34
KUTROSKY**, DR. THOMAS	285
L A TRONICS	191
L.A. WRECKING COMPANY	95
LA BREA BARGAIN CIRCUS	344
LABEL'S HI-FASHION RESALE	146
LACE & SCENTS	64, 127

INDEX – STORES

LADIES SHOES PLUS	156
LAMPMART	243
LARRY & JOE'S PLUMBING SUPPLIES	98
LAX LUGGAGE	340
LAZAR JEWELERS, INC.**, ALEX	253
LE CLUB HANDBAG CO.	117
LE ELEGANT BATH	98
LEATHER CAPITOL	124
LEATHER FACTORY	238
LEE LAWNMOWER**	301
LEON'S FURNITURE	234
LEONARDO'S ITALIAN FASHION**	132
LEONORE'S FUR OUTLET**	124, 138
LESTER CARPET CO., INC.	90
LEVINE & SON, INC., MAX	132
LEVINE, INC., MICHAEL	42
LILA'S GOURMET BASKET	169
LINCOLN FABRICS	43
LINEN CLUB, THE	246
LINGERIE FOR LESS	127
LINOLEUM CITY	91
LIQUIDATION CLUB**, THE	181
LIQUOR BANK & DELI	206
LITTLE PIANO SHOP, THE	275
LLOYD'S CAMERA SURPLUS	299
LOAN MART, INC.	348
LOEHMANN'S	170
LORA BEAUTY CENTER	64
LORD OF THE RINGS**	254
LORE	127
LOS ANGELES UNIFORM EXCHANGE	163
LOS ANGELES WINE CO.	207
LOVE MATCH TENNIS SHOP	108
LUGGAGE OUTLET	340
LUMPY'S DISCOUNT GOLF AND FASHION PLACE	329
LUNA GARCIA	214
LYNWOOD BATTERY MFG. CO., INC	53, 69
M & H CARPETS	91
M. FREDERIC & CO. OUTLET STORE	170
MAGIC JEWELRY	254
MAINLY SECONDS–POTTERY, PLANTS & THINGS	219, 304
MARBLE PRODUCTS OF FULLERTON**	80
MARC'S DISCOUNT LOCK & KEY	318
MARCIA'S RAINBOW FACTORY OUTLET	120
MARV'S U.S.A. AUTO DISMANTLING	56

INDEX – STORES

MATTRESS OUTLET	225
MATTRESS WAREHOUSE**	225
MAX FACTOR OUTLET**	64
MAX FACTORY OUTLET, LEON	112, 171
MAYA	254
MAYA SHOES	155
MC NALLY ELECTRIC	99, 243
MELROSE DISCOUNT CARPET	91
MELROSE DRAPERIES	104
MEN'S CLOTHIERS–MANUFACTURERS' OUTLET	132
MEN'S FASHION DEPOT	133
MERRILL'S MUSIC**	275
METZLER'S HOME FURNISHINGS	235
MEYER'S OFFICE PRODUCTS	278
MICKEY'S AUTO SALES & LEASING	59
MID-VALLEY FLOWER EXCHANGE**	316
MIJANOU'S SILK DESIGNS**	38, 219
MIKASA FACTORY OUTLET	214
MIKO PHOTO-AUDIO-VIDEO CENTER	191, 299
MILLIE'S HANDBAGS AND SHOES	118
MIRMAN'S WESTCOAST TIRE AND BRAKE, BOB	62
MOBILE HOME MANAGEMENT	321
MOBY DISC	264
MODERN SERVICE OFFICE SUPPLY CO., INC	278
MOM'S THE WORD**	129
MONTERREY FOOD PRODUCTS	204
MORAN WAREHOUSE STORE	104
MOTHER GOOSE GARMENT EXCHANGE	140
MOVE IT	108
MOYEN'S JEWELLERY CONNECTION, JOHN**	255
MR. BURKE'S SHOES	154
MR. PRICE	182
MR. SATIN, INC	247
MS. FASHIONS**	171
MS. FITS	171
MUNN'S SILVER SHOP	214
MURREY AND SONS	328
MUSIC EXCHANGE**	264
MY FAIR LADY**	172
NADINES MUSIC	272
NATIONAL AUTO BROKERS, INC	59
NATIONAL STEREO	191
NATURE MART	199
NEW METRO TILE COMPANY	83
NISSAN WOODWORKS INC.	81

INDEX -- STORES

NORDSTROM RACK	113
NORM'S FEED STORE	295
NURSERY LIQUIDATORS	303
NUTONE PRODUCTS DISTRIBUTOR	78
NUTRI/SYSTEM	322
NUTS TO YOU	206
OBALEK TILE & WALLPAPER	83, 100
ODYSSEY VIDEO	268
OFF THE BOLT	43
OFFICE DEPOT	279
OFFICE SUPPLY CO	279
OLD COUNTRY BAKERY	197
OLGA WARNER'S OUTLET	108, 128, 333
OLYMPIC ELECTRONICS	51, 192
ON THE HOUSE	267
ONE NIGHT AFFAIR GOWN RENTALS	139
ORANGE APPLIANCE & VACUUM**	25
ORANGE COUNTY MARKETPLACE	187
ORIENTAL RUG EXCHANGE**	247
ORIENTAL SILK CO	43
OUTLET, THE	161
OZZIE DOTS	164
P F McMULLIN CO.	332
P X DRUGS NO. 2**	259
P.J. LONDON**	147
PACE MEMBERSHIP WAREHOUSE	182
PACIFIC AMERICAN FISH CO., INC.	202
PANEL-IT DISCOUNT STORES	81
PANG!**	29
PAPERBACK TRADER	76
PAR PAINT COMPANY INC.**	96
PARIS GO	165
PARIS PERFUME	65
PARTY CORNER DISCOUNT CENTER**	288, 289
PARTY KING	47, 289
PARTY WORLD	290
PASQUINI	24
PATSY'S CLOTHES CLOSET	147
PEDLEY VETERINARY SUPPLY INC.	295
PENNY LANE	265
PENNY PINCHERS	20
PERFUME CITY	65
PERSONAL SUPPORT COMPUTERS	177
PHILLIPS PHOTOGRAPHY, LYNN	320
PIC-A-SHIRT	137

INDEX -- STORES

PICO CARPET CO.	92
PILLER'S OF EAGLE ROCK	137, 155
PLACE & COMPANY, THE	147
PLAZA CONTINENTAL FACTORY STORES	187
POST TOOLS	105
POTTERY AND FLORAL WORLD**	38, 220, 304
POTTERY MANUFACTURING & DISTRIBUTING	305
POTTERY RANCH, INC.	215
POTTERY STORE, THE	306
POTTERY ETC.**	305
PRATT'S MATTRESS WAREHOUSE, RICHARD	225
PREFERRED GLASS	87
PRESTIGE FRAGRANCE & COSMETICS	66
PRICE BUSTERS SHOE WAREHOUSE**	151
PRICE CLUB	183
PRICE-LESS BRIDALS**	112
PRO GOLF DISCOUNT**	330
QUALITY DRESS SHOP	172
QUICKMED SUPPLIES INC.	261
RADIOLAND/INGLEWOOD ELECTRONICS	51, 195
RAINBOW VACUUM CENTER	26
RAP DISCOUNT AUTO PARTS & MARINE SUPPLY	55, 70
RAP DISCOUNT SAFE CO.	314
RATTAN DEPOT	239
RATTAN DISTRIBUTION WAREHOUSE	239
RAVE REVIEWS-KIDS COTTAGE**	142
RAY'S WOOD FINISHING	106
REAL CHEAP SPORTS	114, 333
RECORD SURPLUS	265
RECYCLED RAGS	143
RED BARN FEED & SADDLERY INC.**	296
RENT-A-WRECK	60
RITZ DRY CLEANERS	150
ROBE OUTLET, THE	128
ROBERT'S INTERIORS	235
ROBERTSON'S INC.	38
ROCKET J'S RECORDS	266
ROGERSOUND LABS	51, 192
ROSCOE FURNITURE LIQUIDATORS**	235
ROSEMAN & ASSOCIATES	133
ROSS DRESS FOR LESS	114
ROUNDHOUSE TRAIN STORE**, THE	45
ROY STEP SHOES**	157
ROYAL DISCOUNT CARPETS	92
RTC MATTRESS WAREHOUSE	226

INDEX – STORES

RUBINFELD-KENNEDY ESTATE JEWELRY**	255
SACKS SFO INC	137
SACKS SFO KIDS	120
SAN DIEGO FACTORY OUTLET CENTER	187
SAN-VAL DISCOUNT INC.	46
SANDLER OF THE VALLEY**	109
SANDY'S ELECTRONIC SUPPLY	196
SANTA FE SPRINGS SWAPMEET	188
SARA DESIGNERS OUTLET**	172
SAV-MOR SHOES	152
SAVE–MOR PLUMBING SUPPLIES	99
SAWYERS & SAWYERS	345
SCOTCH PAINTS FACTORY STORE	96
SEARS CONTRACT SALES	24
SEARS OUTLET STORE	183
SECOND TIME AROUND #2	148
SECOND TIME AROUND RECORDS**	266
SEE ME COLOR**	121, 173
SEYMOUR FASHIONS**	121, 173
SHAKY WIGS OF HOLLYWOOD	67
SHAMROCK GOLF SHOPS	330
SHANES JEWELRY STORE	256
SHE'S FLOWERS	316
SHELL CENTER OF THOUSAND OAKS, THE	56
SHELLY'S DISCOUNT AEROBIC & DANCE WEAR	109, 130
SHELLY'S STEREO HI-FI CENTER	192
SHIPS CONCRETE COMPANY	79
SHIRT MARKET, THE	133
SHOE OUTLET**	152
SHOES BY SHIRLEY	157
SHOES INC	153
SID'S DISCOUNT BABY FURNITURE	121, 238
SIG'S POTTERY & NURSERY	306
SIGHTSINGER MUSIC	272
SILENT PARTNER	148
SILK WAREHOUSE**	39, 220
SILVER ROSES NUTS	206
SIMON'S DISCOUNT CAMERA STORE	300
SINGER BURBANK SEWING CENTER	26
SIT'N SLEEP	226
SITTING PRETTY INC.	236
SIX-PAC FACTORY OUTLET	56
SMART & FINAL	184, 209
SOMETHING FOR BABY**	141
SOMETHING OLD SOMETHING NOUVEAU	20

INDEX – STORES

SOMETHING SPECIAL	316
SONNY'S RADIATOR EXCHANGE**	55
SOUND ENTERTAINMENT	319
SOUNDS GOOD STEREO	52
SOUTHLAND FARMERS' MARKET ASSOCIATION	201
SPA BROKER	312
SPEAKER CITY	52, 193
SPOKES 'N STUFF	324
SPORTS AGAIN	325
SPORTS SPECTACULAR	153
ST. JOHN KNITS, INC.	160
ST. VINCENT JEWELRY CENTER	256
STAMP 'N' DOODLE**	47
STAPLES	279
STAR BABY**	122
STAR DRAPERIES MFG.**	104
STARLIT SOIREE	139
STARS & DEBS**	148
STERLING BEAUTY SUPPLY CO.	66
STERN'S DISCOUNT DRAPERY CENTER	44
STEVEN & CO. JEWELERS	257
STEVEN CRAIG WHOLESALE CLOTHIERS	134
STORK SHOP, THE	122, 238
STUART CLOTHES, INC., ROGER	134
SUNSHINE SPORTS FACTORY OUTLET	333
SUPER POPS RECORD DETECTIVE**	266
SUPER SAVER CINEMAS	268
SUPER-RITE DRUGS INC.	259
SUPERIOR WINDOW COVERINGS, INC.**	105
SURPLUS CITY JEEP PARTS	55
SURPLUS CITY RETAIL CO.**	158, 336
SURVIVAL INSURANCE	61
SUSIE'S DEALS**	173
TELETIRE	62
THAT SPECIAL SHOP	149
THRIFTY KITCHENS, INC.	81
TIFFANY DESIGNER SHOES	157
TIFFANY'S TOYS	326
TILE FOR LESS**	84
TILE OUTLET	84
TILE, MARBLE & GRANITE WAREHOUSE**	84
TILECLUB**	85
TIME-OFF APPAREL	162
TOP TO TOP	153
TOPLINE WINE & SPIRIT CO.	207

INDEX -- STORES

TOWER RECORDS	267
TOWN FAIR BAZAAR	160
TOY LIQUIDATORS**	337
TOYS "R" US	338
TRADER JOE'S	201
TREASURE HUNT	345
TUAZON'S BIKE SHOP	325
TURNER'S OUTDOORSMAN	332
TURNER'S OUTDOORSMAN OUTLET	332
TWENTY TWENTY WINE	208
TWICE TREASURED	142
U.S. SEW-N-VAC	26
UGLY DUCKLING RENT-A-CAR	60
ULTIMAT CAR MATS	54
UNCLE JER'S	174
UNCLE TOM'S TOYS	338
UNDERWOOD MATTRESS FACTORY	226
UNIFORM DEPOT	163
UNITED BAND INSTRUMENT CO	276
VACUUM & SEWING CENTER	27
VALLEY 1-HOUR PHOTO	300
VALLEY BOOK CITY	73
VALLEY CLOCK SERVICE**	220
VALLEY INDOOR SWAPMEET**	188
VALLEY MATTRESS & BUNK BED CENTER**	227
VALLEY SOD FARMS	303
VALLEY TILE DISTRIBUTORS	85
VALLEY UPHOLSTERING	248
VAN DE CAMPER**	57
VAN NUYS ARMY & NAVY STORE	336
VASONA INTERIORS	105
VELVET TOUCH, THE	44
VINOTEMP INTERNATIONAL	24
WALLPAPER BIN	101
WALLPAPER CITY	101
WAREHOUSE DISCOUNT CENTER	25, 99
WAREHOUSE FOOD MART	210
WAREHOUSE OUTLET	115
WATCH CONNECTION**	257
WEINSTEIN INC., M.	257
WEST HOLLYWOOD ATHLETIC SUPPLY**	334
WEST L.A. MUSIC	272
WESTERN EXCHANGE MEAT MARKET	203
WESTON FINE ARTS, EDWARD	30
WESTPORT CARPET INDUSTRIES	92, 248

INDEX – STORES

WHOLESALE INSURANCE SERVICES	318
WHOLESALE LEATHER APPAREL**	125
WHOLESALE MATTRESS DISTRIBUTOR	227
WHOLESALE PRINTING FACTORY 1**	283
WICKER MART	240
WILBURN'S DISCOUNT PARTY CENTER	290
WILD PRICE BOUTIQUE, THE	174
WILSHIRE BEAUTY SUPPLY CO.	66
WILSHIRE WIGS, INC	68
WILSONS LEATHER OUTLET STORE	125
WINE CLUB	208
WINE HOUSE, THE	208
WITH KIDS IN MIND**	319
WOODEN SHIPS WATERBED DISC. WAREHOUSE	227
WOODEN SHIPS WATERBEDS	228
WOODLAND CASUAL	311
WOODLAND HILLS FIREPLACE SHOP**	308
WOODLOWE MUSIC CENTER	273
WOODY'S UN-FINISHED FURNITURE	240
WORK BOOT WAREHOUSE**	158
WORLD OF PLANTS AND GIFTS**	221, 303
WRITE PLACE, THE	320
ZACHARY ALL	134
ZOMMY'S	198

INDEX – CATALOGUES

#1 WALLPAPER	373
A COOK'S WARES	367
A TO Z LUGGAGE	375
AAA-ALL FACTORY, INC.	355
AARP PHARMACY SERVICE	376
ABC VACUUM CLEANER WAREHOUSE	355
ACE LEATHER PRODUCTS	375
ACE SPECIALTY FOODS	363
ADIRONDACK DESIGNS	370
ALAS ACCORDION-O-RAMA	378
ALLIED LIGHTING	371
AMERICAN DISCOUNT WALLCOVERINGS	373
ARCTIC SHEEPSKIN OUTLET	356, 359
ARTIC GLASS & WINDOW OUTLET	358
ASTRONOMICS/CHRISTOPHERS, LTD.	386
BARNES & NOBLE	357
BARRONS	367
BEAUTIFUL VISIONS	362
BEAUTY BOUTIQUE	362
BEAUTY BY SPECTOR, INC.	362
BEVERLY BREMER SILVER SHOP	367
BI-RITE PHOTO AND ELECTRONICS	382
BRASS BEDS DIRECT	370
BURPEE–W. ATLEE BURPEE & CO.	383
BUSCHEMEYER'S SILVER EXCHANGE	368
BUTTON SHOP, THE	353
CABLE FILMS	377
CAMPMOR	384
CAMPUS TRAVEL SERVICE	386
CARTOON COLOUR COMPANY, INC.	351
CAVIARTERIA INC.	364
CELLAR, THE	365
CHADWICK'S OF BOSTON	359
CHARISMA CALIFORNIA	360
CHEF'S CATALOGUE, THE	368
CHEF'S PANTRY, THE	364
CO-OP ARTISTS' MATERIALS ATLANTA AIRBRUSH	351
COLONIAL GARDEN KITCHENS AND HOME	368
COMPANY STORE, THE	372
CONTACT LENS REPLACEMENT CENTER	379
COS-TOM PICTURE FRAMES	351
CRUTCHFIELD	363

INDEX – CATALOGUES

CURRENT	381
DAEDALUS BOOKS	357
DAMARK INTERNATIONAL	366
DEERSKIN PLACE, THE	360
DEFENDER INDUSTRIES, INC	384
DESIGNER DIRECT	360
DOMESTICATIONS	372
E & B DISCOUNT MARINE	384
ELITE EYEWEAR	380
ESSENTIAL PRODUCTS CO., INC.	362
FABRIC CENTER, THE	353
FARMER TO CONSUMER DIRECTORY	364
FIDELITY PRODUCTS	381
FORTY-FIVES	377
FREE THINGS FOR KIDS TO WRITE AWAY FOR	355
FURNITURE BARN OF FOREST CITY, INC.	371
GETTINGER FEATHER CORP	352
GLOBAL VILLAGE IMPORTS	354
HARRIS LEVY, INC	373
HARRIS MORAN SEED COMPANY	383
HIAWATHA HOMES	358
HIDALGO INC	380
HOLABIRD SPORTS DISCOUNTERS	385
INDOOR GARDENING SUPPLIES	383
INTERSTATE MUSIC SUPPLY	378
J.C. WHITNEY & CO.	356
JAFFE BROS. INC.	366
JAMES KAPLAN JEWELERS	375
JAMESTOWN STAMP COMPANY	355
JESSICA'S BISCUIT	357
JOHNSON'S CARPETS	370
KICKING MULE RECORDS, INC.	377
KING'S CHANDELIER COMPANY	372
LEATHER UNLIMITED CORP	360
MARDIRON OPTICS	386
MIDAS CHINA & SILVER	368
MONTERY MILLS OUTLET STORE	373
NATIONAL CONTACT LENS CENTER	379
NEW ENGLAND CHEESEMAKING SUPPLY CO., INC.	365
OKUN BROTHERS SHOES	385
OVERTON'S	385
PEARL PAINT COMPANY	352
PHARMAIL	376
PLEXI-CRAFT QUALITY PRODUCTS CORP	369
PORTER'S CAMERA STORE, INC.	383

INDEX – CATALOGUES

POST WALLCOVERING DISTRIBUTORS, INC. 374
PUBLISHERS CENTRAL BUREAU 358
R.C. STEEL 382
RICK'S MOVIE GRAPHICS 378
RITEWAY HEARING AID CO. 376
ROBIN IMPORTERS, INC. 369
ROBINSON'S WALLCOVERINGS 374
ROCKY MOUNTAIN STATIONERY 382
ROSS-SIMONS 369
ROSS-SIMONS JEWELERS 375
ROUSSEL 352
RUBENS & MARBLE, INC 361
S & S SOUND CITY 363
SAM ASH MUSIC CORPORATION 379
SANZ INTERNATIONAL 374
SEWIN' IN VERMONT 356
SHAMA IMPORTS INC. 354
SHAR PRODUCTS COMPANY 379
SHAW FURNITURE GALLERIES 371
SHOWCASE OF SAVINGS 361
SILVER WALLPAPER, INC. 374
SMILEY'S YARNS 353
SMITH ARTISTS MATERIALS, DANIEL 352
SOBOL HOUSE OF FURNISHINGS 371
SPECIAL INTEREST VIDEO 378
SPORTSWEAR CLEARINGHOUSE 361
SUBURBAN SEW'N SWEEP 356
SUNGLASSES U.S.A. 380
TAPESTRY 369
TAYLOR'S CUTAWAY & STUFF 353
THAI SILKS 354
U.S. GOVERNMENT BOOKS 358
UNITED PHARMACAL CO., INC. 382
VAN BOURGONDIEN 384
VIKING DISCOUNT OFFICE PRODUCTS 381
VITAMIN CO-OP 366
VITAMIN POWER, INC 366
WALLY FRANK, LTD. 359
WAREHOUSE CARPETS, INC. 370
WINE LINK 364
WINTER SILKS 361
WOOD'S CIDER MILL 365

INDEX – STORES
OFFERING DISCOUNT COUPONS

2NDS SHOP**, THE	215
A-1 FURNITURE OUTLET**	221
AAA ETERNAL STAINLESS STEEL CORP.**	211
ABC POOL & PATIO**	309
ACE USED OFFICE FURNITURE WAREHOUSE**	282
ACTION SCREEN & DOOR**	86
AFFAIR OF THE HEART**	109
AIR CONDITIONING EXCHANGE**	77
AL'S DISCOUNT FURNITURE**	228
ALL BED & MATTRESS**	222
ALL IN 1 HOME FURNISHINGS**	229
ALL REASONS TRAVEL**	341
ALPERT'S BEDROOM CITY WAREHOUSE**	222
AMERICAN SURPLUS TRADERS**	282, 335
ASSOCIATED AUTO BODY**	57
BAB'S**	164, 287
BACK ON THE RACK**	141
BAILEY'S**	143
BARGAIN FAIR**	343
BED BROKER**	223
BEDS UNLIMITED**	223
BEDSPREAD CREATIONS**	244
BIG, THE BAD & THE BEAUTIFUL**, THE	123
BILLIARDS & BARSTOOLS**	326
BOOT HILL SQUARE DANCE APPAREL**	165
BOX CITY**	287
BRIDAL FACTORY OUTLET**	110
BUDGET RENTS FURNITURE AND SALES**	241, 282
CANDY FACTORY**, THE	204, 319
CANDY STORE**	204
CARLSON'S T.V. & APPLIANCES**	22
CARPET COLLECTION**	88
CARPET MANOR**	89
CELLULAR WHOLESALERS**	50
CHEAP FRILLS**	107
CONSOLIDATED PET FOODS**	293
CORY'S FURNITURE SHOWCASE**	231
COUNTRY LINENS**	245
CRAFTS PLUS**	35, 46
CRITERIUM CYCLE SPORT**	324
CROWN DISCOUNT BEAUTY SUPPLY**	63

INDEX – STORES OFFERING DISCOUNT COUPONS

CRYSTAL'S LACES & GIFTS**	36
DIAMOND EMPIRE FURNITURE**, NAT	23, 231
DISCOUNT TRAIN WAREHOUSE**	45
DYNAMIC TANGIBLES CORPORATION**	258
E V S PRODUCTIONS**	321
ELLIS**, ROBERT	110, 168
EUROGIFT**	216
EVER-RICH BEDDING**	246
FAUX ART**	217
FERGUSON'S MARINE SPECIALTIES**	47
FOAM MART**	41
FOOT FIESTA**	151
FOOT MART SPORTS**	151
FRAMING OUTLET**	32
FRIEDMAN AND ASSOCIATES**, DR. M.	285
GAINES HANDBAGS, MARLENE**	116
GALAXY OF GOWNS**	111
GAME CITY**	337
GERALD'S FINE JEWELRY**	252
GLAMOUR UNIFORM SHOP**	162
GOLDEN FLEECE DESIGNS INC.**	42, 69
GREAT GATSBY**, THE	168
H R D DISTRIBUTORS**	136
H. LEWIS REX FINE ART**	29
HARTMAN JEWELRY & GIFTS**	180
HIAWATHA HOMES**	94
HOMARUS INC.**	202
HOME COMFORT CENTER**	77
HONEY'S SHOES**	156
HOOPER CAMERA AND VIDEO CENTERS**	298
HOSIERY OUTLET, INC.**	117
IN-A-FLOOR SAFE COMPANY**	313
INTERNATIONAL CUSTOM TAILORS**	150
ITC ELECTRONICS**	50, 195
JEAN'S STARS' APPAREL**	146
KAGAN SURPLUS SALES**	261, 283
KIDS CLUB OUTLET**	120
KIDS FURNITURE WAREHOUSE**	237
KIM-E'S FLOWERS**	315
KITCHEN & BATH WAREHOUSE**, THE	80
KLEIN'S BEAD BOX**	34
KUTROSKY**, DR. THOMAS	285
LAZAR JEWELERS, INC.**, ALEX	253
LEE LAWNMOWER**	301
LEONARDO'S ITALIAN FASHION**	132

INDEX – STORES OFFERING DISCOUNT COUPONS

LEONORE'S FUR OUTLET**	124, 138
LIQUIDATION CLUB**, THE	181
LORD OF THE RINGS**	254
MARBLE PRODUCTS OF FULLERTON**	80
MATTRESS WAREHOUSE**	225
MAX FACTOR OUTLET**	64
MERRILL'S MUSIC**	275
MID-VALLEY FLOWER EXCHANGE**	316
MIJANOU'S SILK DESIGNS**	38, 219
MOM'S THE WORD**	129
MOYEN'S JEWELLERY CONNECTION, JOHN**	255
MS. FASHIONS**	171
MUSIC EXCHANGE**	264
MY FAIR LADY**	172
ORANGE APPLIANCE & VACUUM**	25
ORIENTAL RUG EXCHANGE**	247
P X DRUGS NO. 2**	259
P.J. LONDON**	147
PANG!**	29
PAR PAINT COMPANY INC.**	96
PARTY CORNER DISCOUNT CENTER**	288, 289
POTTERY AND FLORAL WORLD**	38, 220, 304
POTTERY ETC.**	305
PRICE BUSTERS SHOE WAREHOUSE**	151
PRICE-LESS BRIDALS**	112
PRO GOLF DISCOUNT**	330
RAVE REVIEWS-KIDS COTTAGE**	142
RED BARN FEED & SADDLERY INC.**	296
ROSCOE FURNITURE LIQUIDATORS**	235
ROUNDHOUSE TRAIN STORE**, THE	45
ROY STEP SHOES**	157
RUBINFELD-KENNEDY ESTATE JEWELRY**	255
SANDLER OF THE VALLEY**	109
SARA DESIGNERS OUTLET**	172
SECOND TIME AROUND RECORDS**	266
SEE ME COLOR**	121, 173
SEYMOUR FASHIONS**	121, 173
SHOE OUTLET**	152
SILK WAREHOUSE**	39, 220
SOMETHING FOR BABY**	141
SONNY'S RADIATOR EXCHANGE**	55
STAMP 'N' DOODLE**	47
STAR BABY**	122
STAR DRAPERIES MFG.**	104
STARS & DEBS**	148

INDEX – STORES OFFERING DISCOUNT COUPONS

SUPER POPS RECORD DETECTIVE**	266
SUPERIOR WINDOW COVERINGS, INC.**	105
SURPLUS CITY RETAIL CO.**	158, 336
SUSIE'S DEALS**	173
TILE FOR LESS**	84
TILE, MARBLE & GRANITE WAREHOUSE**	84
TILECLUB**	85
TOY LIQUIDATORS**	337
VALLEY CLOCK SERVICE**	220
VALLEY INDOOR SWAPMEET**	188
VALLEY MATTRESS & BUNK BED CENTER**	227
VAN DE CAMPER**	57
WATCH CONNECTION**	257
WEST HOLLYWOOD ATHLETIC SUPPLY**	334
WHOLESALE LEATHER APPAREL**	125
WHOLESALE PRINTING FACTORY 1**	283
WITH KIDS IN MIND**	319
WOODLAND HILLS FIREPLACE SHOP**	308
WORK BOOT WAREHOUSE**	158
WORLD OF PLANTS AND GIFTS**	221, 303

DISCOUNT COUPONS

BUYING RETAIL IS STUPID! DISCOUNT COUPON

2NDS OUTLET
15%

OFF PURCHASE

MAY NOT BE VALID ON CERTAIN ITEMS. EXPIRES 12-31-94

BUYING RETAIL IS STUPID! DISCOUNT COUPON

A-1 FURNITURE OUTLET
10%

OFF PURCHASE

MAY NOT BE VALID ON CERTAIN ITEMS. EXPIRES 12-31-94

BUYING RETAIL IS STUPID! DISCOUNT COUPON

AAA ETERNAL STAINLESS STEEL
10%

OFF PURCHASE

MAY NOT BE VALID ON CERTAIN ITEMS. EXPIRES 12-31-94

BUYING RETAIL IS STUPID! DISCOUNT COUPON

ABC POOL & PATIO
5%

OFF PURCHASE

NOT VALID ON SALE ITEMS. EXPIRES 12-31-94

DISCOUNT COUPONS

BUYING RETAIL IS STUPID!
18345 VENTURA BLVD., SUITE 314
TARZANA, CA 91356

BUYING RETAIL IS STUPID!
18345 VENTURA BLVD., SUITE 314
TARZANA, CA 91356

BUYING RETAIL IS STUPID!
18345 VENTURA BLVD., SUITE 314
TARZANA, CA 91356

BUYING RETAIL IS STUPID!
18345 VENTURA BLVD., SUITE 314
TARZANA, CA 91356

DISCOUNT COUPONS

Buying Retail Is Stupid! Discount Coupon

Ace Used Office Furniture
5%

OFF PURCHASE

MAY NOT BE VALID ON CERTAIN ITEMS. EXPIRES 12-31-94

Buying Retail Is Stupid! Discount Coupon

Action Screen & Door
15% discount + 1 free screen

WITH PURCHASE OF 4 SCREENS

MAY NOT BE VALID ON CERTAIN ITEMS. EXPIRES 12-31-94

Buying Retail Is Stupid! Discount Coupon

Affair of the Heart
100 free personalized napkins

WITH ORDER OF INVITATIONS

EXPIRES 12-31-94

Buying Retail Is Stupid! Discount Coupon

Air Conditioning Exchange
10%

OFF PURCHASE + FREE TAPE MEASURE

MAY NOT BE VALID ON CERTAIN ITEMS. EXPIRES 12-31-94

DISCOUNT COUPONS

BUYING RETAIL IS STUPID!
18345 VENTURA BLVD., SUITE 314
TARZANA, CA 91356

BUYING RETAIL IS STUPID!
18345 VENTURA BLVD., SUITE 314
TARZANA, CA 91356

BUYING RETAIL IS STUPID!
18345 VENTURA BLVD., SUITE 314
TARZANA, CA 91356

BUYING RETAIL IS STUPID!
18345 VENTURA BLVD., SUITE 314
TARZANA, CA 91356

DISCOUNT COUPONS

BUYING RETAIL IS STUPID! DISCOUNT COUPON

AL'S DISCOUNT FURNITURE
5%

OFF PURCHASE

MAY NOT BE VALID ON CERTAIN ITEMS. EXPIRES 12-31-94

BUYING RETAIL IS STUPID! DISCOUNT COUPON

ALL BED & MATTRESS
10%

OFF PURCHASE

MAY NOT BE VALID ON CERTAIN ITEMS. EXPIRES 12-31-94

BUYING RETAIL IS STUPID! DISCOUNT COUPON

ALL IN 1 HOME FURNISHINGS
5%

OFF PURCHASE (CASH OR CHECKS ONLY)

NOT TO BE USED WITH ANY OTHER OFFER. EXPIRES 12-31-94

BUYING RETAIL IS STUPID! DISCOUNT COUPON

ALL REASONS TRAVEL
10%

OFF CRUISE ONLY

MAY NOT BE VALID ON CERTAIN ITEMS. EXPIRES 12-31-94

DISCOUNT COUPONS

BUYING RETAIL IS STUPID!
18345 VENTURA BLVD., SUITE 314
TARZANA, CA 91356

BUYING RETAIL IS STUPID!
18345 VENTURA BLVD., SUITE 314
TARZANA, CA 91356

BUYING RETAIL IS STUPID!
18345 VENTURA BLVD., SUITE 314
TARZANA, CA 91356

BUYING RETAIL IS STUPID!
18345 VENTURA BLVD., SUITE 314
TARZANA, CA 91356

DISCOUNT COUPONS

BUYING RETAIL IS STUPID! DISCOUNT COUPON

ALPERT'S BEDROOM CITY
5%
OFF PURCHASE

MAY NOT BE VALID ON CERTAIN ITEMS. EXPIRES 12-31-94

BUYING RETAIL IS STUPID! DISCOUNT COUPON

AMERICAN SURPLUS TRADERS
10%
OFF PURCHASE

MAY NOT BE VALID ON CERTAIN ITEMS. EXPIRES 12-31-94

BUYING RETAIL IS STUPID! DISCOUNT COUPON

ASSOCIATED AUTO BODY
5%
OFF LABOR ONLY

EXPIRES 12-31-94

BUYING RETAIL IS STUPID! DISCOUNT COUPON

BAB'S (AT RERUN'S)
10%
OFF PURCHASE

MAY NOT BE VALID ON CERTAIN ITEMS. EXPIRES 12-31-94

Discount Coupons

Buying Retail Is Stupid!
18345 Ventura Blvd., Suite 314
Tarzana, CA 91356

Buying Retail Is Stupid!
18345 Ventura Blvd., Suite 314
Tarzana, CA 91356

Buying Retail Is Stupid!
18345 Ventura Blvd., Suite 314
Tarzana, CA 91356

Buying Retail Is Stupid!
18345 Ventura Blvd., Suite 314
Tarzana, CA 91356

DISCOUNT COUPONS

BUYING RETAIL IS STUPID! DISCOUNT COUPON

BACK ON THE RACK
10%

OFF PURCHASE

MAY NOT BE VALID ON CERTAIN ITEMS. EXPIRES 12-31-94

BUYING RETAIL IS STUPID! DISCOUNT COUPON

BAILEY'S
10%

OFF PURCHASE

MAY NOT BE VALID ON CERTAIN ITEMS. EXPIRES 12-31-94

BUYING RETAIL IS STUPID! DISCOUNT COUPON

BARGAIN FAIR
10%

OFF PURCHASE

MAY NOT BE VALID ON CERTAIN ITEMS. EXPIRES 12-31-94

BUYING RETAIL IS STUPID! DISCOUNT COUPON

BED BROKER
5%

OFF PURCHASE

MAY NOT BE VALID ON CERTAIN ITEMS. EXPIRES 12-31-94

Discount Coupons

Buying Retail Is Stupid!
18345 Ventura Blvd., Suite 314
Tarzana, CA 91356

Buying Retail Is Stupid!
18345 Ventura Blvd., Suite 314
Tarzana, CA 91356

Buying Retail Is Stupid!
18345 Ventura Blvd., Suite 314
Tarzana, CA 91356

Buying Retail Is Stupid!
18345 Ventura Blvd., Suite 314
Tarzana, CA 91356

DISCOUNT COUPONS

Buying Retail Is Stupid! Discount Coupon

Bed's Unlimited
5%

OFF PURCHASE

MAY NOT BE VALID ON CERTAIN ITEMS. EXPIRES 12-31-94

Buying Retail Is Stupid! Discount Coupon

Bedspread Creations
5%

OFF PURCHASE

MAY NOT BE VALID ON CERTAIN ITEMS. EXPIRES 12-31-94

Buying Retail Is Stupid! Discount Coupon

The Big, The Bad & The Beautiful
10%

OFF PURCHASE

MAY NOT BE VALID ON CERTAIN ITEMS. EXPIRES 12-31-94

Buying Retail Is Stupid! Discount Coupon

Billiards & Barstools
10%

OFF PURCHASE

MAY NOT BE VALID ON CERTAIN ITEMS. EXPIRES 12-31-94

DISCOUNT COUPONS

BUYING RETAIL IS STUPID!
18345 VENTURA BLVD., SUITE 314
TARZANA, CA 91356

BUYING RETAIL IS STUPID!
18345 VENTURA BLVD., SUITE 314
TARZANA, CA 91356

BUYING RETAIL IS STUPID!
18345 VENTURA BLVD., SUITE 314
TARZANA, CA 91356

BUYING RETAIL IS STUPID!
18345 VENTURA BLVD., SUITE 314
TARZANA, CA 91356

DISCOUNT COUPONS

Buying Retail Is Stupid! Discount Coupon

BOOT HILL SQUARE DANCE APPAREL
5%

OFF PURCHASE

MAY NOT BE VALID ON CERTAIN ITEMS. EXPIRES 12-31-94

Buying Retail Is Stupid! Discount Coupon

BOX CITY
10%

OFF PURCHASE

MAY NOT BE VALID ON CERTAIN ITEMS. EXPIRES 12-31-94

Buying Retail Is Stupid! Discount Coupon

BRIDAL FACTORY OUTLET
$25 Discount

OFF PURCHASE

MAY NOT BE VALID ON CERTAIN ITEMS. EXPIRES 12-31-94

Buying Retail Is Stupid! Discount Coupon

BUDGET RENTS FURNITURE
10%

OFF PURCHASE ONLY

DOES NOT APPLY TO RENTALS. EXPIRES 12-31-94

DISCOUNT COUPONS

BUYING RETAIL IS STUPID!
18345 VENTURA BLVD., SUITE 314
TARZANA, CA 91356

BUYING RETAIL IS STUPID!
18345 VENTURA BLVD., SUITE 314
TARZANA, CA 91356

BUYING RETAIL IS STUPID!
18345 VENTURA BLVD., SUITE 314
TARZANA, CA 91356

BUYING RETAIL IS STUPID!
18345 VENTURA BLVD., SUITE 314
TARZANA, CA 91356

DISCOUNT COUPONS

Buying Retail Is Stupid! Discount Coupon

THE CANDY FACTORY
10%

OFF PURCHASE OR PARTIES

MAY NOT BE VALID ON CERTAIN ITEMS. EXPIRES 12-31-94

Buying Retail Is Stupid! Discount Coupon

CANDY STORE
10%

OFF PURCHASE

MAY NOT BE VALID ON CERTAIN ITEMS. EXPIRES 12-31-94

Buying Retail Is Stupid! Discount Coupon

CARLSON'S TV & APPLIANCES
$10

OFF PURCHASE

MAY NOT BE VALID ON CERTAIN ITEMS. EXPIRES 12-31-94

Buying Retail Is Stupid! Discount Coupon

CARPET COLLECTION
5%

OFF PURCHASE

MAY NOT BE VALID ON CERTAIN ITEMS. EXPIRES 12-31-94

DISCOUNT COUPONS

BUYING RETAIL IS STUPID!
18345 VENTURA BLVD., SUITE 314
TARZANA, CA 91356

BUYING RETAIL IS STUPID!
18345 VENTURA BLVD., SUITE 314
TARZANA, CA 91356

BUYING RETAIL IS STUPID!
18345 VENTURA BLVD., SUITE 314
TARZANA, CA 91356

BUYING RETAIL IS STUPID!
18345 VENTURA BLVD., SUITE 314
TARZANA, CA 91356

DISCOUNT COUPONS

Buying Retail Is Stupid! Discount Coupon

Carpet Manor
5%

OFF PURCHASE

MAY NOT BE VALID ON CERTAIN ITEMS. EXPIRES 12-31-94

Buying Retail Is Stupid! Discount Coupon

Cellular Wholesalers
5%

OFF PURCHASE

MAY NOT BE VALID ON CERTAIN ITEMS. EXPIRES 12-31-94

Buying Retail Is Stupid! Discount Coupon

Cheap Frills
5%

OFF PURCHASE

MAY NOT BE VALID ON CERTAIN ITEMS. EXPIRES 12-31-94

Buying Retail Is Stupid! Discount Coupon

Consolidated Pet Foods
15%

OFF PURCHASE

MAY NOT BE VALID ON CERTAIN ITEMS. EXPIRES 12-31-94

Discount Coupons

BUYING RETAIL IS STUPID!
18345 VENTURA BLVD., SUITE 314
TARZANA, CA 91356

BUYING RETAIL IS STUPID!
18345 VENTURA BLVD., SUITE 314
TARZANA, CA 91356

BUYING RETAIL IS STUPID!
18345 VENTURA BLVD., SUITE 314
TARZANA, CA 91356

BUYING RETAIL IS STUPID!
18345 VENTURA BLVD., SUITE 314
TARZANA, CA 91356

DISCOUNT COUPONS

BUYING RETAIL IS STUPID! DISCOUNT COUPON

CORY'S FURNITURE SHOWCASE
$50

OFF $500 MINIMUM PURCHASE

MAY NOT BE VALID ON CERTAIN ITEMS. EXPIRES 12-31-94

BUYING RETAIL IS STUPID! DISCOUNT COUPON

COUNTRY LINENS
10%

OFF PURCHASE

MAY NOT BE VALID ON CERTAIN ITEMS. EXPIRES 12-31-94

BUYING RETAIL IS STUPID! DISCOUNT COUPON

CRAFTS PLUS
10%

OFF PURCHASE

MAY NOT BE VALID ON CERTAIN ITEMS. EXPIRES 12-31-94

BUYING RETAIL IS STUPID! DISCOUNT COUPON

CRITERIUM CYCLE SPORT
10%

OFF PURCHASE

MAY NOT BE VALID ON CERTAIN ITEMS. EXPIRES 12-31-94

DISCOUNT COUPONS

BUYING RETAIL IS STUPID!
18345 VENTURA BLVD., SUITE 314
TARZANA, CA 91356

BUYING RETAIL IS STUPID!
18345 VENTURA BLVD., SUITE 314
TARZANA, CA 91356

BUYING RETAIL IS STUPID!
18345 VENTURA BLVD., SUITE 314
TARZANA, CA 91356

BUYING RETAIL IS STUPID!
18345 VENTURA BLVD., SUITE 314
TARZANA, CA 91356

DISCOUNT COUPONS

BUYING RETAIL IS STUPID! DISCOUNT COUPON

CROWN DISCOUNT BEAUTY SUPPLY
10%

OFF PURCHASE

MAY NOT BE VALID ON CERTAIN ITEMS. EXPIRES 12-31-94

BUYING RETAIL IS STUPID! DISCOUNT COUPON

CRYSTAL'S LACE & GIFTS
15%

OFF PURCHASE

MAY NOT BE VALID ON CERTAIN ITEMS. EXPIRES 12-31-94

BUYING RETAIL IS STUPID! DISCOUNT COUPON

NAT DIAMOND EMPIRE FURNITURE
10%

OFF PURCHASE

MAY NOT BE VALID ON CERTAIN ITEMS. EXPIRES 12-31-94

BUYING RETAIL IS STUPID! DISCOUNT COUPON

DISCOUNT TRAIN WAREHOUSE
5%

OFF PURCHASE

MAY NOT BE VALID ON CERTAIN ITEMS. EXPIRES 12-31-94

Discount Coupons

Buying Retail Is Stupid!
18345 Ventura Blvd., Suite 314
Tarzana, CA 91356

Buying Retail Is Stupid!
18345 Ventura Blvd., Suite 314
Tarzana, CA 91356

Buying Retail Is Stupid!
18345 Ventura Blvd., Suite 314
Tarzana, CA 91356

Buying Retail Is Stupid!
18345 Ventura Blvd., Suite 314
Tarzana, CA 91356

DISCOUNT COUPONS

BUYING RETAIL IS STUPID! DISCOUNT COUPON

DYNAMIC TANGIBLES
$15.95

SPECIAL PRICE FOR EDUCATIONAL VIDEO

EXPIRES 12-31-94

BUYING RETAIL IS STUPID! DISCOUNT COUPON

E.V.S. PRODUCTIONS
10%

OFF PURCHASE

MAY NOT BE VALID ON CERTAIN ITEMS. EXPIRES 12-31-94

BUYING RETAIL IS STUPID! DISCOUNT COUPON

ROBERT ELLIS
10%

OFF PURCHASE

MAY NOT BE VALID ON CERTAIN ITEMS. EXPIRES 12-31-94

BUYING RETAIL IS STUPID! DISCOUNT COUPON

EUROGIFT
5%

OFF PURCHASE OF IN-STOCK ITEMS ONLY

NOT VALID ON SALE ITEMS. EXPIRES 12-31-94

DISCOUNT COUPONS

BUYING RETAIL IS STUPID!
18345 VENTURA BLVD., SUITE 314
TARZANA, CA 91356

BUYING RETAIL IS STUPID!
18345 VENTURA BLVD., SUITE 314
TARZANA, CA 91356

BUYING RETAIL IS STUPID!
18345 VENTURA BLVD., SUITE 314
TARZANA, CA 91356

BUYING RETAIL IS STUPID!
18345 VENTURA BLVD., SUITE 314
TARZANA, CA 91356

DISCOUNT COUPONS

BUYING RETAIL IS STUPID! DISCOUNT COUPON

EVER-RICH BEDDING
10%

OFF PURCHASE OF $100 OR MORE

NOT VALID ON SALE OR DOWN ITEMS. EXPIRES 12-31-94

BUYING RETAIL IS STUPID! DISCOUNT COUPON

FAUX ART
10%

OFF PURCHASE

MAY NOT BE VALID ON CERTAIN ITEMS. EXPIRES 12-31-94

BUYING RETAIL IS STUPID! DISCOUNT COUPON

FERGUSON'S MARINE SPECIALTIES
10% DISCOUNT + FREE COWRIE SHELL

WITH PURCHASE

MAY NOT BE VALID ON CERTAIN ITEMS. EXPIRES 12-31-94

BUYING RETAIL IS STUPID! DISCOUNT COUPON

FOAM MART
10%

OFF PURCHASE

NOT VALID ON SALE ITEMS. EXPIRES 12-31-94

Discount Coupons

Buying Retail Is Stupid!
18345 Ventura Blvd., Suite 314
Tarzana, CA 91356

Buying Retail Is Stupid!
18345 Ventura Blvd., Suite 314
Tarzana, CA 91356

Buying Retail Is Stupid!
18345 Ventura Blvd., Suite 314
Tarzana, CA 91356

Buying Retail Is Stupid!
18345 Ventura Blvd., Suite 314
Tarzana, CA 91356

DISCOUNT COUPONS

BUYING RETAIL IS STUPID! DISCOUNT COUPON

FOOT FIESTA
5%
OFF PURCHASE

MAY NOT BE VALID ON CERTAIN ITEMS. EXPIRES 12-31-94

BUYING RETAIL IS STUPID! DISCOUNT COUPON

FOOT MART SPORTS
5%
OFF PURCHASE

MAY NOT BE VALID ON CERTAIN ITEMS. EXPIRES 12-31-94

BUYING RETAIL IS STUPID! DISCOUNT COUPON

FRAMING OUTLET
10%
OFF PURCHASE

MAY NOT BE VALID ON CERTAIN ITEMS. EXPIRES 12-31-94

BUYING RETAIL IS STUPID! DISCOUNT COUPON

DR. FRIEDMAN AND ASSOCIATES
5%
OFF PURCHASE OF EYEGLASSES OR CONTACT LENS

EXPIRES 12-31-94

Discount Coupons

BUYING RETAIL IS STUPID!
18345 VENTURA BLVD., SUITE 314
TARZANA, CA 91356

BUYING RETAIL IS STUPID!
18345 VENTURA BLVD., SUITE 314
TARZANA, CA 91356

BUYING RETAIL IS STUPID!
18345 VENTURA BLVD., SUITE 314
TARZANA, CA 91356

BUYING RETAIL IS STUPID!
18345 VENTURA BLVD., SUITE 314
TARZANA, CA 91356

Discount Coupons

Buying Retail Is Stupid! Discount Coupon

Marlene Gaines Handbags
10%

OFF PURCHASE

NOT VALID ON SALE ITEMS. EXPIRES 12-31-94

Buying Retail Is Stupid! Discount Coupon

Galaxy of Gowns
20%

OFF PURCHASE

MAY NOT BE VALID ON CERTAIN ITEMS. EXPIRES 12-31-94

Buying Retail Is Stupid! Discount Coupon

Game City
5% Discount + FREE Game Rental

WITH PAID RENTAL OF ONE GAME

MAY NOT BE VALID ON CERTAIN ITEMS. EXPIRES 12-31-94

Buying Retail Is Stupid! Discount Coupon

Gerald's Fine Jewelry
10%

OFF PURCHASE

MAY NOT BE VALID ON CERTAIN ITEMS. EXPIRES 12-31-94

DISCOUNT COUPONS

BUYING RETAIL IS STUPID!
18345 VENTURA BLVD., SUITE 314
TARZANA, CA 91356

BUYING RETAIL IS STUPID!
18345 VENTURA BLVD., SUITE 314
TARZANA, CA 91356

BUYING RETAIL IS STUPID!
18345 VENTURA BLVD., SUITE 314
TARZANA, CA 91356

BUYING RETAIL IS STUPID!
18345 VENTURA BLVD., SUITE 314
TARZANA, CA 91356

DISCOUNT COUPONS

BUYING RETAIL IS STUPID! DISCOUNT COUPON

GLAMOUR UNIFORM SHOP
10%

OFF PURCHASE

MAY NOT BE VALID ON CERTAIN ITEMS. EXPIRES 12-31-94

BUYING RETAIL IS STUPID! DISCOUNT COUPON

GOLDEN FLEECE DESIGNS
15%

OFF PURCHASE

MAY NOT BE VALID ON CERTAIN ITEMS. EXPIRES 12-31-94

BUYING RETAIL IS STUPID! DISCOUNT COUPON

THE GREAT GATSBY
10%

OFF PURCHASE

MAY NOT BE VALID ON SALE ITEMS. EXPIRES 12-31-94

BUYING RETAIL IS STUPID! DISCOUNT COUPON

H.R.D. DISTRIBUTORS
10%

OFF PURCHASE

MAY NOT BE VALID ON CERTAIN ITEMS. EXPIRES 12-31-94

DISCOUNT COUPONS

BUYING RETAIL IS STUPID!
18345 VENTURA BLVD., SUITE 314
TARZANA, CA 91356

BUYING RETAIL IS STUPID!
18345 VENTURA BLVD., SUITE 314
TARZANA, CA 91356

BUYING RETAIL IS STUPID!
18345 VENTURA BLVD., SUITE 314
TARZANA, CA 91356

BUYING RETAIL IS STUPID!
18345 VENTURA BLVD., SUITE 314
TARZANA, CA 91356

DISCOUNT COUPONS

BUYING RETAIL IS STUPID! DISCOUNT COUPON

H. LEWIS REX FINE ART
10%

OFF PURCHASE

MAY NOT BE VALID ON CERTAIN ITEMS. EXPIRES 12-31-94

BUYING RETAIL IS STUPID! DISCOUNT COUPON

HARTMAN JEWELRY & GIFTS
10%

OFF PURCHASE

MAY NOT BE VALID ON CERTAIN ITEMS. EXPIRES 12-31-94

BUYING RETAIL IS STUPID! DISCOUNT COUPON

HIAWATHA HOMES
10%

OFF PURCHASE

MAY NOT BE VALID ON CERTAIN ITEMS. EXPIRES 12-31-94

BUYING RETAIL IS STUPID! DISCOUNT COUPON

HOMARUS INC.
10%

OFF PURCHASE

MAY NOT BE VALID ON CERTAIN ITEMS. EXPIRES 12-31-94

DISCOUNT COUPONS

BUYING RETAIL IS STUPID!
18345 VENTURA BLVD., SUITE 314
TARZANA, CA 91356

BUYING RETAIL IS STUPID!
18345 VENTURA BLVD., SUITE 314
TARZANA, CA 91356

BUYING RETAIL IS STUPID!
18345 VENTURA BLVD., SUITE 314
TARZANA, CA 91356

BUYING RETAIL IS STUPID!
18345 VENTURA BLVD., SUITE 314
TARZANA, CA 91356

DISCOUNT COUPONS

Buying Retail Is Stupid! Discount Coupon

Home Comfort Center
10%

OFF PURCHASE

MAY NOT BE VALID ON CERTAIN ITEMS. EXPIRES 12-31-94

Buying Retail Is Stupid! Discount Coupon

Honey's Shoes
10%

OFF PURCHASE

MAY NOT BE VALID ON CERTAIN ITEMS. EXPIRES 12-31-94

Buying Retail Is Stupid! Discount Coupon

Hooper Camera and Video Centers
5%

OFF PURCHASE

MAY NOT BE VALID ON CERTAIN ITEMS. EXPIRES 12-31-94

Buying Retail Is Stupid! Discount Coupon

Hosiery Outlet
10%

OFF PURCHASE

MAY NOT BE VALID ON CERTAIN ITEMS. EXPIRES 12-31-94

DISCOUNT COUPONS

BUYING RETAIL IS STUPID!
18345 VENTURA BLVD., SUITE 314
TARZANA, CA 91356

BUYING RETAIL IS STUPID!
18345 VENTURA BLVD., SUITE 314
TARZANA, CA 91356

BUYING RETAIL IS STUPID!
18345 VENTURA BLVD., SUITE 314
TARZANA, CA 91356

BUYING RETAIL IS STUPID!
18345 VENTURA BLVD., SUITE 314
TARZANA, CA 91356

DISCOUNT COUPONS

BUYING RETAIL IS STUPID! DISCOUNT COUPON

IN-A-FLOOR SAFE COMPANY
10%
OFF PURCHASE

MAY NOT BE VALID ON CERTAIN ITEMS. EXPIRES 12-31-94

BUYING RETAIL IS STUPID! DISCOUNT COUPON

INTERNATIONAL CUSTOM TAILORS
10% OFF + 1 FREE HEMMING OF PANTS
WITH $25 OF INCOMING ALTERATIONS

MAY NOT BE VALID ON CERTAIN ITEMS. EXPIRES 12-31-94

BUYING RETAIL IS STUPID! DISCOUNT COUPON

ITC ELECTRONICS
5%
OFF PURCHASE

MAY NOT BE VALID ON CERTAIN ITEMS. EXPIRES 12-31-94

BUYING RETAIL IS STUPID! DISCOUNT COUPON

JEAN'S STARS' APPAREL
10%
OFF PURCHASE

MAY NOT BE VALID DURING SPECIAL SALES. EXPIRES 12-31-94

DISCOUNT COUPONS

BUYING RETAIL IS STUPID!
18345 VENTURA BLVD., SUITE 314
TARZANA, CA 91356

BUYING RETAIL IS STUPID!
18345 VENTURA BLVD., SUITE 314
TARZANA, CA 91356

BUYING RETAIL IS STUPID!
18345 VENTURA BLVD., SUITE 314
TARZANA, CA 91356

BUYING RETAIL IS STUPID!
18345 VENTURA BLVD., SUITE 314
TARZANA, CA 91356

DISCOUNT COUPONS

BUYING RETAIL IS STUPID! DISCOUNT COUPON

KAGAN SURPLUS SALES
5% or 10%

5% OFF PURCHASE UNDER $100, 10% OFF IF OVER $100

MAY NOT BE VALID ON CERTAIN ITEMS. EXPIRES 12-31-94

BUYING RETAIL IS STUPID! DISCOUNT COUPON

KIDS CLUB OUTLET
$5

OFF PURCHASE OF $25 OR MORE

MAY NOT BE VALID ON CERTAIN ITEMS. EXPIRES 12-31-94

BUYING RETAIL IS STUPID! DISCOUNT COUPON

KIDS FURNITURE WAREHOUSE
10%

OFF PURCHASE

MAY NOT BE VALID ON CERTAIN ITEMS. EXPIRES 12-31-94

BUYING RETAIL IS STUPID! DISCOUNT COUPON

KIM-E'S FLOWERS
10%

OFF PURCHASE

MAY NOT BE VALID ON CERTAIN ITEMS. EXPIRES 12-31-94

DISCOUNT COUPONS

BUYING RETAIL IS STUPID!
18345 VENTURA BLVD., SUITE 314
TARZANA, CA 91356

BUYING RETAIL IS STUPID!
18345 VENTURA BLVD., SUITE 314
TARZANA, CA 91356

BUYING RETAIL IS STUPID!
18345 VENTURA BLVD., SUITE 314
TARZANA, CA 91356

BUYING RETAIL IS STUPID!
18345 VENTURA BLVD., SUITE 314
TARZANA, CA 91356

DISCOUNT COUPONS

BUYING RETAIL IS STUPID! DISCOUNT COUPON

KITCHEN & BATH WAREHOUSE
5%

OFF PURCHASE

MAY NOT BE VALID ON CERTAIN ITEMS. EXPIRES 12-31-94

BUYING RETAIL IS STUPID! DISCOUNT COUPON

KLEIN'S BEAD BOX
5%

OFF PURCHASE

MAY NOT BE VALID ON CERTAIN ITEMS. EXPIRES 12-31-94

BUYING RETAIL IS STUPID! DISCOUNT COUPON

DR. THOMAS KUTROSKY
5%

OFF PURCHASE OF LENSES, FRAMES OR CONTACTS

MAY NOT BE VALID ON CERTAIN ITEMS. EXPIRES 12-31-94

BUYING RETAIL IS STUPID! DISCOUNT COUPON

ALEX LAZAR JEWELERS
5%

OFF PURCHASE

NOT VALID ON SPECIAL SALE ITEMS. EXPIRES 12-31-94

Discount Coupons

Buying Retail Is Stupid!
18345 Ventura Blvd., Suite 314
Tarzana, CA 91356

Buying Retail Is Stupid!
18345 Ventura Blvd., Suite 314
Tarzana, CA 91356

Buying Retail Is Stupid!
18345 Ventura Blvd., Suite 314
Tarzana, CA 91356

Buying Retail Is Stupid!
18345 Ventura Blvd., Suite 314
Tarzana, CA 91356

DISCOUNT COUPONS

BUYING RETAIL IS STUPID! DISCOUNT COUPON

LEE LAWNMOWER
10%
OFF PURCHASE

NOT VALID ON SPECIAL SALE ITEMS. EXPIRES 12-31-94

BUYING RETAIL IS STUPID! DISCOUNT COUPON

LEONARDO'S ITALIAN FASHIONS
10%
OFF PURCHASE

MAY NOT BE VALID ON CERTAIN ITEMS. EXPIRES 12-31-94

BUYING RETAIL IS STUPID! DISCOUNT COUPON

LEONORE'S FUR OUTLET
10%
OFF PURCHASE

MAY NOT BE VALID ON CERTAIN ITEMS. EXPIRES 12-31-94

BUYING RETAIL IS STUPID! DISCOUNT COUPON

THE LIQUIDATION CLUB
10% Discount + FREE Membership
OFF PURCHASE

MAY NOT BE VALID ON CERTAIN ITEMS. EXPIRES 12-31-94

DISCOUNT COUPONS

BUYING RETAIL IS STUPID!
18345 VENTURA BLVD., SUITE 314
TARZANA, CA 91356

BUYING RETAIL IS STUPID!
18345 VENTURA BLVD., SUITE 314
TARZANA, CA 91356

BUYING RETAIL IS STUPID!
18345 VENTURA BLVD., SUITE 314
TARZANA, CA 91356

BUYING RETAIL IS STUPID!
18345 VENTURA BLVD., SUITE 314
TARZANA, CA 91356

DISCOUNT COUPONS

BUYING RETAIL IS STUPID! DISCOUNT COUPON

LORD OF THE RINGS
5%
OFF PURCHASE

MAY NOT BE VALID ON CERTAIN ITEMS. EXPIRES 12-31-94

BUYING RETAIL IS STUPID! DISCOUNT COUPON

MARBLE PRODUCTS OF FULLERTON
5%
OFF PURCHASE

MAY NOT BE VALID ON CERTAIN ITEMS. EXPIRES 12-31-94

BUYING RETAIL IS STUPID! DISCOUNT COUPON

MATTRESS WAREHOUSE
Free Bed Frame & Delivery
WITH $250 MINIMUM PURCHASE

MAY NOT BE VALID ON CERTAIN ITEMS. EXPIRES 12-31-94

BUYING RETAIL IS STUPID! DISCOUNT COUPON

MAX FACTOR OUTLET
5%
OFF PURCHASE

MAY NOT BE VALID ON CERTAIN ITEMS. EXPIRES 12-31-94

DISCOUNT COUPONS

BUYING RETAIL IS STUPID!
18345 VENTURA BLVD., SUITE 314
TARZANA, CA 91356

BUYING RETAIL IS STUPID!
18345 VENTURA BLVD., SUITE 314
TARZANA, CA 91356

BUYING RETAIL IS STUPID!
18345 VENTURA BLVD., SUITE 314
TARZANA, CA 91356

BUYING RETAIL IS STUPID!
18345 VENTURA BLVD., SUITE 314
TARZANA, CA 91356

DISCOUNT COUPONS

BUYING RETAIL IS STUPID! DISCOUNT COUPON

MERRILL'S MUSIC
10%

OFF PURCHASE

MAY NOT BE VALID ON CERTAIN ITEMS. EXPIRES 12-31-94

BUYING RETAIL IS STUPID! DISCOUNT COUPON

MID-VALLEY FLOWER EXCHANGE
10%

OFF PURCHASE + FREE BOUQUET OF FLOWERS

MAY NOT BE VALID ON CERTAIN ITEMS. EXPIRES 12-31-94

BUYING RETAIL IS STUPID! DISCOUNT COUPON

MIJANOU'S SILK
5%

OFF PURCHASE

MAY NOT BE VALID ON CERTAIN ITEMS. EXPIRES 12-31-94

BUYING RETAIL IS STUPID! DISCOUNT COUPON

MOM'S THE WORD
10%

OFF PURCHASE

MAY NOT BE VALID ON CERTAIN ITEMS. EXPIRES 12-31-94

DISCOUNT COUPONS

BUYING RETAIL IS STUPID!
18345 VENTURA BLVD., SUITE 314
TARZANA, CA 91356

BUYING RETAIL IS STUPID!
18345 VENTURA BLVD., SUITE 314
TARZANA, CA 91356

BUYING RETAIL IS STUPID!
18345 VENTURA BLVD., SUITE 314
TARZANA, CA 91356

BUYING RETAIL IS STUPID!
18345 VENTURA BLVD., SUITE 314
TARZANA, CA 91356

DISCOUNT COUPONS

BUYING RETAIL IS STUPID! DISCOUNT COUPON

J. MOYEN'S JEWELLERY CONNECTION
10%

OFF PURCHASE

NOT VALID ON LOOSE STONES OR SALES. EXPIRES 12-31-94

BUYING RETAIL IS STUPID! DISCOUNT COUPON

MS. FASHIONS
5%

OFF PURCHASE

MAY NOT BE VALID ON CERTAIN ITEMS. EXPIRES 12-31-94

BUYING RETAIL IS STUPID! DISCOUNT COUPON

MUSIC EXCHANGE
20%

OFF PURCHASE OF RECYCLED GOODS ONLY

MAY NOT BE VALID ON CERTAIN ITEMS. EXPIRES 12-31-94

BUYING RETAIL IS STUPID! DISCOUNT COUPON

MY FAIR LADY
10%

OFF PURCHASE (EXCLUDES BLOW-OUT ROOM)

NOT VALID FOR PARKING LOT SALES. EXPIRES 12-31-94

DISCOUNT COUPONS

BUYING RETAIL IS STUPID!
18345 VENTURA BLVD., SUITE 314
TARZANA, CA 91356

BUYING RETAIL IS STUPID!
18345 VENTURA BLVD., SUITE 314
TARZANA, CA 91356

BUYING RETAIL IS STUPID!
18345 VENTURA BLVD., SUITE 314
TARZANA, CA 91356

BUYING RETAIL IS STUPID!
18345 VENTURA BLVD., SUITE 314
TARZANA, CA 91356

DISCOUNT COUPONS

BUYING RETAIL IS STUPID! DISCOUNT COUPON

ORANGE APPLIANCE & VACUUM
5%
OFF PURCHASE

MAY NOT BE VALID ON CERTAIN ITEMS. EXPIRES 12-31-94

BUYING RETAIL IS STUPID! DISCOUNT COUPON

ORIENTAL RUG EXCHANGE
5%
OFF PURCHASE

MAY NOT BE VALID ON CERTAIN ITEMS. EXPIRES 12-31-94

BUYING RETAIL IS STUPID! DISCOUNT COUPON

P X DRUGS NO. 2
10%
OFF PURCHASE–PRESCRIPTIONS NOT INCLUDED

NOT VALID ON SALE ITEMS. EXPIRES 12-31-94

BUYING RETAIL IS STUPID! DISCOUNT COUPON

P. J. LONDON
10%
OFF PURCHASE

MAY NOT BE VALID ON CERTAIN ITEMS. EXPIRES 12-31-94

DISCOUNT COUPONS

BUYING RETAIL IS STUPID!
18345 VENTURA BLVD., SUITE 314
TARZANA, CA 91356

BUYING RETAIL IS STUPID!
18345 VENTURA BLVD., SUITE 314
TARZANA, CA 91356

BUYING RETAIL IS STUPID!
18345 VENTURA BLVD., SUITE 314
TARZANA, CA 91356

BUYING RETAIL IS STUPID!
18345 VENTURA BLVD., SUITE 314
TARZANA, CA 91356

DISCOUNT COUPONS

BUYING RETAIL IS STUPID! DISCOUNT COUPON

PANG!
10%

OFF PURCHASE OF STOCK ITEMS & CUSTOM FRAMING

NOT VALID ON SALE ITEMS. EXPIRES 12-31-94

BUYING RETAIL IS STUPID! DISCOUNT COUPON

PAR PAINT COMPANY INC.
5%

OFF PURCHASE

MAY NOT BE VALID ON CERTAIN ITEMS. EXPIRES 12-31-94

BUYING RETAIL IS STUPID! DISCOUNT COUPON

PARTY CORNER DISCOUNT CENTER
10%

OFF PURCHASE

MAY NOT BE VALID ON CERTAIN ITEMS. EXPIRES 12-31-94

BUYING RETAIL IS STUPID! DISCOUNT COUPON

POTTERY & FLORAL WORLD
10%

OFF PURCHASE

MAY NOT BE VALID ON CERTAIN ITEMS. EXPIRES 12-31-94

Discount Coupons

Buying Retail Is Stupid!
18345 Ventura Blvd., Suite 314
Tarzana, CA 91356

Buying Retail Is Stupid!
18345 Ventura Blvd., Suite 314
Tarzana, CA 91356

Buying Retail Is Stupid!
18345 Ventura Blvd., Suite 314
Tarzana, CA 91356

Buying Retail Is Stupid!
18345 Ventura Blvd., Suite 314
Tarzana, CA 91356

DISCOUNT COUPONS

BUYING RETAIL IS STUPID! DISCOUNT COUPON

POTTERY ETC.
5%

OFF PURCHASE + FREE 2-1/2 INCH CLAY POT

MAY NOT BE VALID ON CERTAIN ITEMS. EXPIRES 12-31-94

BUYING RETAIL IS STUPID! DISCOUNT COUPON

PRICE BUSTERS SHOE WAREHOUSE
Free 6-Pack of Socks

WITH PURCHASE

MAY NOT BE VALID ON CERTAIN ITEMS. EXPIRES 12-31-94

BUYING RETAIL IS STUPID! DISCOUNT COUPON

PRICE-LESS BRIDALS
5%

OFF PURCHASE

MAY NOT BE VALID ON CERTAIN ITEMS. EXPIRES 12-31-94

BUYING RETAIL IS STUPID! DISCOUNT COUPON

PRO GOLF DISCOUNT
10%

OFF PURCHASE

MAY NOT BE VALID ON CERTAIN ITEMS. EXPIRES 12-31-94

Discount Coupons

BUYING RETAIL IS STUPID!
18345 VENTURA BLVD., SUITE 314
TARZANA, CA 91356

BUYING RETAIL IS STUPID!
18345 VENTURA BLVD., SUITE 314
TARZANA, CA 91356

BUYING RETAIL IS STUPID!
18345 VENTURA BLVD., SUITE 314
TARZANA, CA 91356

BUYING RETAIL IS STUPID!
18345 VENTURA BLVD., SUITE 314
TARZANA, CA 91356

DISCOUNT COUPONS

BUYING RETAIL IS STUPID! DISCOUNT COUPON

RAVE REVIEWS–KIDS COTTAGE
10%
OFF PURCHASE

NOT VALID ON ITEMS ALREADY MARKED DOWN. EXPIRES 12-31-94

BUYING RETAIL IS STUPID! DISCOUNT COUPON

RED BARN FEED & SADDLERY INC.
5%
OFF PURCHASE

MAY NOT BE VALID ON CERTAIN ITEMS. EXPIRES 12-31-94

BUYING RETAIL IS STUPID! DISCOUNT COUPON

ROSCOE FURNITURE LIQUIDATORS
5%
OFF PURCHASE

MAY NOT BE VALID ON CERTAIN ITEMS. EXPIRES 12-31-94

BUYING RETAIL IS STUPID! DISCOUNT COUPON

THE ROUNDHOUSE TRAIN STORE
10%
OFF PURCHASE

MAY NOT BE VALID ON CERTAIN ITEMS. EXPIRES 12-31-94

DISCOUNT COUPONS

BUYING RETAIL IS STUPID!
18345 VENTURA BLVD., SUITE 314
TARZANA, CA 91356

BUYING RETAIL IS STUPID!
18345 VENTURA BLVD., SUITE 314
TARZANA, CA 91356

BUYING RETAIL IS STUPID!
18345 VENTURA BLVD., SUITE 314
TARZANA, CA 91356

BUYING RETAIL IS STUPID!
18345 VENTURA BLVD., SUITE 314
TARZANA, CA 91356

DISCOUNT COUPONS

BUYING RETAIL IS STUPID! DISCOUNT COUPON

ROY STEP SHOES
10%

OFF PURCHASE

MAY NOT BE VALID ON CERTAIN ITEMS. EXPIRES 12-31-94

BUYING RETAIL IS STUPID! DISCOUNT COUPON

RUBINFELD-KENNEDY ESTATE JEWELRY
10%

OFF PURCHASE

MAY NOT BE VALID ON CERTAIN ITEMS. EXPIRES 12-31-94

BUYING RETAIL IS STUPID! DISCOUNT COUPON

SANDLER OF THE VALLEY
10%

OFF PURCHASE

MAY NOT BE VALID ON CERTAIN ITEMS. EXPIRES 12-31-94

BUYING RETAIL IS STUPID! DISCOUNT COUPON

SARA DESIGNERS OUTLET
10%

OFF PURCHASE

NOT VALID ON SALE ITEMS. EXPIRES 12-31-94

DISCOUNT COUPONS

BUYING RETAIL IS STUPID!
18345 VENTURA BLVD., SUITE 314
TARZANA, CA 91356

BUYING RETAIL IS STUPID!
18345 VENTURA BLVD., SUITE 314
TARZANA, CA 91356

BUYING RETAIL IS STUPID!
18345 VENTURA BLVD., SUITE 314
TARZANA, CA 91356

BUYING RETAIL IS STUPID!
18345 VENTURA BLVD., SUITE 314
TARZANA, CA 91356

DISCOUNT COUPONS

Buying Retail Is Stupid! Discount Coupon

Second Time Around Records
5%

OFF PURCHASE

MAY NOT BE VALID ON CERTAIN ITEMS. EXPIRES 12-31-94

Buying Retail Is Stupid! Discount Coupon

See Me Color
10%

OFF PURCHASE

MAY NOT BE VALID ON CERTAIN ITEMS. EXPIRES 12-31-94

Buying Retail Is Stupid! Discount Coupon

Seymour Fashions
10%

OFF PURCHASE

NOT VALID ON SALE ITEMS. EXPIRES 12-31-94

Buying Retail Is Stupid! Discount Coupon

Shoe Outlet
10%

OFF PURCHASE

MAY NOT BE VALID ON CERTAIN ITEMS. EXPIRES 12-31-94

DISCOUNT COUPONS

BUYING RETAIL IS STUPID!
18345 VENTURA BLVD., SUITE 314
TARZANA, CA 91356

BUYING RETAIL IS STUPID!
18345 VENTURA BLVD., SUITE 314
TARZANA, CA 91356

BUYING RETAIL IS STUPID!
18345 VENTURA BLVD., SUITE 314
TARZANA, CA 91356

BUYING RETAIL IS STUPID!
18345 VENTURA BLVD., SUITE 314
TARZANA, CA 91356

Discount Coupons

Buying Retail Is Stupid! Discount Coupon

Silk Warehoue
20%

OFF PURCHASE

NOT GOOD WITH ANY OTHER OFFER OR SPECIAL. EXPIRES 12-31-94

Buying Retail Is Stupid! Discount Coupon

Something for Baby
10%

OFF PURCHASE

MAY NOT BE VALID ON CERTAIN ITEMS. EXPIRES 12-31-94

Buying Retail Is Stupid! Discount Coupon

Sonny's Radiator Exchange
10%

OFF PURCHASE + FREE PERMATEX SEALANT

MAY NOT BE VALID ON CERTAIN ITEMS. EXPIRES 12-31-94

Buying Retail Is Stupid! Discount Coupon

Stamp 'N Doodle
FREE Ink Pad

WITH PURCHASE OF 3 RUBBER STAMPS

MAY NOT BE VALID ON CERTAIN ITEMS. EXPIRES 12-31-94

DISCOUNT COUPONS

BUYING RETAIL IS STUPID!
18345 VENTURA BLVD., SUITE 314
TARZANA, CA 91356

BUYING RETAIL IS STUPID!
18345 VENTURA BLVD., SUITE 314
TARZANA, CA 91356

BUYING RETAIL IS STUPID!
18345 VENTURA BLVD., SUITE 314
TARZANA, CA 91356

BUYING RETAIL IS STUPID!
18345 VENTURA BLVD., SUITE 314
TARZANA, CA 91356

DISCOUNT COUPONS

BUYING RETAIL IS STUPID! DISCOUNT COUPON

STAR BABY
10%
OFF PURCHASE

NOT VALID ON SALE ITEMS. EXPIRES 12-31-94

BUYING RETAIL IS STUPID! DISCOUNT COUPON

STAR DRAPERIES
10%
OFF PURCHASE

MAY NOT BE VALID ON CERTAIN ITEMS. EXPIRES 12-31-94

BUYING RETAIL IS STUPID! DISCOUNT COUPON

STARS & DEBS
10%
OFF PURCHASE

MAY NOT BE VALID ON CERTAIN ITEMS. EXPIRES 12-31-94

BUYING RETAIL IS STUPID! DISCOUNT COUPON

SUPER POPS RECORD DETECTIVE
10%
OFF PURCHASE

MAY NOT BE VALID ON CERTAIN ITEMS. EXPIRES 12-31-94

DISCOUNT COUPONS

BUYING RETAIL IS STUPID!
18345 VENTURA BLVD., SUITE 314
TARZANA, CA 91356

BUYING RETAIL IS STUPID!
18345 VENTURA BLVD., SUITE 314
TARZANA, CA 91356

BUYING RETAIL IS STUPID!
18345 VENTURA BLVD., SUITE 314
TARZANA, CA 91356

BUYING RETAIL IS STUPID!
18345 VENTURA BLVD., SUITE 314
TARZANA, CA 91356

DISCOUNT COUPONS

BUYING RETAIL IS STUPID! DISCOUNT COUPON

SUPERIOR WINDOW
10%

OFF PURCHASE

MAY NOT BE VALID ON CERTAIN ITEMS. EXPIRES 12-31-94

BUYING RETAIL IS STUPID! DISCOUNT COUPON

SURPLUS CITY RETAIL
25%

OFF PURCHASE OF NEW WORK BOOTS

NOT VALID ON RECYCLED OR SALE ITEMS. EXPIRES 12-31-94

BUYING RETAIL IS STUPID! DISCOUNT COUPON

SUSIE'S DEALS
10%

OFF PURCHASE

MAY NOT BE VALID ON CERTAIN ITEMS. EXPIRES 12-31-94

BUYING RETAIL IS STUPID! DISCOUNT COUPON

TILE FOR LESS
FREE BAG OF GROUT

WITH PURCHASE

MAY NOT BE VALID ON CERTAIN ITEMS. EXPIRES 12-31-94

DISCOUNT COUPONS

BUYING RETAIL IS STUPID!
18345 VENTURA BLVD., SUITE 314
TARZANA, CA 91356

BUYING RETAIL IS STUPID!
18345 VENTURA BLVD., SUITE 314
TARZANA, CA 91356

BUYING RETAIL IS STUPID!
18345 VENTURA BLVD., SUITE 314
TARZANA, CA 91356

BUYING RETAIL IS STUPID!
18345 VENTURA BLVD., SUITE 314
TARZANA, CA 91356

Discount Coupons

BUYING RETAIL IS STUPID! DISCOUNT COUPON

TILE, MARBLE & GRANITE WAREHOUSE
10%
OFF PURCHASE

MAY NOT BE VALID ON CERTAIN ITEMS. EXPIRES 12-31-94

BUYING RETAIL IS STUPID! DISCOUNT COUPON

TILECLUB
10%
OFF PURCHASE

MAY NOT BE VALID ON CERTAIN ITEMS. EXPIRES 12-31-94

BUYING RETAIL IS STUPID! DISCOUNT COUPON

TOY LIQUIDATORS
10%
OFF PURCHASE

MAY NOT BE VALID ON CERTAIN ITEMS. EXPIRES 12-31-94

BUYING RETAIL IS STUPID! DISCOUNT COUPON

VALLEY CLOCK SERVICE
10%
OFF REPAIRS ONLY

EXPIRES 12-31-94

DISCOUNT COUPONS

BUYING RETAIL IS STUPID!
18345 VENTURA BLVD., SUITE 314
TARZANA, CA 91356

BUYING RETAIL IS STUPID!
18345 VENTURA BLVD., SUITE 314
TARZANA, CA 91356

BUYING RETAIL IS STUPID!
18345 VENTURA BLVD., SUITE 314
TARZANA, CA 91356

BUYING RETAIL IS STUPID!
18345 VENTURA BLVD., SUITE 314
TARZANA, CA 91356

DISCOUNT COUPONS

Buying Retail Is Stupid! Discount Coupon

Valley Indoor Swapmeet
FREE ADMISSION

POMONA, VAN NUYS OR WOODLAND HILLS

EXPIRES 12-31-94

Buying Retail Is Stupid! Discount Coupon

Valley Mattress & Bunk Bed
5%

OFF PURCHASE

NOT VALID ON SALE ITEMS. EXPIRES 12-31-94

Buying Retail Is Stupid! Discount Coupon

Van De Camper
5% or 10%

5% OFF VAN SUPPLIES OR 10% OFF CATALOGUE ORDERS

MAY NOT BE VALID ON CERTAIN ITEMS. EXPIRES 12-31-94

Buying Retail Is Stupid! Discount Coupon

Watch Connection
10%

OFF PURCHASE

MAY NOT BE VALID ON CERTAIN ITEMS. EXPIRES 12-31-94

DISCOUNT COUPONS

BUYING RETAIL IS STUPID!
18345 VENTURA BLVD., SUITE 314
TARZANA, CA 91356

BUYING RETAIL IS STUPID!
18345 VENTURA BLVD., SUITE 314
TARZANA, CA 91356

BUYING RETAIL IS STUPID!
18345 VENTURA BLVD., SUITE 314
TARZANA, CA 91356

BUYING RETAIL IS STUPID!
18345 VENTURA BLVD., SUITE 314
TARZANA, CA 91356

DISCOUNT COUPONS

BUYING RETAIL IS STUPID! DISCOUNT COUPON

WEST HOLLYWOOD ATHLETIC SUPPLY
5%

OFF PURCHASE OF IN-STOCK ITEMS ONLY

NOT VALID ON SALE ITEMS. EXPIRES 12-31-94

BUYING RETAIL IS STUPID! DISCOUNT COUPON

WHOLESALE LEATHER APPAREL
5%

OFF PURCHASE

MAY NOT BE VALID ON CERTAIN ITEMS. EXPIRES 12-31-94

BUYING RETAIL IS STUPID! DISCOUNT COUPON

WHOLESALE PRINTING FACTORY 1
5%

OFF PURCHASE

MAY NOT BE VALID ON CERTAIN ITEMS. EXPIRES 12-31-94

BUYING RETAIL IS STUPID! DISCOUNT COUPON

WITH KIDS IN MIND
$20

OFF CHARACTER PARTY

(ONE AND A HALF HOUR MINIMUM) EXPIRES 12-31-94

DISCOUNT COUPONS

BUYING RETAIL IS STUPID!
18345 VENTURA BLVD., SUITE 314
TARZANA, CA 91356

BUYING RETAIL IS STUPID!
18345 VENTURA BLVD., SUITE 314
TARZANA, CA 91356

BUYING RETAIL IS STUPID!
18345 VENTURA BLVD., SUITE 314
TARZANA, CA 91356

BUYING RETAIL IS STUPID!
18345 VENTURA BLVD., SUITE 314
TARZANA, CA 91356

DISCOUNT COUPONS

Buying Retail Is Stupid! Discount Coupon

Woodland Hills Fireplace Shop
10%

OFF PURCHASE

NOT VALID ON SALE ITEMS.   EXPIRES 12-31-94

Buying Retail Is Stupid! Discount Coupon

Work Boot Warehouse
$10

OFF PURCHASE (EXCLUDES RUBBER BOOTS)

NOT VALID ON SALE ITEMS.   EXPIRES 12-31-94

Buying Retail Is Stupid! Discount Coupon

World of Plants & Gifts
10%

OFF PURCHASE

MAY NOT BEVALID ON CERTAIN ITEMS.   EXPIRES 12-31-94

DISCOUNT COUPONS

BUYING RETAIL IS STUPID!
18345 VENTURA BLVD., SUITE 314
TARZANA, CA 91356

BUYING RETAIL IS STUPID!
18345 VENTURA BLVD., SUITE 314
TARZANA, CA 91356

BUYING RETAIL IS STUPID!
18345 VENTURA BLVD., SUITE 314
TARZANA, CA 91356

TO ORDER
BUYING RETAIL IS STUPID!

Please enclose a check or money order for $19.95* per book (taxes, shipping and handling already included). Checks or money orders should be made payable to BUYING RETAIL IS STUPID!

```
                                                                  B
_____
   NAME
_____    _____
   ADDRESS                                              APT. #
_____  _____  _____
   CITY                                      STATE     ZIP CODE
_____
   PHONE NUMBER (PLEASE INCLUDE AREA CODE)

Please send _____ copies of BUYING RETAIL IS STUPID!
Enclosed is my check or money order for $ _____
```

MAIL TO:
BUYING RETAIL IS STUPID!
18345 VENTURA BOULEVARD, SUITE 314B
TARZANA, CA 91356

THANK YOU FOR YOUR ORDER.

* For special pricing on orders of 12 or more books please call 818/708-1245. Case pricing is also available.

TO ORDER
BUYING RETAIL IS STUPID!

Please enclose a check or money order for $19.95* per book (taxes, shipping and handling already included). Checks or money orders should be made payable to BUYING RETAIL IS STUPID!

```
                                                                    B
_____
  NAME
_____  _____
  ADDRESS                                                 APT. #
_____  _____  _____
  CITY                                    STATE    ZIP CODE
_____
  PHONE NUMBER (PLEASE INCLUDE AREA CODE)
```

Please send _____ copies of **BUYING RETAIL IS STUPID!**
Enclosed is my check or money order for $ _____

MAIL TO:
BUYING RETAIL IS STUPID!
18345 VENTURA BOULEVARD, SUITE 314B
TARZANA, CA 91356

THANK YOU FOR YOUR ORDER.

* For special pricing on orders of 12 or more books please call 818/708-1245. Case pricing is also available.

BOOKS AVAILABLE FROM NMI PUBLISHERS

HAPPINESS THROUGH SUPERFICIALITY: THE WAR AGAINST MEANINGFUL RELATIONSHIPS by Jerry Newmark and Irving S. Newmark (176 pages, 1992…$11.95)

This book lifts your spirits, makes you laugh, challenges you to rethink your values and shows you how to lead a happier, more fulfilling life. The Doctors Newmark offer fresh perspectives, in a humorous and often provocative way, on many of the most serious aspects of life—sex, marriage, parenting, work, health, education, money, love, lawyers, doctors, psychotherapy and much more. You will learn how to stop taking everything too seriously—especially your self and how to come through the '90s whole and happy.

THIS SCHOOL BELONGS TO YOU & ME: EVERY LEARNER A TEACHER, EVERY TEACHER A LEARNER by Gerald Newmark (431 pages, 1976…$9.95)

First published in 1976, this book remains an important resource for anyone interested in improving education. It describes a new kind of learning community—an exciting school where students, parents, teachers, staff, and administrators are turned on to learning and to working cooperatively with each other. "This School Belongs to You & Me" offers a detailed plan for the redesign of an entire school into a vibrant learning community. It is also a rich resource book of educational ideas and practices which can be used by individual teachers to improve any existing program or classroom. Developed from a seven-year, Ford Foundation supported project in inner-city elementary schools, the ideas presented can be applied to all school levels, whatever their geographic, ethnic, or soci-economic characteristics, in exciting, cost-effective ways.

To order additional copies of **BUYING RETAIL IS STUPID**, **HAPPINESS THROUGH SUPERFICIALITY** or **THIS SCHOOL BELONGS TO YOU & ME** send a check for the amount of the book, plus $3.00 for tax and shipping (add $1 for each additional book) to:

NMI PUBLISHERS
18345 VENTURA BLVD., SUITE 314
TARZANA, CA 91356

(For Credit Card orders call: 818/708-1244)